# A TASTE OF WAR

# A TASTE OF WAR

EYEWITNESS ACCOUNTS
OF WORLD WAR II

Edited by

## HAROLD ELK STRAUBING

Sterling Publishing Co., Inc.   New York

**Library of Congress Cataloging-in-Publication Data**

A Taste of War : eyewitness accounts of World War II / compiled and edited by Harold Elk Straubing.
    p.    cm.
   Includes index.
   ISBN 0-8069-7206-8
1. World War, 1939-1945—Personal narratives.   I. Straubing, Harold Elk, 1918-
   D811.A2T35    1992                                    91-44011
   940.54'8—dc20                                        CIP

10  9  8  7  6  5  4  3  2  1

Published by Sterling Publishing Company, Inc.
387 Park Avenue South, New York, N.Y. 10016
© 1992 by Harold Elk Straubing
Distributed in Canada by Sterling Publishing
*c/o* Canadian Manda Group, P.O.Box 920, Station U
Toronto, Ontario, Canada M8Z 5P9
Distributed in Great Britain and Europe by Cassell PLC
Villiers House, 41/47 Strand, London WC2N 5JE, England
Distributed in Australia by Capricorn Link Ltd.
P.O. Box 665, Lane Cove, NSW 2066
*Manufactured in the United States of America*
*All rights reserved*

Sterling ISBN 0-8069-7206-8

**D**edicated to my nephews and grandnephews, who escaped military service due to the accidental time of their births: Richard, Scott, Barry, and Jeremy Mozlin, and Geordie Straubing. Also to my nephew, Howard Mozlin, who tasted the bitter pill of Vietnam. And to the men and women of my generation who were born at the "right" time to spend a long period in the hell-on-earth called World War II.

# Contents

# CONTENTS

CONTENTS

# 8. The War's End

# 9. The Occupiers

# INTRODUCTION

The truce between World War I and World War II was rocky at best. New nations came into existence, and language barriers fell with old boundary lines. Physically mangled and mentally broken survivors could be encountered on street corners in major European cities. Mustard-gas victims, some blind, coughed and hacked in public places. Bombed-out buildings, bridges, and roads pockmarked the landscape, physical evidence of war's devastation. Those unwelcome invaders, poverty and inflation, crossed all borders. All classes suffered, except for the very rich and the ruling classes, who feared a spread of communism that would erase their wealth and power. In Germany the wealthy few cast about for a leader who had the potential to take over the reins of government, stop communism, and preserve the status quo.

Adolf Hitler caught their eye, a daring young man with a plan guaranteed to touch the patriotic streak in every German citizen. His simple concept: They were the master race, and no matter what their education or competence in any given field, the Germans were superior. With platitudes, slogans, and sabre rattling, Hitler gathered a loyal clique that helped him worm his way through government offices until he *was* the government.

Among the Allied officials who survived World War I, not one, at least publicly, recognized the danger this demagogue presented to the civilized world. Plans were soon under way among the Hitler clique, as "der Führer" climbed the rungs of government, to divide the human race into two parts: those with a right to life and those with none. Aryans, the superior race, would be the leaders, the supervisors. Non-Aryans would be the slaves, serving the Aryans in any capacity the rulers deemed necessary. Those who had no right to life, Jews, Catholics, Gypsies, the aged, the infirm, etc., would be exterminated.

The population of Europe in the early Twenties was in a state of shock in the aftermath of World War I and found it difficult to face the possibility of another war. Despite mutual assistance treaties between the former allies, they quaked at the thought of opening hostilities once again. The more they hesitated, the more Hitler demanded. When Germany invaded Poland, there was no armed resistance from any world power, and Germany's new war was on the march.

The United States had turned inward since the end of World War I. Large corporations grew larger and richer, but the working man grew poorer as jobs dried up at the war's end. Labor troubles were quelled by violence. American troops had

11

even fired on destitute war veterans marching on the White House to demand a bonus for their war service.

The theory of "America First" grew simultaneously from a war-tired citizenry and a U.S. Congress prompted by protectionist big business. Newspapers picked up the cry. Let Europe fight its own wars! The United States was distant enough so that no matter who was victorious, they would not affect Americans or America.

In less than six months, the "America Firsters" claimed 60,000 members and one of their spokesmen, Charles A. Lindbergh, the flying hero of 1927, said, soon after being royally entertained in Berlin by Field Marshal Göring, "Let us stop this hysterical chatter of [German] invasion." He concluded, "The three most important groups which have been pressing this country towards war are the British, the Jewish, and the Roosevelt administration."

The "America Firsters" sat out the civil war in Spain that saw Germany contribute arms and men to Francisco Franco. The Spanish Civil War gave Hitler an opportunity to try out some of his new weapons, and to give German soldiers combat training. The isolationists watched as Italy's Mussolini sent men and arms to help General Franco subjugate the Spanish people. They clucked sympathetically as Italy invaded Ethiopia. Conscience-stricken men and women in the United States formed the Abraham Lincoln Brigade and volunteered their services to the Loyalist Spanish government to halt the armies of the dictators, but because of inadequate arms and training, they only ended as cannon fodder on the bloody fields of Spain.

It wasn't until 1940 that concerned Americans began to question the progress of the Nazi movement. In the eastern United States, Nazi Bunds were organized in contemplation of a European victory. The followers wore Nazi uniforms, and organized special camps in New Jersey and New York for drilling their men. Uniformed men wearing the bold red swastika on their sleeves would wander known Jewish neighborhoods and beat up innocent civilians. From Germany, atrocity stories of concentration camps began to circulate. The Nazis were killing not only Jews, but Catholics and Lutherans. Priests were being jailed. People in conquered lands had been moved to Germany as slave labor. Hitler's all-out war was finally recognized as being a threat to all civilized mankind.

Conscription in the United States became a reality in September 1940 despite the urgings of several hundred citizen's committees that doubted the wisdom of the drift toward war. "America Firsters" still beat the drums of neutrality and slowed the start of the manufacture of war materiel. There were no firearms available for draftees, and many recruits performed their army drills using broomstick handles for rifles; automobiles and trucks were utilized with large signs on their sides labelling them "tanks"; lead pipes were labelled mortars, and large felled trees were marked in bold signs as cannons.

Winston Churchill convinced Franklin Roosevelt that without American participation their cause might be lost and all Europe overrun by the Nazi troops. The President inaugurated a Lend-Lease program for the fighting Allies, while the young American army grew in numbers, and arms manufacture began to increase.

Some, like Douglas Miller, author of the best-selling book *You Can't Do Business with Hitler* (published in June 1941) cautioned against complacency. Once

Adolf Hitler was victorious over England, he warned, the Führer would rule all of Europe, Africa, and Asia Minor. The United States could not expect to do business at the same old stand because of the many essential raw materials that would be denied. The United States could fall without firing a shot. "The Nazis often said," Douglas Miller wrote, "that there are two opposite poles in the world: Germany, the pole of order, discipline, and scientific progress; and the United States, the pole of democratic anarchy, decadent Christianity, and the degeneration and loss of efficiency which accompanies a system of free enterprise. Hitler's conquest is only partial and incomplete until we (the United States) are brought into his world system."

Miller's book attracted much attention, but it took the bombing of Pearl Harbor to crack isolationism and unify the country in its war effort. In the early hours of December 7, 1941, Japanese aircraft transported on naval carriers attacked the U.S. Pacific fleet anchored at Pearl Harbor in Hawaii. They sunk or severely damaged eight battleships, three cruisers, three destroyers, a minelayer, a repair ship, a seaplane tender, and a large floating dry dock.

Of 202 Navy planes at Kaneoha Marine Base, 80 were destroyed, 70 damaged, and only a few of the remaining 52 were able to take off due to the flaming debris on the runways. Of 273 Army planes, 93, including 23 bombers, were destroyed at Hickam, and 66 planes were blown up at Wheeler Field, with almost as many severely damaged.

In all, eighteen ships were sunk or badly damaged. Planes and ammunition, buildings and supplies had been destroyed at a cost of nearly half a billion dollars. 2,383 men were killed, 1,842 were wounded, some of whom later died, and 960 were missing.

The United States was stunned. By this one act, the Japanese solved President Roosevelt's most pressing problem: how to get the United States into the war against the Axis powers without firing the first shot.

For many years after the war, there persisted a conspiracy theory, that the Japanese were forced to attack the United States because of the economic demands made on them. Since August 1940, the Japanese secret diplomatic code had been broken and the State Department informed of the contents of all messages. There are many who believe that the planned attack on Pearl Harbor was well known in advance. In addition, the American ambassador to Japan, Joseph C. Grew, notified the State Department in January 1941 about talk of an attack on Pearl Harbor should the discussions between the United States and Japan break down. In November of that year he again cautioned the State Department that Japan's war preparations were not just sabre rattling.

The administration in Washington was aware that Japan could never acquiesce to American demands that Japan withdraw from its Asian conquests, and so Admiral Stark and General Marshall sent war warnings to U.S. commanders of Pacific installations. The message from Japan turning down the American proposals started coming in on December 6, but the communication was so long that it was not complete until December 7. It was delivered to the White House at 1:00 P.M., Washington time. After a short delay, General Marshall sent an additional warning to all commanders in the Pacific regarding the possibility of war, but the warning failed to arrive in time, and an hour later, Washington learned of the attack on Pearl Harbor.

The United States had been forced into war.

Why a book on World War II at this time? Especially a book on a war that ended almost fifty years ago. At this writing, World War II is still the only war to have seen participation by the entire world. It is the only war in which all resources of all countries were mobilized and dedicated to one purpose—to win at any cost. Men and women were joined in uniform, and civilians were placed on strict rations. Disobedience was punished by fines and jail sentences.

Most adults today don't realize the hardships endured by all the participants in the war on both sides. The following pages attempt to convey the experiences of those who fought the war on land, sea, and air, and on the home front. These are the personal stories of people many of whom lost health, personal fortune, and immediate family. Most of this material was written during the war, or soon after, while memories were the freshest and emotions at their highest. For those fortunate enough to have never gone through the rigors of war, the following excerpts will paint a graphic picture of the daily heartbreak, disappointment, and general hardship endured by victor and vanquished alike at a time when the free world was fighting for its life.

# 1
# Prelude to War

## OBERSALZBERG

from
*Inside the Third Reich:*
*Memoirs by Albert Speer*
Translated from the German by Richard and Clara Winston
New York: The Macmillan Company, 1970

*We empathize with our friends and co-workers on a day-to-day basis. We understand their goals, ambitions, disappointments and joys. But what if among our acquaintances we have someone like Adolf Hitler? How far can we reach out with understanding and encouragement? In his later years, Hitler resembled the devil, but in his youth, Hitler was just another man with a dream. He had an inner fire that attracted people and magnetism that would draw people even if they did not fully share his vision.*

*One such man, Albert Speer, was bewitched by Hitler's charm when he met him in 1930. Speer was the product of an upper-middle-class family. Although his father read the liberal press, he himself had no strong political beliefs. An unemployed architect, he joined the National Socialist party because of a speech given by Hitler to university and technical students about a revitalized Germany. Hitler's speech seemed to be an answer to communism and to the futility of the Weimar governments.*

*He did odd jobs for the party quickly and efficiently, and when the young Führer learned that Speer was an architect, a friendship was formed. Hitler, a frustrated architect, who was refused admission to an art school because his "original" drawings were recognized as copies, looked to Speer to help plan new state offices, stadiums, and supercities.*

*Speer never embraced the party's principles, but he was so enamored of the architectural tasks given him that he felt one could dismiss the Nazis'*

15

*anti-Semitism as no more than a "children's disease" if one liked the rest of the program. And he was obsessed with the opportunity to create buildings and cities for a new Germany.*

*Although Speer seemed politically detached, Hitler made him minister of armaments and war production, where he proved to be so effective that he has been given credit for prolonging the war.*

*At Nuremberg Speer was sentenced to twenty years for crimes against humanity and other war crimes. He served the complete sentence at Spandau, where he managed to write his memoirs, smuggling them out with the aid of a member of the prison staff, a Dutchman who had been a slave laborer. Speer's memoirs include his impressions of Adolf Hitler and opinions expressed by the Führer of the various leaders of the Nazi party.*

In the Ostertal, a remote mountain valley in the Bavarian Alps, I had located a small hunting lodge, big enough to set up drawing boards, which with a bit of crowding could accommodate my family and a few associates. There, in the spring of 1935, we worked away at my plans for Berlin. That was a happy period for my work and for the family. But one day I made a crucial error; I told Hitler about this idyll. His response was: "Why, you can have all that and more near me. I'll put the Bechstein house at your disposal. There's ample room for your office there in the conservatory." (At the end of May 1937 we moved from the Bechstein house into a studio building which Hitler had Bormann build from my design.) Thus I became the fourth "Obersalzberger," along with Hitler, Göring, and Bormann.

Naturally I was happy to be granted so obvious a distinction and be admitted to the most intimate circle. But I soon came to realize that the change had not been exactly advantageous. From the solitary mountain valley we passed into an area guarded by a high barbed-wire fence which could be entered only after identity checks at two gates. It was reminiscent of an open-air enclosure for wild animals. Curiosity-seekers were always trying to catch a glimpse of some of the prominent inhabitants of the mountains.

Bormann was the real master of Obersalzberg. He forcibly bought up centuries-old farms and had the buildings torn down. The same was done to the numerous votive chapels, despite the objections of the parishes. He also confiscated state forests, until the private area reached from the top of the mountain, which was some sixty-four hundred feet high, to the valley at an altitude of two thousand feet, and embraced an area of 2.7 square miles. The fence around the inner area was almost two miles long, around the outer area nine miles long.

With total insensitivity to the natural surroundings, Bormann laid out a network of roads through the magnificent landscape. He turned forest paths, hitherto carpeted by pine needles and penetrated by roots, into paved promenades. A barracks, a vast garage building, a hotel for Hitler's guests, a new manor house, a complex for the constantly growing number of employees, sprang up as rapidly as in a suddenly fashionable resort. Dormitory barracks for hundreds of construction workers clung to the slopes; trucks loaded with building materials rumbled along the roads. At night the various building sites glowed with light, for work went on in two shifts, and occasionally detonations thundered through the valley.

On the top of Hitler's private mountain Bormann erected a home that was luxuriously furnished in a somewhat rusticated ocean-liner style. You reached it by a precipitous road that ended in an elevator blasted into the rock. Bormann squandered between twenty and thirty million marks merely on the access route to the eyrie, which Hitler visited only a few times. Cynics in Hitler's entourage remarked: "Bormann has created a gold-rush town atmosphere. Only he doesn't find any, he spends it." Hitler regretted the hubbub but commented: "It's Bormann's doing; I don't want to interfere." Another time he said: "When it's all finished I'll look for a quiet valley and build another small wooden house there like the first." It never was finished. Bormann conceived a never-ending succession of new roads and buildings, and when the war finally broke out he began building underground quarters for Hitler and his entourage.

The gigantic installations on the mountain were, in spite of Hitler's occasional sarcasms about the tremendous effort and expenditure, characteristic of the change in the Führer's style of life and also indicative of his tendency to withdraw more and more from the wider world around him. Fear of assassination cannot explain it, for almost daily he allowed thousands of people to enter the protected area to pay homage to him. His entourage considered such behavior more dangerous than spontaneous strolls on public forest paths.

In the summer of 1935 Hitler had decided to enlarge his modest country house into one more suitable for his public duties, to be known as the Berghof. He paid for the project out of his own money, but that was nothing but a gesture, since Bormann drew upon other sources for the subsidiary buildings, sums disproportionately greater than the amount Hitler himself provided.

Hitler did not just sketch the plans for the Berghof. He borrowed drawing board, T-square, and other implements from me to draw the ground plan, renderings, and cross sections of his building to scale, refusing any help with the matter. There were only two other designs on which Hitler expended the personal care that he applied to his Obersalzberg house: that of the new Reich war flag and his own standard as Chief of State.

Most architects will put a wide variety of ideas down on paper, and see which lends itself best to further development. It was characteristic of Hitler that he regarded his first inspiration as intuitively right and drew it with little hesitation. Afterward, he introduced only small retouchings to eliminate glaring defects.

The old house was preserved within the new one, whose living room joined the old through a large opening. The resultant ground plan was most impractical for the reception of official visitors. Their staffs had to be content with an unprepossessing entry hall which also led to the toilets, stairwell, and the large dining room.

During official conferences Hitler's private guests were banished to the upper floor. But since the stairs led down to the entry hall, private visitors had to be cleared by a guard before being allowed to go through the room and leave the house for a walk.

A huge picture window in the living room, famous for its size and the fact that it could be lowered, was Hitler's pride. It offered a view of the Untersberg, Berchtesgaden, and Salzburg. However, Hitler had been inspired to situate his garage underneath this window; when the wind was unfavorable, a strong smell of gasoline penetrated into the living room. All in all, this was a ground plan that would have been graded D by any professor at an institute of technology. On the other hand, these very clumsinesses gave the Berghof a strongly personal note. The place was still geared to the simple activities of a former weekend cottage, merely expanded to vast proportions.

All the cost estimates were exceeded by far, and Hitler was somewhat embarrassed. [He commented:]

> I've completely used up the income from my book, although Amann's given me a further advance of several hundred thousand. Even so there's not enough money, so Bormann has told me today. The publishers are after me to release my second book, the 1928 one, for publication. [Hitler's so-called second book was not published until 1961.] But I'm certainly glad this volume hasn't been published. What political complications it would make for me at the moment. On the other hand it would relieve me of all financial pressures at one stroke. Amann promised me a million just as an advance, and beyond that it would bring in millions. Perhaps later, when I'm further along. Now it's impossible.

There he sat, a voluntary prisoner with his view of the Untersberg, where, legend has it, the Emperor Charlemagne still sleeps, but will one day arise to restore the past glory of the German Empire. Hitler naturally appropriated this legend for himself: "You see the Untersberg over there. It is no accident that I have my residence opposite it."

Bormann was linked to Hitler not only by his vast building projects on the Obersalzberg. He contrived at the same time to take over administration of Hitler's personal finances. Not only were Hitler's adjutants tied to the purse strings that Bormann controlled, but even Hitler's mistress was dependent upon him, as she candidly confessed to me. Hitler left it to Bormann to attend to her modest needs.

Hitler praised Bormann's financial skill. Once I heard him relate how Bormann had performed a significant service for the party during the difficult year of 1932 by introducing compulsory accident insurance for all party members. The income from this insurance fund considerably exceeded the expenditures, Hitler said, and the party was able to use the surplus for other purposes. Bormann also did his bit to eliminate Hitler's financial anxieties permanently after 1933. He found two sources of ample funds. Together with Hitler's personal photographer Hoffmann and Hoffmann's friend Ohnesorge, the Minister of Posts, he decided that Hitler had rights to the reproduction of his picture on postage stamps and was therefore entitled to payments. The percentage royalty was infinitesimal, but since the Führer's head appeared on all stamps, millions flowed into the privy purse administered by Bormann.

Bormann developed another source by founding the Adolf Hitler Endowment

Fund of German Industry. Entrepreneurs who were profiting by the economic boom were bluntly requested to show their appreciation by voluntary contributions to the Führer. Since other party bigwigs had had the same notion, Bormann obtained a decree assuring him a monopoly on such contributions. But he was clever enough to return a part of the donations to various party leaders "in behalf of the Führer." Almost all of the top party functionaries received gifts from this fund. The power to set the living standards of the Gauleiters and Reichsleiters did not attract attention; but fundamentally it conferred on Bormann more power than many other positions within the hierarchy.

The powerful men under Hitler were already jealously watching one another like so many pretenders to the throne. Quite early there were struggles for position among Goebbels, Göring, Rosenberg, Ley, Himmler, Ribbentrop, and Hess. Only Roehm had been left by the wayside, and before long Hess was to lose all his influence. But none of them recognized a threat in the shape of trusty Bormann. He had succeeded in representing himself as insignificant while imperceptibly building up his bastions. Even among so many ruthless men, he stood out by his brutality and coarseness. He had no culture, which might have put some restraints on him, and in every case he carried out whatever Hitler had ordered or what he himself had gathered from Hitler's hints. A subordinate by nature, he treated his own subordinates as if he were dealing with cows and oxen. He was a peasant.

Hitler's stays on "the mountain" provided him, as he often stressed, with the inner calm and assurance for his surprising decisions. He also composed his most important speeches there, and it is worth noting how he wrote them. Thus, before the Nuremberg Party Rally he regularly retreated to Obersalzberg for several weeks in order to work out his long speeches on basic principles. As the deadline drew nearer, his adjutants kept urging him to begin the dictation and kept everyone and everything away from him, even architectural plans and visitors, so that he would not be distracted from the work. But Hitler postponed the task from week to week, then from day to day, and would reluctantly set to work on it only under extreme time pressure. By then it was usually too late to finish all the speeches, and during the Rally, Hitler usually had to stay up nights to make up for the time he had squandered at Obersalzberg.

I had the impression that he needed this pressure in order to be able to work, that in the bohemian manner of the artist he despised discipline and could not or would not force himself to work regularly. He let the content of his speeches or his thoughts ripen during these weeks of apparent idling until all that had accumulated poured out like a stream bursting its bounds upon followers or negotiators.

Our move from our secluded valley to the bustle of Obersalzberg was ruinous to my work. The very sameness of the day's routine was tiring, the unchanging group around Hitler—the same coterie who regularly met in Munich and in Berlin—was boring. The only difference from Berlin and Munich was that the wives were present on the mountain, and also two or three women secretaries and Eva Braun.

Hitler usually appeared in the lower rooms late in the morning, around eleven o'clock. He then went through the press summaries, received several reports from Bormann, and made his first decisions. The day actually began with a prolonged afternoon dinner. The guests assembled in the anteroom. Hitler chose the lady he would take in to dinner, while Bormann, from about 1938 on, had the privilege of escorting Eva Braun to the table; she usually sat on Hitler's left. That in itself was proof of Bormann's dominant position in the court. The dining room was a mixture of artistic rusticity and urban elegance of a sort which was often characteristic of country houses of the wealthy. The walls and ceilings were paneled in pale larchwood, the chairs covered with bright red morocco leather. The china was a simple white; the silver bore Hitler's monogram and was the same as that used in Berlin. Hitler always took pleasure in its restrained floral decoration. The food was simple and substantial: soup, a meat course, dessert, with either Fachinger mineral water or wine. The waiters, in white vests and black trousers, were members of the SS bodyguard. Some twenty persons sat at the long table, but because of its length no general conversation could arise. Hitler sat in the middle, facing the window. He talked with the person opposite him, who was different every day, or with the ladies to either side of him.

Shortly after dinner the walk to the teahouse began. The width of the path left room for only two abreast, so that the file resembled a procession. Two security men walked at the head. Then came Hitler with one other person, with whom he conversed, followed in any order by the dinner company, with more guards bringing up the rear. Hitler's two police dogs roamed about the area and ignored his commands—the only oppositionists at his court. To Bormann's vexation, Hitler was addicted to this particular walk, which took about half an hour, and disdained using the mile-long paved forest roads.

The teahouse had been built at one of Hitler's favorite lookout points above the Berchtesgaden valley. The company always marveled at the panorama in the same phrases. Hitler always agreed in much the same language. The teahouse itself consisted of a round room about twenty-five feet in diameter, pleasing in its proportions, with a row of small-paned windows and a fireplace along the interior wall. The company sat in easy chairs around the round table, with Eva Braun and one of the other ladies again at Hitler's side. Those who did not find seats went into a small adjoining room. According to taste, one had tea, coffee, or chocolate, and various types of cake and cookies, followed by liqueurs. Here, at the coffee table, Hitler was particularly fond of drifting into endless monologues. The subjects were mostly familiar to the company, who therefore listened absently, though pretending attention. Occasionally Hitler himself fell asleep over one of his monologues. The company then continued chatting in whispers, hoping that he would awaken in time for the evening meal. It was all very familial.

After about two hours the teatime ended, generally around six. Hitler stood up, and the procession moved on to the parking area, about twenty minutes' walk, where a column of cars waited. After returning to the Berghof, Hitler usually withdrew to the upper rooms, while the retinue scattered. Bormann frequently disappeared into the room of one of the younger stenographers, which elicited spiteful remarks from Eva Braun.

Two hours later the company met again for supper, with repetition of the afternoon ritual. Afterward, Hitler went into the salon, again followed by the still unchanged company.

We found places on the sofas or in one of the easy chairs in either of the sitting areas; the two tapestries were raised; and the second part of the evening began with a movie, as was also the custom when Hitler was in Berlin. Afterward the company gathered around the huge fireplace—some six or eight persons lined up in a row on the excessively long and uncomfortably low sofa, while Hitler, once more flanked by Eva Braun and one of the ladies, ensconced himself in one of the soft chairs. Because of the inept arrangement of the furniture the company was so scattered that no common conversation could arise. Everyone talked in low voices with his neighbor. Hitler murmured trivialities with the two women at his side, or whispered with Eva Braun; sometimes he held her hand. But often he fell silent or stared broodingly into the fire. Then the guests fell silent also, in order not to disturb him in important thoughts.

Later, during the war, Hitler gave up the evening showings, saying that he wanted to renounce his favorite entertainment "out of sympathy for the privations of the soldiers." Instead records were played. But although the record collection was excellent, Hitler always preferred the same music. Neither baroque nor classical music, neither chamber music nor symphonies, interested him. Before long the order of the records became virtually fixed. First he wanted a few bravura selections from Wagnerian operas, to be followed promptly with operettas. That remained the pattern. Hitler made a point of trying to guess the names of the sopranos and was pleased when he guessed right, as he frequently did.

To animate these rather barren evenings, sparkling wine was handed around and, after the occupation of France, confiscated champagne of a cheap brand; Göring and his air marshals had appropriated the best brands. From one o'clock on some members of the company, in spite of all their efforts to control themselves, could no longer repress their yawns. But the social occasion dragged on in monotonous, wearing emptiness for another hour or more, until at last Eva Braun had a few words with Hitler and was permitted to go upstairs. Hitler would stand up about a quarter of an hour later, to bid his company goodnight. Those who remained, liberated, often followed those numbing hours with a gay party over champagne and cognac.

Eva Braun was allowed to be present during visits from old party associates. She was banished as soon as other dignitaries of the Reich, such as cabinet ministers, appeared at table. Even when Göring and his wife came, Eva Braun had to stay in her room. Hitler obviously regarded her socially acceptable only within strict limits. Sometimes I kept her company in her exile, a room next to Hitler's bedroom. She was so intimidated that she did not dare leave the house for a walk. "I might meet the Görings in the hall."

In general Hitler showed little consideration for her feelings. He would enlarge on his attitude toward women as though she were not present: "A highly intelligent man should take a primitive and stupid woman. Imagine if on top of everything else I had a woman who interfered with my work! In my leisure time I want to have peace. I could never marry. Think of the problems if I had children! In the end they would try to make my son my successor. Besides, the chances are slim for someone like me to have a capable son. That is almost always how it goes in such cases.

Consider Goethe's son—a completely worthless person! Lots of women are attracted to me because I am unmarried. That was especially useful during our days of struggle. It's the same as with a movie star; when he marries he loses a certain something for the women who adore him. Then he is no longer their idol as he was before."

Hitler believed that he had a powerful sexual appeal to women. But he was also extremely wary about this; he never knew, he used to say, whether a woman preferred him as the Chancellor or as Adolf Hitler, and as he often remarked ungallantly, he certainly did not want witty and intelligent women about him. In making such remarks he was apparently not aware of how offensive they must have been to the ladies present. On the other hand Hitler could sometimes behave like a good head of a family. Once, when Eva Braun was skiing and came to tea rather late, he looked uneasy, kept glancing nervously at the clock, and was plainly worried that she might have had an accident.

Eva Braun came of a family of modest circumstances. Her father was a schoolteacher. I never met her parents; they never appeared and continued to live as befitted their station until the end. Eva Braun, too, remained simple; she dressed quietly and wore the inexpensive jewelry that Hitler gave her for Christmas or her birthdays; usually semiprecious stones worth a few hundred marks at most and actually insulting in their modesty. Bormann would present a selection, and Hitler would choose these trinkets with what seemed to me petit-bourgeois taste.

Eva Braun had no interest in politics. She scarcely ever attempted to influence Hitler. With a good eye for the facts of everyday life, however, she did sometimes make remarks about minor abuses in conditions in Munich. Bormann did not like that, since in such cases he was instantly called to account. She was sports-loving, a good skier with plenty of endurance with whom my wife and I frequently undertook mountain tours outside the enclosed area. Once Hitler actually gave her a week's vacation—when he himself was not at Obersalzberg, of course. She went to Zürs with us for a few days. There, unrecognized, she danced with great passion into the wee hours of the morning with young army officers. She was very far from being a modern Madame Pompadour; for the historian she is interesting only insofar as she set off some of Hitler's traits.

Out of sympathy for her predicament I soon began to feel a liking for this unhappy woman, who was so deeply attached to Hitler. In addition, we were linked by our common dislike for Bormann, although at that time what we resented most was the coarseness with which he was raping the beauty of nature at Obersalzberg and betraying his wife. When I heard at the Nuremberg Trial that Hitler had married Eva Braun in the last day and a half of his life, I felt glad for her—even though I could sense even in this act the cynicism with which Hitler had treated her and probably women in general.

I have often wondered whether Hitler felt anything like affection for children. He certainly made an effort when he met them, whether they were the children of acquaintances or unknown to him. He even tried to deal with them in a paternally friendly fashion, but never managed to be very convincing about it. He never found the proper easy manner of treating them; after a few benign words he would soon turn to others. On the whole he regarded children as representatives of the next generation and therefore took more pleasure in their appearance (blond, blue-eyed), their stature (strong, healthy), or their intelligence (brisk, aggressive) than in their nature as children. His personality had no effect whatsoever upon my own children.

What remains in my memory of social life at Obersalzberg is a curious vacuity. Fortunately, during my first years of imprisonment, while my recollections were still fresh, I noted down a few scraps of conversations which I can now regard as reasonably authentic.

In those hundreds of teatimes questions of fashions, of raising dogs, of the theater and movies, of operettas and their stars were discussed, along with endless trivialities about the family lives of others. Hitler scarcely ever said anything about the Jews, about his domestic opponents, let alone about the necessity of setting up concentration camps. Perhaps such topics were omitted less out of deliberate intention than because they would have been out of place amidst the prevailing banality. On the other hand, Hitler made fun of his closest associates with striking frequency. It is no accident that these particular remarks have remained in my mind, for after all they involved persons who were officially immune from all criticism. Hitler's private circle was not held to these rules, and in any case Hitler considered it pointless to attempt to keep women from gossiping. Was it self-aggrandizement when he spoke disparagingly of everything and everyone? Or did such talk spring from his general contempt for all persons and events?

Thus Hitler had little sympathy with Himmler in his mythologizing of the SS. [Hitler said:]

> What nonsense! Here we have at last reached an age that has left all mysticism behind it, and now he wants to start that all over again. We might just as well have stayed with the church. At least it had tradition. To think that I may some day be turned into an SS saint! Can you imagine it? I would turn over in my grave... .
>
> Himmler has made another speech calling Charlemagne the "butcher of the Saxons." Killing all those Saxons was not a historical crime, as Himmler thinks. Charlemagne did a good thing in subjugating Widukind and killing the Saxons out of hand. He thereby made possible the empire of the Franks and the entry of Western culture into what is now Germany.

Himmler had scientists undertake excavations of prehistoric sites. Hitler commented:

> Why do we call the whole world's attention to the fact that we have no past? It isn't enough that the Romans were erecting great buildings when our forefathers were still living in mud huts; now Himmler is starting to dig up these villages of mud huts and enthusing over every potsherd and stone axe he finds. All we prove by that is that we were still throwing stone hatchets and crouching around open fires when Greece and Rome had already reached the highest stage of culture. We really should do our best to keep

quiet about this past. Instead Himmler makes a great fuss about it all. The present-day Romans must be having a laugh at these revelations.

Amid his political associates in Berlin, Hitler made harsh pronouncements against the church, but in the presence of the women he adopted a milder tone—one of the instances where he adapted his remarks to his surroundings.

"The church is certainly necessary for the people. It is a strong and conservative element," he might say at one time or another in this private circle. However, he conceived of the church as an instrument that could be useful to him. "If only Reibi [this was his nickname for Reich Bishop Ludwig Müller] had some kind of stature. But why do they appoint a nobody of an army chaplain? I'd be glad to give him my full support. Think of all he could do with that. Through me the Evangelical [Protestant] Church could become the established church, as in England."

Even after 1942 Hitler went on maintaining that he regarded the church as indispensable in political life. He would be happy, he said in one of those teatime talks at Obersalzberg, if someday a prominent churchman turned up who was suited to lead one of the churches—or if possible both the Catholic and Protestant churches reunited. He still regretted that Reich Bishop Müller was not the right man to carry out his far-reaching plans. But he sharply condemned the campaign against the church, calling it a crime against the future of the nation. For it was impossible, he said to replace the church by any "party ideology." Undoubtedly, he continued, the church would learn to adapt to the political goals of National Socialism in the long run, as it had always adapted in the course of history. A new party religion would only bring about a relapse into the mysticism of the Middle Ages. The growing SS myth showed that clearly enough, as did Rosenberg's unreadable *Myth of the Twentieth Century.*

If in the course of such a monologue Hitler had pronounced a more negative judgment upon the church, Bormann would undoubtedly have taken from his jacket pocket one of the white cards he always carried with him. For he noted down all Hitler's remarks that seemed to him important; and there was hardly anything he wrote down more eagerly than deprecating comments on the church. At the time I assumed that he was gathering material for a biography of Hitler.

Around 1937, when Hitler heard that at the instigation of the party and the SS vast numbers of his followers had left the church because it was obstinately opposing his plans, he nevertheless ordered his chief associates, above all Göring and Goebbels, to remain members of the church. He too would remain a member of the Catholic Church, he said, although he had no real attachment to it. And in fact he remained in the church until his suicide.

Hitler had been much impressed by a scrap of history he had learned from a delegation of distinguished Arabs. When the Mohammedans attempted to penetrate beyond France into Central Europe during the eighth century, his visitors had told him, they had been driven back at the Battle of Tours. Had the Arabs won this battle, the world would be Mohammedan today. For theirs was a religion that believed in spreading the faith by the sword and subjugating all nations to that faith. The Germanic peoples would have become heirs to that religion. Such a creed was perfectly suited to the Germanic temperament. Hitler said that the conquering Arabs, because of their racial inferiority, would in the long run have been unable to contend with the harsher climate and conditions of the country. They could not have kept down the more vigorous natives, so that ultimately not Arabs but Islamized Germans could have stood at the head of the Mohammedan Empire.

Hitler usually concluded this historical speculation by remarking: "You see, it's been our misfortune to have the wrong religion. Why didn't we have the religion of the Japanese, who regard sacrifice for the Fatherland as the highest good? The Mohammedan religion too would have been much more compatible to us than Christianity. Why did it have to be Christianity with its meekness and flabbiness?" It is remarkable that even before the war he sometimes went on: "Today the Siberians, the White Russians, and the people of the steppes live extremely healthy lives. For that reason they're better equipped for development and in the long run biologically superior to the Germans." This was an idea he was destined to repeat in far more drastic tones during the last months of the war.

Rosenberg sold his seven-hundred page *Myth of the Twentieth Century* in editions of hundreds of thousands. The public regarded the book as the standard text for party ideology, but Hitler in those teatime conversations bluntly called it "stuff nobody can understand," written by "a narrow-minded Baltic German who thinks in horribly complicated terms." He expressed wonderment that such a book could ever have attained such sales: "A relapse into medieval notions!" I wondered if such private remarks were carried back to Rosenberg.

Hitler believed that the culture of the Greeks had reached the peak of perfection in every field. Their view of life, he said, as expressed in their architecture, had been "fresh and healthy." One day a photograph of a beautiful woman swimmer stirred him to enthusiastic reflections: "What splendid bodies you can see today. It is only in our century that young people have once again approached Hellenistic ideals through sports. How the body was neglected in earlier centuries. In this respect our times differ from all previous cultural epochs since antiquity." He personally, however, was averse to any kind of sports. Moreover, he never mentioned having practiced any sport at all as a young man.

By the Greeks he meant the Dorians. Naturally his view was affected by the theory, fostered by the scientists of his period, that the Dorian tribe which migrated into Greece from the north had been of Germanic origin and that, therefore, its culture had not belonged to the Mediterranean world.

Göring's passion for hunting was one of his favorite topics. [Hitler said:]

> How can a person be excited about such a thing. Killing animals, if it must be done, is the butcher's business. But to spend a great deal of money on it in addition.... . I understand, of course, that there must be professional hunters to shoot sick animals. If only there were still some danger connected with hunting, as in the days when men used spears for killing game. But today, when anybody with a fat belly can safely shoot the animal down from a distance.... . Hunting and horse racing are the last remnants of a dead feudal world.

After dramatic negotiations Hitler was apt to deride his opposites. Once he described Schuschnigg's visit to Obersalzberg on February 12, 1938. By a pretended fit of passion he had made the Austrian Chancellor realize the gravity of the situation, he said, and finally forced him to yield. Many of those hysterical scenes that have been reported were probably carefully staged. In general, self-control was one of Hitler's most striking characteristics. In those early days he lost control of himself only a very few times, at least in my presence.

Some time around 1936 Schacht had come to the salon of the Berghof to report. We guests were seated on the adjacent terrace and the large window of the salon was wide open. Hitler was shouting at his Finance Minister, evidently in excitement. We heard Schacht replying firmly in a loud voice. The dialogue grew increasingly heated on both sides and then ceased abruptly. Furious, Hitler came out on the terrace and ranted on about this disobliging, limited minister who was holding up the rearmament program. He had another such fit of rage at Pastor Niemöller in 1937. Niemöller had once again delivered a rebellious sermon in Dahlem; at the same time transcripts of his tapped telephone conversations were presented to Hitler. In a bellow Hitler ordered Niemöller to be put in a concentration camp and, since he had proved himself incorrigible, kept there for life.

Sometimes I asked myself: Why can't I call Hitler my friend? What is missing? I spend endless time with him, was almost at home in his private circle and, moreover, his foremost associate in his favorite field, architecture.

Everything was missing. Never in my life have I met a person who so seldom revealed his feelings, and if he did so, instantly locked them away again. During my time in Spandau I talked with Hess about this peculiarity of Hitler's. Both of us agreed that there had been moments when we felt we had come close to him. But we were invariably disillusioned. If either of us ventured a slightly more personal tone, Hitler promptly put up an unbreakable wall.

Hess did think there had been one person with whom Hitler had had a closer bond: Dietrich Eckart. But as we talked about it, we decided that the relationship had been, on Hitler's side, more a matter of admiration for the older man, who was regarded chiefly in anti-Semitic circles as a leading writer, than a friendship. When Eckart died in 1923 there remained four men with whom Hitler used the *Du* of close friendship: Hermann Esser,* Christian Weber, Julius Streicher, and Ernst Roehm. Even toward Eva Braun he was never completely relaxed and human. The gulf between the leader of the nation and the simple girl was always maintained. Now and then, and it always struck a faintly jarring note, he would call her *Tschapperl*, a Bavarian peasant pet name with a slightly contemptuous flavor.

Hitler must already have realized the immense drama that his life was, the high stakes he was playing for, by the time he had a long conversation with Cardinal Faulhaber at Obersalzberg in November 1936. Afterward Hitler sat alone with me in

---

* Hermann Esser was one of the very first party members and later became the state secretary for tourism. Christian Weber, also one of the earliest party members, was reduced to a rather limited role after 1933; among other things he was in charge of the horse races at Riem. Ernst Roehm was head of the SA and was murdered by Hitler in 1934. Julius Streicher was Germany's foremost anti-Semite, editor of *Der Stürmer* and Gauleiter of Franconia.

the bay window of the dining room, while the twilight fell. For a long time he looked out of the window in silence. Then he said pensively: "There are two possibilities for me: To win through with all my plans, or to fail. If I win, I shall be one of the greatest men in history. If I fail, I shall be condemned, despised, and damned."

# THE PROTOCOLS OF
# THE WISE MEN OF ZION

from
*Der Fuehrer:*
*Hitler's Rise to Power*
by Konrad Heiden
Translated by Ralph Manheim
Boston: Houghton Mifflin Company, 1944

*Before World War I, strong socialist parties in every European nation had made all political and military leaders wary of this growing faction. In a sense, that war had been welcomed by the current rulers, for it had enabled them to restrict the growing socialist parties, and they had been quite effective in stopping the spread of socialism by directing all efforts towards winning the war.*

*Once the war was over, the socialist stirrings were felt again on the continent. Although the treaty foisted by the Allies on the defeated German nation and its war partners splintered the Socialist Party in Germany, hunger and unemployment encouraged the founding of small rebellious political cells. One spin-off was the German Workers Party which became the nucleus for the National Socialist Party, or Nazis. The chief theoretician in this group was Gottfried Feder, who advocated certain socialist reforms, like state ownership of land and the nationalization of the banks. Early members of the party's socialist cell included discontented war veterans like Hitler, Rudolf Hess and Hermann Göring, social misfits like Julius Streicher, and frustrated intellectuals like Paul Goebbels and Alfred Rosenberg.*

*Probably no one man influenced Hitler more in promoting the hatred and destruction of the Jews of Europe than Rosenberg. He convinced Hitler that to save the country it was necessary to destroy the members of a "German Jewish conspiracy" who were the betrayers of the fatherland and "the international Jewish bankers" who were dedicated to the destruction of Germany as a nation. Rosenberg clinched his argument with the booklet* The Protocols of the Wise Men of Zion.

*What makes* The Protocols *especially important is that this forgery, which is responsible for inducing the destruction of millions of men, women and children, is still being circulated in different languages throughout the world.*

27

*The creation of* The Protocols *and Rosenberg's introduction to them was graphically described by Konrad Heiden, an ardent anti-Nazi since 1921, when he had attended his first National Socialist meeting. In 1923, as a student, he engaged in fistfights in the street with Hitler and his bullies. Heiden followed Hitler's career very carefully, and put together an authoritative work on Hitler's life.*

*At the beginning of 1918, the Bolshevik revolution was spreading, frightening Alfred Rosenberg. He packed his few belongings and the* Protocols of the Wise Men of Zion, *and fled from Moscow to his native city, Reval. The Germans had taken the city earlier, and Rosenberg made an effort to join the German forces fighting the Bolsheviks, but the commandant didn't trust this German-Russian and rejected him. Rosenberg was forced to take a job teaching until the end of the year, when the Bolshevik army advanced on Reval and the German army retreated.*

*Once more Rosenberg packed his suitcase and his precious booklet,* The Protocols, *and ran. This time he headed for Munich, where he found his way to a conspiratorial group that called itself the "Thule Society" after the legendary kingdom of Nordic mythology. Here he became acquainted with a young soldier, Rudolf Hess, and with Dietrich Eckart, an elderly writer. Rosenberg brought to them* The Protocols of the Wise Men of Zion, *and very soon a German edition appeared. The little book gave birth to a cause, and the backers chose to remain anonymous. It became the book of the hour in Germany, and then the British newspaper,* The Post, *reprinted it in a series. The London* Times *demanded an investigation to learn if there was any truth to* The Protocols, *but there was no investigation, only added publicity. The poison continued to spread.*

The Protocols *was published in America, Italy, Hungary, Turkey and elsewhere. The little volume gave Germany and her World War I allies a scapegoat for the loss of the war. They felt they had attained a military victory but been betrayed by the Jews. The resulting Depression had been caused by the Jews, and since* The Protocols *had come from Russia, was it not fair to infer that Communism was a Jewish plot, and Communist Russia was the instrument through which Jews would dominate the world?*

*The forged* Protocols of the Wise Men of Zion, *composed in a Russian cellar by secret police in the pay of the tsar, was given to the world by Alfred Rosenberg, half German, half Russian, half architect, half engineer, and half Jewish.*

One day in the summer of 1917 a student was reading in his room in Moscow. A stranger entered, laid a book on the table, and silently vanished. The cover of the book bore in Russian the words from the twenty-fourth chapter of Matthew: "He is near, he is hard by the door."

The student sensed the masterful irony of higher powers in this strange happening. They had sent him a silent message. He opened the book, and the voice of a demon spoke to him.

It was a message concerning the Antichrist, who would come at the end of days. The Antichrist is no mythical being, no monkish medieval fantasy. It is the portrait of a type of man who comes to the fore when an epoch is dying. He is a man with white skin, in everyday clothes, dangerously contemporary, and a mighty demagogue. He will talk with the masses, and at his word the masses will rise up and turn a culture to ashes, a culture which has deserved no better, since it has borne the Antichrist in its own image and for its own destruction. The great Russian philosopher Soloviev described him. The Antichrist "does not look like what he is," and therein precisely lies the danger. He is a young man with a strong personality and seductive power of speech and writing. He is an ascetic and a vegetarian. He will win fame first by a book in which "respect of the ancient traditions and symbols stands side by side with a bold and thorough radicalism in social and political problems... absolute individualism with an ardent fidelity to the common weal. ...' Then in Berlin he will become ruler of the "United States of Europe"; he will conquer Asia and North Africa; America will submit to him voluntarily. He is an absolute genius, and he may, says Soloviev, wear a small mustache.

This is the demon who speaks out of the book.

"We shall talk with the people on the streets and squares," says the demon, "and teach them to take the view of political questions which at the moment we require. For what the ruler says to the people spreads through the whole country like wildfire, the voice of the people carries it to all four winds.

"We"—the demon always says "We"—"shall create unrest, struggle, and hate in the whole of Europe and thence in other continents. We shall at all times be in a position to call forth new disturbances at will, or to restore the old order.

"Unremittingly we shall poison the relations between the people and states of all countries. By envy and hatred, by struggle and warfare, even by spreading hunger, destitution, and plagues, we shall bring all peoples to such a pass that their only escape will be in total submission to our domination.

"We shall stultify, seduce, ruin the youth.

"We shall not stick at bribery, treachery, treason, as long as they serve the realization of our plans. Our watchword is: force and hypocrisy!

"In our arsenal we carry boundless ambition, burning avidity, a ruthless thirst for revenge, relentless hatred. From us emanates the specter of fear, all-embracing terror."

A gabbling demon, and self-conceited, too:

"We are the chosen, we are the true men. Our minds give off the true power of the spirit; the intelligence of the rest is instinctive and animal. They can see, but they cannot foresee; their inventions are purely corporeal. Does it not follow clearly that Nature herself has predestined us to dominate the world?

"We shall not submit the unique greatness of our ultimate plan, the context of its particular parts, the consequences of each separate point, the secret meaning of which remains hidden, to the judgment and decision of the many, even, of those who share our thoughts; we shall not cast the gleaming thoughts of our leader before the swine, and even in more intimate circles we shall not permit them to be carped at.

"We shall paint the misdeeds of foreign governments in the most garish colors and create such an ill-feeling toward them that the peoples would a thousand times rather bear a slavery which guarantees them peace and order than enjoy their much touted freedom. The peoples will tolerate any servitude we may impose on them, if only to avoid a return to the horrors of wars and insurrection. Our principles and methods will take on their full force when we present them in sharp contrast to the putrid old social order.

"Outwardly, however, in our 'official' utterances, we shall adopt an opposite procedure and always do our best to appear honorable and cooperative. A statesman's words do not have to agree with his acts. If we pursue these principles, the governments and peoples which we have thus prepared will take our IOU's for cash. One day they will accept us as the benefactors and saviors of the human race.

"If any state dares to resist us; if its neighbors make common cause with it against us, we shall unleash a world war."

And then the demon spreads his wings, conceals the sky, darkens the world:

"By all these methods we shall so wear down the nations that they will be forced to offer us world domination. We shall stretch out our arms like pincers in all directions, and introduce an order of such violence that all people will bow to our domination."

Who is this "we"? Who is it that brags so absurdly?

To the student it is not absurd. It sounds fantastic, but it is not a mere tissue of lies. He turns back the pages and discovers that all this accursed wisdom, all these diabolical plans, were hatched out by a group of old Jews, who met together in a back room in Basel, Switzerland, in the year 1897. The demon aiming to devour the world is a Jewish club. It stands there in black and white, described at length, with place and date. Twenty years had passed before this knowledge found the right man. And thus *The Protocols of the Wise Men of Zion*, since become so famous, fell into the hands of Alfred Rosenberg.

A mysterious occurrence. Rosenberg himself has often told how the unknown suddenly stepped into the room, laid down the book, and silently departed. To Rosenberg it was a sign from heaven. Both the place and the hour were significant. Moscow, 1917. Far to the west, the German-Russian phase of the First World War was drawing to an end in crumbling trenches; in the streets of the capital, the Russian Revolution was ebbing and flowing. Alfred Rosenberg, the son of a shoemaker, born in Reval (Tallinn) on the Baltic, was then twenty-four years old; he was of German descent but as an Estonian, he was a subject of the Russian tsar. He had been raised in the German and Russian languages; he had first studied engineering and architecture at Riga, also on the Baltic; then, when the German army occupied Riga, he had fled. Now he was studying in Moscow.

The globe was afire. The tsar's empire was crumbling. Perhaps there would never again be peace. Perhaps this book would tell him why. The demon, who had incited the nations against each other, had spoken. Perhaps he, Alfred Rosenberg, understood him better than others; for in his own soul he could feel more strongly than others the mesh woven by hatred and love between the nations. He came from the tsar's Baltic, German provinces. He could scarcely say whether he was more Russian or more German. But today there were greater things concerning which he must achieve clarity. Here in Russia's holy city, in Russia's language, he had received a message. Judah, a book has brought forth thine innermost thoughts! He, the student, would close his eyes and believe it all his life, as firm as a rock. Was a new epoch of world history beginning in Moscow at that hour? Surely one of the most astounding, far-reaching, and bloody conspiracies of all time was bound to that hour. He who could read would go far.

"The nations," says the demon, "love and honor audacity in statesmen. Faced with an act of violence, they say: that was vile but clever! A scoundrel's trick, but wonderfully executed! With what insolence! Our leaders must move toward their goal with unparalleled boldness. Then we shall break all resistance in our path." The vision sends forth an icy chill and a breath of deadly truth.

The demon of world domination has spoken. He has proclaimed the great secret: the world can be dominated. Bowed with weariness, the peoples demand subjection. And those who resist will be tamed by terrible blows and sufferings. Modern society is charged with a magical current which in all men creates the same thoughts. The masses expect great things of their rulers. And for that reason, great things are easy.

This is the true sense of the secret writings which we today know as *The Protocols of the Wise Men of Zion*. Everything else in them develops from the basic idea that world domination is possible in our time: with sovereign contempt it is shown with what relative ease it can be achieved. Later, at third, fourth, and fifth hand, these profound thoughts were woven together with a figment of forgeries and purposeful lies which confused and obscured the whole document to the point of unintelligibility. But precisely in that condition it could be swallowed without understanding by millions of readers, and this gave it its great effect.

Today we are in a position to re-create the original content of the document. Its content is how to establish dictatorship with the help—and abuse—of democratic methods. The genesis of Caesarism is described. We are told that democracy, if carried to its extreme conclusion, provides the usurper with his best weapons. Furthermore, democracy, in the international field actually offers a dictator, who has firmly entrenched himself in one country, the possibility of world domination. This is the true content of the famous *Protocols*. Three generations ago a brilliant thinker wrote this secret formula for the achievement of world domination. We know little concerning his life. He was a French lawyer named Maurice Joly. He was, at the time he wrote his little book, a conservative, legitimist and monarchist. He had no thought of writing a secret document; on the contrary, he had in mind a satire against Napoleon III, then emperor of the French. Whether he ever perceived that he was leaving behind him the prophecies of a great seer; whether he ever guessed that his book embraced a political doctrine of world-shaking force, we do not know. The work was published in Brussels in 1864 by A. Mertens et Fils, as an illegal propaganda pamphlet; it was written in French and bore the title: *Dialogue aux enfers entre Machiavel et Montesquieu, ou la politique de Machiavel au XIX<sup>e</sup> siècle, par un Contemporain.* (Dialogue in hell between Machiavelli and Montesquieu, or the politics of Machiavelli in the nineteenth century by a contemporary.) His anonymity did not avail the author. The police of the French emperor discovered him, he was sent to prison for fifteen months. His book was published in a second edition, then it was forgotten, and today scarcely any copies of it can be found.

For the author had seen the secret disease of his epoch, and that is something which men do not like. Today we read Joly with quite different eyes. Today the evils are no longer secret. To us, living in the present day, some of the sentences of this forgotten book seem like a lightning flash, bathing the present in dazzling light. They are unpleasant truths, but great truths, and they come down to us from great sources. Joly gathered his wisdom from Machiavelli and Montesquieu; the Italian political philosopher of the fifteenth, the French political philosopher of the eighteenth century, step forward in his book and utter the ideas of their great works, *Il Principe* and *L'Esprit des Lois*. Chiefly the ideas of Machiavelli were retained in the book's later form, *The Protocols of Zion*. Joly applied these ideas to the technique of dominating the modern masses; that was his contribution. In the final version the conception is broadened to cover the masses of whole continents, of the entire globe...

Maurice Joly had understood the meaning of domination. He knew the modern mass and its state of mind. He had seen a master guide it. The master was Napoleon III, conspirator, usurper, and for nearly twenty years emperor of the French; at once nationalist and socialist, democrat and tyrant, pacifist and conqueror, dictator by virtue of bayonets and the plebiscite; applauded by the masses whom he had politically raped. Joly had written his book with him in mind. He was meant when the demon spoke: we shall stultify the people, we shall promote disturbances in Europe and elsewhere, we shall create a mighty central power, we shall commit crimes, and the people will admire us for them. If gallstones had not made a wreck of this third Napoleon, he might have died in power and glory.

Joly's magnificent portrait of modern tyranny underwent a strange fate. After thirty years of oblivion, its great day came. It was discovered by a group of Russian conspirators. Not, to be sure, by the Russian revolutionaries of that day, the Nihilists, Social Democrats, or Social Revolutionaries; but by a few crafty agents of the counter-revolution, members of the Ochrana, the tsar's secret police. They wanted to frighten the tsar and drive him to bloodshed. To this end they persuaded him that the Jews of the whole world had devised a secret conspiracy to achieve domination, first over Russia, then over the whole world.

Claims of this sort were not new; they lay to a certain extent in the air. In the nineteenth century the Jews had nearly everywhere—though not in Russia—achieved civil equality and thus taken their place in modern society. Some had amassed great wealth, a few—for example, the house of Rothschild—had even attained real influence, and inspired a venomous anti-Semitism. Soloviev, for example, quotes a French priest who wrote that "he lived by anticipation of that glorious day when, the skin stripped off... the Jews will be used for making cheap carpets."

This epoch lies behind us. Today Rothschild is a memory, no longer a power. Anonymous, massive concentrations of power in industry and finance have relegated the Jewish bankers and big merchants—once so impressive—to second or third rank. There is a Jewish problem; this book will not attempt to deny it. As a modern Jewish leader, Theodor Herzl, said, "The Jewish question exists wherever Jews live in any considerable number... The longer anti-Semitism lies dormant, the more furiously it must break out." Nevertheless, painful as it is, it principally concerns the Jews themselves; it is not and never was the chief problem of society as a whole, which has other and graver worries. But in the nineteenth century, it was possible for imaginative minds to be frightened by the aura of political power surrounding certain Jewish names. In 1868, Hermann Gödsche, a German signing himself Sir John Retcliffe the Younger, wrote a novel entitled *Biarritz*. In it twelve rabbis from all corners of the earth meet in the Jewish cemetery in Prague. There they set up a cry of Satanic glee, for through accursed gold, through its mighty bankers, Judah has conquered the world, bought kings and the princes of the Church; Judah is wallowing in vice and glory. The rabbis represent the twelve tribes of Israel and speak Chaldaean. Subsequently this chapter, somewhat revised, was printed in pamphlet form and translated into foreign languages. And now, lo and behold, we have an "authentic document," proving the existence of a Jewish world conspiracy.

Gödsche's text was childish and none too convincing. But suppose you take these rabbis conspiring in their cemetery and give them the worldly wisdom, the contempt for humanity, the seductive power of Joly's tyrant. Don't just make them avaricious braggarts; make them subtle and crafty; make them speak the accursed satirical wisdom of Machiavelli, but in deadly earnest; finally, confound the fabulous nocturnal conspiracy with an international Jewish congress which actually did convene to discuss such sober matters as the problem of emigration. Then we have before us, in all its bloody romantic horror, the demon of Jewish world domination gathered in a congress and fixed in a protocol.

That is what happened. The group of Russian conspirators dug up Joly's forgotten book; they were also familiar with the horror story about the Jewish cemetery in Prague; they knew by the newspapers that in 1897 the Jewish Zionist movement had very publicly been founded at a congress in Basel; finally, they knew only too well the golden awe emanating from the ancient fame of the Rothschilds. The ingredients of a magnificent conspiracy lay at hand, requiring only to be mixed.

The Ochrana, the tsarist secret police, furnished the means and the brains. First General Oryevsky, one of its heads, had a pamphlet prepared, based on the rabbis' conspiracy in Gödsche's story. The novelty was that the pamphlet was written in the form of protocols; this gave it a much more serious look. The pamphlet served as a frame to which Joly's ideas were embroidered in glowing colors. This was the work of General Ratchkovsky, the leader of the French division of the Ochrana. For the Ochrana had divisions for all countries. Everywhere it tracked down the activities of Russian, and not only Russian, revolutionaries. It was a kind of world conspiracy; a net of spies, intriguers, bribe-givers, and political agitators, which Russian tsarism had cast over the world.

With his eye for conspiracy, Ratchkovsky saw the explosive power inherent in Joly's timeworn and seemingly harmless work. It described modern dictatorship, its secret and yet so open methods; laid bare its cogs and springs. A real tyrant would never have spoken so self-revealingly; only a hostile satirist could have put such words of braggadocio into his mouth. The effect was a terrible self-indictment of modern dictatorship. This presumably is why the material appealed so strongly to these conspirators of dictatorship. They were confronted with their own image.

They could scarcely have pondered the matter very deeply, but it is precisely in the unconscious acts of men that history is most clearly revealed. The Ochrana men knew that this was good material, that they could make use of it. That was enough. In one or two evenings, over a pipe and a cup of tea, you could adapt this colorful but rather anonymous document for any purpose, put any label on it. Where Joly speaks in the first person singular, puts his speeches in the mouth of Machiavelli, means Napoleon III, and is actually denouncing modern Caesarism as such, just substitute "We Jesuits," "We Freemasons," "We Englishmen," or "We Jews"—the result would be a fragment of perverted truth, hence not entirely incredible. As for Ratchkovsky and his clique, they were interested in the Jewish angle.

Their plan was more than a simple palace conspiracy. It was the first great attempt at a mighty national counter-revolution against the democratic and socialist revolution of the nineteenth century. The plan was to fuse the passion of the people and the cold power of the state into a mighty counter-revolutionary force that would shake society to its foundations. If the movement had succeeded, it would most likely have transformed the old autocratic tsarism profoundly from within, made it a hundred times more powerful. In Holy Russia, at the beginning of the twentieth century, it would probably have created a new phenomenon in many respects resembling the later fascist dictatorships. Society in Russia was further advanced in its spiritual disintegration, inwardly more prepared for revolution than anywhere else in the world; at the same time the state power was stronger than anywhere else. Hence, it is understandable that this first attempt at a state-directed revolution should have been made here. It is in any case worth thinking about. Through this conspiracy, Russia became the spiritual mother country of modern fascism, as it later became the world center of communism.

As nucleus of the counter-revolutionary popular movement, a new party was formed. A certain Butmy was its leader. This party was military in organization. Its storm troops rode through the country performing "propaganda by action." Chief among their activities was a bloody persecution of the Jews, the aim being to call attention to the Jews as the ostensible cause of bad conditions. Always strike the minority was their principle—for when a minority is punished, it is guilty in the eyes of the masses. The name of the movement was "The Black Hundreds," which meant simply: the black guard. *The Protocols of the Wise Men of Zion* became the program of this movement; with it they were born, and with it they grew. Even the primitive version, based on Gödsche's nocturnal conspiracy of rabbis, had a terrible effect. It was circulated widely, and in 1903 gave the signal for the Kishenev pogrom, in which several thousand Jews were massacred.

By its very nature every fascist movement strives to harness both the people and the state power to its will. The men who cooked up the *Protocols* wanted not only to stir up the masses, but also to take in the credulous tsar. To this end, they gave the book a political timeliness. A first version had been prepared toward the end of the nineties by Golovinski and Manuilov, two journalists in the service of Ratchkovsky. This version included Joly's most impressive bits. For some reason or other the bombshell was left unused for a few years. It was not hurled until political developments offered a particularly grateful target. In 1904-05, the pamphlet was

34

refurbished as an attack on Prince Svatopulk-Mirski, minister of the interior, and Count Witte, the finance minister, who were too liberal for the Ochrana. A pamphlet on financial policy, by a certain Sharapov, attacking Count Witte was appended. References to the unfortunate Russo-Japanese War and to Witte's rôle as peacemaker were woven in. All this, of course, beneath the paper-thin trimming of a Jewish conspiracy. Other propaganda works represented the Jews as warmongers; now, on the contrary, they had to be peacemongers; for if Witte made peace with the Japanese, he did so—say the *Protocols*—on the instigation of the Jews, who were opposed to a Russian victory. They did not want a Russian victory, because it would have thwarted their plan for world domination.

This is the origin of the supposed textbook of Jewish world domination. Today the forgery is incontrovertibly proved, yet something infinitely significant has remained: a textbook of world domination, pure and simple. The leaders of the Black Hundreds had written this great method of demagogy, the tsar's secret police had given it plastic form. Or, to call this clique of political officials, venal writers, conspiratorial officers, by their proper name: the armed intellectual was out to seize power over the masses. He denied it, to be sure; he said: no, no, this was not my work. The Jew devised these plans; I only stole them and brought them to light for the salvation of mankind. But today we know better. An impartial court has established the truth, even anti-Semitic propagandists have today dropped the myth of the Jewish conspiracy in Basel and admitted Joly's authorship. At first the anti-Semites comforted themselves with the idea that Joly was a Jew and that a "Jewish spirit" had impelled him to write his book; but then Joly's baptismal record was found, exploding this last hope; since then, some anti-Semites have declared merely that the *Protocols* are "deeper wisdom," beyond any possibility of documentary proof. Actually they do contain a deeper truth; but the demonstrable history of their origin shows that this truth involves not a Jewish but a fascist world conspiracy.

# THE SIEGE OF MADRID

from

*Looking for Trouble*

by Virginia Cowles

New York: Harper & Brothers, 1941

*The first large metropolitan city to get a preview of the warfare to follow during World War II was Madrid, the capital of Spain. For hundreds of years, Spain's turbulent leadership had vacillated from monarchy to dictatorship. Whatever the leadership in power, strikes and uprisings were invariably suppressed with great brutality. In 1923 an outbreak in Catalonia, though quickly and bloodily repressed, resulted in a national military dictatorship under Primo de Rivera. Several years later he was forced to resign, and in 1931 a republic was formed, resulting in the deposition of King Alfonso XIII. The first elected president, caught up in the continuing conflict between church and state, resigned in protest against anticlerical legislation.*

*The shifting of public sentiment from left to right to left precipitated a military rebellion. The insurgents, under the command of Francisco Franco, embraced the monarchy, the industrialists, and the landowners. Franco's sympathies paralleled those of the current European dictators, and he soon accepted men and arms from Hitler and Mussolini with which he slowly and efficiently destroyed the short-lived Spanish democracy.*

*Observers recognized that what was happening in Spain might be a forerunner of things to come in other countries. Reporters from around the globe flocked to Madrid to tell the world of the brutal enslavement of the Spanish people by Franco's fascist forces and their allies.*

*In 1937 a slim, young woman reporter, Virginia Cowles, arrived in Madrid. A Boston debutante with a flair for writing, she had served her apprenticeship as a society columnist and later as a writer for fashion magazines, but she was unhappy writing about the fluffy society she had been born into and wanted serious assignments.*

*At that time, women were expected to write from the "woman's angle." Straight news was handled by men. Nevertheless, Cowles persuaded the manager of the Hearst papers to let her go to Spain in 1936. She said, "The only way a girl can cover a war is to tell the paper of her choice that she is going anyway and would they like some stories."*

*Virginia Cowles arrived the week after the battle of Guadalajara to investigate the Loyalist (Republican) side. Once in Madrid, she visited with correspondents Martha Gelhorn, Kennedy of the Associated Press, and Ernest Hemingway, to get help with her assignment.*

*Nearly arrested as a spy, Cowles escaped to Paris and wrote up her interviews with American soldiers and others at the fighting fronts, including a special interview with a Red Army general (the Communists had sent men and arms to help the Loyalists). She continued covering the area until she moved on to England to cover the battle of Britain.*

*A critic said of her book,* Looking for Trouble, *that it had authenticity and charm but that the author was sometimes fatuous. Perhaps he had in mind Cowles's disappointment in the International Brigade for not looking like swashbuckling soldiers of fortune.*

*Published before the bombing of Pearl Harbor,* Looking for Trouble *ends with a plea for help for England and for a declaration of war on Germany by the United States.*

M y room, on the fifth floor of the Hotel Florida, stamped me as an amateur; knowledgeable people lived as close to the ground as possible as a precaution against aerial bombs. The hotel was crowded, however, so the best the manager could do was to switch me to a large outside room on the fourth floor; but this, too, had its disadvantages. It faced a broad square and overlooked a jumble of grey rooftops that dwindled into a distant landscape of rolling green hills. And these hills belonged to the enemy. Although this placed me in the direct line of shell-fire, the desk clerk refused to let me move. He said the inside rooms were dark and stuffy, and, besides, the hotel was not a military objective, so if a shell went through my room it would only be a mistake.

Madrid, dark and gloomy at night, was transformed into a new world with the daylight. The sun was shining and the air resounded with the clatter of humdrum business. I leaned out of the window to find the square thronged with people. Khaki-clad militiamen with red ties around their necks threaded their way into a café across the street, while black-shawled housewives with children tugging after them hurried off to do the day's marketing. A trio of peroxide blondes swayed along the rough pavement on high-heeled shoes to the intense interest of a group of young men in dark blue berets who stood in the sun prodding their teeth with toothpicks. Donkey-carts rumbled across the cobble-stones, newspaper sellers shouted their wares, and from a movie house half a block away came a lively melody from Al Jolson's *Casino de Paris*. For a city subjected to daily bombardments Madrid seemed as unreal as a huge movie set swarming with extras ready to play a part.

The telephone rang with a message from Sefton (Tom) Delmer of the London *Daily Express*, who offered to show me the sights of Madrid. I had often heard of Tom, who was noted for his quick wit and had the reputation of being one of the shrewdest journalists in Europe. He was a large bulk of a man with a smiling face. He greeted me by asking hopefully if I had brought any food from France. The fact that I hadn't I soon realized was an unforgivable oversight.

We strolled down the streets and Tom told me he had covered the war on the Nationalist side until he made the mistake of writing the story of Knickerbocker's trip to Burgos. The latter's plane had been mistaken for an enemy machine and fired upon by anti-aircraft guns. Tom pointed out in his story that Knickerbocker had been unaware of the episode until he was informed of it by the aerodrome authorities. The Nationalists claimed this was an attempt to cast reflection on their anti-aircraft defences and Tom was thereby expelled. Since then he had been covering the war from Madrid: "All Spaniards are mad," he said, "but the people over here are less dangerous to England."

We walked along the main streets and passed dozens of holes blasted out of the pavements where shells had fallen; many buildings bore jagged wounds, and on the *Castellana* a huge stone lion stared gloomily into space as though it knew its nose had been chipped off by shrapnel.

There was a good deal of traffic on the streets. Ministry of War cars, evacuation lorries, bicycles and ambulances all raced past us, and once a despatch rider on a motor-cycle roared by headed for the front. Parked on a side street we saw a brown and green camouflaged truck bearing proud white letters that said: "Captured from the enemy at Guadalajara."

At many of the corners stone barricades were erected across the streets—barricades that had been built in November when Franco boasted that his generals would soon be drinking in the *Puerta del Sol.* "If Franco takes Madrid," said the people, "he'll have to fight for it inch by inch."

And yet the atmosphere of the city was not one of war. Although it had become transformed into a village behind the front, bombs and shells had been unable to erase the daily routine of life. It was this that lent the city its curious air of theatre. Bright yellow tramcars rattled peacefully down the avenues, shop windows displayed Schiaparelli perfume, silver fox furs, jewellery, gloves and ladies' handmade shoes; movie houses advertised Greta Garbo in "Anna Karenina" and the Marx Brothers in "A Night at the Opera." A store on the *Gran Via* held a gala exhibition of war posters; they were ultra-modern posters, screaming out in reds, oranges and blues for the people of Spain to defend the Republic against Fascism. There was a small jagged hole in the ceiling where a shell had come through; beside it a card had been tacked "Art as practised by General Franco."

The shell-holes, the camouflaged trucks and the stone barricades seemed as unreal as stage props; the sun was too warm, the people too nonchalant for war. Only the queue lines carried a sense of tragedy. On a side street a procession of women and children were lined up before a grocery store, with empty baskets over their arms. Some leaned wearily against the building, others sat on the curb staring into space with a strange Oriental impassiveness. All over Madrid these queue lines were formed. The city's main diet was beans, bread and rice, but food was so scarce that only a limited number could be served. Tom said that often the lines waited from midnight till noon the next day.

We crossed the *Puerta del Sol* and Tom stopped at a small shop to look at some cavalry cloaks which he was thinking of taking back to England as presents. We had to step over an old peddler woman who was selling red and black anarchist ties and small tin ornaments made in the shapes of tanks and aeroplanes which she had carefully spread over the pavement.

The proprietor welcomed Tom warmly and brought out an assortment of capes of different lengths and cuts with a variety of brightly coloured linings. They discussed them for some time and Tom decided to come back again. When we said good-bye he asked the proprietor how his business was going and the man sighed and shook his head: "It is very difficult, Señor. There are so few gentlemen left in Madrid." Outside, Tom said, "It is obvious where *his* sympathies lie."

As we were walking down the *Gran Via* on the way back to the hotel I asked Tom how often the city was shelled and he stopped and looked meditatively at his watch. "It's past noon now. They usually drop a few before lunch." Scarcely a moment later I heard a noise like the sound of cloth ripping. It was gentle at first, then it grew into a hiss; there was a split second of silence, followed by a bang as a shell hurtled into the white stone telephone building at the end of the street. Bricks and timber crashed to the ground and dust rose up in a billow. A second shell plunged into the pavement thirty yards away and a third hit a wooden block of flats on a corner. Everyone started running, scattering into vestibules and doorways, like pieces of paper blown by a sudden gust of wind.

Tom and I took cover in a perfume shop and the explosions continued one every minute. My heart pounded uncertainly; the crash of falling bricks and breaking glass and the thick dust that rose up to blot out the sunshine seemed like some fearful Bible plague tuned up and mechanized for the twentieth-century appetite. The proprietress of the shop, however, appeared to be far more concerned with the preservation of property than possible death. She hastily began removing the perfume bottles from the window and laid them in neat rows on the floor. With each explosion she broke into a fresh flow of expletives. Tom explained she was afraid the windows would break. And glass, she said, was very dear.

The bombardment lasted about half an hour. When it was over we walked down the street; the pavements were strewn with bricks and shrapnel and a telephone pole leaned drunkenly across one of the buildings, the wires hanging down like streamers. The second floor of a hat-shop had a gaping hole and at the corner an automobile was a twisted mass of steel. Nearby, the pavement was spattered with blood where two women had been killed.

Desolation hung over the thoroughfare, but the loudspeaker was still screaming a tune from the *Casino de Paris*. Trucks rolled up and men got out and began to clear up the debris, the music ringing in their ears as they worked. Groups of people gathered on the corners and little boys ran out to collect pieces of shrapnel as souvenirs, and newspaper sellers drifted back to their boxes, the bootblacks called for customers and the shopkeepers re-arranged their wares. Two hours later the rubble was in neat piles along the curb. Automobiles hooted their way over the cobblestones, and once again people sauntered arm-in-arm in the sunshine. That, I learned, was Madrid. Mr. Hyde had vanished and Dr. Jekyll once more had control of the city.

I had never before felt the sort of fear that sends the blood racing through your veins. As intense an emotion as it was, I was surprised to find that with the passing of danger it disappeared so completely it was difficult even to recall the sensation. More curious still, it left no hang-over of apprehension. In between bombardments you literally forgot about them. Why this was I don't know; Nature, I suppose, taking its course. At any rate, the whine of a shell never failed to come as an utter surprise, and, to my way of thinking, a very nasty one at that. I greatly admired the indifference, often bordering on nonchalance, with which the Spaniards accepted these bombardments.

Strategically, Madrid was a third-line trench and the population had received their training. Civilian ears had become so acute that the ordinary man or woman could judge the proximity of a shell by the sound of the whistle. When shells fell at four- and five-minute intervals it indicated that only one battery was firing and there was always "a safe side" of the street. But if the explosions came fast it meant a cross fire—then there was nothing to do but take cover and trust to luck. During the innumerable shellings I never once saw a sign of panic. People conducted themselves as coolly as trained soldiers; narrow escapes became so much a part of daily life they were not even major topics of conversation.

I soon discovered that food was much more of a preoccupation than danger. Occasionally, when a donkey-cart, filled with lettuces or bread, moved through the streets a crowd gathered and tagged it breathlessly to its destination. In spite of this terrible shortage of essentials, the cognac and gin supplies had held up well and every afternoon the cafés were crowded. One of the most popular cafés was on the *Puerta del Sol*. A bomb had gone through the top of the building and you could see chunks of sky through the roof, but the ground floor did a thriving business.

The two gayest meeting-places, however, were the once fashionable Chicote's and Molinero's. Although these cafés were on the *Gran Via*, the most frequently bombarded street in Madrid, every afternoon they were crowded with soldiers with guns dangling from their hips and platinum blondes whose hair was growing out very black due to the fact that all the peroxide had been confiscated by the hospitals.

At Molinero's you found a last lingering badge of class-conscious Spain. The waiters were the same waiters who used to serve the wealthy *Madrileños* and they were dressed in the conventional uniform of black suit and white shirt. Some pushed their way through the noisy, singing throngs with obvious disdain; others took advantage of the *camarada* spirit and served you with unshaven faces and cigarettes hanging from their mouths.

The owners of Chicote's and Molinero's and most of the big shops and hotels had either been shot, were in gaol, or had fled from the city. Their concerns had been taken over by the Trade Unions and many were run collectively by the employees. Palaces and country villas were used as ministries and headquarters. Often journalists went to get their permits from officials in sweaters and leather jackets, reclining in sixteenth-century chairs in rooms with carved walls and priceless tapestries. More than once interviews were brought to a halt while the "comrade" proudly insisted upon your making an inspection of the books and paintings, and even the statues in the garden.

During those first few days in Madrid, it all seemed like a strange carnival to me. It was only at night when the capital was swallowed up in a suffocating darkness that the atmosphere took on a note of grim reality. The buildings jutted up so blackly the sky looked almost white, and as you threaded your way along the pavement, guards moved noiselessly out of the doorways and asked to examine your credentials.

Everything was deserted and still. The only noise was a distant one: the noise of fighting on the *Casa del Campo*, a mile and a half away. You could hear the dull thud of trench mortars like far-off thunder, and the thin crack of rifles like sheets snapping in the wind. And as you walked through the night, stumbling over shellholes, you wondered whether this was just the beginning and how long it would be before the lights went out somewhere else.

Madrid was honeycombed with Fifth Columnists and spies, and the Republicans had a large secret police force working to combat the leakage of information. Dossiers were kept on thousands of suspects, including the entire foreign press, and garish posters pasted on the buildings warned the population of the dangers of spies even among friends. A favourite poster showed a green-faced man with a hand cupped to his ear and in front of him a *señorita* with fingers raised to her lips saying, "Sh! Comrades! not a word to brothers or friends or sweethearts!"

None of us knew the full activities of the secret police or what went on behind the prison walls of Madrid. There is no doubt, however, that the Government was

waging a desperate struggle against Fifth Columnists who were supplying the enemy with a steady stream of information by radio and courier. There is no doubt,
either, that many thousands of innocent persons were dragged from their beds and
shot without trial.

Although I never witnessed any "atrocities" myself there is one episode that
stands out in my mind. I was having lunch at the *Gran Via* restaurant with Ernest
Hemingway and Josephine Herbst when a bombardment started. Shells were dropping on the street outside the café and it was impossible to leave, so we sat lingering
over our coffee. At the next table I noticed a fastidious-looking man dressed from
head to toe in dove grey. He had the high forehead and long fingers of the intellectual and wore horn-rimmed spectacles which added to his thoughtful appearance.

"That," said Hemingway, "is the chief executioner of Madrid."

Ernest invited him to join us and he accepted on the condition we would allow
him to buy us a carafe of wine. His manner was ingratiating to the point of syco-
phancy, but I shall never forget the look in his bright, marble-brown eyes. Perhaps it
was my imagination, but to me they mirrored all the traditional sadism of Spain.
Hemingway was passionately interested in details of death and soon was pressing
the man with questions.

"Have many people died in Madrid?"

"A revolution is always hasty."

"And have there been many mistakes?"

"Mistakes? It is only human to err."

"And the mistakes—how did they die?"

"On the whole, considering they were mistakes," he said meditatively, "very
well indeed; in fact, *magnifico!*" It was the way he said it that sent a shiver down my
spine. His voice rose on the last word to a note of rapture and his eyes gleamed with
relish. He reached out for the carafe of wine and filled my glass. It gurgled into the
tumbler, thick and red, and I could only think of blood.

When we got out of the restaurant, Hemingway said, "A *chic* type, eh? Now
remember, he's mine." When I read his play, *The Fifth Column*, many months later,
I was not surprised to find the following lines:

PHILIP: And, Antonio. Sometimes there must have been mistakes, eh? When
you had to work in a hurry perhaps. Or you know, just mistakes, we all
make mistakes. I just made a little one yesterday. Tell me, Antonio, were
there ever any mistakes?

ANTONIO: Oh, yes. Certainly. Mistakes. Oh, yes. Mistakes. Yes. Yes. Very
regrettable mistakes. A very few.

PHILIP: And how did the mistakes die?

ANTONIO (proudly): All very well.

Hemingway was greatly admired in Spain and known to everyone as "Pop."
He was a massive, ruddy-cheeked man who went around Madrid in a pair of filthy
brown trousers and a torn blue shirt. "They're all I brought with me," he would
mumble apologetically. "Even the anarchists are getting disdainful." Although he

had been wounded four times in the World War, the trenches had a fascination for him. On days when the front was quiet, he used to prowl around trying to borrow cartridges to go out to the country and shoot rabbits.

Hemingway's room (on the second floor of the Florida) was presided over by Sydney Franklin, a rough young American bull-fighter. He had often fought in the bull-rings of Spain and had a collection of rings and heavily-embossed cigarette-cases which had been presented to him by various fans. When I asked him how he had happened to come to Madrid, he said: "Well, see, one day Ernest rings me up and says:'—'lo, kid, want to go to the war in Spain?' and I says, 'Sure, Pop. Which side we on?' "

One of the most interesting trips I made was to the front where the International Brigades were fighting. This was on the Morata front where they were defending the Madrid-Valencia road, the last link between the capital and the outside world. Although Franco had launched fierce and repeated attacks, and the Republicans had suffered heavy loss of life, the lines had held. In May, this front was regarded as the most important sector in Spain and was commanded by a Soviet General.

In spite of being common knowledge that the Russians had sent nearly two thousand staff officers, technicians, airmen and tank experts to train the Republican Army, the subject was taboo. Journalists were not allowed to come into contact with them and the headquarters from which they operated was shrouded in secrecy. By accident I visited the Morata Headquarters and was "detained" there by the Soviet General for three days.

It happened in an odd way. One afternoon I drove out to Morata with Kajsa, a Swedish girl, and Jerome Willis of the *Agence d'Espagne*. We got lost and instead of reaching Brigade Headquarters wound up before a ramshackle old mill which we discovered was serving as Divisional Headquarters. The sentry led us into a garden where we were confronted by the commanding officer, a middle-aged man with a broad Slavonic face and sullen green eyes. He had an interpreter with him and spoke a language I thought was Hungarian. His manner was cold and hostile and he curtly cut off our attempts at conversation.

"Have many Fascist planes been over here?" Jerome asked.

"They fly."

"Do you think the enemy will make another drive soon?"

"Who knows?"

We explained that we hoped to talk to some of the American and English soldiers fighting in the Brigade but received a blunt refusal. "No visitors are permitted at the front." Although we argued that several journalists had been taken through the lines a few days before, it was to no avail. As we were leaving he walked over to one of the rosebushes, snapped off a spray of flowers and handed them to me, saying, with a studied sarcasm apparent even through the mouth of the interpreter, "You can write your story from the garden. No one will know the difference; and here is a souvenir to remind you of your adventure at the front."

I replied by passing the flowers to a surprised sentry and walking angrily out to the car. On the way home I asked Kasja if the officer was a Hungarian, and she nodded; but the rest of the trip she was unusually quiet.

I thought no more about the incident until a week later, when I was lunching in the *Gran Via* restaurant. A tall, serious-faced soldier spoke to me in English, introduced himself as "Santiago," and asked if I had paid a visit to Morata a few days previously. I nodded, and he said: "The commanding officer wishes to offer his apologies and says that perhaps you will come to lunch one day." I was surprised by the invitation and wondered what had caused the officer's sudden change of heart. I wasn't particularly anxious to go, but as it was my only chance to visit Brigade lines I accepted; the following noon Santiago arrived in the pouring rain to drive me out.

The General's manner was scarcely more cordial than before. He received me with a salutary smile and led the way to the mess hall. The room was shabby and the paint was peeling off the walls: there was a leak in the ceiling and the raindrops dripped slowly into a large tin placed on the floor. Standing around a long table in the centre were about a dozen officers; eight blond-haired Russian staff officers, two Hungarians, two Spaniards and a Russian-born American, David Jarrett, who acted as interpreter. I was introduced all round, but only Santiago and David could speak English my conversation was limited.

We sat down to lunch of partridges, fresh vegetables, bread and butter and wild strawberries. There was an air of great formality and I had a feeling everything had been carefully arranged, even to the large bowl of flowers in the middle of the table. I sat next to David Jarrett, a clean-cut man with a pleasant smile. He spoke eight languages fluently and told me that he had given up a job in New York as a Court interpreter to come to Spain. General Gal (whether or not this was a pseudonym I don't know) didn't address me till lunch was nearly over, then he instructed David to translate the following remark: "I may take you to the front this afternoon, but first you will have to remove those gold bracelets you are wearing. The enemy would be sure to spot them."

Everyone laughed and I seized the opportunity to press home the point about the front. "You are too soft," he replied. Then he looked disapprovingly at my black suede shoes. "You would get tired and want someone to carry you."

He was deliberately provocative, but I managed to keep a civil tongue, and an hour later, much to my surprise, my request was granted. The General, David and I got into a car and started for the front.

The front was about three miles away; it was raining hard, and as we neared the lines the woods on either side of the road became alive with tanks half hidden among the wet trees. Field-kitchens and first-aid stations were set up in the clearings and when we swung around a bend we passed a large truck with a container on top that looked like a gasolene tank; this was "the bath truck" that went up to front once a week with gallons of hot water.

The noise of gunfire grew louder and every now and then the dull grey sky lighted up with a flash as a shell travelled through the rain somewhere in the distance. At the bottom of a long slope our car stopped. The lines ran along the top of a hill and the ground between was scarred with shell-holes and mortar pits. There was the constant crack of rifle-fire and the bullets whined over our heads like angry wasps. The General explained that the climb up the hill involved a risk and told us to walk as quickly as possible. It was certainly one of the most uncomfortable experiences I have had; several shells burst near us and the only thing that kept me from bolting in the opposite direction was fear of the General's contempt.

When at last we reached the trenches we found them ankle deep in mud. They were deep, carefully-constructed lines that twisted and turned for four miles through the rolling fields. Men were standing at intervals firing through the openings in the sandbags. None were equipped with mackintoshes or tin hats, but wore an assortment of sweaters and jackets with mufflers tied around their necks. Most of them were soaked to the skin. The General led the way through the mud and we passed soldiers of every creed and nationality: Germans, Slavs, Jews, Frenchmen, Italians, Englishmen and Americans. They were each formed into their own companies and as we went along the General shook hands with them, patted them on the back and made light remarks that David translated into half a dozen languages.

The men looked strained and sick and I learned they had been in the front line for seventy-four days without a break. Most of them had been recruited by the Communist parties of the world and they struck me as a pathetic group. They had none of the swagger of the traditional legionnaire who fought for the joy of adventure; they were idealists and down-and-outs, many of them ill-suited for soldiering. They had fought bravely but already half their thirty thousand had been buried on the plains and plateaux of Castille.

When we reached the American section the men crowded around eagerly and pressed me with questions about "the States." One of them was an American Negro who had arrived at the front only a day or two before. The General asked him how he liked it and his dark face broke into a wide smile. "Ah appreciates de glory, suh, but to tell the truth ah was puffickly satisfied in de rear."

There were factory workers from Massachusetts, miners from Pennsylvania and farmers from Mississippi. Their manners were light-hearted but their faces were worn. "You might suggest to the General we get a vacation," said one. "Not that we have any kick about the neighbourhood but the view is getting monotonous." I left wondering how many would ever see the American continent again and a few weeks later heard that three-quarters of them had been wiped out in a fresh attack.

# POLAND ON THE BRINK

from

*The Armies March:*
*A Personal Report*
by John Cudahy
New York: Charles Scribner's Sons, 1941

*In 1933, as Hitler's revolutionary ideas were beginning to send shock waves throughout Europe, John Cudahy, an attorney whose interests ranged from law to real estate, was appointed ambassador to Poland.*

*Poland was creeping into the age of industrialization, and the old ways of life were changing reluctantly and slowly. The nobility had lived in splendor for more than a thousand years surrounded by a populace that had grown used to its level of poverty. The nation was trying to hold on to traditional values and maintain the illusion that everything would remain the same, only better.*

*The ruler of Poland, Josef Pilsudski, was a national hero. Every home that could afford a bust or a photograph of Pilsudski sported one in a conspicuous place. He seemed a hardy pioneer, a robust two-fisted warrior. Pilsudski ruled as a virtual dictator. He had no respect for the Sejm, the Polish parliament, and his language when he addressed them shocked sensitive people. In Poland he enjoyed much the same stature as did Hitler in Germany and Lenin in Russia.*

*Ambassador Cudahy writes of his meeting with Pilsudski, Foreign Minister Joseph Beck, and others of the Polish hierarchy.*

When I arrived in Poland in the late summer of 1933, the tension between Poland and Germany had reached the breaking point. Since Versailles, the Corridor and Danzig were constant threats to the peace of Europe, and there had been a sharp controversy over the administration of the Free City. The Polish army was strong. The country had been starved for the army. Probably two million men at that time could have been placed in the field. Pilsudski believed that he could defeat Hitler and he was realistic enough to recognize that if he waited he might well lose military preponderance over the German dictator. The time had come for a show-down, and the Polish Ambassador in Berlin, Lipski, was instructed to tell Hitler in undiplomatic language that he could have war or peace and to make up his mind in a hurry. The German-Polish treaty of January 23, 1934, was the consequence of this vigorous demarche. Germany agreed for a period of ten years to settle any difference with Poland at the conference table and in no event to resort to war.

Shortly afterward I called on Pilsudski at Belvidere Palace, Lazienki Park, where he lived in Warsaw. He was an ailing old man then, with caricaturish profile, outthrust chin and beetling brows over deep-sunk eyes. He wore the gray uniform of a field marshal, his skin had that dull gray lifelessness which proclaims a malignant, fatal disease, and his whole color note, his hair, his profuse brows, his eyes—all were gray. He was an ailing old man, although only sixty-seven years, doomed for an early death.

I spoke to Pilsudski about the peace he had made with Germany and was bold enough to ask him what he thought would be the state of Polish-German relations when the agreement reached expiration. I can see now, as I write, his piercing gray eyes and their twinkle as he leaned over and put his hand on my knee, "Young man, politicians used to build for their countries a generation in the future; now any man who thinks ahead a whole year is thinking a long, long time, and any one who plans for ten years is just an idiot."

Just five years and six months after this conversation German Stukas were screeching over Polish towns and panzer divisions were making their pulverizing advance over Polish soil.

I wonder if he knew what would happen to Poland and realized there was no escape. He had a faculty of divination that was almost preternatural, knew Europe well, and was seldom deceived on the fundamentals of the international situation.

Colonel Josef Beck, the Foreign Minister, was a faithful disciple of Pilsudski, with the brittle realism of the Talleyrand school of diplomacy. He believed that the purpose of words was to conceal ideas. Always from my meetings at the Foreign Office, I came away with the feeling that he had held back on me. There was an innate caution in his make-up, and he made a rule of concealment. He was clever and affected cleverness which wasn't too clever. Negotiations between governments are the same as any other negotiations. Only candor and honesty, or the appearance of these qualities, can beget confidence, and without confidence no negotiation can carry conviction.

Beck was very proud of Poland and his position, and always insisted that the Polish nation be recognized as one of the great powers of Europe with Great Britain, France, Italy and Germany. I found him unable to conceal his elation upon the conclusion of the ten-year pact with Germany, this traditional enemy of his country which three times had brutally despoiled Polish territory.

I always thought of the hardship on the poor Poles caused by the great weight of armament. One half of the budgetary outlay was required for the military establishment, and now that the German agreement was concluded, I inquired of the Foreign Minister (Col. Josef Beck) whether the load could not be lightened by demobilizing several divisions, but Colonel Beck dismissed this suggestion peremptorily with characteristic cynicism by saying that the agreement would never have been reached if Hitler had not feared Polish military force. This made me ponder on the durability of this forced peace with Hitler, for the population of the Reich was over twice that of Poland. The German ruling passion was soldiering. By tradition and training Germans had been great warriors since the days of Tacitus, and while the Polish divisions outnumbered them today, what would be the situation next year, five years from now? But I kept my speculation to myself, for Colonel Beck would have been offended if I had given utterance to what I considered the truth about his country and its future.

The truth, if you define truth as reality, had little bearing upon the life of Poland. The aristocracy lived in the grand manner with sweeping, seignorial gesture. They lived gallantly, gracefully, and with no sense of social or political responsibility. They lived successfully, unconscious of the afflicting poverty of the people, and life was a pleasant experience on their great estates, one of them, that of Prince Radziwill, the area of Delaware and Rhode Island combined.

Everyone lived off the earth. Land was the only wealth and there was not nearly enough to go round, but these great proprietors saw no anachronism in this grotesque, uneven distribution of the Polish soil. Once at a shoot, with my irrepressible Americanism, I spoke to Prince Radziwill of the social revolution which, since the reign of the Bolsheviks, was sweeping the world. I said, with typical undiplomatic openness, that Poland was a relic of feudalism and could not escape the universal transition in the division of individual possessions. We were witnessing in Poland the last stand of Feudalism. More and more the State was taking command of our lives and property, soon all would have to march in the regiment as common

46

soldiers. I predicted that in a few years these great shoots with their medieval magnificence would be a thing of memory. But he looked so hurt I was sorry I had spoken. You do not tell a victim of cancer about his fatal disease, and there was something profane in the crass suggestion that there might be an end to the Polish aristocracy and their happy status—immutable as the law of seasons and of stars.

A shooting party on one of the properties like that of Count Morinski's was like a page from Turgeniev and had no relation to the prosaic utilitarian temper of our twentieth century. At a comfortable hour the guests were driven from the castle in a high vehicle that in my day was known as a tallyho. Everything was flawlessly smart, the patent-leather top hats of the liveried servants and the cockade, the Morinski Crest, and the fine spanking horses. Magnificent beings of another world, we made our impressive way through the squalid, thatch-roofed poverty of the village just beyond the Prince's domain, where ragged people bowed and lifted their hats deferentially, the Prince acknowledging their obeisance with a salute of assured authority beyond condescension. I know that the dramatic contrast between our sybaritic elegance and this debasing indigence, which struck me with such painful embarrassment, passed entirely over his head, for he dismissed the suggestion with a light gesture when I spoke of it. The common people had always lived in this humble fashion, he said. They had always accepted the Morinski family and their eminence as one would accept any other permanent institution. But it was more than acceptance, the people took a pride in this fine elegance, they loved all the show, the panoply of power, and experienced a sense of splendor in this fairylike grandeur. Something dramatic, like the Christmas myth of childhood, would be taken from them, if the great castle were to close its gates, Prince Morinski explained with an air of benevolence.

We left the dirty little village and crossed a broad, flat land to a dark forest of tall, slim pines, where a group of two hundred odd peasants, formed in a double line like an infantry company on parade, were assembled for the shoot. The First Forester and his three assistants, in a uniform the color of the pine trees, were drawn up before the beaters and at our approach they sounded a call to the hunt from great curling trumpets. Then the Chief Forester approached Prince Morinski, bowed and kissed his hand. The whole scene was invested with an unreal air of regality of another age and might have been a hunting party of the Sun Monarch at the forest of Fontainebleau.

Now the beaters moved out, and, still in our tallyho, we drove to another quarter of the forest where the guns got out along a clearing and took positions fifty paces apart. The clearing cut a narrow course through the trees like an alley. It was only four yards across and from the time the game emerged and flashed to the cover of the thick underbrush on the other side was one and one half to two seconds. During that time you had to bring your rifle to the shoulder and get in a directed shot. The British military attaché in Warsaw, Colonel Conan Rowan, had been at several Polish shoots with me and we were always hopelessly outclassed by the Poles, for we could never get over the thought of our neighbors to left and right, the danger of hitting them if we shot too impetuously, and this hesitation of the trigger finger always brought off a miss.

White-haired President Moscicki, who was such a passionate sportsman that at shoot he was like a boy of five before a Christmas tree, told us scornfully that the Anglo-Saxon co-ordinating processes were too slow for this Polish art of flash shooting, a skill of instinctive co-ordination, brain, muscle, and nerve reflexes one had to cultivate very young, and there was nothing in the shooting performance of the British and American representatives in Poland to contradict him.

The scene this February day at Morinski's had the enchantment of a fairy scene with the white forest garlanded and festooned with snow, through which we peered like eager hounds as a distant horn announced the beginning of the beat. After an interval of ten minutes, we slipped off our huge fur coats and hung them over our backs, ready for action. Suddenly there was the snap of a twig and, as I shot, the snow tossed up underneath the shadow flashing across the clearing.

An instant later two rifle blasts sounded so close together you could hardly distinguish one from the other. The beaters came out a few minutes later. The beat was over. Twenty paces beyond the clearing lay a huge boar, hit in two vital places, the head and high up in the shoulder. Prince Morinski came up now with the other sportsmen, and my neighbor on the left, Count Von Frum, a young German from the Corridor, was congratulated on every side. The prince broke off a little sprig of pine, dipped it in the boar's blood and fastened it, an accolade of merit, in Von Frum's hat band. The boar was a big "solitary" with tusks well over six inches and probably weighed two hundred fifty kilos, General Frabisy, who was a great authority on the chase in Poland, said. After the tension of the beat, there was much excited talk and laudatory comment on his distinguished shooting, for the young man, who, through all the hullabaloo, bore himself with great modesty.

That night there was a great party in the castle. A bountiful meal, zakonski, was served with boar meat, spiced fish, and caviar, liberally drenched with starka, and then we went in to the dining room for a dinner of nine courses, which Prince Morinski himself, a famous gourmet, had supervised. There were many delicate dishes that only one of refined, cultivated palate could savor, borszcz, sandre ala Forwitee, saddle of mutton Archiduc, turkey polonaise, Heres 1885, rare burgundy of 1870, Moët et Chandon champagne. With the champagne there was much ceremonial lifting of the glasses. Everybody shook hands with his dinner partner and thanked her, then your partner thanked you for having thanked her, and after that all got up and went shaking hands and thanking all around the table. Prince Druska thanked the host and extolled him as an exponent of the richest traditions in Polish sport, and the host responded with thanks to Prince Druska for his thanks and thanks for the presence of all his gifted guests. Prince Radziwill was reduced to tearful eloquence over the nobility of the true Polish aristocrat and might have wept unrestrainedly if someone had not interrupted with "Nie zgi," which cannot be translated, but means something like long life, like "Vive" in French. Every one took up "Nie zgi" and the whole pleasant company started to sing "Sto Lot, Sto Lot, may you live 100 years, sans tears, may you live 100 years."

After dinner this bounding exuberance subsided a little and most of the guests settled down to bridge, but since I never play bridge when I can escape, and because I knew an outraged stomach would exact retribution in the morning, I asked young

Count Von Frum, who was on the bridge sidelines also, if he wanted to go out and walk with me in an effort to recover from the toxic accumulation of the evening.

Outside a great moon filled the scene with luminous, misty radiance, and the white stillness was oppressive like suspended breath. We walked the road across the long plain which ended in the forest, somber against the snow, where we had shot during the day, and I turned the conversation to the interests of youth and the future. He would finish at Heidelberg that summer, young Count Von Frum said, and he hoped to become an advocat. I was an humble member of the same noble profession and predicted for him a career at the bar as brilliant as his shooting that afternoon. "No, Excellenz," he said quietly, and turned away with a renunciation so final that I was disturbed. When I persisted in asking an explanation, he told me factually and with no heroics that his generation was caught in the convulsion of the great war which was coming within a few years. "There can be no individual life," he said with an air of mysticism, "our lives belong to the Führer, and all that belongs to us. Most of us will die. What is the use of planning for the future, when most of us must die for Germany"—his voice dropped in reverential respect—"and our Führer?"

"Why in hell do you want to die for Germany and your Führer?" I blurted with uncontrolled irritation. "Why don't you live for them? Don't you want to take a position, get on in the world? Isn't there a girl somewhere?" But he seemed unaware of my irritation, the conversation fell dead after that, and we walked almost in silence till we turned back to the castle.

I often thought of this episode when I visited Germany and listened in great assemblages to a little man who might have been a waiter, but not a head waiter, with a grotesque toothbrush mustache and a plastered mop of mouse-colored hair, as he exhorted his countrymen to avenge the humiliation of Versailles. Vehemently they cheered him. They listened with the rapt attention one might accord an emissary from on high. He was their führer with the mission of a Messiah to save Germany. Men were going back to work this year 1935. Soon, our Embassy reported, there would be no unemployment. The sullen air of defeatism had vanished before a vibrant, dynamic energy which charged the air everywhere. Germany was on the march, and millions like the young Count Von Frum were marching with blind devotion and the exaltation of fanaticism behind the little man with the tooth-brush mustache.

It was in Brussels, six months after the invasion of Poland, that I heard that Ober Lieutenant Von Frum had been killed in the attack on Warsaw.

*Ambassador John Cudahy attempted to interview some of the German leaders, but was generally met with rebuffs due, he said, to the petty jealousies, and general envy among the lower bureaucrats. He managed a meeting with Von Ribbentrop, but everything that was said was "off the record"; therefore the ambassador's report concerned only the attitude of the Minister of Foreign Affairs. All that is written of the meeting is that Von Ribbentrop displayed buoyant confidence in a soon-to-be-had German victory.*

*Cudahy's talk with Dr. Paul Goebbels, Chief of the Propaganda Ministry, was short. Goebbels wanted to know why Americans were so unfriendly to*

*Hitler's Reich. The ambassador explained that there were several reasons, but the primary one was that the people feared German conquest might extend to the Americas. Goebbels laughed at this. It was a military feat, that as far as he was concerned, was impossible. This comment prompted such headlines in the United States as "Nazis Admit They Have Considered Invasion of Western Hemisphere."*

*The aim of interviewing Adolf Hitler was thwarted by all the bureaucrats. The ambassador was told that a talk between Hitler and himself was impossible for if the matter of peace was brought up, it could be viewed as a sign of German weakness. Cudahy suggested they not talk about peace, but the American people were very interested in Hitler's reaction to the Lend-Lease bill that President Roosevelt had just recently signed into law.*

*The chance for an interview seemed hopeless and the ambassador made arrangements to leave Germany for Spain. On the day of his planned departure, he received word that Adolf Hitler would speak to him.*

Few people had ever heard of Berchtesgaden a few years ago. Now there are very few where language is printed or spoken who have not heard of this little old town in the Bavarian Alps with its white-gabled cottages and well ordered stability, clean as the mountain air, and the man on the mountain there.

At the hotel, on a flagstone sun-lighted dining veranda, Herr Schmidt, the celebrated interpreter, was waiting. A big, well-set-up man, he had about him an air of electric energy, his whole brisk bearing indicative of his photographic quinlingual mental processes. No man in the world hoards more momentous secrets, and no one could be more miserly about them. Silence is the first requisite of an interpreter, as he interprets his role, and he says, "If silence is golden, I am many times a millionaire." He speaks, thinks and acts in German, French, Spanish, English, and American. He is especially proud of the last accomplishment and knows all our idioms and cracks, which he says he absorbed from the motion pictures.

As we talked on I noticed people on the veranda stretching their necks, observing us with undisguised curiosity, and you could see excitement, palpable as a breeze, pass from one table to another. They could tell we were speaking English and that was enough, Schmidt said, to start the rumor of a visiting peace delegation. The whole countryside, he said, would soon be buzzing with gossip and before evening the war would be well on the way of being ended.

Our conversation rattled on in this engaging way until suddenly it was time to leave. We got into a big black Mercedes-Benz automobile and drove down a curving road by a row of shops under a medieval arcade, passing two churches, one with the bulbous cupola of Byzantium and the other with the delicate needle spires of the Gothic West. The plastered cottages by the roadside were white as milk in the sunshine, with broad brown eaves overreaching balconies gay with flowers. We left town and climbed up a long incline where there was a gate with a lodge. The custodian poked his head out of the door, gave one quick look, and we went on. A quarter of a mile further we were stopped at another gate and there was a colloquy. The gatekeeper knew the chauffeur, who was in German military uniform, and he knew well the big shining black automobile, but nothing is left to chance in guarding the

Führer of all the Germans. "He is shy of civilians," Herr Schmidt explained, "no one ever comes this way now, except people from the army." Not before we had established our identity beyond question were we permitted to proceed.

A little farther on, the mountain road took a sharp turn and we stopped before a white cottage resembling a double-decked California bungalow. Hitler's ruling passion is architecture. In *Mein Kampf* he admits his outstanding talent and tells how his original ambition was to be a builder. He has collected one of the most outstanding libraries in the world on architecture, especially that concerned with the theatre. Architecture, as he conceives it, should be the symbol of cities, reflect their spirit and he deplores the lack of expression, taste, and character in the silhouette of most German urban centers. But I saw nothing original or very decorative in the first aspect of the Berghof.

In the hall of the Berghof my attention was arrested by a portrait of Bismarck by Lenbach, so distinguished that I stopped to study it for a minute. Then we went along a passageway where servants appeared every few steps, as if by magic. They looked thoroughly capable, thoroughly businesslike, and beneath their brass-buttoned uniforms you could detect the contour of lithe, well-muscled figures. I had seen lions on the Sarengetti African plains look me over with the same quick, all-encompassing appraisal which these liveried men-in-waiting gave me in the Berghof. I think there must have been at least six of them and they missed not a single detail of my entry, my conduct, or the content of my pockets, between the hallway and the anteroom where we left our hats and coats before we passed through the double doorway to enter the most unique room I have ever seen. It was obviously intended by architect Hitler for a salon, but had the amplitude and vast proportions of a hall. Three marble steps, which descended from the doorway, extended in a line across the floor and divided the room into two levels; but the commanding feature was the great bay window, like a shop window, which filled nearly the whole front and looked out upon the dramatic spectacle of the Untersberg, gleaming white and magnificent in the sunshine. Far below was the little village of Obersalzberg, people working in the plowed fields, and, across a green valley of light and shadow, Salzburg dreamed in the distance.

During my conference with Hitler I had an opportunity to study the detail of this strange hall-like room, haunted by the memories of so many momentous interviews which have darkened the world for millions. The white-plastered walls were panelled with shellacked oak to a shoulder height and square oak-shellacked panels covered the high ceiling, from which hung two circular chandeliers of imitation wax tapers with frosted electric bulbs. In one far corner at the rear was a short stairway of the same marble as the steps which divided the room, with a black iron banister, ascending to an arched doorway, and in the center of the rear wall, a fireplace with a mantel of marble surrounded by benches, with cordwood piled up alongside. Opposite us as we entered, a massive cabinet, probably ten feet in height, with closed doors, looked like the arcanum of sinister mystery. Facing each other near the huge bay window were tapestries with figures in the costume of the Frederick the Great period and the Flemish horses of Rubens's imagination, whose great quarters contrasted with their small, grotesque heads. The back part of the room was hung

51

with oil paintings and the color note of the whole scene was strawberry, the carpet which covered the floor, the furniture covering, the marble of the steps and fire-place—all this same tint. When we sat down for the interview I scrutinized the designs interwoven in the cotton velvet furniture covering and saw they were tiny swastikas.

The furniture, all modern, standardized, styleless, might have been made in Grand Rapids, easy chairs, a comfortable sofa and three or four tables, one of them ranged alongside the great show window. Near this, a globe, and a little farther back, a grand piano with a bronze bust of Richard Wagner, whom Hitler often has pro-claimed as one of the noblest exponents of Germanism. We always think that one's character and individuality are reflected by the atmosphere of his domestic sur-roundings and Schmidt had told me every minute feature of Berchtesgaden had the Hitlerian touch. But the impression was one of conventional commonplace taste and the only books in the room to sustain Hitler's reputation as an assiduous student were a few brightly decorative volumes, in a small open bookcase near the piano, which looked as if they had rarely been opened.

There were many flowers about, yellow calla lilies and white ones on the low table by the window, a bowl of carnations on the low table about which we sat, and, grouped throughout the room, marguerites, zinnias, pansies and hydrangeas.

But the commanding feature in the scene and the one which held us fascinated was the great mountain through the window, its color and line and the lurid light and shadow. I stood looking for a moment, forgetful of all else, until Schmidt suddenly galvanized to rigid attention and whispered, stagelike, "The Führer."

Hitler stood at the threshold, accompanied by Walter Havel, his liaison officer with the Foreign Office. Schmidt crossed the room and raised his hand on high, to which Hitler replied with the same gesture. Without a word he extended his hand to me and shook hands limply with no display of enthusiasm. I had seen Hitler at Brown Shirt meetings when I visited Berlin during my four years in Poland and only two weeks before in the Reichstag when he addressed that body on the campaign in Greece. In these appearances he had looked so much taller, so much more impres-sive, that at first I could hardly identify him with the slight figure before me now, whose melancholy fragility reminded me of Harry Hopkins. Above all I was struck by the unhealthy pallor of his skin. He had the same look as prisoners who have been denied the sun during a long period of confinement. He looked as if he might be the victim of a gall bladder, dog-tired, with swollen, puffed eyes, febrilely bright. You could believe the stories that he got less than four hours' rest each night. He gave the impression of being utterly fatigued, one whose nervous energy was nearly spent from overstrain.

Directly after our introduction, Hitler crossed the room and without a word sat down in an easy chair by the round table near the window. A grandfather clock in the corner struck three; Hitler was on time, to the dot. I stood awaiting an invitation from my host to sit down until Schmidt whispered that I should take the seat next to the Führer while Schmidt sat at my right and Havel sat directly opposite Hitler. Hitler stared at me and I stared back. He continued to stare so long that I wondered if this staring duel would ever end. His expression was one of cold hostility. Finally he dropped his eyes and after that only glanced at me casually from time to time. His eyes were truly remarkable and gave the impression of light, so intense they were. They were the arresting feature of his face, harsh, metallic eyes, indicative of an intense, indomitable will, geared to a frenzy. In color they were so pale that at first you could not identify the pigment of the iris. Perhaps they had been seared by gas blindness at Ypres during the last days of fighting in 1918. As our talk developed, I had a chance to examine Hitler's eyes carefully and decided they were that pale translucent green one sees in certain moods of the sea. Above all they were hard, unyielding, fanatical eyes, harsh as the facial lineaments were harsh, without one compromising note of sympathy or kindliness.

As we sat there, Hitler's attitude was that of a man who faced a disagreeable ordeal and wanted to get it over with as soon as possible. He crossed his knees and teetered one foot up and down impatiently. He was dressed in a gray-green coat, like a military tunic, with a double row of brass buttons and wide lapels, wore dark civilian trousers, a white shirt with a soft collar and black tie with a silver swastika scarf pin. After we had talked for a few minutes, he draped one arm about the back of his chair and I had an opportunity to study the hand, a small hand with short square finger tips, a white and lifeless hand of unseen veins like the hand of one dead. All through the conversation he held his hand motionless and never did he gesticulate with either hand.

There is more in any talk than what is spoken. A test of this is to put a wall of paper between you and the person with whom you are talking. Instantly you become detached, that strange magnetism of visual human presence and expression and the connotation of the unspoken word taken away completely. The same thing in some measure is true when speaking through an interpreter, for it seems silly to look at one and address one directly in a language which is meaningless as Chinese or pidgin jargon. So in this conversation my questions were directed to the interpreter, Schmidt, but Hitler strangely when he answered, spoke to Havel, an old comrade of the first Putsch days, and seemed to find a response and receptiveness in him, rather than in the interpreter.

No written questions were submitted before the interview and Hitler had no intimation of what I would ask him. The issue of convoys was agitating the American people and the ignorance on this subject was unbelievable. We Americans are a land people and know little about nautical terms or anything touching upon the sea. Many persons in states like my own Wisconsin had no conception of what was meant by a convoy or its significance, so I considered the most important issue to be clarified was this matter of convoys and Hitler's attitude if American ships should escort war materials to Britain. He told me very simply and with no show or dramatics in answer to this question, that convoys meant war and went on to say that the action of escorting munitions and deadly weapons to an enemy with armed naval forces had always been considered a warlike act, the legal precedents had been determined by Anglo-Saxon maritime powers and were thoroughly well known and understood by all legalistic authorities the world over.

I had always been told that Hitler's mental processes were emotional rather than intellectual, but that was not my experience at this meeting. He spoke concisely, consecutively, and more responsively than many men of state I had interviewed under the cloak of confidence and secrecy when I was in the Foreign Service. His voice had the harsh, frayed quality one associates with political orators at the close of a hard campaign and was utterly lacking in any sympathetic timbre. I did not find Hitler a monologist or given to a great volume of words. So many people had told me about his ranting and raving, yet in this conference his voice was never once raised and never did he give sign of any agitation; nor did he gesticulate, but spoke with the utmost composure, never betraying vocally the intensity indicated by the taut lineaments of his face.

His hair was a plastered mouse-brown mop. His mustache showed a few gray hairs and there was a hint of gray commencing at the temple and back of the ears. The forehead showed a remarkable protuberance above the eyebrows, which the phrenologists call the perceptive cranial area. The upper forehead receded and did not indicate great contemplative capacity. The nose was thick and heavy, without clean-cut line, and the lower face, although not heavily boned or projected, gave an impression of great power of will, great energy, and aggressiveness.

I told Hitler that the reason the United States had passed from stage after stage of hostility to one of non-combative belligerency was because many Americans feared first the probability of invasion and next the competition of German goods in world commercial markets. These were the primary reasons for American hostility to Germany in the war, I said, and referring to the first of these I said there was widespread sentiment among the American people that the security of the Western Hemisphere was threatened by German aggression. It was argued that the German conquest might go on and on and with Europe conquered, the next logical step for the German military adventure was the two American continents. He laughed a harsh, strident laugh, disagreeable as a rasping automobile gear and his face looked as if it had taken a long holiday from honest, spontaneous laughter when he said that the idea of Germany invading the Western Hemisphere was about as fantastic as an invasion of the moon. I replied that fantastic or not, an eventual attack by Germany was feared by a large number of thoughtful American people. He said he could not believe this, he had too high an opinion of American intelligence and good sense. He turned on me sharply and asked the opinion of American military experts on the subject. I told him I did not know, but believed that the Chief of Staff and Chief of Naval Operations had never been quoted. He went on then to say he was convinced that if they were ever heard from they would confirm what he had first said. This invasion story was, he was certain, put out by warmongers against their better knowledge, men who wanted war in the belief that it would be profitable for business, but this was an erroneous conception since the last great war had demonstrated war was ruinous to business.

He declared that the German High Command regarded an invasion of either American continent as wildly imaginary. He asked why the British did not send more troops to Greece and North Africa in the campaigns in these countries and answered the question by saying it was because sufficient transports were not available, although the distances were comparatively short. He assured me that the combined shipping tonnage of the British, United States, and German marine would likewise be hopelessly inadequate to transport the army of millions which would be required for a successful conquest of the Western Hemisphere. The German army, he assured me, was not concerned with military expeditions for the sake of showing off or in order to demonstrate that nothing was impossible for German arms. The undertaking of invading Crete over one hundred kilometers of open water and England over forty kilometers of open water were formidable enough, and he said the thought of an attack over the four thousand kilometers of open water between Europe and the United States was simply unthinkable.

Somewhat irrelevantly he then declared that nobody in his hearing had ever said that the Mississippi was the German frontier in the same spirit that the Prime Minister of Australia had referred to the Rhine as the frontier of that country, but since the Rhine was their frontier, he had decided to send some Australian prisoners to the famous German river so that they might acquaint themselves with the frontier atmosphere. He assured me that Germany had too many serious problems in Europe ever to give any thought to an American invasion.

Many people, I told the German Führer, shared his view that military science had not yet developed to such a point that the Atlantic could be brushed aside as an obstacle of defense for the Western Hemisphere, but many people believed that the greatest menace of a triumphant Germany was to the economic life of the United States, and that German victory would mean disaster to American business. This conviction, I said, was predicated upon the assumption that the standard of living in Germany was far lower than that in the United States. Also the working hours imposed and the regimentation of German labor would never be accepted by working people in the United States. Therefore, it was only logical to assume that American industrial output could not compete with that of Germany. He did not like the inference that the living standard of the German worker was a low one, and said the controlling purpose of National Socialism from the beginning had been to improve living conditions for labor. The war had interrupted this effort, but it would be renewed with redoubled force when peace came. He said one of the controlling ambitions of his life was to improve the lot of the common man in Germany and among other things he hoped to see every laboring man own an automobile. He reminded me then that Germany with a population density of 140 per square kilometer had conquered the depression and provided jobs for all so that there was no longer any unemployed in the country, while the United States with eleven to the square kilometer was unable to cope with its serious unemployment problem. Why, he asked me, did we single out Germany as the outstanding menace to American economy, when Germany had a physical area of six to seven million square kilometers, and a population of eighty-five million, while the British Empire comprised four hundred million kilometers, Japan one hundred million kilometers, Russia one hundred seventy million, and the other nations of the world four hundred million. These national areas, he intimated, were far more menacing to American economy than Germany was. He asked why if German competition was so greatly feared, were her colonies taken away from her, and went on obliquely to say that development of these colonies would have provided a great outlet for German industrial output. Why, he asked me, was the United States so opposed to German organization of

Europe in order to provide a market for German goods, thereby lessening competition with the United States in the world markets? He talked at some length of southeastern Europe, which he said was the natural complement to German economy, because the Balkan countries had surplus agricultural produce which they could exchange for German industrial output. He declared there was an "iron rule of trade" which was that no country could buy from another unless it could also sell. Assuming the verity of this rule, he asked how the United States, with great agricultural surpluses, could take further farm produce from southeastern Europe, which was the only payment that area could make for needed American manufactured articles. I inquired whether or not he envisaged a trade union for Europe with suppression of quotas, tariffs, currency restrictions, etc. He replied that he thought all commercial relations between all countries could only be assured by long-term trade treaties permitting the partners thereto a profitable arrangement and suppressing the element of speculation, which he said had always cursed business. He did not believe in trade relations based on borrowed money and declared loans have to be paid and the end of borrowing often is disillusion and bankruptcy. The future trade of Germany, he insisted vigorously, would not be based on paper but upon exchange of commodity for commodity with an absolute exclusion of all speculation. The professors, he said sneeringly, had scorned these economic theories of his, but in twenty or thirty years, he predicted, they would be teaching them in the universities. He was frank in saying he saw no prosperous future in the trade relations of the United States and Germany, for the reason that Germany had no gold with which to buy the raw materials which it would need and the United States would not take in payment German manufactured goods to compete with its own output, except perhaps in a limited field of electrical equipment, optical goods and possibly dyes.

I asked about gold and its function in the future international trade of Germany. He said that reparations had deprived Germany of all of its gold and forced him to devise a system of international trade without gold, but I was surprised when upon further questioning, he admitted the usefulness of gold in providing a more elastic method of mercantile dealing and as a basis of credit between nations. He said quite openly that Germany was forced to trade by barter and had been driven away by necessity from the use of gold.

I then turned to the countries occupied by German military forces and, although I had been warned that the Führer would not discuss this subject, I pressed him to indicate his thought with reference to such nations, telling him frankly that my question was inspired by a violent prejudice among Americans that German domination of Europe would mean suppression of native national language, customs, and institutions in the occupied territories. His unresponsive answer was that Germany had not commenced this war, the war had been declared by England and France against Germany and it was strange to hear the British discourse on world domination when they went on suppressing millions of Indians, Egyptians and Arabs. "We shall settle relations with our neighbors in such a way that all will enjoy peace and prosperity," he summarized. I became more specific and referred to the case of Belgium, explaining that my interest had a personal angle because I had lived in the country. His answer was that his formula for the future of Europe was "Peace, prosperity and happiness." Germany, he said, was not interested in slaves or the enslavement of any people.

As we talked on, the clock in the corner struck at several intervals with rasping regularity. And during one of these clanging outbursts, the Führer rose to his feet in the same abrupt, ill-mannered fashion in which he had sat down. He shook hands with me with the same unmollified hostility he had displayed at the outset, saying that he had tried to answer all my inquiries with clarity and without reservation but he believed the interview was a waste of time, since no matter what he said his words would be distorted by the American press. I told him I would report what he said honestly and objectively without comment, but I had no idea of how American editors might construe and interpret his remarks. We mounted the marble steps and at the threshold of the Berghof, Schmidt turned and raised his hand ceremonially in farewell. Then we went away.

This interview was submitted to Hitler and approved by him without change. It was then cabled to *Life* and Time Publishing Company and published a week later simultaneously by *Life Magazine* and the newspapers in the syndicate North American News Alliance. *The New York Times* printed it with an editorial disparaging Hitler's words and pointing to his many broken promises. *Life* also published a caption making its position clear that it did not subscribe to anything he said.

The interview covered three salient points, of which the only important one dealt with the question of convoys. On this Hitler spoke succinctly and unequivocally, in saying that the convoy of war materials to England by armed American naval vessels would mean war. It was strange not a single editor or commentator passed upon this, although it was the only significance of what Hitler said to me.

The second subject concerned invasion of the Western Hemisphere. Opinions on this differ, and a very useful purpose would have been served if American experts had replied to Hitler's statement that the German military establishment had decided that an invasion of the Western Hemisphere was not practicable. Instead American journalistic opinion and politicians all declared Hitler had said that he had no designs on the Americas. Editorial after editorial ridiculed and derided such a hypocritical, lamblike attitude and held up his shameless record in Poland, the Low Countries, Austria, Czechoslovakia, etc., to prove that under no circumstances could his word be trusted. But Hitler never said anything about his intentions. His answers to questions dealing with the Western Hemisphere were confined solely to the military aspect of the situation and mentioned nothing else.

This phase of Hitler's utterance absorbed editorial and political attention so exclusively that nothing was said about the third feature, German-American competition in world markets after the war. On this also opinions differ, and a number of very competent business men in this country believe that American industry can never compete with German industrial output because of lower German labor costs and the barter system of German international trade. Mr. Bernard Baruch takes the opposite view and, in a discussion with him a few weeks after my return, he said most emphatically that he believed that American mass production could easily undersell German manufactured goods in any world market. The subject is a very important, far-reaching one and should be discussed and analyzed on its merits without prejudice.

Unlike *Life* and *The Times*, editors, commentators, columnists, and politicians did not confine their criticism to Hitler's words. They directed their remarks to the interviewer, stating openly in some cases and intimating by broad inference in others, that he had been influenced—even bribed—by the Nazis. Others accused him of dopily acting as a mouthpiece for Nazi propaganda and deplored his gullibility, guilelessness, and naïveté. The import of the whole assault was that it was the duty of the reporter to evaluate and comment upon Hitler's utterance instead of recording factually what was said and letting the words speak for themselves. Almost without exception all reviewers did not analyze what was said. They drew conclusions and made assumptions from Hitler's words. This is a familiar practice with which every trial lawyer is familiar and always occurs among ignorant witnesses and those of little mental discipline. Prejudice could have the same blinding influence as ignorance, it appeared. Many prominent educators insist there is no such thing as the judicial faculty or the objective mind. I had a feeling of profound depression, not because of barbs thrown at me personally, but at this exposure of our intellectual level.

# BRITAIN BRACES FOR WAR

from

*Assignment to Catastrophe. Volume I:*
*Prelude to Dunkirk—July 1939 - May 1940*
by Major-General Sir Edward Spears
New York: A. A. Wyn, Inc., 1954

*In England, there was curious inaction instigated by Prime Minister Neville Chamberlain, who had been looking for a solution other than war since September 1938, when Hitler had demanded the right of self-determination for the Sudetenland. After rioting broke out in Czechoslovakia prompted by Konrad Henlein, the leader of the German Nationalists, Chamberlain met with Adolf Hitler at Berchtesgaden for their first conference. Hitler demanded annexation of Czechoslovakian border areas in the Sudetenland where German was the dominant language. Here began the policy of appeasement that was to be the hallmark of Chamberlain diplomacy. Although both Britain and France were pledged to defend Czechoslovakia against aggression, they acquiesced to Hitler's proposal. At a second meeting between Hitler and Chamberlain, at Bad Godesberg, Hitler increased his demands, but these proved too much even for Chamberlain, and he rejected the new proposals.*

*The unavoidable war was put off for the moment when, at the urgings of*

*President Roosevelt and Benito Mussolini, a new conference was scheduled at Munich. Britain was represented by Chamberlain and Halifax, France by Edouard Daladier and Georges Bonnet, Italy by Mussolini and Galeazzo Ciano, and Germany by Hitler and Joachim von Ribbentrop. Czechoslovakia was not represented, nor was Russia invited, even though it had offered the Czechoslovaks military aid in accordance with their 1935 treaty.*

*In a few hours England and France surrendered to Hitler's demands. The Munich pact dated September 29 permitted immediate occupation by Germany of the Sudetenland. There were also provisions for a plebiscite, but those provisions were never carried out. France and Britain now promised to guarantee the new Czechoslovak boundaries. When Chamberlain returned to London from Munich he announced to a cheering crowd that he had secured "peace in our time."*

*The appeasement policy made the position of Czech President Benes untenable and he resigned. Czechoslovakia was dissolved in March 1939 by Adolf Hitler without a shot being fired on its behalf by France or England.*

*In September the Hitler juggernaut swept over Poland. Only Germany knew what it wanted and when, while the rest of Europe specialized in rhetoric, with little or no action. England and France had a pact with Poland and were supposed to spring to its defense, but inaction and speeches marked continuous delays. France, with 3,000,000 men under arms, wanted time to mobilize 3,000,000 more, and additional time to move about 1,000,000 civilians from projected war zones. In England there was much sound and fury as to the pros and cons of moving children out of London.*

*In the United States the "America Firsters," a noisy minority, held out to prevent the U.S. from siding with countries involved or about to be involved in hostilities. When Poland was conquered in 27 days, the U.S. War Department awakened. The United States Army was ranked 17th in the world in total manpower and weapons, much lower than those of Poland that had been crushed by Hitler's forces in less than a month! They began to dust off the munitions factories.*

*Sir Edward L. Spears, a decorated veteran of World War I writes of his experiences in the early days of World War II as he saw it in and out of the British government.*

## August 1st–23rd, 1939

Winston [Churchill] thought war was imminent, but he was certain the German General Staff would try to dissuade Hitler from becoming involved in a war on two fronts. What was the real attitude of Russia? Although an Anglo-French Military Mission was discussing plans in Moscow, he felt grave doubts concerning Stalin's policy. He thought, as I did, that we had deeply, perhaps irretrievably, offended the Russians at the time of Munich, and that they would not hesitate to turn the tables on us, as they considered we then had on them, if they considered it to their advantage to do so.

Nothing, he thought, was better calculated to encourage the Germans, and for that matter the Russians, in the belief that as always we inclined to a policy of *laissez-faire*, than that the House should adjourn for the long summer recess as the Prime Minister planned.

What worried Winston most, apart from fearing the Government would run out over Poland as it had over Czechoslovakia, was our weakness in the air. He came back to this again and again. He spoke of the French Air Force, but about this I had no information save that it was notoriously poor. On the other hand, we were both full of admiration for the French Army. The review at Versailles in honour of our King's visit had epitomised in a magnificent display all the traditions of a force that was, I thought, the very embodiment of the essential virtues of France. I could not recall that occasion without pleasure and confidence. I was very fond of the French Army and shared in the martial pride of its officers and men. I had spent much of the last war with them and acquired that spirit of comradeship which comes of enduring good and bad days with men one likes and respects. I was always flattered when the French said I knew their Army better than they did themselves.

That afternoon I asserted that the French soldiers, sons of the big-hearted, patient, brave men I had known in 1914, were worthy of their fathers.

Then we spoke of the immense advantage which had accrued to Germany by her seizure of Czechoslovakia. Neither of us doubted that in the year that had since elapsed Germany had armed infinitely faster than had either the French or ourselves.

I knew Czechoslovakia well. There was no doubt that the already vast German arms industry, driven at furious pace, had gained an enormous accession of strength by the possession of the Skoda and Witkowitz works.

[The trip] began on August 14th, 1939 when Winston Churchill and I became the guests of General Georges. We met for lunch at a restaurant in the Bois de Boulogne. The place was empty, for the world of fashion had deserted Paris a month ago. Four of us sat in a shady corner, General George, his A.D.C. [aide-de-camp], Winston Churchill and myself. It gave me great pleasure that my two old friends so evidently liked each other. Indeed, I felt a kind of proprietary satisfaction in Georges as he explained why we should visit this point and that during the tour of the Rhine defences we were to begin next day. Lucid, forceful and clear as always, he obviously impressed Churchill.

Georges was convinced war was almost upon us, and that the Germans, unless given all they wanted, were prepared to launch it. It went without saying that if Poland gave way, they would present other demands which would be insisted upon the more arrogantly because their might and confidence would have grown.

As we ate wood strawberries soaked in white wine, it emerged that there was no more doubt in General Georges' mind than in ours that it was the Germans rather than we who had benefitted by the time gained at Munich, always supposing they had really intended fighting then, which he doubted. He thought Hitler had been bluffing. He pointed out, as proof of the good use the Germans had made of the time granted them, that a year ago they had no defences facing France. Now they had the Western Wall, a formidable obstacle built according to modern ideas, in great depth, whereas the

Maginot Line was linear. And another thing; a year ago the French artillery was incomparably superior to the Germans, but now? And Georges lamented, as a major disaster, the gain by Hitler of Skoda, one of the greatest armament firms in the world.

And the air? All agreed that the Germans had forged ahead and that the results were very serious; all we could do now was to build and build, and place the largest possible orders in the United States.

This led me to put a question to which I did not receive a satisfactory answer then or at any other time. If the Germans had air superiority, would they not in fact be able virtually to besiege the Maginot Line with its garrison of hundreds of thousands of men? Could not even a weaker air force do this? A vast number of trains were required daily to supply the garrison. Supposing this point or that on the line was attacked day after day and night after night, would not the result be to weaken the garrison as if it were effectively besieged?

Was it possible for motor transport to replace trains over a long period, and would they not be subject to the same disabilities as rail transport, even though in mitigated form? There must be railheads somewhere.

One question in particular, I remember, preoccupied Churchill. It was the shoulder of the Maginot Line, the point where it came to an end about Montmédy and was thence prolonged by field works opposite the Ardennes, and on to the sea. I have no note of what Georges answered. He doubtless said what I had many times heard, that the nature of the subsoil from Montmédy onwards did not lend itself to the deep excavations required by the Maginot plan of fortifications; he may also have said they were too expensive, but I'm not sure.

What I do remember, for I recalled it a few months later with great vividness, was Churchill's pursed mouth, his look centered on the fruit on the table as if he were crystal-gazing. His face had ceased smiling, and the shake of his head was ominous when he observed that he hoped these field works were strong, that it would be very unwise to think the Ardennes were impassable to strong forces, as he understood Marshal Pétain had held in his time. "Remember," he said, "that we are faced with a new weapon, armour in great strength, on which the Germans are no doubt concentrating, and that forests will be particularly tempting to such forces since they will offer concealment from the air."

Churchill was, I knew, for we had discussed it, aware of a contradiction in the French strategic plan. If the French intended to wage a purely defensive war, then presumably they would have fortified their whole frontier, including that facing Belgium, perhaps the most likely one the Germans would select for their onslaught. But this would mean holding a line running through France's richest industrial areas, that is, condemning them to destruction, or one behind the industrial area, abandoning it to the enemy without fighting, which was inconceivable.

Fears concerning what the King of the Belgians would do in case of war were apparent in what Georges told us of the French plans. Leopold was reputed to be much under German influence. He apparently intended standing alone, holding the Western Allies at arm's length, relying on his coolness toward them to obtain German indulgence.

The Belgian attitude was all the more important now that the French were considering an offensive policy, that is, not only a rush through Belgium, as soon as that country's permission was obtained, so as to line up on its eastern frontier, but an actual offensive aimed at turning the German attacking armies and the unfinished Siegfried Line. But was the French Army, so long trained to the defensive, and presumably equipped for it, capable of offensive action against so powerful and aggressive an opponent as the Germans?

I gained the impression that this question worried Churchill, but the matter in hand, and therefore the one on which he was concentrating, was the Maginot Line and the possibility, which Georges considered very great, of a violation of Swiss territory and an attack through Basle.

We saw some of the amazing forts of the Maginot Line with their underground railways, their garrisons that could remain for months hundreds of feet below the surface. We saw miles of tank obstacles, turned-up rails with sharpened points as if the countryside had been sown with dragon's teeth. We gazed across the Rhine at the immense Black Forest which, the French told us, was full of ammunition dumps. Loaded convoys were for ever driving into its depths and coming out empty. We drove through enchanting Alsatian villages bathed in sunshine, their little crooked houses painted robin's egg blue, with cherry-coloured shutters, all ablaze with flowers in their window-boxes.

We visited the strong points on the Rhine, the line of defence running through the Haguenau forest and the great barrage of Kembs and the power station built well into the river. As it furnished electricity over a wide area and was within rifle-range of the Germans, we wondered what would happen in case of war. In the upshot they were careful not to damage it.

We saw the great guns sited to shell the passages at Basle if the Germans came that way. Field works were being constructed whilst peasants reaped the golden harvest with immense scythes having a basket attachment.

We also visited the organisations of Glaserberg which were the hinge of the Vosges and Jura defences.

It was all very remarkable and, at the moment, comforting.

The trip tore to shreds any illusion that it was not Germany's intention to wage war and to wage it soon. There was no mistaking the grim, relentless and barely concealed preparations she was making, in spite of the fact that silence and secretiveness characterized the right bank of the Rhine. Every commander had tales to tell and they all led to the same conclusion.

The nightly discussions had borne on the efficacy of the tank obstacles, the danger from parachutists, and attacks in a fog or under cover of artificial fog, which Churchill strongly emphasised. Georges was certainly worried about the lack of depth of the Maginot Line, for he referred to it again, saying it must be doubled by field works and that nothing could dispense with the necessity of having powerful reserves behind it. Our backwardness in tank construction was deplored, and the consensus of opinion certainly favoured the heaviest type that bridges could carry, unless indeed means could be found of lightening a tank for river-crossings or devising machines capable of crossing river-beds. As I listened I remembered how in 1915 I had heard this same Winston developing his theory of "land cruisers" to a French General and his staff on the Vimy Ridge, and how heartily they had laughed, after he had gone, at this absurd idea. "Your politicians are even funnier than ours," they had exclaimed.

At Strasbourg, looking at the Rhine flowing under the Kehl Bridge, on which French and German posts stood watch within pistol-shot of each other, and remembering that later the river passed through German territory on either side and under bridges of all kinds vital to their mobilisation, I suggested that mines should be launched in the stream on the declaration of war. It seemed to me that mines linked by cables and urged on by the current would lash themselves round the piers of the bridges and explode, while shoals of smaller mines could blow a way through the nets the Germans would certainly endeavour to stretch across the river. Churchill thought at the time this was not a good plan, but that tiny submarines might possibly be useful to blow up bridges further down-stream. Later he put my suggestion into practice, but by then he believed it was his own idea; and so it was, for he carried out what would have been, had he not taken it up, a fancy leaving no more trace than a butterfly's shadow on running water.

On [August] 17th we were back in Paris. Next day we separated, Churchill to join his family in Normandy, I to visit French friends in South-Western France.

Again I found the atmosphere heavy with apprehension. The fear of war was casting its gloom over uncomprehending people. Why, they asked, had the world gone mad? Our own generation had been cut down as with a scythe, the land must die if the present generation was also to be decimated. What was the matter with that clamorous lunatic house-painter, Hitler? But was there not some foundation for his claims? The Peace Treaty had not been wise, that was a fact. Could not a settlement be found that would avoid war? My hosts, while belonging to the same milieu as the people I had seen in Normandy, moved in a less worldly circle. They were not bitter about England although resentful that we as allies had so little to contribute to the common cause. If war did come it was France again that would be bled white. They did not think Britain was manoeuvring so as to bring about a war, with France as her shield, but they did think, reasonably, that if we had made up our minds to challenge Hitler, we should have provided ourselves with the means of doing so. The people of the neighbourhood, the villagers, the shopkeepers in the little town, considered it the duty of the Government to avoid war. It was bad enough to have to defend France like last time, but to fight for Poland, that was just crazy! But they still wondered uncomfortably at the strident Nazi campaign demanding that Danzig should be returned unconditionally to the Reich, and even the short memories of modern electors could not but note the complete similarity between the German propaganda concerning the Poles today and that employed against the Czechs so short a time ago.

One thing had greatly impressed the inhabitants of the towns and villages for miles around, and that was the flight of a large formation of Wellingtons that had gone from England to Bordeaux and back without landing. They had seen the great machines, which may have accounted for British stock being higher here than elsewhere.

One morning, a knock at the door heralded, not the white-jacketed butler with coffee, but my hostess, looking pale and serious as she held out a local paper. "This is very bad news, isn't it?" she said. It certainly was. The Soviet-German non-aggression pact was announced. It was the 22nd of August.

So this was it. We had been double-crossed, beautifully fooled.

## August 24th—September 2nd, 1939

On the afternoon of Thursday, August 24th, I listened from my usual seat on the third bench above the gangway to the Prime Minister, Neville Chamberlain, explaining why Parliament had been summoned in special session.

The house was packed and the atmosphere the very opposite of what it had been in the Munich days. Fear, the mental attitude that is the equivalent of the physical gesture of warding off a blow, had disappeared, and Members now seemed to be on the watch to detect, and resent, any sign of weakness in the Prime Minister's statement. When he said that at the beginning of the week German troops had begun to move towards the Polish frontier, and that since a crisis of the first magnitude was imminent the Government had concluded that the approval of Parliament must be sought for further measures of defence, the serried ranks of Members registered quite definite though silent approval.

The House received even more favourably his statement that the Germans seemed to be labouring under the dangerous illusion that under the new circumstances created by the Russian *volte-face* neither France nor Britain would fulfill their obligations to Poland. How could we with honour go back on these?

The emphatic cheer which this statement received left no doubt as to what the Commons felt about it.

The measures we were taking were in no sense a menace to Germany, the Prime Minister declared. As no one could imagine circumstances arising under which the Chamberlain Government could be conceived as threatening Hitler or anyone else, this comment was allowed to fall, it seemed to me, in critical silence. If war were forced upon us, he went on, we should not be fighting for Danzig, but for principles the destruction of which would bring to an end all possibility of peace and security for the peoples of the world.

Chamberlain was followed by Arthur Greenwood, deputising for Attlee, away ill.

Greenwood may perhaps be no great statesman, but on that day and on those that followed he showed himself equal to a great occasion. "I wish to make it unmistakably plain to those beyond the seas…" he said, "they will not find here a disunited people. Unity on that issue will be complete, and the issue will be faced with confidence and fortitude."

The House adjourned for a week, but was recalled five days later.

The Prime Minister's speech on this occasion caused the anti-Munichers, of whom I was one, some uneasiness. As I have to use this term it is necessary to describe its meaning, all the more so in that it was in the main the Conservative anti-Munichers, the men who had at the time of Munich lost faith in the Prime Minister and his colleagues, who finally brought about the fall of his Administration. We were not many who openly and persistently laid claim to this extremely unpopular description, but we were in desperate earnest. I for one have never been through such an ordeal as that of Munich. Like most people, I have had my private sorrows, but there is no loss that can compare with the agony of losing one's country, and that is what some of us felt had happened when England accepted Munich. All we believed in seemed to have lost substance.

Recalling the Munich days, there were many in the House and outside who watched the French Government with some suspicion, more than half-expecting it to abandon the Poles as it had the Czechs. After all, the same Ministers were in power in Paris. It was therefore with great relief that I heard from my friends at the French Embassy that the Germans had tried to detach the French from the Poles on the 25th but had been turned down.

By the 29th it seemed beyond all doubt that Hitler intended to attack Poland. This meant we must be prepared for war at any moment or accept dishonour with the further consequence of becoming to all intents and purposes a satellite of Germany. Yet on Wednesday, the 30th, the Prime Minister told the C.I.G.S., General Ironside, that there would be no war. So the latter told General Sir Frederick Maurice. This was extraordinary. I lunched with Generals Ironside and Kirke at the Carlton on the 29th, but the former said no word of this to me. I should have been surprised had he done so.

At 5:30 A.M. on September 1st the German Army invaded Poland.

The house met at 6 P.M.

The Prime Minister's opening words were what we all expected. "The time has come when action rather than speech is required." Most of us must have been sorry for him, I certainly was, when he went on: "Eighteen months ago in this House I prayed that the responsibility might not fall upon me to ask this country to accept the awful arbitrament of war. I fear that I may not be able to avoid that responsibility." What a world of shattered illusions those words conveyed! Gone was the faith that he, the simple, direct businessman, together with the ubiquitous Horace Wilson, had discovered a new approach to diplomacy. I wondered if he heard, as I did, the echo of his own words of a year ago: "I have brought back peace with honour," and if he saw as I did the German monster, though still belching from a surfeit of Czechs, getting ready to devour Poland as a next meal, with, no doubt, an eye on Britain for dinner. Well, Hitler's menu had gone wrong. The Poles were not going to be served up to him spitted and trussed as the Czechs had been.

We would oppose force by force, said Chamberlain, which undoubtedly gave great satisfaction to the House. Then he went on to tell us of the latest events which demonstrated that Hitler had not failed on this occasion to re-edit the dismal farce which was his stock curtain-raiser to the murder of a nation. It was always the same, which alone proclaimed him a criminal. He might have been a disciple of Joseph Smith, the Brides-in-the-Bath murderer, when he once more produced the little scenario he had found answered so well: Polish provocation, persecution of German minorities, impossible terms presented at the last moment—all the props.

65

The Prime Minister told us that only the night before (the 31st) the Polish Ambassador in Berlin had told Ribbentrop his government were prepared to negotiate with Germany. The German reply had been the invasion of Poland. They were at that moment bombing open towns.

Mr. Chamberlain then read the document the French and British Ambassadors had been instructed to hand to the German Government. It stated that unless the German Government was prepared to give His Majesty's Government satisfactory assurances that the German Government had suspended all aggressive action against Poland and was prepared promptly to withdraw their forces from Polish territory, His Majesty's Government in the United Kingdom would without hesitation fulfill their obligations to Poland. The Prime Minister went on: "If a reply to this last warning is unfavourable, and I do not suggest that it is likely to be otherwise, His Majesty's Government's Ambassador is instructed to ask for his passports."

The House seemed puzzled. These were fine words, but the plain fact was that by the terms of our treaty with Poland we should by now have come to her help. Again Arthur Greenwood voiced the feelings of the majority. "We shall," he said, "at whatever cost, in the interests of the liberty of the world in the future, use all our resources to defend ourselves and others against aggression." He went on to say that the Prime Minister had left a loophole and given the German Government an opportunity of withdrawal, but there could be no withdrawal now, and the nation was in honour bound.

Greenwood was careful not to be critical of, still less hostile to, the Government. His manner was perfect. He evidently intended that no words of the Opposition Leaders should provide a pretext for inaction, and that Hitler should be left in no doubt that Great Britain was at one in her undertakings.

After Sir Archibald Sinclair, speaking for the Liberals, had given the Government eloquent support, a batch of Bills was immediately dealt with and the Government was granted £500,000,000 beyond the ordinary grants of Parliament.

But the House was restive in the absence of positive action by the Government, and uneasiness grew as the hours passed. A rumour got about that the Italians had put forward proposals which the French had eagerly seized upon as a pretext for running out on the Poles.

The overwhelming majority of the Conservative Party felt very much as had the anti-Munichers a year before: we must now stand and fight. The Socialists and Liberals were solidly of that opinion.

September 2nd was a day of acute suspense.

At a conference of the small group of Conservative M.P.s led by Anthony Eden, it was reported that Daladier was wobbling badly, and that Georges Bonnet, the Minister for Foreign Affairs, had given a very unsatisfactory interview to the Polish Ambassador in Paris, which had caused Count Raczinski, the young and admirable Polish Ambassador in London, to seek explanations at Downing Street.

No wonder the Poles were disturbed. The French Ministers may only have been trying, as they contended, to gain time for their mobilisation programme, but what Bonnet actually said when the Polish Ambassador protested against the delay of the French Government in carrying out their clear Treaty obligations to give Poland air support was: "You don't expect us to have a massacre of women and children in Paris." Considering what had been happening in Poland for the last 36 hours, the remark was abominable.

I was so disturbed that I called up Roland de Margerie, the very active First Secretary of the French Embassy. As I was waiting to get through, I heard a Member in the booth next door informing his family that the French had ratted. This I told Margerie. It was indeed the general feeling. I went on to tell him it was essential Paris should realise how dangerous the situation was. Collaboration with France would be a thing of the past unless she acted promptly. Anger was growing, confidence was waning; this was, I said, a bad start for the adventure we were about to embark upon, presumably together. Margerie appeared to be very much of my way of thinking.

When I returned to the House I noted that, in a long experience covering many critical periods, I had never seen the Commons so stirred, so profoundly moved, as it was that afternoon. It was dawning upon even the most uncritical of the Government's supporters that Great Britain's honour, of which we were the collective guardians, was in danger. And I noted something else. Churchill was obviously advancing from the wings on to the stage of the political scene. His name was on many lips. The more the Cabinet vacillated the more numerous were the eyes turned towards him. The Government seemed not to know what to do. Everyone was aware that he saw clearly the path to follow while others were still groping. The change was the more remarkable in that there was a persistent and deep-rooted prejudice against him amongst Conservatives. Prominent Conservatives in my constituency had warned me in the past that too enthusiastic support of Churchill and his ideas would do me harm locally.

Even some members of the group led by Eden, to which I belonged and which included several of Winston's personal friends and genuine admirers, held that Churchill was not trusted by the public, which was convinced that he was erratic and dangerous. This was the avowed reason for his not being a member of Eden's group, though I privately thought that fear of his dominating it, as he invariably did any body of men with which he was connected, had weight with some.

No later than the previous evening I had told members of the group of the difficulties my uncompromising support of Churchill had caused me in my constituency, but that within the last day or two I had had many communications, some by long-distance telephone, asking for Churchill. The majority of the group had nevertheless held that mine must be a special case, that he was as yet not acceptable to the public, and too close contacts with him would weaken the effectiveness of our body.

The weary evening dragged on. Everyone was restless. Few sat in the Chamber. Men moved from group to group, in the smoking-room, on the terrace, back to the lobbies. When it became known that the Reichstag had passed a law annexing Danzig to the Reich, I do not think anyone was left with the least doubt that Germany had unmasked her batteries and that our only choice was between ignominious surrender and war.

Sir John Simon, the Chancellor of the Exchequer, had announced when the House met that the Prime Minister would make a statement later in the sitting. This was what all were waiting for.

Soon after 6 P.M. the Speaker suspended the sitting until the Prime Minister should make his statement. We had been told by the Whips that this would be about 7 P.M., but it was not until 7:45 that the bells rang throughout the House sending Members at their best speed to the Chamber. The benches were packed. The unbearable suspense was about to be relieved. One and all were keyed up for the announcement that war had been declared. Most were ready to show their intense relief that suspense was ended by cheering wildly. But as we listened, amazement turned into stupefaction, and stupefaction into exasperation. This is what Mr. Chamberlain told us:

Our Ambassador in Berlin had delivered the previous night at 9:30 the "warning message" which had been read to us the previous day. Ribbentrop had said he must submit this to Hitler. So far, no answer had been received.

The delay might have been caused, Mr. Chamberlain said, by a proposal put forward by the Italian Government that hostilities should cease and that there should be an immediate conference between Great Britain, France, Poland, Germany and Italy.

His Majesty's Government, went on the Prime Minister, would find it impossible to take part in a conference while Poland was being subjected to invasion, her towns bombarded and Danzig annexed by unilateral action.

The Government would be bound to take action unless German forces were withdrawn from Polish territory.

They were in communication with the French Government "as to the limit of time within which it would be necessary for the British and French Governments to know whether the German Government were prepared to effect such a withdrawal. If the German Government should agree to withdraw their forces, then His Majesty's Government would be willing to regard the position as being the same as it was before the German forces crossed the Polish frontier."

He concluded by saying that His Majesty's Government would not recognise the annexation of Danzig.

Members sat as if turned to stone. The shock was such that for a moment there was no more movement than there was sound when the Prime Minister sat down. Not a single "Hear hear" could be squeezed out of the packed assembly.

There was a kind of ripple. Someone was being betrayed. Who? The Poles, certainly; were we as well? By whom? The French? Our own Government? It was inconceivable that anyone should believe Hitler meant to turn back. It was unbelievable that anyone not bent on surrender would be prepared to treat now with the Germans, who would only negotiate so as to gain further military advantage.

Arthur Greenwood got up, tall, lanky, his dark, fair hair hanging to either side of his forehead. He swayed a little as he clutched at the box in front of him and gazed through his glasses at Chamberlain sitting opposite him, bolt-upright as usual. There was a moment's silence, then something very astonishing happened.

Leo Amery, sitting in the corner seat of the third bench below the gangway on the Government side, voiced in three words his own pent-up anguish and fury, as well as the repudiation by the whole House of a policy of surrender. Standing up he shouted across to Greenwood: "Speak for England!" It was clear that this great patriot sought at this crucial moment to proclaim that no loyalty had any meaning if it was in conflict with the country's honour. What in effect he said was: "The Prime Minister has not spoken for Britain, then let the Socialists do so. Let the lead go to anyone who will." That shout was a cry of defiance. It meant that the House and the country would neither surrender nor accept a leader who might be prepared to trifle with the nation's pledged word.

Greenwood then made a speech which I noted that night as certain to be the greatest of his life; a speech that would illuminate a career and justify a whole existence. It was remarkable neither for eloquence nor for dramatic effect, but the drama was there, we were all living it, we and millions more whose fate depended on the decisions taken in that small Chamber.

He hoped the Prime Minister would be able to make, he must make, a further statement when the House met at 12 next day, Sunday. He must make a statement. Here many shouted "definite statement." Every minute's delay imperilled the foundations of our national honour. There must be no more devices for dragging out what had been dragged out too long. The moment we looked like weakening the Dictators would know we were beaten.

Before the universal cheers had died down, the Liberal Leader, Sir Archibald Sinclair, was on his feet. Handsome, eloquent, he stammered his indignation.

The House was evidently in so furious a mood that the Prime Minister thought it advisable to get up again. He would be horrified, he said, if the statement he had made gave the impression of the least weakening in either the French or British attitude.

He suggested that there were great difficulties in coordinating action between two Governments, and declared he would have been glad had he been able to announce that the French were agreed on giving the Germans the shortest possible time in which to accept or reject the proposals.

He felt certain he would be able to make an announcement next day and indicated that, but for a miracle, it would be to announce we were at war. He assured the House he would have to be convinced that the Germans were in good faith before believing in any action they took.

Again he sat down without a cheer. Even this declaration, though far more precise than the earlier one, had not dispelled the deplorable impression he had made. The House was oozing hostility. Dismay is the only word that can describe the feelings of Members. I was told that one elderly Conservative, distinguished more for his fidelity to his leader than for his critical faculties, was in tears, and another, of spherical construction, who had lately formed a group of like-minded wobblers with the express object of creating a pro-Chamberlain *claque*, said he felt sick. An attendant told me that two members actually were sick.

As I stood in the lobby talking to someone, A. V. Alexander said as he passed: "Well, Spears, are you still proud of being an Englishman?" Such were the feelings of Members when the House dispersed. Suspicion and distrust centred, however, on the French. We knew the Government were now fully aware that the House would not accept any further procrastination.

## September 3rd, 1939

On Sunday, September 3rd, there was a meeting of the Eden Group at Ronnie Tree's charming house in Queen Anne's Gate. If there were any who doubted that we should be at war before the day was out, they were not in that room. The discussion in the main centred on the inevitable Cabinet changes. It was by then known that Churchill would be asked to join it and would become the standard-bearer of the men sitting there with me and of those outside who thought as we did. Conversation became general, but the voices were quiet and casual. The view was expressed that Eden should also be in the Cabinet to give Churchill support. On the other hand, nothing should be done that would give the Prime Minister any pretext for excluding Winston. In view of the general quality of the Government, his presence was essential. It was also necessary to look to the future. If he were ever to lead the country he must be in the Government now.

A servant appeared at the door and said Corbin, the French Ambassador, wanted to see me urgently. I went at once to the French Embassy at Albert Gate. Dalton was with the Ambassador, so I went in to see Margerie, who was at pains to explain that the reason the French had delayed sending their ultimatum to Germany was the absolute insistence of the French General Staff that they must be given time to complete mobilisation.

They had 3,000,000 men with the colours, and general mobilisation meant the calling up of 3,000,000 more, which, together with the evacuation of the front line zone, meant that 10,000,000 people were on the move in France. This figure was probably an exaggeration, but there seemed to be no doubt that the French General Staff had asked for time. The obvious answer was that they should have started mobilising earlier. But then so should we. We were hardly in a position to throw stones at the French from the brittle precincts of our own glass-house. Had not Chamberlain (so Vansittart told me) informed a Labour delegation the previous day that he could not sanction the evacuation of the London children as this would be provocative! When I did see Corbin, I was able to tell him I felt sure Margerie had given me all the news, so there was no need to repeat it. I was in a great hurry, and come what may must be in the House when it met. Was there anything else he had to say? Yes, would I please assure my colleagues it really was all right, that France would be at war by 5 p.m. that afternoon? I now knew the reasons for the delay and could explain to my friends, for I understood the immense problems of a continental mobilisation and the risks involved. A premature enemy air-raid and days might be lost that might make the difference between victory and defeat.

Was he absolutely sure, I asked? Yes, he said, absolutely. He had told Winston, he had just convinced Dalton.

I believed Corbin; he was so obviously relieved himself.

In a very few minutes I was back at Tree's house, where the meeting was breaking up. Some had already started walking to the House, others piled into my car. We stopped to pick up one or two, including Eden, on the way. Then the sirens raised their banshee wail for the first time. Loud and urgent came the unexpected, frightening sound which seemed to be heralded by a pre-sound: the rushing of myriads of invisible wings. Such was the impression sirens always made on me.

As we turned into Great George Street leading into Parliament Square, we saw scores of people running, many carrying small children, towards some shelters supposed to exist in St. James's Park. My feeling was one of exasperation, for the public had been warned against taking children into the streets. The people who ran were not, I observed, either panicky or frightened.

There was a jam in Parliament Square. Drivers were flustered. Some of my passengers jumped out. The remainder kept me company till I parked in the Speaker's Courtyard.

At six minutes past noon Neville Chamberlain told us we were at war. It was simple and inevitable. There was no sign of the strain of the previous night; the House was relaxed and serene.

# THE FALL OF FRANCE, 1940

from
*All Gaul Is Divided:*
*Letters from Occupied France*
Anonymous
New York: The Greystone Press, 1941

*France lost its war with Germany in less than two months (May-June 1940). Sixty thousand men were killed, and 2 million more were surrendered without firing a shot. The country had been taxed heavily for years to pay for weapons that had never been ordered. The money had disappeared within the high levels of government.*

*Marshal Pétain, the 84-year-old French ambassador to Franco's Spain, was recalled to sign an armistice with Germany. It was felt that this World War I hero, who had stopped the Germans at Verdun in 1916, would boost the morale of the average Frenchman. Pétain sought to improve the plight of the French prisoners by collaborating "honorably" with the Germans, but as he was forced to yield continually to ever harsher Nazi demands, his popularity decreased.*

*In the days that followed defeat, the French knuckled under to German military rule. Once the shock of occupation started to fade, German propaganda*

*began to encourage a strong dislike for former French allies—a hatred of Britain
for continuing the war, and a growing irritation with the United States for sup-
porting England with weapons and materiel. Blame for French hardships slowly
transferred from the Germans to the British and the Americans. Many believed
that if Britain would give up the war, French living conditions would improve.*

*The following anonymous communications are from a series originally pub-
lished in the New York* Herald Tribune *and later reprinted in a slim volume containing sixteen letters. They were all unsigned, unaddressed, and undated. The
writer, or the original recipient of the letters, evidently feared reprisals. The letters give us a frightening picture of the German occupation. Both the invaded and
the invader trod carefully to maintain the delicate balance of their day-to-day
existence. And each day, the vanquished lost a little bit more.*

A t ten minutes to noon a German motorcyclist left a pink slip with the mayor
that sixty rooms would be required for nine o'clock that evening. It had been
rumored that the enemy was north of the Gironde, but no one dreamed that
they could be so close to us. The *garde champêtre* hurriedly posted notices upon the
church, the hotel and the corner house, inviting the population to be calm, dignified,
and about their ordinary pursuits. For once the women did not have much to say. In
groups of three and four they stood in the middle of the street, whispering.

By four o'clock a stream of swift vehicles, lead-colored, solid-tired, was
purring and rumbling toward Le Verdun, our nearest port; slender-nosed artillery,
trailed by trucks of ammunition, motorcycles with side cars, plastered with spare
wheels; three-seated open cars, four soldiers to a seat, each with a short rifle
between his knees. Many of the men, arms folded, sitting erect, were sunk in a sleep
of exhaustion. Fully half of them were under twenty years of age, blond, big-boned,
thin, with the waxy complexion that one associates with short rations.

An officer's car pulled into the alley beside the pork store. While the officer
made his rounds, the driver slipped into the store, bought a boudin (blood sausage),
concealed it under his arm, retired to the closed court in the rear. I was in the back
room of the bicycle shop and watched him through a crack in the door. Throwing a
glance to right and left, to make sure that he was not observed, he tore into the drip-
ping meat like a wild animal, swallowed the whole two pounds without apparent
mastication, wiped his lips on his sleeve, regained his chauffeur's seat.

Their machinery is magnificent. From behind a plane tree I viewed the procession until darkness shut it out, without hearing a bolt rattle or a spark plug falter. At
the cross-roads, men with half-moons of white metal marked Field Police about
their necks, directed traffic. No one saw them come, no one saw them go, but they
were there, at the right place, as long as they would be effective. In signalling they
used what looked like red phonograph discs at the end of short handles.

The evening our village had its first glimpse of regimented amusement. At the
entrance of the woodbine arbor of Mère Lafon's café, a sergeant took his station.
Behind him was strung out a line of men in uniform. The sergeant let the first three
men enter. Eyes front, iron hats on their heads, they ordered and consumed a cup of

coffee or a glass of beer, clumped out the door in their cowhide boots. As they emerged the sergeant permitted three more revellers to enter.

Between the newcomers and the civil population amicable relations are making a halting but undeniable progress. Members of the invading force receive, day by day, strict instruction as to their conduct. On the first and second day they walked abroad in couples, wearing green cloth gloves, uttering no sound, woodenly expressionless.

The third day there was a slight unbending. One of them stopped to play with a puppy outside the butcher's. Another waved his hand to a little girl who was gathering string beans in her front yard. The maidenly clerk in the fruit store called across to the girl in the dry goods shop, *"Ils sont de beaux gars, quand même."*

After the lapse of a week, although still reserved and keeping to themselves, they had become integrated with the landscape. The village had ceased to accord them much attention. They stood in line beside the pumps, stripped to the waist, for their morning turn at the cold water. They shaved before pocket mirrors balanced upon fence posts. But the novelty, except for the more impressionable girls, had worn thin.

Mathilde Guitard, circulating in her donkey cart of milk cans, amended her cry; *"Lait und Milch; zwei pfennigs ou deux francs."* Women who went early to the washing pool found it drained dry. Half a dozen young men, waist deep in the ooze, were capturing eels. The baffled washladies were placated by the wherewithal for a dish of anguille-à-la-matelote. And the pool was deepened by a good two feet, which is unquestionably a community benefit.

Eighteen hours after the soldiers, the women and commercial travelers arrived. The women wore short skirts, carried attaché cases, were quiet and ladylike, and principally of two age groups, those under twenty-five years, and those over forty. But they didn't stay long, as they were seeking particular individuals, none of whom was billeted in our commune. In a region where the feminine form is draped in black, except when it makes its first communion or enters wedlock, these guests from beyond the Rhine moved about like exotic flowers or tropical birds. Through the medium of color contrast, their costumes were designed to administer a shock to the peasantry. They did. Mauve jersey above a green skirt; black suit with white hat, belt, gloves and stockings; a yellow suit within a purple coat.

The commercial travelers are all of a type, speaking good French, dressed in grey, a portfolio of catalogues in one hand, a sample case of hardware, aluminum, and celluloid novelties in the other. Four teams, of two men each, visited the trade in the smaller towns. They offered quick delivery, long credit, relatively low prices, which are three effective arguments with merchants whose shelves are becoming bare.

The occupation of central and southern France has been achieved without untoward incident. The invaders have been correct, disciplined, prepared to accede to reasonable requests. Regulations which work a hardship to working people have been modified. For example, the decree of "everyone indoors and lights out at eight o'clock" was not practicable at this season of vintaging and harvesting, when people stay in the field until nightfall. The hour has been extended to eleven o'clock.

The rule that the swastika flag should float over the town halls has been annulled. It was a gratuitous humiliation of docile elderly people who are doing their best. The unwritten, but insisted-upon custom that the clerks of a store should drop other customers when a German enters, and serve him first, has fallen into the discard. They take their places in the line like the rest of us.

It is obvious that the invaders wish to accomplish their task with a minimum of friction. To date, they are pulling their punches. Sentimentally and commercially, they want to alienate France from Britain. They are treading French soil with velvet-shod boots, hoping to assure France's neutrality, if not her co-operation, in the conflict with England. As to the future, our village is holding its breath, with its fingers crossed. Now and again there is a stray straw in the wind. The boys who occupy our pink guestroom find the color effeminate. They say that if I will buy the paint and wallpaper they themselves will do the manual work of redecoration, in the best Munich manner.

"But do you think it will be worth the trouble, for so short a time?" I question.

"Oh yes. They say that we are to be with you for five years."

We have always recognized that the primary fortune of France lies in her rich plowland. At present, however, and in a quite different sense, supplementary wealth is being added to that soil. All sorts of people, panic-stricken or of deliberation, in their orchards, or hit or miss along the highways, are burying treasure.

It is a veritable mass movement, with no means of placing a figure upon the total amount that is being secreted. Family silver, jewelry, precious stones, bars and coins of gold, stocks and bonds of foreign countries, are being tumbled hurriedly into holes in the ground, among the roots of apple trees, in the corner of cellars, at the end of the seventh row of grape-vines.

Half a dozen circumstances are impelling householders to adopt this primitive protection for their valuables. First and foremost, the safe deposit vaults of banks are no longer safe. That is to say, they are no longer private. Nor are they a person's own property. The government of occupation has placed them under supervision, for such of their contents as it may wish to levy upon. An individual may no longer visit his strong box save in the presence of a representative of the German Treasury.

It is unlawful for a resident of the occupied zone to possess gold metal in any form, unset precious stones, any non-French security, any currency other than German marks and French francs. If objects in these categories are found in the box, the bank management holds them at the disposal of the German Treasury.

But before the above rule was put into effect, a whispered warning ran along the grapevine telegraph. There was a run upon the bank cellars. In our bank I saw plump diamond dealers of Antwerp and Amsterdam puffing out to their cars, under trunks ponderous enough to make a gangster's mouth water.

Nine million people, in northern and central France, were stampeded by fear. It was a contagion of terror. Like October leaves before a hurricane, they precipitated themselves south. With each day's quota of fresh rumor they became more desperately in haste. Each carried what he could on his back, on his bicycle, in the baby's perambulator, in a superannuated car that broke down or ran out of gas. They became blistered, footsore, lost the way. What they carried grew less and less, cached piecemeal along the road, beside a stump or stone that they fondly hoped to identify later. At one hill, on Route Nationale Number 7, between Vendôme and

Tours, 54 cars, crowned with mattresses, top-heavy with packages, victims of tire trouble, engine trouble, fuel trouble, have been pushed into the ditch and abandoned.

An American widow, with maid and chauffeur, arrived at our farm, seeking shelter for the night. By rights, she has no cause for apprehension. She holds an American passport, and her nation is not at war. But the blind epidemic of fear flogs her on. After supper, through the shutter, I overheard her asking the advice of our fourteen-year-old child, as to the safest place to hide jewelry.

No, not in the ground. The Germans are wise to that. They look where the surface of the ground has been stirred, and pour on water. Where the soil settles, makes a depression, they dig. Under the tiles of the roof? But wouldn't that make the roof suspiciously bumpy? In a hollow tree? Yes, that is worth considering, unless it blows down before I can get back. Many of my friends have been to their tailors, had the padding removed from the shoulders of their coats, and replaced by thousand dollar bills wrapped in oiled silk. Another good way, if you can stop in one place, is to roll your money tight and pack it in the middle of a bottle of epsom salts. Or rings and a necklace can be put in a box of baking soda, and pushed to the back of the shelf. I know a man who has his whole fortune inside his typewriter. He dismounted the machine, rolled the bills into tight cylinders like pencils, and pushed them into the tubular frame.

At the Spanish frontier, to which most of the well-to-do fugitives make their way, French fiscal agents apply a rule which is responsible for as much burying of treasure, as is the German control of bank accounts and safe deposits. Between the towns of Hendaye and Irun flows a narrow stream, the Bidassoa. Crossing this river is a hundred-foot-long international bridge, at either end of which is a white bar, like the gate of a grade crossing. In the exact middle is an iron post, bearing a tricolor shield upon its northern face, and the red and yellow ensign of Spain upon the reverse.

To thousands of unhappy people this a veritable Bridge of Sighs. Each week, for one or two days, Spain has closed the frontier, padlocked the white bar, and posted sentries with fixed bayonets. Then occur scenes of hysterical profligacy. In the long line of motors, women have locked themselves in their limousines for 48 hours at a stretch. Packards and Rolls-Royces are forsaken, trunks of lingerie discarded, as distracted men and women attempt to cross the bridge on foot.

The obstacle at the bridgehead, to which I referred above, is the German-inspired French law that no precious metal, no precious stones, no foreign currency or security, and not more than two hundred francs in money, per head, may leave French territory. As this rule prohibiting the exportation of capital is generally known, it becomes apparent why fleeing citizens see the necessity of finding a place of concealment for their valuables before they arrive at the international bridge. Which means, practically speaking, since banks are taboo, that somewhere on the road between Angoulême and Hendaye the fugitive must select some tree or stone or ruined cottage, to be the repository of his wealth. In parenthesis, and in explanation, it may be mentioned that many who seek asylum in Spain are Jews. Rightly or wrongly, they mistrust the measures which the Aryan invaders may enforce against their race and possessions.

The present burying of treasure is a temporary expedient. It will pass. But for the moment, the soil of France, rich by nature, is being made artificially richer by the panic of human nature. What cannot ever be known is the proportion of this vast concealed wealth which will never be recovered.

Money is a good subject with which to introduce what is actually happening in France. What people are using for money, what is its purchasing power, its foreign exchange value, its probable future acrobatics? Money is the facet of public policy which most intimately touches the civilian.

In occupied France we carry two kinds of currency in our jeans, French francs and "occupation" marks. The occupation mark is neither a Reichsmark nor a tourist mark, and is legal tender only in the occupied zone. It has no metal coverage and no worth other than the power of the military authority to impose its acceptance.

Lumbering along with the army of occupation came printing presses on wheels. Notices upon the walls and the voice of the broadcaster informed merchants and hotel keepers that the two-toned brown notes, on stiff crackly paper, were to be accepted at the ratio of one mark to twenty francs. The ambulant presses operate in the provincial cities, grinding out small denomination notes by the million. A finance commissioner regulates their output, so that they shall not drown the market.

I have said that the occupation mark has no metal backing, but, as a matter of reality, neither has the French franc. Since the governor of the Banque de France has become a German, and the gold reserve has been sequestered, the value of the franc is more than shadowy. The above statements apply to currency within the occupied zone, but before this letter arrives in New York the distinction between "free" and "occupied" France may have disappeared, and all France be on the occupied footing. Already gauleiters (supervisors) function in cities of the free zone, and the frontier between the free zone and Spain is guarded by German troops.

With occupation marks, the military who control France pay themselves the equivalent of forty francs a day, which is exactly fifty times what French soldiers on active duty receive. With occupation marks, supplies are purchased for the upkeep of the garrisons. With these worthless notes, the shelves of stores are being stripped. Merchants of antiques, jewelry, kodaks, radios, linen and women's costumes, shoes, are obliged to keep their shops open for business, even though the stocks disappear with no replacements in sight. On an average, one store in three is empty, and stands with shutters closed. Butter, eggs, meat, grain are purchased in carload lots, before the stuff can arrive at the Paris market. Trains are re-routed to beyond the Rhine.

To print money in any volume desired, to be under no obligation to redeem it, and to oblige venders to accept this currency for merchandise of intrinsic value is an invisible form of confiscation. One can call it velvet-glove looting.

The business areas of Tours, Poitiers, Bordeaux, as well as of Paris, are dotted with trucks and trailers bearing the insignia of transport companies of Dresden, Munich, Stuttgart, Hamburg, and Berlin. Loaded to the roof, they are transferring the contents of French stores, hotels and civilian households into Germany. Yesterday I saw two trucks backed up before Robert Rothschild's home—the famous Richelieu Palace, at the corner of Place de la Concorde and Rue St. Florentin. Men in field-grey uniforms, like a swarm of bees, were packing the priceless collections. I asked what was going forward. "We are carting this junk away, because we need the place for a soldiers' dormitory." The sides of the trucks were marked Bremen.

But it has been the opening of the safe-deposit boxes, and particularly the sneaking way it was done, that has killed the last spark of courage in many a French heart. One of the first acts of the invaders was the announcement that there would be no interference with bank deposits nor with the contents of safe-deposit boxes. The promise was printed in the papers and repeated over the radio in French, English, and German. Citizens were urged to leave their cash and valuables undisturbed. People breathed a sigh of reassurance and accepted the promise at face value. But it was an anesthetic.

The experience of the present writer may be multiplied by tens of thousands. My wife and I had railway bonds, the coupons of which were payable on August 1. On visiting the bank we were told, without warning, that access to our deposit box could be allowed only in the presence of a finance comptroller. Three weeks later we were advised to be at the vault the next morning, with our keys.

Pasted on the door of my box was a certificate, signed and sealed by the legation of my country, which, though small, has a heroic history and is not at war with Germany. The certificate stated in German and French that the contents of the box were the property of a citizen of a non-belligerent nation, temporarily domiciled in France for the purposes of trade. This information did not cause a second's pause on the part of the comptroller. Neither did he know, nor would it have affected him to know, that the contents of that box represented the lifetime savings of the owner, upon which he depended for the education of his children and the support of his old age.

From my box the German removed everything which can be marketed in a foreign currency, stock certificates of Royal Dutch, Rand Mines, Crown Mines, General Motors, General Electric. A jeweler, who weighed and appraised the stones and the gold and platinum in my wife's jewelry, accompanied the examiner. The items were placed in the custody of the bank management until such date as the Reich requires delivery.

The seance finished, and all the boxes rifled, the examiner made a speech. I did not hear well, because of the noise of a Belgian woman who had lost $3,700, everything she possessed.

"What is taking place here today," said the representative of the Reich, "is happening in every banking and safe deposit institution in occupied France. Here is the reason for it. Germany at present is administering France upon the basis of an armistice. Eventually the peace terms will be arranged. Among those terms it is certain that there will be one requiring the vanquished to pay the victor a cash indemnity.

"After the war of 1914-'18 there was delay and complaint both in the fixing and in the collecting of the indemnity which the Allies solicited of Germany. There was a Dawes plan, a Young Plan. No plan was successful. Germany could not be made to pay.

"At the close of the actual war," continued the treasury man acidly, "we do not propose to be hampered by delay, excuse-making or concealment of assets. The contents of safety boxes and of the bank deposits in foreign currencies, are being added up. We shall have a pretty clear notion of the liquid capital of this country. It will be safe in our hands before we begin to discuss peace terms. That total sum will be the initial cash payment on the war indemnity which we shall demand of France."

That every phase of manufacturing and trade be rapidly and comprehensively resumed is, in a nutshell, Germany's business policy for France, and she is correct in believing that social health will improve when men and women get back to the accustomed jobs.

From its headquarters in the Hotel Crillon the German high command has issued printed orders to executives, big and little. Merchants with closed shops will reopen them. Managers of idle plants will start the wheels turning. It is to be done, moreover, within sixty days. Otherwise there looms the penalty of having the property appropriated and the business conducted by a personnel of the invader's selection.

The breweries and the newspapers are two cases in point. The French make good beer, but the flavor did not appeal to the occupying soldiery. Also the stream did not flow fast enough. In consequence the Germans have installed their own maltsters and are running the breweries twenty-four hours a day. There is certainly more beer, and it is presumably in the Munich manner. At the capitulation of Paris the majority of the newspapers transferred their offices to Vichy. Two, however, remained, *Le Matin*, a morning paper, and *Paris Soir*, an evening paper. Both had been pronouncedly Anglophile. It was disturbing for their penmen to execute a right-about overnight, to denounce the loyal comrades of yesterday as unspeakable monsters in tomorrow's issue. The Germans found the editorial invective of both papers tepid. They therefore walked in, sat down at the typewriters and took over. There was no question of purchase, only of eminent domain and public policy.

The military order for the resurrection of French business also stipulates that each enterprise shall employ its pre-war staff, or their numerical equivalent, at the same wages and on a five-day week. In other words, business shall reopen under the same conditions as were in force during the first six months of 1939, whether or not raw material is procurable, whether or not a market exists for the output.

On the other hand, as a stimulant to entrepreneurs, the army of occupation promises an absence of labor trouble. At the first tremor of unrest the French police, officered by Germans, plus the garrisons from beyond the Rhine, will crack down on agitators with an iron hand inside an iron glove. The C.G.T. (French Federation of Labor) is supposedly disbanded. Of a certainty it has not uttered a whisper of remonstrance.

The foreign exchange value of the French franc is disconcertingly low—12 francs to the Swiss franc, 10 francs to the Spanish peseta, 100 francs to the dollar. Nevertheless, the cost of life has not risen proportionately. And although wages have been reduced by two-thirds, working people still manage to keep afloat. The rationing of essential foods is severe as to quantity, but the price of these staples is strictly controlled. Canned goods are not rationed, but an impish practice prevents the housewife from accumulating a hoard. In selling a can of condensed milk or green peas the grocer punches a hole in the can. The contents must thus be consumed the same day.

As a warning, newspapers print the names of establishments which have been guilty of overcharging. The grocery which my family patronizes is in disgrace. The doors are locked, and the front window exhibits a placard, "Closed for Ten Days Because of Attempted Speculation." As the season advances, however, and eatables become rare, and as the status of the franc becomes increasingly dubious, the pressure toward higher prices must become intense. Wheat, oat, potato and bean crops have been better than normal. If the Germans would allow occupied France to retain these home-grown supplies there would be sufficient nourishment to go around. Unfortunately, this is not the fact. The cream of the crop is being skimmed off for the army of occupation. A still further quantity is being shipped into other German-controlled lands. Hitler, it should be recalled, faces a food shortage everywhere. He has ninety million mouths to feed, and it comes after an agricultural season during which his man power has been not on the land but under arms.

French retailers are being cheered by the promise that Hebrew merchants are to be squeezed out. My next-door neighbor owns five popular-price drygoods stores. They are modeled on the five-and-tens. The toughest competition in his line comes from Jewish colleagues. A scout of the National Socialist party, in the official brown uniform of the party, has assured my friend that not a Jewish merchant will be in business after November 1. Naturally our neighbor is enchanted. He calls the invaders the saviors of gentile trade and has presented the local kommandantur with ten cases of champagne. But in my opinion he is myopic. He does not foresee that the same machinery which is now suppressing his competitors and throwing their stocks upon the market in forced sale may equally be directed against himself at the whim of the dictators.

If the Germans honestly desire the revival of French business it is a puzzle to know why they are detaining two million young Frenchmen in prison camps. These young fellows are crazy to get home and into harness. Farm labor, railway employees, civil servants, the shock troops of agriculture and transportation have already been released. Why are these other two million potential workers held in enforced idleness, four-fifths of them on foreign soil? Is Germany fearful of revolution while she still has England on her hands?

The hair-trigger danger to France, particularly to rural France, during the 1940-'41 winter lies, it seems to me, in the social unrest which must accompany the liberation of the war veterans. These men are already angered at being so long, so uselessly and so inexplicably interned. Rightly or wrongly, they believe that they were betrayed and sold like droves of cattle by their top commanders and by the pre-armistice government.

If, as and when these two millions, nursing their sense of injury, return to their homes, to find their communities stripped to the bone, to find many of their sweethearts and wives pregnant, their dependents hungry, their jobs vanished, their farms overrun by foreigners, they will be dynamite. If packs of desperate men roam the countryside, burning barns and haystacks, seizing animals and foodstuff, looting the houses of the well-to-do, I, for one, will understand it and will sympathize with their mood.

In such an emergency will Germany maintain public order? Or will she welcome the boiling over of the pot and seize upon it as an excuse for planting her cowhide boot more firmly upon her former rival? This is the anguishing question that can be answered only as the months go by.

To sum up this ambiguous situation: With one breath Germany purports to desire full steam ahead in French industry; with a second breath she commands the imprisonment and inaction of the very labor which is essential to French industry. She cannot face two ways, nor order the business man to forge ahead and to halt simultaneously. Speaking as one who has been in business in this country fifteen years, I am terribly afraid that the invader is storing up grief for himself and for enslaved France during the cold nights of January and February.

My brother, who is a colonel, talked with one of Pétain's top men at Vichy. "Our country," said the latter, "is a boxer who has had a knockout blow. He is beginning to come out of the fog. But all he knows is that he still breathes."

This state of semi-consciousness, when sales resistance is low, is being fruitfully played upon by the German idea-conditioners. They know that what is dinned into people's ears and spread before their eyes, hour after hour, day after day, is bound to leave an imprint. When the one side of a story is repeatedly presented, it takes a stout intellect to compose a formula which will successfully contradict it.

I find myself shocked to discover the extent to which many of my intimates and relatives have been converted to Hitlerian dogma. It does not seem possible that they should be so bat-eyed. They used to believe in popular government, in the will of the masses. They don't any more. They have been driven into a corner, starved for outside news, and are being shown a single way out.

As a result of German influence, these friends and relatives of ours, erstwhile straight thinkers, say that the sun is going down on democracy: they say that France is suffering from, and has been betrayed by, too wide an application of the democratic principle. The rank and file are not capable of rule. Democracy may work among the Anglo-Saxons, with their long experience in self-government, but not among the Latins. The Latin is too flamboyant, too politically passionate. This applies to the Spanish and the Italians, as truly as to the French. With the Latin a potent central authority, the less diffused the better, responsible only to itself, can alone guide and administer with success.

Behind the unctuous wording of the Nazi propagandist one discerns his clear intent. He aims to obliterate from the mind of the French all memory of France's three disappointing fliers in popular government. He wants to replant confidence in the close-knit oligarchy. Once that is achieved, the next step will follow smoothly. And that step is the popular acceptance of an oligarchy, or council, not exclusively French. It may even, during its trial flights, be presided over by a gauleiter. By imperceptible stages, the national mind is being jockeyed into the desired coma of passivity.

It is useless to deny that a large number of the French—presumably a majority of those who retained sufficient sang froid to be able to reason at all—viewed the assumption of power by Germany with considerable relief. Profound as was their grief at the nation's collapse, they were nevertheless glad to be rid of a parliament and a cabinet which had forfeited the respect of its constituents. For a decade the

French voter has been blundering about, endeavoring to revamp a system of government which no longer represented the people. At every point the parliamentarians
checkmated the exasperated citizen. People were restive, disgusted, more and more
determined to clean the vermin out. Gen. Maxime Weygand might have been dictator had he not been so much of a legalist.

Building upon this existing French antipathy toward the administrators of its
late republic, anti-British propaganda has hammered away upon the alleged fact that
a British victory will mean the triumphant return of the Mandels, the Reynauds, the
LaChambres and the whole venal crew who conducted the nation to the abyss.

The backlog of Nazi disparagement of England, however, as uttered over the
French radio and in the French press, is Britain's willfully stupid tenacity in continuing the war. The bulldog is too dumb to stop fighting. This stubbornness has
angered and astonished Germany. They blame every inconvenience and distress to
which France is now subjected upon those condemned Britons. Is Paris without fuel,
without medicine, on short commons? Are the pet dogs being suppressed, do the
hens not lay? The fault is with Britain.

Are French women, because of the lack of textiles, about to be garbed in a
standardized, unadorned, gray uniform, as are the frauen of the Fatherland—which
is no light matter with women who have a flair for self-decoration—Britain and her
blockade are alone to blame. All would be well if only those ivory-headed English
could know when they are whipped.

The "Blame Britain Campaign," in experienced Nazi hands, is being plausibly
done. Unfortunately, it carries weight. Men who ought to see clearer say to me:
"Isn't it criminal the way the English are retarding Hitler's Federation of Europe?
For people who pretend to be our friends, they are certainly doing us dirt."

It goes without saying that press and radio nearly leave their senses at any intimation that America may throw her full resources to the side of Britain. German
voices on the air and German-inspired articles in French journals assume a tone of
airy incredulity. In fact, they might be dealing with some bed-time tale in the nursery. But no one is deceived. The entry of full American aid into this war is the
supreme nightmare. The French fear it, because it will inflict a painfully extended
period of stagnation and near-starvation. For, officially, France is now Germany,
and it will involve an involuntary quarrel between peoples who have always been
friends. The German people fear it, because it will assure the eventual loss of the
struggle, revolution in their homeland, and a flare-up in every country upon which
Germany has planted her boot. A terrible feature of this war and the Germans
already foresee it, is that it has sown the seed for a dozen future revolts.

I overhear German soldiers talking quietly among themselves in café corners.
Back on our farm, I used to hear them, under the trees on Sunday afternoons. They
are not aware that we understand their language. At first this was Germany's personally conducted war; she struck where she would, when it suited her. The soldiers are
noticing that this is no longer true. They say that it must be finished before next
summer, so that they can go home, or some may go home anyway. They say that
America must not mix in this. Last time it was over-sea material that turned the
scales. Lieber Gott in Himmel, if America should do it again!

We are trying to face the future rationally, neither too hopefully, nor too despondingly. Before me is an article by the esteemed scholar Georges Claude of the Institut de France. It is entitled *Au Seuil d'un Monde Nouveau*. And we keep asking ourselves, as we shall cross that threshold, how will our poor, dismantled, manacled France fit into the framework of a new world? More than that, will this heralded New World be one whit better than previous new worlds? After the victory of 1918, weary peoples pinned faith in a Europe Nouvelle, pacified, disarmed, based upon justice, ruled by law and not by men, and under the leadership of Democracy. It has been a dud. And now, with the victory of Germany, is there justification to believe that she can command a new order with any greater success? We are at present below par, physically and emotionally, and would give anything to be able to stop thinking. But the question of a Federation of Europe, and our place within it, will not let us alone.

It becomes evident that the partitioning of France into two, or even three, zones had been long-thought-out, and is intended to be permanent. The people of the northern departments are alarmed that there will be still further surgery, and that a strip of France will be added to the southern boundary of Belgium. That will leave us of the occupied zone to be the Province of West Frankreich, or Atlantic France. We shall be a unit of, say, 22 million people, living upon two-thirds of the pre-disaster French territory, which contains the seaports on the western ocean, the better portion of the grain land and the factories, and the leading cities, save Lyons and Marseilles.

At the threshold of Professor Claude's New World, we of the West Frankreich will need to start from scratch. Our capital will be gone. We shall be unarmed and without even domiciliary defense. Our livestock will have been requisitioned, our working gear will be worn out. Our reserves will have been consumed. My most serious anxiety is lest, when the new era does dawn, we may find that our spiritual reserves may also have disappeared, and our will to work, our will to live uprightly with self-respect and free-mind. After so long a spell of impaired vitality, with no visible escape through the barbed wall of force, courage is bound to weaken.

We have been repeatedly warned that we of the occupied zone—the West Frankreich Province—are to be a predominantly agricultural district, with only such manufactures as have no connection with war-making. We are to specialize in grain, wine, the elegancies, and exportable luxuries. Above all, metallurgy is to be transferred elsewhere. The scheme of suppressing iron-work among a population which may be tempted to re-arm and revolt is extremely ancient. The Philistines enforced the same rule against the restive children of Israel. See I Samuel, Chapter 13, for a detailed preview of the Führer's regulation. No smithy was allowed in Canaan, lest the Hebrews should make for themselves swords and spears. The Israelites were obliged to trek down into Philistia to sharpen their axes and ploughshares. This is already literally taking place, as our agricultural machinery can only be delivered from the Reich.

A second restriction to be imposed upon the West Frankreich touches superior education. Three military schools were the pride of old France: St. Cyr, (Infantry at Versailles); St. Maxence, (Higher Mathematics and Artillery); and Saumur,

(Cavalry, west of Tours). The first two of these famous schools have been moved into the Pétain zone, to Aix-en-Provence, the hoary classical university, 18 miles north of Marseilles. The Saumur establishment, home of the most beautifully trained high-school horses in the world has ceased to function. At the moment when this is penned, the Sorbonne and the College de France, in Paris, are momentarily closed. The ostensible reason is lack of coal, but the actual reason is believed to be penal. The Germans have suspended a Damoclean sword over higher education in our zone. It was college students who rioted at the shrine of the Unknown Soldier on November 11th, the single hostile demonstration since the Germans took over. Machine guns cleared the avenues converging at the Etoile and a number of students were killed, while a larger number were sent to prison in Germany. Universities are notoriously the nurseries of a turbulent nationalism.

Men, whatever their dissatisfaction, are unable to stage an effective revolt without two things—arms and a leader. Our conquerors plainly intend to deprive our West Frankreich of both. There is to be no metal industry, which might surreptitiously fabricate firearms. There is to be no liberal schooling, to train an elite, from among whom might arise leaders.

Arranging our facts in order, the prospect is dreary for occupied France. For if love laughs at locksmiths, so does the spirit of patriotic youth disdain garrisons and undercover police. It must, from its very essence, aspire, ferment, break into action. It will associate itself into secret societies, keeping alive the cult of nationalism. There will be the blockade running of arms. There will be—there already is—communication with plotters overseas, like the de Gaulle force, like the Ottawa stalwarts. We must foresee a society honeycombed with emancipation movements. The hardiest, most idealistic of our boys will be involved. There will be secret agents, informers among our very kin, repressive measures, heart-breaking executions. It is the inevitable sequence when tyranny nails down the lid upon a people who have known liberty and must know it again.

Among our neighbors and friends I find that the mood of fatalism is on the increase. It has, of course, a physical basis, but it transforms them into people whom one hardly recognizes. Their emotions are drained to the last drop. They pine for the absent. They sit numb about their fireless hearths. Let no well-fed man or woman condemn the mother who, in alternating waves of apathy and rage, watches her children grow whiter and whiter above their plates of thin soup. She can do nothing but feel. She does not think in terms of nations or continents. She thinks in terms of a kitchen and dooryard. Her responsibility is bounded by a cookstove and the crowded untidiness of a bedroom. Lack of the roughest essentials presses heavier and heavier. She bites her lip to keep going. She dare not stop. She gets to the stage where she will accept any capitulation, if only life can be a little more right. Of course fatalism grows, the dumb, drugged acquiescence of bone-tired people to anything that can promise a few breaths of respite. It is the animal instinct of self-preservation, the maternal instinct of self-immolation to protect its young.

As the residue of such months a hatred of war and warmakers remains. It is a white-heat of disdain and loathing that the uninitiated may not comprehend. I know a family in which the custom of morning prayers has been revived, but with no respectable motive. The master of the house assembles his dependents for no other purpose than to pour out before Almighty God the anathema of his outraged feelings against those who have led helpless masses into suffering and tears. It makes the blood run cold to hear the curses which he beseeches God to visit upon the malefactors in high places. He almost gives God the names and addresses.

There is one miracle of which we dare not allow ourselves to think. We are led to believe that the objective of England, and co-operating with her, of the United States, does not extend beyond the repulse of German attack upon their shores. If that be the fact, what I have written above, as to the probable future of the West Frankreich, must stand, I believe, without correction.

But if, through some unpredictable and unhoped-for turn of event, the German should be forced to relinquish his strangle hold upon our French land and our French folk, the period of enslavement, for our lifetime, and the painful and bloody period of regaining liberty, upon the part of our children, might be shortened, even evaded.

Should the democracies land their forces upon our soil, it will involve the destruction of such man-made improvements as may remain, before they finally possess it. Should the German be driven from France, he has let it be known that, as a chapter in his program of frightfulness, he will pillage and violate to his utmost, as he retires. Furthermore, he will immediately commence preparation for renewed invasion. Whether he remain with us, therefore, or withdraw from us, we are to be the victim, and he to be the ruthless overlord.

We of the occupied zone are thus between the horns of a dilemma. Either course, so far as the human eye may see, is a dismal road. On the whole, however, even at his preannounced price, we shall prefer to have the German ousted. A mad dog, followed by an obedient, hypnotized pack, is loose upon our world. For the moment no one can say or think much further than that.

# SHANGHAI, 1941

from

*They Call It Pacific:*

*An Eye-Witness Story of Our War Against Japan from Bataan to the Solomons*

by Clark Lee

New York: The Viking Press, 1943

*As 1940 began, those countries not actually engaged in combat were beginning to experience war jitters. Only in the United States was there any complacency; the citizenry felt safe because two vast oceans separated them from the war zones.*

*Egged on by Winston Churchill, as England and her allies were being defeated on several fronts, and advised by economists who feared that, with Hitler victorious in Europe and the Japanese in Asia, the United States would fall without firing a shot, President Roosevelt began to discuss the possibilities of a peacetime draft. Strategic materials, it was feared, would be denied to the United States by Germany and Japan. World markets would be closed to American products. The whole structure of the free enterprise system would collapse. Could the United States allow this without getting directly involved?*

*When, because of the unpreparedness of American armed forces, the President talked seriously about instituting the draft, he was immediately labeled a "warmonger" by the isolationists in Congress. Sen. Burton K. Wheeler, an "America First" leader, claimed that if the draft became law, then Hitler would have achieved a cheap victory, and Rep. Martin L. Sweeney, a fervent Irishman, shouted against the draft: "If the draft law is passed," he thundered, "then America has surrendered to the British."*

*As the year progressed, the German army gained momentum. In April, Germany declared war on Norway and Denmark, and in the next month on the Netherlands, Belgium, and Luxembourg. The "war climate" in the United States began to change. Although the "America Firsters" still loudly voiced their objections to the American draft, the isolationists were losing ground. One of Wheeler's colleagues was overheard to say after one of the senator's harangues, "Since he's been talking, Hitler has taken another country!"*

*May 1940 was a black month for the Allied forces, as the English retreated from Dunkirk. Nine hundred ships of various shapes and sizes took almost 350,000 troops across the English channel, including more than 25,000 French troops. As Britain left the shores of the European mainland, Belgium surrendered to the Nazis. Italy's Mussolini declared war on Great Britain and France a few days after the Dunkirk debacle, and with an air of bravado, Britain and Canada declared war on Italy.*

*By the end of June, Vichy France signed an armistice with Germany, and two weeks later the Nazis began their systematic bombing of English cities. On the other side of the world, by the end of September, Japan went on the march and invaded Indochina.*

*In the United States, President Roosevelt, breaking a 144-year precedent, was running for a third term against Wendell Willkie, a man who the Republicans felt would be a strong contender. The rumpled Willkie, whose clothes looked slept in, never seemed to comb his hair, never carried a watch, and never owned an automobile (he never learned to drive). He was attractive to the Republican hierarchy because, although he looked like a country bumpkin, he was, in fact, the president of a large utility company. At the height of the Depression he had earned $75,000 a year.*

*There were cries of dictatorship and dynasticism hurled at Roosevelt, but the U.S. national income was $40 billion above the point to which it had sunk during the Hoover administration, and there was little difference between Willkie's approach to the draft and armaments and Roosevelt's. The third-term issue and other charges seemed unimportant to most voters.*

*A record number of people went to the polls in November, and more than 50 million votes were cast. Although 22 million people voted for Willkie, it wasn't nearly enough to unseat President Roosevelt.*

*With the presidency once more in his grip, Roosevelt began to make new plans. The draft in place, he began to advance his "Lend-Lease" ideas that would provide aid to any country whose defense the President deemed vital to the defense of the United States. The isolationists were outraged but outnumbered. Lend-Lease became law and guns and food began to flow to England. On the drill fields throughout the country young American men were turned into a fighting force.*

*All eyes were on Europe. The continuous bombings of England and the atrocity stories transmitted daily from countries under the heel of German forces riveted American interest to that theater of the war. Except for the foreign correspondents and military personnel stationed in the Orient, few noted the gradual buildup of Japanese forces and the more and more outspoken talk of war with the United States.*

*One such correspondent was Clark Lee, a journalist employed by the Associated Press, who accompanied the Japanese army as a war reporter during its campaigns in China and Manchuria ("Manchukuo"). Lee wrote of the growing danger that lay in wait for the United States. Lee describes his flight from Shanghai to Manila just weeks before Pearl Harbor.*

Sergeant Hajime Matsui of the Imperial Japanese Army leaned closer to me across the table and said in a low voice, "I have a message for you from the colonel."

He glanced cautiously around the windowless, smoke-filled room. In the booth next to us two husky Japanese privates in weather-beaten khaki were flirting loudly with a moon-faced girl recently imported from Nagasaki to help entertain the Emperor's soldiers in China.

On the other side a Japanese captain was sprawled face up across a table, snoring noisily. Beer had spilled down the unbuttoned coat of his uniform; his sword dangled from his belt to the floor.

"It was at the colonel's suggestion," Matsui continued, "that I asked you to meet me here. The colonel says he believes that you appreciate Japan's national problems and are personally friendly to the Japanese people. He says that during your trips to the front with the Japanese Army, on which he served as your escort, he has grown to like you—personally; even though your newspaper stories have been highly critical of Japan's conduct in China."

Matsui's English was perfect, for he was a native of Southern California. In other ways, too, he was not an ordinary Japanese sergeant. His family was one of the most prominent in Japan: one uncle was a general; another uncle an important official of the foreign office. Talking to Sergeant Matsui wasn't exactly the same as talking to Premier Tojo or Foreign Minister Togo, but from my point of view it was better. The sergeant knew what was going on in Japan, and would talk about it.

"The colonel has been informed," he continued, "that at the Japanese army press conferences you have recently made inquiries as to whether the Japanese barracks at Kiangwan, outside of Shanghai, would be used as an internment camp for Americans in the unfortunate event of war between Japan and America."

I began to get the picture: a friendly tip regarding internment camps and how to stay out of them.

Matsui went on, "It has also been called to the colonel's attention that you plan to go to the United States on home leave in about two months. You have been quoted as saying you 'hoped to get home and back before the shooting started.' "

"That's right," I said. "It's been five years, six months and sixteen days since I left San Francisco. I've been two years in Hawaii and the rest of the time in China and Japan. I want to get home just long enough to visit my family, and maybe see a football or baseball game again. Then I'll be glad to come back to the Orient for the duration."

"The colonel takes the liberty of reminding you," Matsui continued, "that there have been no regular transpacific ship schedules from Shanghai for some months. He wishes to point out that except for two Dutch vessels and one French, no departures are scheduled from Shanghai. There is a possibility that after the next ten days there may not be any way to get out."

The pieces of the puzzle fell into place. The shooting might start anytime after the next ten days.

"Then the powder keg—" I began.

"Is almost certain to explode shortly and blow up the Orient with it," the sergeant concluded. "Mr. Kurusu, who is now on his way to Washington, will tell Mr. Hull that Japan is anxious for peace on Japan's terms, terms that cannot involve surrender of any of the territory which Japan has taken in the past four years at the cost of so much blood and treasure. Mr. Kurusu—"

This time I interrupted. "Mr. Kurusu will be told that Japan's terms are impossible. And then we will go to war!"

Matsui had said as much as he could. I asked him, "And what about yourself?"

He took a sip of tea, sucking it in noisily in Japanese fashion. "I'm here for the duration, or until I get killed. As a youngster I thought of myself as an American. I was born there and went to college there. I failed to find a place in my native country compatible with my education and background. People would not accept me as an American, because I look Japanese. I went back to Japan and they put me in uniform. Here I am."

I shook hands with him. "Good-by, Jimmy. I won't see you until after the war, unless we happen to come face to face in a trench. But I won't forget what you have told me. And thank the colonel for me."

I walked out into the sparkling afternoon sunshine and crisp fall air of Shanghai. The date was November 14, 1941.

My ricksha boy started weaving through the traffic, dodging speeding Japanese army trucks, a camouflaged light tank, swarms of rickshas and slow-moving coolies tugging heavily loaded carts by long ropes. Japanese soldiers, sailors, and marines crowded the sidewalks, jostling Japanese girls in bright-colored kimonos. This part of Shanghai was part of Japan's New Order now.

I directed the ricksha puller, "Garden Bridge. Chop-chop." I intended to act quickly on the advice that Matsui had given me. What he had said merely re-emphasized my own conviction that war had to come. For months, in stories and letters, I had been writing that it was inevitable.

Several other Japanese officers and civilians had given me "friendly" warnings that I would be wise to leave Shanghai as soon as possible, but none had been as specific as Matsui.

The Japanese made it perfectly clear that unless the United States surrendered completely and discontinued its moral aid to Generalissimo Chiang Kai-shek—aid backed by a few planes and other war materials being sent into Free China—there could be no settlement of Japanese-American difficulties. They said Japan had no intention of getting out of Manchukuo, China, Indo-China, and Hainan Island and going back to Japan itself. Those were the American terms, and they were not much less stringent than the terms that would be imposed on a defeated Japan.

The Japanese were playing for much bigger stakes than the areas they had already conquered. To go on playing power politics, they had to gain free access to certain raw materials they had been purchasing from the United States and from European colonies in the western Pacific. They needed oil, aluminum, iron, nickel, tin, tungsten, chrome, manganese, and rubber. All these, except iron, were ready to hand in Malaya, the Netherlands East Indies, and the Philippines. The iron was, and is, in Shansi province in North China. To get those things meant fighting the United States, Britain, and the Dutch, and taking away our Asiatic possessions.

Once having these sources of raw materials, Japan would become potentially the strongest power in the world. The next step, then, would be to unite the races of Asia under Japanese leadership and domination, and to embark on the program of world conquest that Japan's militarists and statesmen had outlined long before.

As for the United States, we could not afford to let Japan seize the wealth of the Orient without fighting. So war had to come, and for a long time nearly every American and every Japanese in the Far East had seen it coming.

My ricksha man pulled up at Garden Bridge, which led across Soochow Creek to the heart of the International Settlement. Rickshas were not allowed to pass the Japanese sentries on the bridge. I walked across, dropping my cigarette before reaching the sentries. They considered themselves representatives of Emperor Hirohito, and many foreigners had been slapped or clubbed for "disrespectfully" smoking in front of Imperial Representatives. The Chinese walking ahead of me suddenly stumbled to the pavement. He had forgotten to remove his hat and the sentry struck him a slashing blow across the face with the butt of his rifle. I kept my hat on and walked past rapidly. There was nothing I could do about it—yet.

Across the bridge I took another ricksha. "Take me corner Szechuen Road, Foochow Road," I directed the puller. "One dollar for go chop-chop." The grinning Chinese youngster sprinted up the Bund in his bare feet, passing the tall, solid buildings from which flew the national flags and house flags of American, British,

Japanese, French, Italian, and German banks, steamship companies, and business firms. He darted into a side street and halted outside of the Java-China-Japan-Lijn office.

I had been keeping in close touch with the steamship offices, both for news stories and because of my plans for home leave, which The Associated Press had approved for "late December or early January." There had been no ships, until the *Tjibadak* came in.

Since the American freezing of Japanese credits in July, transpacific shipping had been nearly at a standstill. American ships were going directly from Honolulu to Manila and then back to the United States. Most of Japan's big liners had been diverted from their regular runs and sent to bring Japanese nationals home from the United States, the Philippines, Singapore, Batavia and Australia. Early in November the Japanese announced that the *Tatsuta Maru* would sail for California on a similar trip on December 2. A grim-faced naval attaché in Shanghai told me, "That is a trap and we know it very well. They are trying to get us to send our ships out here for them to grab. They'd certainly like to get the *Coolidge* and four or five other big ones on the first day of war."

In the Java-China-Japan-Lijn offices, the Dutch agent recognized me and called to me over the heads of a group of foreigners and Chinese crowded anxiously against the counter. "If you want to leave," he said, "you are just in time. There has just been a cancellation. One cabin is available on the *Tjibadak* tomorrow morning. It is going to Manila and you may be able to connect with the *President Coolidge* for the United States."

The agent beckoned a man standing near by. "This will be your roommate." I found myself shaking hands with an old friend, Señor Roberto Mujica Lainez of the Argentine Embassy in Tokyo. Roberto had been trying for weeks to get passage from Shanghai to his new post in San Francisco.

I paid for my ticket and went over to The AP office to tell the Chief of Bureau, Morris Harris, that I was jumping the gun on my home leave. Jimmy White of our Peiping Bureau was on his way to Shanghai so our office would be well staffed.

"If I can get even as far as Manila, I can help cover the war from there," I said to Harris. "Or if I make the *Coolidge* and reach Honolulu, I can be assigned to the Pacific Fleet. There is no use of all three of us getting interned in Shanghai."

Weeks before, I had planned ways and means for escaping from Shanghai when the Japanese should take over the entire city, as they were certain to do on the first day of war. With a group of other Americans I established contact with headquarters of the Chinese New Fourth (former Chinese Communist) Army, just outside the city. They sent an emissary who slipped through the Jap lines and met us in a back room of the King Kong restaurant. We ate spicy Szechuen duck, and, as is the custom in China, said nothing whatever about the purpose of our meeting. He was looking us over.

As a result of the dinner, a young American-born Chinese came quietly into our office one day. He introduced himself as Washington Woo. He told us, "Buy Chinese gowns, caps and dark glasses, and Bibles." We never did find out what the Bibles were for.

89

We mapped a half-dozen possible routes through the mazes of the International Settlement, across the French Concession and the Badlands, and finally over the barbed wire guarding the Shanghai-Hangchow Railway and thus to Free China and a 1,400-mile hike to Chungking. We knew it would be touch and go getting out, for Shanghai was already a huge concentration camp. Its streets were crisscrossed with barricades and patrolled by sentries, and the entire city was surrounded by double lines of barbed wire. In September we burned most of our AP office files, after some Nazi friends warned us that the Japanese Army was getting impatient and might take over the entire Settlement at any time. There were a lot of data in the files that the local Japanese had never seen, and we knew it would go hard with us if they ever discovered the source of some of the stories that had been printed in American newspapers concerning the Japanese Army and Navy in China. Those stories had gone out under Manila or Hong Kong datelines, having been smuggled from Shanghai, where the Japanese operated an illegal and surreptitious mail censorship.

In some of the smuggled stories I had reported Japan's war plans and preparations. During the summer and fall Japan had carried out a gigantic military mobilization and had called home from the Seven Seas her vast merchant fleet totaling more than 5,000,000 tons of shipping. The ships were turned over to the Army and Navy.

Major Frank Merrill, American military attaché in Tokyo, came over to Shanghai en route to his new post in Chungking, and gave me details of the mobilization. "The Japanese have got every able-bodied man, and some who aren't so able-bodied, in uniform. They have 2,670,000 men under arms. Of these 1,667,000 are combat troops. Their reserves number 3,300,000. They have a total of 10,500,000 men to draw from, but some of those are undoubtedly essential to their industry.

"They now have only sixteen divisions in Manchukuo. Since October the first the others have been moving southward, probably to Hainan Island and Saigon. They are getting set to jump."

I kept in close touch with the Japanese military and the information they had given me coincided with Major Merrill's.

One Japanese officer, Captain M. Takada, graduate of Columbia University and army spokesman in Peiping, came down to Shanghai for a visit. We had christened him "Baroness Takada," because of the mock elegance of his manners—manners which he had so far forgotten one night in our home in Peiping as to chase our comely Chinese amah around and around the garden in the middle of a snowstorm—(she won the race!) Takada was good-humored and informative, although indirectly so.

He told me, by indirection, that although the Japanese mobilization had taken place in Manchukuo, it would be "quite easy" for Japan to move her troops to other areas, as necessity might dictate. He said what happened in Manchukuo would depend on the fighting on the Moscow front. "War with Russia is inevitable someday, of course."

Lieutenant Colonel Kunio Akiyama, the Japanese spokesman in Shanghai who looked exactly like a caricature of Japanese Militarism but who was a friendly and even a timid person underneath his military trappings, made a hurried trip to Tokyo to report. He told us on his return that he had found all Japan hopeful that an agreement would be reached in the Washington talks between Japanese Ambassador Kichisaburo Nomura and Secretary of State Cordell Hull, but, alas, "agreement would be possible, ah, only if United States recognize Japan's true position as leading nation of Orient!" With appropriate gestures, he told us the American embargo was "strangling Japan," and Japan could not put up with it much longer.

The Japanese Army and Navy liaison men entertained the American correspondents more frequently than formerly, but in smaller groups. There were fewer geisha girls, less *sake* and more serious conversation than at previous similar dinners in the Japanese restaurants of Hongkew. At those dinners we discussed war plans and possibilities and invariably they asked the question, "Will America fight?" Our answer was always, "We certainly will."

One night a Japanese naval captain asked an American Marine officer and me to dinner. He said, "The Japanese Navy is invincible in the western and southwestern Pacific. We will capture your bases. If you send your ships out to try to retake them, our dive-bomber and torpedo-plane pilots will crash their planes on your decks and sink your ships."

The Marine officer answered, "Nobody doubts the suicidal courage of your pilots, my dear Muriyama-san. But when your ships come into our waters our pilots will go just as low and just as close as necessary to get home their bombs and torpedoes. And if it is necessary to crash-dive on your ships, they will do that too."

Underlying the conversation of many of our Japanese friends we sensed their fear that Japan in the long run could not win, and a hope that the United States would back down at the last moment. There was never any suggestion that Japan could recede from a position which it considered to be honorable and just.

Those Japanese who hoped that war would be averted were mostly businessmen and a sprinkling of Army and Navy officers who had traveled in the United States and knew our potential strength. The only reason that they did not want to fight was that they thought Japan would lose. They did not abhor war, nor did they lack sympathy with Japan's desire to rule the Orient. They were just afraid of the ultimate outcome.

Reports from Chungking said the Japanese had, in recent raids, ceased their aimless "area" bombing of the Chinese capital and had suddenly begun to hit their targets on the nose. They hinted at a new bombsight.

Late in September I had a close-up of the Japanese Air Force. Together with a few other correspondents I flew with the Japanese Army over the Changsha battlefield. Changsha, seven hundred miles from the seacoast, was one of the gateways to Chungking, and the Japanese advance was of great importance because of the possibility that they might at last be attempting a knockout blow against China. Twice, since 1937, the Japanese had been turned back outside of Changsha, but this time they took the city in a lightning drive which covered more than ninety miles over plains and mountains in ten days. They plunged on southward for fifteen miles past Changsha—and then withdrew.

When the Japanese quit Changsha we reported the withdrawal as voluntary and surmised that the Japanese drive was primarily combat training of troops. We didn't guess, of course, that within less than three months those same troops would be using the same tactics in the Philippines and Burma and Malaya.

We saw Army "97" dive bombers and fast Navy fighters in action that may have been Zeros, although we had never heard of Zeros at the time. We took movies and still pictures of the Japanese planes on the ground and in flight, and by devious methods succeeded in getting our pictures past the Japanese military censorship and turning them over to quarters where they should have done the most good.

We were surprised at the extensive and extremely effective use the Japanese made of dive bombers.

The Nazi correspondent said, "These Japanese monkey men haf learned well dere lesson from der Führer, ja!"

He elaborated. Since the Chinese invented gunpowder every weapon had served the same purpose: to shoot lead or steel and explosives from one place to another and kill your enemy and destroy his own guns and his fortifications, cities and ships. The airplane was the greatest artillery piece ever invented. It had its own eyes and unbeatable mobility. Would anyone deny that a sufficient number of 18-inch guns firing into New York City or any other city could devastate the city and force its occupants to surrender? Would anyone deny that enough airplanes could accomplish the same end? To do so was to deny that steel and TNT could win wars.

"If der Führer had only had enough airplanes to continue to blitz England for three more weeks..." the Nazi correspondent continued. And so on.

Our sympathy with the Chinese redoubled on that trip, because we saw what an army was up against without artillery, and most of all without airplanes. We saw how the Japanese Air Force co-operated perfectly with the ground troops. When the ground forces ran into a strong point they would radio back for a plane. The dive bombers would come over, locate the Chinese machine-gun nest or pillbox, and swarm down on it. Then the Chinese would be dead and the Japanese ground forces would march on past or drive on in their trucks and tanks.

It was about this time that Japan's future enemies missed a chance to learn about the Mitsubishi Zero fighter plane that was to astound and confound them a few months later. A report came in to Chungking, the capital of Generalissimo Chiang Kai-shek's Free China, that a new, fast Japanese fighter had made a forced landing on an airfield in Western China and had been captured intact by the Chinese Army. A special plane was put at the disposal of the American and British air attachés in Chungking to fly over and inspect the Japanese aircraft. But when they arrived they found the pursuit plane a messed-up wreck on the airfield. Only the wing tips, with their bright-red "Rising Sun" insignia, were undamaged. An over-anxious Chinese army pilot had taken the Zero up for a test flight and had found it too hot to handle.

When I returned to Shanghai from the Changsha trip I found further signs that Japan was on the march. The youthful Japanese soldiers who had been on guard duty around Shanghai had disappeared. They had been a tough, cruel lot, whose officers had taught them to cultivate what we called the "China Face" with outthrust jaw and sneering down-turned mouth. They were replaced by thin, undernourished reservists—office workers and older men who looked ill at ease in their uniforms.

The Chinese were greatly pleased at the change, because the newcomers kicked and beat them less often at the barriers and barricades around Shanghai.

Through the Chinese secret service I learned that the younger Japanese troops had been put in transports and sent, not to Manchukuo, but to the south. That could mean only one thing: the Japanese had abandoned their plans for attacking Siberia.

The Kwantung army generals, the rulers of Manchukuo, had wanted to fight Russia first, while the Japanese Navy had always argued that its "historic destiny" lay to the south. If Moscow had fallen the Kwantung Army would probably have had its way and Japs would have attacked Vladivostok and surged across the Amur River into Siberia.

But when Moscow held and the Siberian winter came on, and simultaneously the United States began to tighten its pressure on Japan, the Kwantung army generals agreed with the admirals, finally, that the blows must be struck to the south and must be all out.

One by one the Japanese commanders in China went home to confer with the new premier, General Tojo, with the general staff, and with the admirals. Prince Chichibu, brother of the Emperor, flew down to Indo-China to tie up the loose strings there. Shortly after his visit Japan took over all of southern Indo-China, including the excellent harbor of Camranh and the southern capital of Saigon, which was the obvious jumping-off place for an attack on Malaya and the Dutch East Indies.

In a series of stories written for The AP in February of 1941 I had said, "When the Japanese mass troops and ships and planes at Saigon in large numbers, the danger of war between the United States and Japan must be reckoned from day to day or even from hour to hour, since the practice of the Japanese has always been to strike first, and explain afterward."

Now, on the evening of November 14, they were quickly massing troops, ships, and planes at Saigon "in large numbers." I was glad that I was leaving Shanghai—getting out of Japanese territory—the next morning. I wanted to see the war, but not from an internment camp.

I took a ricksha back to my rooms at the Metropole Hotel and told the amah to start packing my clothes. "Everything—this time."

I had moved to the hotel after my wife had gone home in August, following a very polite suggestion from Japanese Army and Navy officers that "perhaps, in view of growing tension in Orient, it would be more better if Mrs. Ree returning Honoruru." We got the point, even if the Japanese always pronounced the letter "l" as "r."

Most of the Americans had left Shanghai months before, heeding our State Department's thrice-repeated advice that all American women, children and "nonessential" men return to the United States from the Orient. The American businessmen, whose import and export trade had collapsed as a result of Washington's embargo on shipments of strategic materials to the Far East and as a result of Japan's bayonet-enforced monopolies of trade in the Yangtze River hinterland, had little to do except roll dice for drinks at the American club. As many of them as could get space on ships, left for Manila or for home. We expected every ship to be the last one.

Carroll Alcott, the Far East's favorite radio commentator, had gotten out just in time. He boarded a ship for home under the escort of a Marine bodyguard. The Japanese hated Alcott and had tried to kill him three times. Of the five American newsmen on the original Japanese "blacklist," only J. B. Powell remained in Shanghai to continue in his *China Weekly Review* a courageous and dangerous exposé of Japan's murderous outrages in China and of the war lord's preparations to fight America. Powell stayed too long, and when he finally returned to the United States both his feet had been amputated as a result of an infection contracted during six months in a Japanese jail.

Colonel Samuel Howard, Major "Duke" Hamilton, and the other officers of the Fourth U.S. Marines entertained the American community on the occasion of the Marine Corps' 166th birthday party on November 10. It seemed more like a funeral wake than a celebration. The sole topic of discussion was war, and the only questions talked about were: "How soon will the Japanese attack?" and "What will become of us?"

There were only a handful of American women present. The women and their husbands were keeping their eyes on the Marines, who had come to China sixteen years before to protect American interests and who had always been the trouble barometer for Americans. The husbands said, "When the Marines go, we'll send our families." But when the Marines left on the *President Harrison* late in November, it was too late for others. There were no more ships. On its return trip to pick up additional Marines and a few American men, women and children from North China, the *Harrison* was captured off Chinwangtao by Japanese destroyers.

That last night in Shanghai I went out on the balcony for a last look at the city that had been my home for three years, except for assignments in Japan, Manchukuo, and North China, and trips to the front with the Japanese Army.

In the twilight, Shanghai sprawled vast and uneasy from the massive buildings of the Bund through the jumbled tangle of slums where four million Chinese lived in space built for half that many; and then on out to the residential areas where American, Britons, Frenchmen, and the people of a score of nations had tried to reproduce the atmosphere of their own home countries on the mud flats of the Yangtze delta.

Shanghai and the other great cities of the eastern coast were all in the grip of Japanese military rule; a regime characterized by corruption, graft, violence, poverty and narcotics. Beyond and between the Japanese lines was the real China of four hundred million people, free and unconquerable, but sadly underarmed. They had been unable to fight against a Japanese war machine which American airplanes, gasoline, steel, scrap iron, and automobiles had made great and powerful.

I recalled that if Shanghai could last until 1942 it would be one hundred years old. But the chances seemed slim. Since 1937, Shanghai had been in its death throes as a white man's city. For more than four years Shanghai had been living practically in a state of siege, with bombs, bullets, and barbed wire for its daily diet, with its streets stinking of the death, starvation, misery and corruption of war. The sound of assassins' pistols and the explosion of terrorists' bombs had become a part of everyday life.

There was too much champagne in Shanghai, and not enough rice. The price of rice kept going up and up, and so did the number of starved Chinese whose bodies were picked up from streets each morning.

From my hotel balcony I watched the wretched and tattered Chinese street scavengers follow the rice trucks along Foochow Road. They carried short brooms and dust pans, and fought for the few crumbs of rice that tumbled to the pavement when the trucks passed. Sometimes they chased the trucks and slit the bags with long knives, ignoring the blows rained on their heads by truck guards armed with bamboo poles.

That was one of the last street scenes I saw in Shanghai. Some friends came in during the evening to say farewell, and shortly afterward I was notified that two Japanese army officers were waiting for me in the hotel grill. They were Lieutenant Colonel Akiyama, the army spokesman, and his interpreter, Sublieutenant K. Matsuda, ex-Princeton and graduate of the University of Missouri. At first I thought that perhaps their spies had overheard my conversation with Sergeant Matsui that afternoon. Then I saw Matsuda was carrying a carefully boxed package containing a beautiful gold lacquer vase.

Akiyama made a little presentation speech before handing me the package. "You have traveled great deal with Japanese Army in past three years. You have ridden in our military planes, seen our bombers operate and our troops fight. This present is in appreciation your effort to report truthfully true intentions of Imperial Japanese Army in bringing peace and order to East Asia." Since I had always tried very diligently to report the "true intentions" of the Japanese Army, I accepted the gift.

Akiyama wiped the remains of his second cocktail from his black mustache and added, "Japanese Army still hoping United States, Japan not going war, but situation now very difficult. Mr. Kurusu-san was ordered by Emperor himself to ask America recognize Japan's honorable intentions. If America refusing—"

Colonel," I said, "it looks like war."

He replied gravely, "*So desu, ne!* (That is true!) Very unfortunate."

Matsuda, who had once worked for The AP in Tokyo, said, "Well, if we are both alive after it, maybe we can have some more tennis games."

No flowers to fill the gold vase were forthcoming from the Japanese Navy. They had recently traced to me the authorship of some stories reporting how Japanese officers were making fortunes by selling safe conducts for ships to run their blockade of the China coast and how the Imperial Navy had engaged in wholesale piracy. I was on their black list.

I went back up to my room, and an American naval officer from the gunboat out in the Whangpoo called me aside. I told him what Akiyama had said, and asked him if we would have trouble defeating the Japanese Navy. He replied with the estimate of our future enemies then fashionable among our Navy officers. "Their ship handling is superb, their morale and discipline are excellent. Their gunnery is not so good and they lack imagination and daring. They haven't fought since they beat a battered Russian fleet in Tsushima Straits in 1904."

I reminded him, "Well, as a Navy we haven't fought since Dewey sailed into

Manila Bay and shot up the outnumbered and demoralized Spanish fleet. The last real knock-down, drag-out fight was between the *Monitor* and the *Merrimac*."

Another American officer had joined us. "I don't know exactly how good or how bad the Japs are," he said, "but I am dead sure we are going to fight them. And I'm just as sure that I'll never see the United States again."

A few days later he was transferred to Manila where he found his new orders awaiting him. He was assigned to the *U.S.S. Houston* just before she went down with all hands in the Java Sea.

On the morning of November 15, I went aboard the *Tjibadak*. My Argentine friend, Señor Mujica Lainez, made it by the skin of his teeth. Out of touch with his government, he was without funds. Rear Admiral William C. Glassford, commander of the United States Yangtze patrol and once naval attaché in Buenos Aires, heard of Roberto's plight and put the Good Neighbor policy into practical effect by advancing the necessary money.

Riding down the Whangpoo by launch to the docks where the *Tjibadak* was moored, I experienced the sensations of a condemned man who is granted a last-minute reprieve. As we passed the last Japanese destroyer anchored in midstream even the air seemed freer. I was leaving behind the gigantic prison camp that was Shanghai.

The 8,000-ton *Tjibadak* was in war paint, her hull a dark gray and her masts light brown. Her captain wasted no time in casting off and heading down the curving Whangpoo and into the vast, muddy Yangtze delta.

"This is the last trip that we shall make here." he told me nervously. "Maybe we were foolish to make this one. My government in the Netherlands East Indies believes that Japan will attack soon."

We promptly christened the *Tjibadak* the "S.S. Jitterbug." Our fellow passengers in first and second class included an American authoress who had spent seven years making an "esoteric study of exotic religions." She insisted on instructing the Standard Oil official in Yogi. The grass widow from Batavia wanted Roberto to give her tango lessons on the blacked-out moonlit deck. The Mexican, who was engaged in the dangerous business of carrying forbidden currency from Oriental country to country for a profit, sat in the smoking room for hours at a time, taking potshots at cockroaches with a toy .45 which fired BB shot. He was a crack marksman. The naval commander who had tried to drink Shanghai dry—and like thousands before him had failed—was watched constantly by his two Medical Corps "escorts."

In Amoy, two days south of Shanghai down the China Coast, we ran into trouble. I snapped a few pictures of Japanese ships and shore installations, and then luckily changed the roll in my camera before taking one more. A Japanese patrol boat spotted me and Marine officers in khaki uniform, with their swords swinging threateningly, hurried on board and demanded that I be brought to the bridge. They examined the camera. I had not turned the crank on my Rolleiflex after taking one shot and the shutter would not click and the indicator pointed to "1." I told them that meant no pictures had been taken. The interpreter, anxious to show his knowledge of cameras, confirmed my statement, "Hai! Yes! That is so. I mysefu having Rorreifrex." The senior officer, who had given no sign that he understood English, said, "Okay, you can go."

The officers searched the ship for other cameras, found and confiscated a few, and then went ashore to develop the films. The *Tjibadak*'s captain was sweating blood, fearing his ship would be held up indefinitely, but they let us proceed.

We steamed southwestward down the coast for twenty-four hours and next day sailed into Hong Kong's beautiful harbor. A patrol boat pitched on the sparkling blue waters at the harbor entrance and a bearded English naval officer challenged us through a megaphone. Our captain shouted back, "Her Imperial Netherlands Majesty's ship *Tjibadak*, sailing under British Admiralty orders." Then the patrol boat guided us through the mine fields, while an ancient "Singapore" flying boat, with twin puller and pusher motors, lumbered overhead.

That, and a few other planes of similar vintage, were Hong Kong's air force. Great Britain had neither the men nor airplanes nor guns to spare for the defense of this once mighty bastion of Far Eastern Empire. But the high hills of the Kowloon Peninsula, behind which lurked the Japanese Army, looked formidable, and Victoria Island, on which the city of Hong Kong is located, bristled with guns and machine-gun posts.

Nearly all the foreigners ashore were in uniform, with Canadian and Indian troops predominating. Most of the British families were gone, but a few officials were congratulating themselves on evading the evacuation order and keeping their wives and families among them. There were blockhouses and barbed wire along the waterfront, and across the island at Repulse Bay. The Royal Navy was represented by a few torpedo boats and a destroyer or two in the harbor.

The town was as filthy, in the crowded water-front areas, as ever, and as magnificent from the soaring Peak. People were still dancing in the Hong Kong and Gloucester Hotels, and some of the more beautiful Chinese and Eurasian girls had as many as five handsome, uniformed escorts. Everybody was talking about the recent defense scandal which revealed that part of the funds set aside to build air raid shelters had found its way into the bank account of Mimi Lau, a young Cantonese beauty. At least one official had taken the honorable way out: a single shot through the temple.

On our strolls through the city Roberto would stop aghast, and stare angrily, as he saw for the first time what the British Colonial thought of the Chinese. Time after time we saw amiable-appearing British businessmen push Chinese who got in their way on the sidewalks, or urge on ricksha men with a few light strokes of a cane. It was all done casually, as something in the normal course of events.

The Canadian troops had just arrived and their transports and a light cruiser were still in the harbor. Their first day ashore some Canadians went into the Gloucester lounge for tea and were told no men in uniform, except officers, would be served. They went out muttering, "So we came here to fight for democracy. Oh yeah, what democracy?" A few days later the order was changed and the Canadians went wherever they pleased until December 8.

As in Shanghai, business for foreigners was dead in Hong Kong, and nobody thought much about the future except that it was obvious that something had to break soon. With no shipping, it was impossible to plan.

Some of our Hong Kong friends recalled the prophecy of a Chinese historian in 1841, when the British first took Hong Kong, that "British rule will last exactly one hundred years." I told them that the Japanese plan called for the capture of Hong Kong within nine days after the initial attack. That information came from my ex-friend Major T. Nishihara of the Imperial Japanese Army, who had spent four years in Hong Kong as a "language student," and who at a Shanghai party one night amused us by drawing a map of Victoria Island and sketching in every one of Hong Kong's big gun positions. Actually, Hong Kong held for eighteen days.

Entering Manila Bay we glanced only casually at the Bataan Peninsula and the impressive saddle of Mt. Mariveles. The channels through the mine fields led us close to the shore of Bataan, although we didn't know at the time that it was Bataan. The peninsula looked forbidding and uninhabited. We turned our glasses on the vast bulk of Corregidor, with its huge barracks atop the highest point and the American flag waving over them. Somebody pointed out the radio masts at the Cavite naval base as we passed.

Behind the breakwater in Manila Harbor we saw the *Coolidge* tied up, with an American cruiser in battle paint beyond it. Tanks and trucks and boxes of ammunition and crated planes were being unloaded from many ships of a convoy just in from the United States.

The harbor seemed to be full of the submarines and destroyers of Admiral Thomas C. Hart's Asiatic Fleet. Navy catapult planes buzzed overhead and an occasional pursuit and four-engined bomber. Those were the first American war planes I'd seen in more than two years.

I called to Roberto, "Look at those American ships and planes. Don't they make you feel good?" Roberto, who like all Argentines is meticulous about the use of the adjective "American," replied, "You mean those United States of North America ships and planes, my amigo."

I said, "Well, American or United States of North America as you please. They certainly are beautiful. When the Japs come down here, they'll be playing in the Big League for the first time in their lives."

# 2
# The Recruits

## REVEILLE

from
*See Here, Private Hargrove*
by Marion Hargrove
Garden City, NY: The Sun Dial Press, 1943

*When the United States entered World War I in 1917, a Selective Service Act was passed that required the registration of all men between the ages of 21 and 30. By 1918, the age limit was stretched to include all males between 18 and 45. The men were chosen by lottery with the "winners" being sent off to training. There were several exemptions to the draft: men who had physical disabilities or dependents, members of religious organizations with pacifist principles, and those engaged in vital defense industries. More than 2,500,000 men were garnered through the draft in World War I.*

*The first peacetime draft in American history was adopted in September 1940. The Selective Service Act called for an army of 900,000 men between the ages of 21 and 35 who were to serve for one year. Many young men, rather than wait for the draft, enlisted to "get it over with." After the attack on Pearl Harbor, the law was revamped to include all males from 18 to 45 and to extend the stay in the armed forces to the duration of the war plus six months.*

*Early draftees marching into induction centers included many who had never lived away from home before and had seldom, if ever, travelled. To many, this was the beginning of a one-year "lark" away from family and friends; a chance for a fling that they might never have again. Others entered army life fearing the unknown.*

*Outside the training camps, there was a great thirst for knowledge about what kind of experience the citizen-soldier was having. Fortunately for the civilian population, President Roosevelt sent his greeting to Marion Hargrove, a young journalist working on a small Southern newspaper. In short order, there was a book explaining the ordeal and the stress of becoming a soldier, as experienced by "Private" Hargrove. The nation chuckled at the misadventures of the making of a private and at the training that turned a civilian into a soldier.*

W e are now soldiers.

This morning—our first morning in the Recruit Reception Center—began when we finished breakfast and started cleaning up our squadroom. A gray-haired, fatherly old private, who swore that he had been demoted from master sergeant four times, lined us up in front of the barracks and took us to the dispensary.

If the line in front of the mess hall dwindled as rapidly as the one at the dispensary, life would have loveliness to sell above its private consumption stock. First you're fifteen feet from the door, then (whiff) you're inside. Then you're standing between two orderlies and the show is on.

The one on my left scratched my arm and applied the smallpox virus. The only thing that kept me from keeling over was the hypodermic needle loaded with typhoid germs, which propped up my right arm.

From the dispensary we went to a huge warehouse of a building by the railroad tracks. The place looked like Goldenberg's Basement on a busy day. A score of fitters measured necks, waists, inseams, heads, and feet.

My shoe size, the clerk yelled down the line, was ten and a half.

"I beg your pardon," I prompted, "I wear a size nine."

"Forgive me," he said, a trifle weary, "the expression is 'I wore a size nine.' These shoes are to walk in, not to make you look like Cinderella. You say size nine: your foot says ten and a half."

We filed down a long counter, picking up our allotted khaki and denims, barrack bags and raincoats, mess kits and tent halves. Then we were led into a large room, where we laid aside the vestments of civil life and donned our new garments.

While I stood there, wondering what I was supposed to do next, an attendant caught me from the rear and strapped to my shoulders what felt like the Old Man of the Mountain after forty days.

"Straighten up, soldier," the attendant said, "and git off the floor. That's nothing but a full field pack, such as you will tote many miles before you leave this man's army. Now I want you to walk over to that ramp and over it. That's just to see if your shoes are comfortable."

I looked across the room to where an almost perpendicular walkway led up to and over a narrow platform.

"With these Oregon boots and this burden of misery," I told him firmly, "I couldn't even walk over to the thing. As for climbing over it, not even an alpenstock, a burro train, and two St. Bernard dogs complete with brandy could get me over it."

There was something in his quiet, steady answering glance that reassured me. I went over the ramp in short order. On the double, I think the Army calls it.

From there we went to the theater, where we were given intelligence tests, and to the classification office, where we were interviewed by patient and considerate corporals.

"And what did you do in civil life?" my corporal asked me.

"I was feature editor of the Charlotte *News*."

"And just what sort of work did you do, Private Hargrove? Just give me a brief idea."

Seven minutes later, I had finished answering that question.

"Let's just put down here, 'Editorial worker.'" He sighed compassionately. "And what did you do before all that?"

I told him. I brought in the publicity work, the soda-jerking, the theater ushering, and the printer's deviling.

"Private Hargrove," he said, "the Army is just what you have needed to ease the burdens of your existence. Look no farther, Private Hargrove, you have found a home."

This was a lovely morning. We began at daybreak and devoted all the time until noon to enjoying the beauties of nature. We had a drill sergeant to point them out to us. We marched a full twenty miles without leaving the drill field. Lunch, needless to say, was delicious.

We fell into bed, after lunch, determined to spend the afternoon in dreamland. Two minutes later, that infernal whistle blew. Melvin Piel, guardhouse lawyer for Company A, explained it all on the way downstairs. We were going to be assigned to our permanent stations.

The sergeant called off the first list of names and the boys fell out. I heard him tell them that they were going to Virginia. "That's nothing," said Piel. "We're next and we're going to California." Guardhouse Lawyer Piel smiled happily.

The sergeant began the second list. "Moscowitz! Goldberg! Pinelli! Jones! Smith! Brown—" He stopped short. Then he started looking down the front line, choosing men to fill out the list. I smiled brightly from under my floppy denim cap at him.

"What's your name?" he asked.

"Hargrove, sir."

"Groves?"

"Hargrove, sir."

"All right, Grove. Fall in with those men over there."

I fell in and a corporal led us off down the street. I could feel the California palm trees fanning my face. We stopped at Barracks 17 and the corporal led us inside.

"Do we go to California, corporal?" I asked.

"Naah," he said.

"Where do we go?" I asked him, a little disappointed.

"To the garbage rack," he said. "Double quick." He thumbed Johnny Lisk and me to the back of the barracks.

At the garbage rack we found three extremely fragrant garbage cans. Outside, we found more. Lisk and I, citizen-soldiers, stared at them. The overcheerful private to whom we were assigned told us, "When you finish cleaning those, I want to see my face in them!"

"There's no accounting for tastes," Lisk whispered. Nevertheless, we cleaned them and polished them and left them spick and span.

101

"Now take 'em, outside and paint 'em," said the private. "White. Git the black paint and paint 'HQCO—RRC' on both sides of all of them!"

"This is summer," I suggested. "Wouldn't something pastel look better?"

The sun was affecting the private. "I think you're right," he said. So we painted them cream and lettered them in brilliant orange.

All afternoon, in a blistering sun, we painted garbage cans. The other Charlotte boys waved to us as they passed on their way to the ball park. Happy voices floated to us from the post exchange. The supper hour neared.

The straw-boss private woke up, yawned and went away, telling us what would happen if we did likewise. He returned soon in a truck. He motioned peremptorily to us and we loaded the cans into the truck. Away we went to headquarters company—and painted more garbage cans. It was definitely suppertime by now.

"Now can we go home, Private Dooley, sir?" asked Lisk. I looked at Lisk every time the blindness left me, and I could see the boy was tired.

The private sighed wearily. "Git in the truck," he said. Away we went back to our street. We stopped in front of our barracks and Private Dooley dismounted. "The truck driver," he said, "would appreciate it if you boys would go and help him wash the truck."

We sat in the back of the truck and watched the mess hall fade away behind us. Two, three, four miles we left it behind us. We had to wait ten minutes before we could get the wash-pit. It took us fifteen minutes to wash the truck. By the time we got back to the mess hall, we were too tired to eat. But we ate.

"There's one thing to be thankful for," said Lisk. "Tomorrow can't be this bad."

On the way to our barracks we met Yardbird Fred McPhail, neat and cool, on his way to the recreation hall. "Good news, soldiers," said Yardbird McPhail. "We don't have to drill tomorrow."

We halted and sighed blissfully.

"No, sir," said McPhail. "They can't lay a hand on us from sunup until sundown. The whole barracks is on kitchen duty all day."

It was through no fault of mine that I was a kitchen policeman on my sixth day. The whole barracks got the grind. And it was duty, not punishment.

It was all very simple, this KP business. All you have to do is get up an hour earlier, serve the food, and keep the mess hall clean.

After we served breakfast, I found a very easy job in the dining hall, where life is much pinker than it is in the kitchen. A quartet was formed and we were singing "Home on the Range." A corporal passed by just as I hit a sour note. He put the broom in my left hand, the mop in my right. ...

There was a citizen-soldier from Kannapolis to help me clean the cooks' barracks. For a time it was awful. We tried to concentrate on the floor while a news broadcaster almost tore up the radio trying to decide whether we were to be in the Army ten years or twenty.

We finished the job in an extremely short time to impress the corporal. This, we found later, is a serious tactical blunder and a discredit to the ethics of goldbricking. The sooner you finish a job the sooner you start on the next.

The corporal liked our work, unfortunately. Kannapolis was allowed to sort garbage and I was promoted to the pot-and-pan polishing section. I was Themos Kokenes's assistant. He washed and I dried. Later we formed a goldbricking entente. We both washed and made Conrad Wilson dry.

Pollyanna the glad girl would have found something silver-lined about the hot sink. So did I. "At least," I told Kokenes, "this will give my back a chance to recover from that mop."

When I said "mop," the mess sergeant handed me one. He wanted to be able to see his face in the kitchen floor. After lunch he wanted the back porch polished.

We left the Reception Center mess hall a better place to eat in, at any rate. But KP is like woman's work—never really done. Conrad Wilson marked one caldron and at the end of the day we found that we had washed it twenty-two times.

Jack Mulligan helped me up the last ten steps to the squadroom. I finally got to the side of my bunk. "Gentlemen," I said to the group which gathered around to scoop me off the floor, "I don't ever want to see another kitchen!"

The next morning we were classified and assigned to the Field Artillery Replacement Center. Gene Shumate and I were classified as cooks. I am a semi-skilled cook, they say, although the only egg I ever tried to fry was later used as a tire patch. The other cooks include former postal clerks, tractor salesmen, railroad engineers, riveters, bricklayers, and one blacksmith.

But we'll learn. Already I've learned to make beds, sweep, mop, wash windows, and sew a fine seam. When Congress lets me go home, will I make some woman a good wife!

"Just look at me," the exercise sergeant roars in a voice that would go four miles against the wind. "Just look! I weigh two hundred and eight pounds and I'm in the worst physical condition I've ever been in! I ought to be busted for the way I've allowed myself to get fat and flabby! I'm ashamed!"

You look at the exercise sergeant and wonder what he's leading up to. To you he looks like the "after taking" part of a malted yeast advertisement. He could probably lick his weight in police dogs.

His next statement explains everything. "Now I'm going to show you an exercise that's so simple it's almost ridiculous. Even I can do it. Now, I don't want to hear anybody down there admitting he's in worse shape than I am. If I can do it, you can do it—or else!"

He outlines the exercise and you begin wondering how a contortionist happened to wind up at Fort Bragg. This self-styled "fat and flabby" calisthenics master doesn't have any knees or elbows. You stand there waiting to hear his spine fall apart under the strain, but he comes up all in one piece.

"That's the way I want you boys to do it," he says, beaming cheerfully. You begin to feel your face getting gray and you wonder why a bolt of lightning doesn't come to deliver you from the prospective torture.

"One. Two. Three. Four. Five. Six. Seven. Eight. One. Two—"

The first three or four times are the hardest. After that, you get the swing of it. It's really tame stuff, you decide.

"The next exercise," says the sergeant, "is what we call the quarter, half, and full knee bend. It goes like this." He shows you. When you see it, the corners of your mouth go up in a sneer of derision (unless the corporal is looking). Ho hum, you say to yourself. Why do they take up my time with this play?

"Exercise—one, two, three, four—" Quarter, half, full recover. Your knees get That Tired Feeling after the third time. After the sixth time, you feel your eyes getting glassy. After the ninth, you're floating in space. By the time the exercise is over, nothing matters any more.

The exercise sergeant sighs with bubbling energy and bounces exuberantly on his toes. "Didn't that feel good?" he asks. You nod feebly, expecting to collapse at any minute.

A messenger from the battery orderly room mounts the platform and talks for a while to the exercise sergeant. The sergeant's face falls. He turns to the ranks with disappointment written all over his face.

"Sorry to tell you this, boys," he says, "but we'll have to stop here. No more exercise this morning. All play and no work—you know what that means. You have to take your typhoid shots now."

Before you have marched off the drill field you notice that you still haven't collapsed. In fact, you find to your disappointment that you're beginning to feel good. All limbered up.

I told our platoon sergeant that it was just like carrying papers. The bag is sometimes so heavy to the route-carrier that when he sets it down he feels as if he's floating.

"There you go, Hargrove," the sergeant sighed. "Always looking at the dark side of life!"


A mess sergeant, according to military legend, is a cook whose brains have been baked out. This does not apply to the mess sergeant in our battery, whose feelings are easily hurt by cruel remarks and who weeps tears into the mashed potatoes when he's picked on. This is simply the old Army definition of a mess sergeant.

All of us rising student cooks are eligible to become mess sergeants, Staff Sergeant Adams told us in our first cooking class yesterday morning. Then we can sit out in the cool dining rooms and yell back orders for the cooks to yell at the kaypees.

This is not the beautiful goldbricking life that it seems, though. The mess sergeant has to make requisitions and keep records on all the rations, he has to make out the menus, see that the food is prepared properly and supervise the work of the cooks, the student cooks, and the kaypees. Besides this, he must listen to all the gripes about his food and to the threadbare jokes about cooks who get drunk from lemon and vanilla extract.

All this he must do, with his brains baked out.

The cook, lucky little rascal that he is, also leads an ideal life. He is allowed to believe that he knows more about cooking than the mess sergeant will ever know, although he is not supposed to tell the mess sergeant that he does. He works one day and sleeps the next two.

If the cook is not feeling cheerful, he can pick on at least one student cook and at least five kaypees. On the battlefield, he is in the safest position behind the lines, since the food is endowed with more sentimental value than the top sergeant. The jokes about Army cooks being shot at from both sides are not based upon fact.

However, friend cook has to greet the morn before the morn gets there. On the days when he works, he has to get up between 3:00 and 3:30 o'clock in order to prepare a substantial breakfast for about two hundred healthy, growing boys whose appetites are exceeded only by the size of their mouths and the power of their lungs.

Yesterday we started to school, with cookbooks and manuals and loose-leaf notebooks for our homework. The only way in which it differed from public schools was that the naughty boys didn't have to go and sit with the girls. Also, the dunce seat, instead of being in the corner of the classroom, was said to be behind a large sack of potatoes in the battery kitchen.

The only hope for an easy time in class was gone in this school. There's no percentage in bringing a shiny red apple to a teacher who has the key to at least one well-stocked pantry.

Tomorrow, after lunch, each of us will be taken to one of the sixty-four Replacement Center kitchens. There we will present ourselves to the mess sergeant, who will sigh wearily at the sight of us and show us where to change our uniforms. Then we will proceed to prove, in our respective kitchens, the old saw about too many cooks.

We will be railed at by the mess sergeant and the first cook and, if we want to and know how to, we can rail at the kaypees in turn. When the boys in line make sneering remarks about having spinach again already, we can jaw back at them. It will be wonderful to be able to jaw at someone again. Life has loveliness to sell.

Private Sher and I were sitting out on the back steps to dodge the cleaning work going on inside when we saw the sergeant bearing down on us from the other end of the battery street.

"It's no use scooting inside, Hargrove," said Sher. "He's already seen us. Look tired, as if you'd already done your part of the work." Private Sher is the goldbricking champion of Battery A and always knows what to do in such an emergency.

We both draped expressions of fatigue over our faces and the sergeant skidded to a halt before us. He reached into his hip pocket for the little black book and aimed a finger at both of us.

"Bums!" he shouted. "Bums! I worked my fingers to the bone yesterday morning getting this platoon to pretty up the barracks for inspection. Comes inspection and two privates have dirty shoes lying sprawled all over the floor under their bunks! Private Hargrove and MISTER Private Sher! Report to Corporal Farmer in fatigue clothes."

We reported to Corporal Farmer, who looked at his list of jobs. "As much as you don't deserve it," he said, "you two goldbricks are in line for canteen police."

Mr. Private Sher and I walked up the battery street toward the canteen.

"Is this canteen police business good or bad?" I asked.

"Oh, so-so," he said. "You have to clean up the papers and cigarette butts around the post exchange first thing in the morning. Then you come around and check up three or four times during the day."

I stopped, aghast. "What do you do betweentimes?"

"Just be inconspicuous," said Sher. "That's all there is to it. Pick up that candy wrapper over there. My back aches."

We cleaned up the grounds around the post exchange and sat for a while in the shade, watching a battery going through calisthenics. With beautiful precision, the soldiers swung their rifles up, down to the right, to the left. They went through the quarter, half, and full knee bends and the shoulder exercises and the rest of the routine.

"Those boys seem to be improving, Mr. Sher," I said.

"Result of hard work," said Maury. "Personally, I get awfully tired watching this. We'll wear ourselves out. Let's go over to my kitchen and handshake for a bottle of milk."

"No," I protested. "We must go to my kitchen."

"To avoid a tiring argument," suggested Private Sher, "we will go to both our kitchens. We can't be thrown out of both of them."

After successful forays on both kitchens, Private Sher began to yawn with boredom. "My dear Hargrove," he said, "we must stimulate our minds. Let us adjourn to my place for a game of checkers." Private Sher's "place" was only one flight of stairs removed from my squadroom, so we adjourned.

After two games of checkers, Private Sher waved his arms. "This is folderol," he said. "You are no checker player, Hargrove. You have no idea of tactics. Let us sit by the window and watch our comrades drill. There is something stirring in the sight of fine young men perfectly executing a marching order."

While we were sitting there being stirred, another corporal disturbed us. He wanted us to go with him to haul coal.

"Much as we would like to help you haul coal, my good man," said Maury, "we are now actively engaged in the work of policing up the post exchange. Feel free to call upon us at any other time."

The corporal placed his hands on his hips and stared at us. "You're being punished," he asked, "with canteen duty?"

There's no need to be vulgar," said Sher. "If you will excuse us, it is time for us to go again to look for cigarette butts around the post exchange. Coming, Mr. Hargrove?"

"Coming, Mr. Sher. And a good day to you, corporal!"

Somewhere on the wild coast of South Carolina, the battalion in which I cook is being treated to a weekend to combine business with pleasure. We can romp in the Atlantic while we get a "taste of the field." With the wind blowing the sand into kitchens and pup tents alike, it will be nice to get back to Fort Bragg for a taste of the food we eat. A vexed soldier here doesn't grate his teeth. He crunches them.

We made the trip here in lorries, which are the mechanical age's nearest approach in appearance to covered wagons. You've probably seen them rolling noisily but smoothly through town—large canvas-topped trucks with a folding bench down each side inside. You'd expect to be hauled out of one of them, beaten to death, at the end of a 130-mile trip. They give a tolerably bumpy ride, just tolerably.

When we started pitching camp, about a quarter of a mile back from the beach, we found the place already inhabited—by cannibals. These creatures, which masquerade as harmless flies and even camouflaged by the harmless sounding name of sand flies, must have vampire blood back in the line somewhere.

I don't bear any grudge against the easygoing, good-natured housefly—in fact, I feel rather cruel when I squash one for tickling me—but it arouses my pioneer fighting spirit to see a stunted horsefly light on my bare leg, make himself sassily comfortable and start draining off my life's blood. But what can you do? Slapping one only serves to make him mad at you.

At night we sleep, or at least we simulate sleep, in pup tents, made by our own hands with loving care, blood, sweat, tears, two pieces of waterproof cloth, two lengths of rope, and a handful of turned lumber.

I share my little duplex with Private Warren, the new student cook. When I stumbled home last night, primed to the gills with a blend of sand and salt water, I discovered that we had an overnight guest! The chief cook on our shift, in the task of packing the field kitchen, had neglected to put his own field pack (tent half, blankets, etc.) on the truck, so he decided to drop over and have us put him up for the night.

A pup tent, as you probably don't need to be told, will accommodate two men, provided neither of them walks in his sleep. If three men are to sleep in one tent, at least two of them must be midgets or babes in arms. Cooks should never sleep two in a tent, because of their tendency toward plumpness.

We arranged ourselves in the tent by wrapping around the tent poles, putting all feet outside for the night and raising one side of the tent high enough to make a rustic sleeping porch of the whole affair.

The guest proved to be one of those loathsome creatures who pull all the cover to their side of the bed. We had quite a lot of trouble with him, since he slept in the middle and rolled up in both our blankets. We remedied this by waiting until he started snoring, then recovered our blankets, rolling ourselves in them and throwing a raincoat over him.

The three-man arrangement was very uncomfortable for a while, but when I woke the next morning I found that the night had been comfortable on the whole. When I finished opening my eyes by scooping the sand from them, I found that I had rolled out through the opened side of the tent and spent the night under a myrtle bush ten yards down the slope.

During my first off hour, I succeeded in getting a tan which must have darkened the very marrow of my bones. My chest, back, and legs looked the color of a faded danger flag and smelled like the roast pork that the cook forgot to watch. After that, the surf and the sun went their ways and I went mine.

My sole amusement now, when I can sneak away from the field kitchen, is in sitting on the porch of a drink stand, mooching ice cream from passing friends. The jukebox inside has played incessantly since we first came here. Of the past 390 selections played, at least 389 have been "$21 a Day Once a Month." The boys all know the lyrics verbatim now and drown out the vocalist, which is some relief.

Whatta you say we go home now?

# THE RECRUITS

I'm getting to a point where I throw down any magazine which has an article about the draft army. No matter what phase of the life they discuss, I usually get a tired feeling before I finish reading.

An article guaranteed to give me that tired feeling is one, usually written by an oldster who managed to get out of the last war, which stamps and snorts about the sissiness of the draftees and their routine. "These selectees are a bunch of cream-puffs who don't know what an army is. They act like Boy Scouts and they're trained and handled as if they were all senators' sons. They aren't soldiers like we were!"

The back of my neck to you, grandfather.

I'm a student cook in the Army. Cooks are supposed to have the easiest work and the most comfortable positions the Army affords. Compared to the boys in the gun batteries, the signal corps, the antitank units, we're almost white-collar men.

We student cooks—the future "happiness" boys of the Army—have to get up for reveille at the usual hour, beating the sun to the rise every morning. We get an hour of calisthenics, directed by a noncom who's in good physical shape and expects us to be the same way. Then we drill for an hour and hell hath no fury like that unleashed on the recreant who doesn't come up to standard in drill. We attend class for two hours and there's no foolishness there.

After lunch, we report to our kitchens, where we work until seven o'clock, taking our trade practically, taking part in the preparation of food for over two hundred hungry and fastidious soldiers. The next morning finds us in our kitchen at three or four o'clock and we stay there until one. We're supposed to have the afternoon off—unless there's something that has to be done in the line of battery duty.

When we leave those kitchens for the afternoon, we go back to our barracks for rest and sleep, which we need badly after the twenty-four-hour shift at huge coal-burning stoves. Reading is a popular diversion during the time, unless you pick up a magazine which tells you what slackers you are because you aren't like the author was in the Real war.

Then there's another altogether different type of article that is equally nauseating. It tells of the poor little soldier boys, who give up everything to go into training thousands of miles from mother's lap and who will have to spend their time leaning against urban lampposts—because nothing is being done for their morale.

You're talking about entertainment, Gertrude—not morale. In the matter of entertainment, there's plenty of that to be found, even if it isn't like being back home toasting marshmallows with Her. There's so much being done here for entertainment that you can't get halfway to the Service Club without being drafted for a battery show or a volleyball game.

Morale, to my way of thinking, is not a matter of entertainment. It isn't a feeling that fills you when you play spin the bottle.

Morale is the spirit that gets you when you're out on the regimental parade ground with the whole battalion for retreat parade. Every mother's son there wants to look as much the soldier as the Old Man does. Not another sound can be heard before or after the one-gun salute to the colors or when the band crosses the field to a stirring march in the Display of the Colors. And when your battery passes in review before the colonel, you're firmly convinced that there isn't another battery on the field that makes as good a showing as your battery.

It's the enormous feeling you know when you sit in pitch dark before a pup tent in the field and watch the fort's searchlight cut the sky. It's the feeling you know when you can look across a great space and see long lines of Army trucks moving along every road you can see.

That's morale. Just a matter of pride.

The top sergeant stuck his head out of the supply room and beckoned with his arm. "Come 'ere, you!" I dropped my stable broom in the battery street and hastened toward him, as one always does when summoned by the top kick.

"Well, Private Hargrove," he said, "this is a red-letter day for you." "You mean you're going to let me go out and drill like the other fellows?" "Noooo, Private Hargrove," he said. "I mean I'm going to let you turn in all your equipment. You are no longer to be a rookie, Private Hargrove. You are going to be an important working cog in the great wheel of national defense. You are leaving us, Private Hargrove."

I leaned against a filing cabinet to figure it out. "You should be very happy, Private Hargrove," he said tenderly. "I thought you would have been in this three-month training cycle for at least six years. You make me proud of you." "What's the deal?" I asked. "Where do I go and what do I do?

The sergeant chuckled and leaned back in his chair. He sighed ecstatically twice. "Would you really like to know, son, or would you rather put it off as long as you can?"

"Well," I said thankfully, "you can't be sending me out as a cook, because I don't know anything about cooking."

The sergeant sat back and drummed happily on the table.

"Great gods!" I shouted. "I'm not going to be a cannoneer, am I?"

The top sergeant rocked back and forth on the hind legs of his chair and hummed half a chorus of "Maple on the Hill" (No. 2). "No, Private Hargrove," he said after another long pause, "you're not going to be a cannoneer. We're going to give you a job where you can use your natural talents."

There was a distinctly sadistic tone in his voice. I waited.

"You're going to be a first cook, Hargrove," he said fondly. "Not just a plain cook. A head cook! A king in your own kitchen, a man of responsibility. Ain't that lovely?"

I was appalled. I clawed silently for air while Sergeant Goldsmith resumed his soft humming of "Maple on the Hill" (No. 2).

"You can't do this to me!" I roared, when my breath returned. "It's against every decent human law! I don't know anything about cooking! I want to be a cannoneer!"

Sergeant Goldsmith's eyes wandered guilelessly to the ceiling. "You don't know anything about cooking, huh? That's bad, boy, that's bad! Why, you're supposed to be on shift right now."

"Sergeant," I said, "I couldn't fry an egg right now if it had directions on the package."

"You're in the cooks' battery, ain't you? You've been going to cooking school and you've been sent to a kitchen for all these weeks. You're supposed to be graduated any day now. What have you been doing in the kitchen I put you in?"

"Making jerk-ade," I explained, "chopping celery, peeling onions. They say I get in their way. They say I keep spirits too high and production too low."

"I feel for you," the sergeant said. "I deeply sympathize. You're going to be a mighty unpopular little boy in your new home. If that supper tonight don't melt in them boys' mouths and send them clamoring for more, they'll either massacre you or run you over the hill. That's one thing the boys won't allow—bum cooking!"

"Sergeant Goldsmith, sir," I implored him, "can't somebody else go in my stead? Somebody who can cook? Look at me—a digger of ditches, a mopper of floors, a scrubber of kitchens, a ministering angel to undernourished grass plots, but a cook never! You don't know what you're doing to me!"

The top kick looked dreamily through the orderly-room door. "Son," he said, "you're going to make a perfectly breath-taking Horrible Example!"

I had nothing more to say. The sergeant crossed his right foot over his left knee and sat watching a fly on the window screen. He took a cigarette from his pocket, lighted it and settled back into reverie.

Then he rose and walked back into the supply room. "Thomas," he said, "check in this yardbird's equipment."

Sergeant Israel looked up from his Form Thirty-Two records. "Don't he like his equipment?"

"Check in everything but his clothing," the top kick said. "Get a truck to take him to Headquarters Battery, FARC."

Sergeant Thomas W. Israel looked up in faint amazement. I looked in sheer bewilderment.

"They had to figure some way to stop his cooking career and save the morale of some battery as would get him as a cook," said Sergeant Goldsmith. "So he's being palmed off to Center Headquarters as a public relations man."

"The Lord giveth," said Sergeant Israel, "and the Lord taketh away."

"Blessed be the name of the Lord," said the top kick.


# WE MARCHED DOWN THE HILL

from
*An Apple for the Sergeant*
by Anthony Cotterell
London: Hutchinson & Co. (Publishers), Ltd., 1945

*In recent wars, the citizen-soldier has played a most important role. Every country selects young men, usually of sound mind and body, and places them in an environment where every part of waking life is scheduled. They are told what to do, how to dress, what and where and when to eat. They are restricted in their living quarters and recreational facilities. The work is arduous and dangerous. Once accepted for military service, inductees walk through Alice's magic looking-glass into a new world with its own rules and regulations. There is no turning back.*

*Some find army life to their liking. For the first time they have real security: food, shelter, clothing, and medical care. They don't have to think; it's done for them, to the last detail. Even the training field is really a game. Win, lose or draw, they will find a hot dinner waiting and be told what time to go to bed. Existence is safe, wholesome, and worry-free, for the moment. Others can't forget they are free souls. When it's hot, they wish to put on cool clothes no matter what the regulation. When it's cold, they wish to dress warmly no matter the uniform of the day. They want leave to consort with old friends and family, or members of the opposite sex. The restrictions become more than can be borne.*

*It is the army's job to turn these citizens into killing tools and to teach them that the battle objective is to be gained without any regard to their health or safety. This is a slow process, but eventually the army prevails. When the troops move out to take their place on the battle lines, they usually acquit themselves heroically, win or lose.*

*The transformation from civilian to soldier is fraught with conflict. In each war the transformation to a new life shocks some conscript into writing of the amazing lifestyle just discovered. And in every war there is an audience to follow that story vicariously.*

*Almost all newly inducted personnel, after a few weeks, begin to look about for a niche where the work is minimal and the rewards are greatest. Just such a niche was sought and found by Anthony Cotterell of the British army in 1940, but as most soldiers soon learn, whatever relief is found is only for the moment. The army, any army, has its own methods for catching up with its personnel.*

*Anthony Cotterell eventually attained the rank of Major before the war was over. The following recounts his early experiences in the British army, which in many respects resemble those of soldiers the world over.*

M arching along I felt rather pleased with myself. The first eight weeks of Army life had been successfully survived; we had passed all the accepted tests of elementary aptitude and in general were beginning to feel quite professional. We seemed to have been in the Army a long time. Writing now, four years later, it is difficult to see how we got that impression; but when everything is new, when you are constantly learning new things and making progress, every week takes on the dignity of months.

We marched along the lane down the hill on which most of the town of Dorchester is planted and right-wheeled opposite the Chequers. A few hundred yards down the side street we came to a corner house across the road from the town's modest, second-string cinema. This corner house was the H.Q. of 'S' Company, the specialist Company which we were now joining to be trained as signallers, carrier drivers or M.T. drivers. Each of us felt some sense of personal triumph in coming to this company, because we had been selected from a large number of candidates.

I think I had been one of the first in our platoon to realize that to become a specialist would probably involve much less marching and tedious physical exertion than to continue training as an ordinary rifleman. I had checked this by cross-questioning members of 'S' Company I met about the place, and decided to get there if I could. I tried to dissuade others from providing any formidable competition for my own candidature by painting lively stories of the discomfort, the long hours, the poor quarters and repressive discipline involved. But in vain—the prospect of having something technical to tinkle with (which was the only deterrent as far as I was concerned) was the main attraction for most people.

When we got to 'S' Company H.Q. we waited outside for some time and were then split into three batches. As far as I remember about ten of us went to the Signals, and other, larger batches were divided between the Carrier Platoon and the M.T. Platoon. The sergeant-major of 'S' Company was superintending these proceedings. At first sight he was no sweetheart; there was a reptilian calm about him—an air of self-contained efficiency bordering on the sinister. He walked in and out of the Company Office smoking a pipe and wearing his side cap squashed on his head in a way which we had been contemptuously taught to discard soon after our arrival. But these irregularities counted for nothing in the general picture of ding-dong efficiency which he produced. We were called to attention and stood at ease to hear a few words of welcome from our new Company Commander, a tall, dark and handsome individual. He assured us that a high standard of cleanliness, enthusiasm and technical competence was not only demanded in his Company but by one means or another consistently obtained. After he had disappeared again into his office we went on waiting.

"I don't fancy this very much," said Daly, who was standing next to me. The sergeant-major's head appeared out of the window.

"Second man from the end, rear rank. Take his name. Talking on parade," he barked, and disappeared, evidently psychic. His victim, Daly, had been my closest associate up to this time: a plump, portentous, pink-faced youth with a moustache, who smoked a pipe, talked like your grandfather, and managed an extraordinary equanimity in face of the criticisms evoked by his pompous approach to our extremely unpompous life.

Being a soldier consists mostly of being inconvenienced; of waiting in a line to be fed, to be paid, to buy a stamp, and so on. A surprising proportion of your time is taken up in petty processes of personal administration and supply. You are inspected, expected and suspected every minute of the day. You are urged to use your initiative and simultaneously prevented from doing so.

Presently three sergeants appeared. One of them summoned us—"Right, all men for Signal Platoon fall in over here—sharp. Now come on, move it. Nawh—not there—here. Come on, hurry up—haven't got all day. Fall in in three ranks. Squad properly at ease. Squad 'TCHUN—move to the right—right TURN—by the left, quick march—left-right, left-right."

Our particular sergeant was a dark, saturnine little man with a jaundiced approach to life, especially Army life. He would tell us that much to his regret he had been a regular soldier—and now he had been called back as a reservist. He marched us down the road, round the corner and back on to the main London road again. We crossed the road and halted in a yard round the back of a modern pub.

"Right, now stand easy," said the sergeant. "I 'ave just got one thing to say to you. If you don't muck about with me I won't muck about with you. But if you do muck about with me then I will muck about with you accordingly. Now you're going to be here for some months, at the end of which time you will pass out—or it's to be hoped you will pass out—as trained regimental signallers. My privilege is to teach you. Any questions?"

"Sergeant," said a small man I did not know, coming to attention.

"What is it, lad?"

"Is this the Signals Platoon, Sergeant?"

"Why, now you come to mention it, I think it is," said the sergeant, "but if you like it better we could call it something else."

"I think I come to the wrong place, Sergeant."

"I thought things were going too well," said the sergeant.

Another sergeant appeared who might have been the sergeant-major's favourite son. Physically very like him, but not yet quite so strongly flavoured.

"You ought to have called the roll," he said.

"I ought to have done a lot of things," said our sergeant, and started calling out our names.

"Baker, Potton, Scuse, Smith, Cotterell, Wallace. ..."

Presently the missing man was identified, and the wrong man was sent to fetch him.

"You can't be all together. You'll have to sleep where we can fix you in, but that won't be a bad thing, because you will be with men more advanced than yourselves and they'll be able to help you. Now, any two of you special friends?"

I thought this presented possibilities of comfort, so I seized the man next to me, whom I had never spoken to before, and said firmly, "Yes, we are."

He was a very tall, rather serious-looking young man whose name I subsequently discovered to be Baker.

"Right, you two wait here—the rest come along with me," said the Sergeant.

"I hope you're right," said Baker to me, and I didn't feel any too sure.

We looked around the yard in which we were waiting. There were some wooden stairs up to a loft, where the sergeant had just led three or four of the rest of them. He now reappeared and, calling us to follow behind, took the others through an outer barnlike apartment, which had been fitted up as a class-room, into a dormitory. It was quadrilaterally shaped, with a low ceiling supported by thin metal pillars. Most of the space was taken up with a closely packed row of beds along each wall. A high standard of cleanliness and order was prevailing. In the middle of the room was a table with two benches. There were about half a dozen men sitting at the table with a sergeant at one end, tapping out Morse on a W.T. set. Three or four other men were sitting on the beds, all of them intently engaged on taking dictation from the Morse. It was immediately obvious to me that I should never be able to learn the Morse code. The sergeant looked annoyed at the interference, and so did some of the class.

Five of us were allotted beds here, and then the sergeant led Baker and myself along a narrow passage leading out of the other side of the room, and finally into a small room with just enough space for two plank beds and a packing-case, off which a mouse jumped and scurried away as we entered the room.

"We keep the bread in here," said the sergeant, "so you're liable for a lot of rats and mice, but if you like privacy it's a very nice little bunk. Right—I'll leave you in here; I want you fallen in outside in the yard—ten minutes' time. Get it?"

He disappeared, and we started looking round, which was quickly done. The floor and the walls and ceiling were all of flimsy, ramshackle wood in unconventionally angled planes, but the window gave out on to a pleasantly picturesque little garden, and by craning out of it you could catch sight of what must have been the River Frome, or, anyway, a branch of it. Gingerly—I am not very fond of either rats or mice—I looked into the packing-case. There were two large tins of jam and half a loaf.

"Better than no bread," I said.

The beds consisted each of three narrow planks, supported on miniature trestles at the head and foot. They did not look very snug after the pull-out beds we had had up at the barracks.

As soon as we fell in outside we were marched off to a stable over in another part of the town, calling at the Company stores to collect a palliasse for each man. The stable was full of straw, which we stuffed into our palliasses. We marched back to the Company stores, where we queued up for about an hour to be issued with three blankets, all of which we carried back to the billet. We were then required to return to the Company office to collect our kit-bags, which had been brought over on a truck, a convenience which did not, for some reason or other, extend to delivery at our platoon billet or stable.

It was now time for dinner—served and eaten in the barrack room. Baker and I took ours and ate it in our bunk, which provided a pleasant illusion of private retreat. There was no hot water afterward, so it was difficult to wash up.

In the afternoon our signal training started. We sat crammed on two backless benches on either side of a trestle table while Sergeant Ensor addressed us, supported by two lance-corporals whose duties seemed, shall we say, light. One of them was a young man, who disappeared after a day or two—I forget where; the other was an old soldier who didn't say much.

The first job was to learn the Morse code. We were horrified to hear that we were expected to have learned this by the following day. That is to say, to have learned what the various letters and numbers were represented by in terms of dots and dashes. I have never been able to remember anything by heart, and I was afraid this would be the case with Morse. In fact, we were all afraid. I think being in the ranks gives one a pleasantly modest conception of one's capabilities.

It wasn't an ideal classroom, having a sloping stone floor and a carriage driveway entrance unprotected against the lively prevailing winds, so that anything which could blow away did blow away. We were watched all the time by a horse, which was quartered a few feet away. The sergeant issued us with note-books and then drew the Morse dots and dashes on the board for us to copy down in our note-books. While he was doing this the platoon officer appeared. We hadn't seen him before. He was extremely young and was carrying a fishing-rod. He stood behind the class for a minute or two rather uncertainly before he asked us our names one by one. Then he went away.

After we had all copied down the symbols on the board—some of us were slower than others—the sergeant told the corporals to set up the lamp. They set up a miniature search-light on a tripod, and the sergeant started to describe it. "This is the lamp signalling daylight short range," he said, and continued, without batting an eyelid or showing any evidence that he knew what he was talking about: "The lamp can be read under average conditions in daylight at a distance of two miles with the naked eye and three–four miles with the telescope. At night six miles with the naked eye and nearly twice that distance with the telescope. The beam of light from the lamp is visible for forty yards on either side of a station one mile distant, and proportionately farther at longer ranges." The corporals then showed us the thing in detail and we had to take notice of the way it worked and how to test it. Half-way through, the other younger sergeant came in with an order that we were to interrupt the class for the purpose of emptying our palliasses. "But we've only just filled 'em," said someone. "You don't interest me," said the sergeant. We collected the palliasses from our beds, fell in outside, and marched across the town to the stables, where we emptied the straw into the same barn from which we had collected it. There may even have been some good reason for this, but we were given no information.

I was sent with two others to fetch the tea, which meant carrying two large buckets of it about a quarter of a mile. They were extremely heavy, and I got my best battle-dress trousers soaked on the journey. We had tea in our bunk again. There was a most luxurious sense of ownership about having this half-share in a ground-floor attic. After tea Baker and I went across the road to a secondhand furniture and general dealer. Here we managed to find a white cupboard about three feet square and two feet deep standing on four legs, which we bought for five shillings. We scrubbed it out and placed it, still soaking, between our beds. As the beds were only just off the floor and the cupboard legs were about four feet high, it didn't seem right somehow, so we guillotined the legs and used them as a support for the packing case with the food in it. We hoped that this might make things more difficult for the mice and rats, but as it turned out they found it no inconvenience.

The Chequers, which was a pleasant little house, was only about fifty yards up the street, and I met Daly there in the evening. He and the rest of the Carrier Platoon were billeted in a Church Hall. They didn't seem to have done so well as we had.

I left Daly after a bit and went back to the billet, where Baker was already sitting trying to memorize the Morse alphabet. Funnily enough, he wasn't doing too well, though he was just the sort of man whom you might expect to learn it immediately. And he was very young, 23 or 24, which, we had been told, was a help in picking it up quickly.

Presently we went round to the canteen for some food and then came back to bed. It was hardly ten o'clock, but we had had a tiring day.

The process of moving living-quarters from a barrack hut at one end of a little country town to a stable at the other may not seem a very spectacular or exciting change, but we had found it so.

The absence of straw in our palliasses became sharply evident when we went to bed, especially in my case, because one of the three planks was more resilient than the others. It hung in a rounded curve which enabled the development of a sharp pinching action if I moved at all suddenly.

We were woken early next morning by the golden voice of young Sergeant Cheetah, whose bunk was immediately next door to ours. We peered at him through one of the many holes in the thin wooden wall. The sergeant was singing, as he was subsequently to sing every day, a song which he soon taught us word for word.

We went along the passage to wash. Up in the barracks we had had a properly appointed wash-house; here there were simply a limited number of tin bowls. It was discouraging washing in a crowded stable in cold water on a cold morning, after having waited fifteen minutes for a tin bowl. Also, we were the new boys. Everyone else knew their way around and exchanged enviable familiarities. The sense of professional experience which we had felt marching away from the barracks yesterday was now at low ebb. And I had not realized that I was mess orderly. I had to run the quarter-mile to the cookhouse and try to run the quarter-mile back carrying two buckets of tea, haunted by the communal impatience which had been expressed at my late start. But I must say the breakfast wasn't bad at all. A considerable improvement on the food we had had up at the barracks. It is extraordinary how the quality of Army food varies from place to place—from plain terrible to not bad at all.

One mistake I had made was not to realize how quickly it was hoped that we should appear on parade for P.T. We were fallen in outside in the yard and double-marched very briskly about a quarter of a mile on to a piece of common land about the size of a large football field, surrounded by houses. Here the rest of the Company were already paraded; it seemed to be a matter of bitter concern to Sergeant Cheetah that we had been the last platoon to arrive. The sergeant-major was in charge of the proceedings, which he started with a few snarling remarks to the effect that any sign of half-heartedness in the exertions would be dealt with in no half-hearted manner. As I said before, he was extremely impressive, this sergeant-major.

We were hunted and chased about the place for half an hour or so every morning, ending in a run round the outskirts of Dorchester, which I personally preferred to the games which preceded it. I don't like competitive games, especially the ones where you are liable to personal injury. As I was one of the last ten to return from the run round the houses I had to run a substantial part of the way again, so my bed wasn't made up. I had folded and arranged the blankets but, in the unexpected hurry of being mess orderly and then having this extra run to do, I hadn't had time to complete the rest of the detailed arrangements required. I was therefore arraigned before the sergeant, who said that evidently I was a slow, clumsy type of man and that I really must learn to be quicker and smarter. My boot weren't clean, he said, and my cap badge didn't look as if it had been touched. I said I had done my best, and he pointed out that, if only I'd smarten myself up a bit, the Signals Platoon offered many opportunities for technical training which might help me to a more remunerative job in after-life. The Post Office were always looking for ex-Army signallers, and once in the Civil Service who knows what might not happen. In the end he became quite fatherly.

We spent the morning learning Morse, with a twenty-minute break, during which I repaired to a dairy where, at that earlier stage in the hostilities, you could still get things made with Dorset cream, also chocolate. I had again become a keen addict to the pleasures of the tuck-box. After the break we were marched with our empty palliasses round to the stable again. We filled them with the same straw with which we had filled, and subsequently emptied, them yesterday. It didn't seem to be any better or worse for its night in the stable.

It was a warm evening, so Baker and I walked out into the fields to continue learning the Morse code. It was quite extraordinary how interested we became. To my surprise and complacence I picked it up very quickly. It is the only military activity for which I have shown more than mediocre aptitude. You become a sort of mental athlete with off-days and on-days so far as your speed and accuracy in sending and receiving Morse is concerned. Your whole life is permeated with de-de-de-da-de. After a day devoted to arms drill or weapon training you have no particular conviction of progress and not often any means of assessing it. But here we spent the day with the sergeant reading us blocks of letters or news stories from the *Daily Mirror* in Morse dots and dashes. We had to write them down, then hand them in to be marked. You could see how you were getting on.

Most of the time we spent in the stable doing this or listening to lectures. Every day we would march out in a little crocodile, armed with our pencils and note-books, and stand in pairs reading a lamp which one of the corporals was operating several fields away. You took it in turns, one man reading the lamp, the other writing down the letters as he read them out. The great attraction was that it occupied your mind and made the time pass very quickly. You had to learn to send Morse ten words a minute W.T. and eight words a minute with the lamp. Your whole life was devoted to obtaining this proficiency. It is a tangible skill, with a pleasant sense of expertness attaching to it, and most people get interested in it.

Every day before lunch we had twenty minutes' arms drill. Although we only had this twenty minutes, we drilled much more smartly than most of the Rifle Company platoons who were doing far more arms drill and weapon training. The reason was that we were let off as soon as we had reached a certain standard and therefore had something to gain by doing the thing well.

Things were going too smoothly to last for long. We were all very comfortable so we were moved. Though a frequent change of scene is a great help during the monotony of training, it is always disconcerting when it happens. You can't help feeling that it is bound to be a change for the worse. There were plenty of grounds for believing that this was to be a change for the worse. The B.E.F. were falling back fast, so presumably things were going to change progressively for the worse from now on. There were the usual rumors which accompany any impending move. Cartloads of tropical kit had been seen being unloaded into the Company stores, not to mention Polar equipment and luggage labels printed 'Troop Convoy to France'.

What it finally boiled down to was that we were being shifted to a half-built hutted camp on the hill behind the barracks.

Baker and I had considerable discussion as to whether we should be allowed to keep our privately bought furniture in a barrack room. We didn't know whether to ask for permission or not. He was for asking permission—I was for the *fait accompli*. It always seems to me that the very fact of asking permission raises in the mind of the person you are asking a light of doubt, and the horrible prospect of a responsibility to be taken. It seems absurd to be exercised about whether or not we could have a small wooden cupboard. But it had made a considerable difference to our standard of living and was therefore valuable. It was a symbol of self-determination. Finally, we waited until the truck was half loaded, then stuck it in the middle and camouflaged it with military equipment.

Our new quarters were a little too spartan for my liking. There were about thirty-six in the Signals Platoon and thirty of us were quartered in one of the standard-type barrack huts. The room was furnished quite simply with a fire extinguisher. Before we left our ex-billet we had had to scrub down our plank beds, and pile them neatly in a corner. We had assumed from this that there would be other plank beds waiting for us in our new quarters—but not so. This made us all radiantly happy, especially when Sergeant came in and ordered us to parade at the Company stores for the purpose of relinquishing one of our three blankets.

The rest of the Company were quartered in similar huts, about half a dozen of them, planted on a hillside by a railway line overlooking the barracks and the prison, but with a large expanse of rolling grassland behind, so that it was by no means unpleasantly situated. It might be worse, we thought, as we filed in to dinner. After all, there was a proper dining hut with tables and benches, and though it had been pleasantly informal to eat in the room where we slept and worked, these more elaborate arrangements were probably more satisfactory. But it started raining as we queued up for dinner. It was only then that I, for one, realized that the dining hut had no roof, nor any glass in the windows, nor any door to the doorway. It was more of gesture than anything.

About the same time we discovered that it was very difficult to keep our clothes and boots clean, owing to the rich nutty chalk subsoil which clogged on to everything and made the whole process of personal maintenance much more of a chore than it had been back in the stable down in town. However, our cupboard had survived with no more than a few sarcastic comments from the sergeants. The sergeants slept up one end of the room. Those who wished to ingratiate themselves with the authorities slept as near the sergeants as possible. Of course, Baker and I were passionately anxious to ingratiate ourselves with the authorities, but our approach was more subtle. We played hard to get and slept right down the other end of the room.

Sleeping on the floor is another technique again. We had two blankets and a ground sheet. With these we had to establish some sort of arrangement with the wooden floor. For a pillow we could use a partly emptied sector of our kit bags. Briefly, the difficulties were that if we lay flat or prone we ricked our backs, and if we lay on our sides the floor lacked the voluptuous resilience which makes this position practical in an ordinary bed. I won't say that I didn't sleep the first few nights, but I felt as if I had been for a long cross-country run when I got up. I felt that it must have done me good, otherwise I wouldn't feel so terrible. By and by, helped by watching the approach and technique of one of the stray dogs round the camp, I managed to make myself fairly comfortable. After a day or two I was just as reluctant to get up off the floor in the morning as I am to get out of my bed at home.

We had to be up early next morning to march down to the town and scrub out our old billets. When I see that there is no further chance of evading some activity of this kind I usually try to throw myself into it whole-heartedly on the theory that, if I can possibly interest myself in it, time will pass quicker. This constructive and enthusiastic mood usually lasts for several minutes. It isn't long before someone more manually agile gets impatient with one's clumsiness and does the job himself.

"Do it properly or not at all, Cotterell. Here, give it to me."

I always give them anything they want and retire modestly to the background and watch. As a matter of fact there isn't usually any need to do much on these mass fatigues if you don't want to, because there is never enough equipment to go round. We usually get about seven mops and three buckets for use by seventeen men—a state of affairs which obviously leaves many loopholes for the less determinedly energetic. The surprising thing is that most men fret at inactivity. So there are usually enough people fretting to keep the mops and buckets occupied.

Our daily routine soon settled into pattern. I believe reveille was at 6:15, but we didn't get up until nearer seven o'clock. The first practical attempts to rouse us were from the N.C.O.'s, who had sleeping-out passes in the town and had to report into the camp very punctually at a prodigiously early hour in order not to lose this privilege. There was one healthy helot among the recruits who also slept out. The N.C.O.'s nearly all had Welsh or West-country accents. There was one fat corporal who was usually the centre of these celebrations. He would come in and clump his way up and down the room, pulling off the blankets and making all the usual early-morning jokes.

"Roize and shoine. It's what cooms of thik yere luxury beds. It's vicious lying yere, that's what it be—vicious. Coom arn. Coom arn. Roize 'n shoine. Jello!"

Jello was the word they used for 'double up'; I think it comes from India.

There were no taps in the camp except one, which sprung mysteriously out of the side of the hill and was always surrounded by people and mud—inches deep. It wasn't easy to wash or shave.

The proper wash place was about half a mile through the rest of the half-built and, as yet, untenanted hutted camp; down a hill to a piece of open ground. There were half a dozen rows of wooden trestle-work wash-stands, each about thirty feet long, with taps at intervals. On a lovely morning it was pleasant to wash in the open air. On a non-lovely morning it was not at all pleasant. When it was cold I used to walk a little further and go to the old wash-house we had used during our first eight weeks. This was properly fitted up with mirrors and hot water, but it was forbidden ground, and if identified as belonging to another Company you were liable to be reported and punished. The only thing is that no one feels much like identifying and punishing people at that time of day when aggressiveness and self-confidence are at their lowest ebb.

Breakfast was served out in the open air. Usually the weather was fine. It was that wonderful 1940 summer. Our eating equipment wasn't lavish. We had a knife, fork and spoon and a tin bowl. For breakfast we usually had porridge, a bit of bacon and fried bread, then bread and jam or marmalade and, of course, the rich, dark brown, treacly Army tea which bears no relation to any other tea, but appeals to me. I managed to get a tin plate after a day or two, but until I had thus supplemented the official arrangements, eating a meal required a certain amount of planning, unless you were content to throw the whole thing into your tin bowl and eat it as a kind of porridge and bacon salad. The queue for meals was about 80 yards long at its maximum. The way to deal with queues is either to come very early or come very late and take a chance on there being anything left. Often, of course, there might be plenty left; it depended on how frugal the mess orderlies had been. We had to take it in turns to be mess orderlies, which involved fetching the food from a cook-house, located, for no reason that I could see, about half-way across the county, over rich and loamy agricultural land. The process of washing up the dishes was again difficult, as there was no hot water. You could get so far scraping them out with grass, but it wasn't altogether satisfactory. Young Daly just never bothered; he kept a clean bowl for inspections and another one for use which was never washed—except partially, by the passage of subsequent food or tea—from one week to another.

"If they treat me like a pig, I'm going to act like a pig," he said.

After breakfast we had P.T. From a medical point of view it was undoubtedly the wrong way round, and is, I believe, officially forbidden. No doubt if I had indulged in violent exercises immediately after a meal in civil life I should have felt the worse for it, but many of these natural laws don't seem to apply in the Army. They seem to be able to ill-treat you with medical impunity. We did P.T. as a company, accompanied by those high-pitched, nasal, sexless, zealot voices.

"Warn, tew, three; warn, tew, three; warn, tew, three. When I say change keep circling in the same manner with the left leg and right arm. Keep the stomach in and the head out. Warn, tew, three. CHANGE. Warn, tew, three. Now what's the matter with the last man in the third row? Swing properly with a warn, tew, three."

The first thing after this was Morse reading. We sat there with pencils and scraps of paper reading the messages tapped out by the sergeant. They might be this kind of thing—"Rations consumption 8 June delivered Chichester 0430 hours 14 June. Submit future indents your Battalion H.Q. Petrol available cans Brigade." Or they might be from a newspaper, like this—"A big offensive against the U-boats is on the way, I have been seeing the preparations for it. Scotland Yard are to help the local police in their enquiries into the death of a thirty-three-year-old woman whose body was found in a garage."

The speeds were gradually working up. When we started, two or three words a minute seemed bewilderingly fast. After a week or two, the same speed was disconcertingly slow. You even made more mistakes because your attention had time to wander. It is a good training in mental concentration.

I had been invited out to dinner at Upwey, down near Weymouth, about eight miles away. It was a little village quite a way off the bus route to Weymouth, but I was anxious to go. I was going to dinner at a perfectly delightful house, with all the comforts which are totally lacking in a camp. The properly furnished bathroom, the books and bottles, the gramophone records and manicured hands, the scent and voice were very welcome. Women are a great idea. You don't realize how arid a barrack room is until you are reminded that the other kind of life still goes on.

# WOMEN AT WAR

from

*Angel of the Navy:*
*The Story of a WAVE*
by Pharmacist's Mate Joan Angel, U.S.N.R.
New York: Hastings House, 1943

*In its rush to build up its fighting forces, the United States allowed women into the Army, Navy, Marines, and Coast Guard in 1942. They were to take over the "desk-jockey" jobs stateside and allow trained male personnel to be moved to the war fronts.*

*For women, service was voluntary, but once in the branch they chose, they were under military discipline. If a woman joined the Marines, she was a Marine, but in the Army she became a member of the Women's Army Auxiliary Corps (WAAC), in the Coast Guard she was a SPAR (short for the Coast Guard motto, Semper Paratus, Always Ready), and in the Navy she became a member of the WAVES (Women Appointed for Voluntary Emergency Service). Training was brisk, and differed from organization to organization.*

*In basic training, they were all indoctrinated into the way their service oper-ated. They were taught to march in formation, to drill, to wash and clean the Army/Navy way. In addition they were graded on their personal skills and soon assigned to specialized training so that they could replace technicians in any of several fields. Women usually filled clerical and secretarial posts, but many were trained as cartographers, medical technicians, and air traffic controllers, or in naval air navigation, photography, and communications.*

*Early training camps were all over the country—New York, Wisconsin, Iowa, Oklahoma, and Indiana. By 1943 a newly commissioned Coast Guard Training Station was opened in a luxurious hotel in Florida.*

*The women in the Marine Corps found a sterner program. They received their basic training at Parris Island, South Carolina, and were given additional instruction in the care of and the firing of small arms. There were also field exer-cises, and lessons in water safety survival.*

*The first WAAC Training Center was at Ft. Des Moines. Classrooms were erected in converted stables with reworked plumbing, while separate housing for men was erected. At the clothing warehouse, all the fitters were from local department stores. While the chocolate-colored undergarments fitted decently, the uniform itself was very disappointing. The skirts were cut to fit men's hips, the material buckled and wrinkled across the stomach, and when the women marched, their skirts hiked up above the knees. The hot, stiff, cotton jackets seemed like straitjackets and the unbecoming caps cut into the forehead and were easily warped, crushed, and soiled. All outer garments were large and needed extensive alterations.*

*The WAACs were constantly pulled out of classes before getting their regular assignments to do KP at their own mess, or the officer's mess, or the consolidated mess. They scrubbed classroom floors and the theater daily, cleaned offices, orderly rooms, day rooms, store rooms, cleaned the outside of buildings, washed windows, and scrubbed down the white pillars in zero-degree weather. One recruit noted that on her first day, before she received her uniform, she was sent out to scrub up one of the offices.*

*By the war's end almost 300,000 women were in uniform in all branches of the service. Although women in all branches were demobilized in 1945, the following year the WAAC asked for reenlistments to meet the growing need for hospital staff. In 1948 Congress passed a bill incorporating the WAAC into the regular army. The WAVES were enlisted into the regular navy, but the SPARS were not to be reactivated until 1973 when the women's reserve became an integral part of the Coast Guard and was no longer a separate branch.*

*The SPARS, activated in November 1942, had 10,000 enlisted and 1,000 officer women by the end of World War II. Only highly qualified women were allowed in this unit. Of the 1,130 enlisted women enrolled in the first year of its existence, 56 had college degrees, 282 had at least one year of college, and 745 had high school diplomas. Today, all enlisted women have a high school diploma or its equivalent, and nearly all the officers are college graduates, some with advanced degrees.*

*The part women played in the winning of World War II cannot be emphasized enough. They were all volunteers who willingly gave up their families and careers to help their country in a time of crisis.*

*The following excerpt from a book written by a WAVE can only induce envy in all who served in other branches of the armed services during World War II.*

T hree weeks after I was sworn in, I got my orders. On December 13 I was to leave New York for my boot training at the Iowa State Teacher's College in Cedar Falls, Iowa. As a member of the V-10 class of Apprentice Seamen (pay, $50 a month) I would be given a five-week indoctrination course, after which I could go on to whatever specialty the Navy assigned me.

I was to get a $200 clothes allowance, of course, but the uniform would be bought at the training center after about two or three weeks, during which time I would wear my own clothes. Also, I had to bring my own shoes, gloves and underwear, along with any other miscellaneous items which might come in handy.

The evening of the 13th I was jittery with excitement. I had been told to report to Penn Station at ten o'clock. I hadn't seen Pennsylvania Station for a long while, so I was completely unprepared for the dark, cavernous depths of it.

Soldiers and sailors drifted through its huge waiting-rooms. But most conspicuous of all were the little clusters of people that dotted the entire floor—two or three hundred would-be WAVES from the Third Naval District and their well-wishers. Seeing some of my future shipmates brightened me up again. After all, a bunch of well-dressed, attractive girls can make even Pennsylvania Station in wartime look a little cheerful.

Then suddenly from the other end of nowhere, a voice boomed. "ANGEL— UP FRONT!"

It didn't take long for the names of other girls to be called. We stood in a group, shifting our weight in an attempt to keep at least one foot at a time off the cold floor.

For three more hours, we stood there in Penn Station, wondering if maybe they were out laying tracks for us to ride on.

"Wish we were joining the British Navy," said the girl next to me. "Maybe then at least we'd get a quota of grog to warm us up a little."

After what seemed like a chilly eternity, the gates finally opened, and there was a wild rush into the train. It was a special WAVE section, with five Pullmans and dining-car, but accommodations were arranged by rule of domain. Being fleet of foot and used to getting a seat quickly even in crowded Radio City Music Hall, I snared a precious lower berth.

The next day we all made the acquaintance of Raymond, "our host." Raymond was a mahogany-skinned, pearly-toothed porter who had been probably selected for his complete charm and thoughtfulness. He treated us like a group of favorites he had watched grow from "tiny mites." We watched in awe the precision with which he made a bed, little thinking that in a week or so we would be able to outdo even him. He brought water for some of the girls' fast-wilting corsages—dug us up some cards for gin rummy—hovering over us like a mother chicken. Even our loud singing of "Give us some men who are stout-hearted men" as we made brief station stops didn't seem to upset him.

Because of some other troop movements (*we* were a troop movement, too, you know), our train was routed through Canada. So it wasn't until December 15th that we hit Iowa. The train did not go directly to Cedar Falls. Probably as a psychological move, our first stop was a town bitingly called "Waterloo." Here we had lunch and dropped postcards, or sent telegrams home, and freshened up. Then we got on the train again and traveled a few miles to Cedar Falls.

We were singing as we rode in the crowded buses from the station up to Iowa Sate Teacher's College, which was to be our boot camp for the next five weeks. It was a merry ride. The bus-driver had all he could do to keep his eyes on the road as one of the Southern girls in the back of the bus kept shrieking, "But it's so *white*! And it's all *over* the place!" She had never seen snow before.

We were a varied group of almost a thousand girls as we poured into Bartlett Hall that day. There were representatives from nearly every State in the Union, plus Hawaii and Washington, D.C. There was a Korean girl from California. A Seaman

Seamann from Norton, Virginia, and her friend Seaman Divers from Roanoke, Virginia. There were girls from big cities and small towns, girls who seemed terribly young and others whom it was rather difficult for a twenty-year-old pip-squeak like me to consider as "girls" at all.

Miggs, the cute redhead from Dobbs Ferry, had suggested that she and I stick together at the registration desk so there'd be more of a chance of our being billeted in the same room. Luckily, it worked out exactly that way.

I'll never forget the way Miggs and I wandered around the labyrinth of wings in S.S. Bartlett Hall, looking for Billet 206-B. They say the new Pentagon War Department building in Washington is confusing—but it has nothing on the impression Bartlett Hall gives a poor, bewildered boot, her arms stacked high with bed-linen!

The room was as bare as a cell. Two unmade double-deckers, their springs showing, were up against the blank walls. There was one desk, one dresser with mirror, two wooden chairs, two closets, a medicine-cabinet, and a GI wastebasket. The windows had no curtains—just shades. The floor had no rug—just boards. We heaved our linen down on the bunks and took a deep breath. So this was home! My heart sank.

I could write a whole book about sleeping in an upper. It was especially fascinating at Bartlett Hall, because the ladders which had been ordered were still on their way. That made getting in and out of bed a gymnastic procedure somewhat related to mounting a bronco. One minor accident during our boot training occurred when a girl fell out of an upper berth. Possibly it had something to do with her system of somersaulting out instead of doing the "double-decker-swing."

Just a word about the noble Navy institution of the platoon. In case you have never heard of a platoon, let me explain that in the WAVES it is a group of sixty boots who do everything—with few exceptions—together. For, as a WAVE, you just don't wander about from class to class by yourself—or suddenly get a yen to take a walk around campus. *WAVES must muster*—and mustering means lining up and counting off in platoons, then marching off together wherever you happen to be going.

Where do you muster? Aaaah, that's easy. Almost everywhere. You muster to go to class. You muster to go down for chow. You muster to go to church, the doctor's office, to town on a shopping tour. About the only occasion not calling for a muster is a trip to the head—Navy term for what we females usually refer to as the johnny. Even here, a favorite trick to clear the decks and snatch a seat for yourself is to stick your head in the door and yell, "Muster!" Someone always comes out in a hurry.

We didn't have to muster that first day, luckily. But we did have to wait on line for chow, since the messroom was not large enough to hold us all at one time, but served two hundred and fifty at a time, eating in hasty fifteen-minute shifts.

The messroom was a big, cheery place, filled with long, mahogany-colored tables. We served ourselves in semi-cafeteria style, on the regular Navy chow trays which are divided into six parts. It takes some skill to arrange your courses chronologically in the various segments, and that first night my tray was rather a mess. But the meal they served had chop-suey as the main dish (a gesture to our Chinese allies, no doubt), so it didn't matter much that things got somewhat mixed up.

Our waitresses throughout training were college girls from the regular section of the campus. They got paid for their work, of course, but it soon became clear that their jobs also had another advantage. We WAVES had to send our civvies home eventually, you see, and the college girls would offer to save us the trouble by buying whatever struck their fancy. For instance, I came down to chow one night in a pale blue cashmere sweater that had set me back a young fortune in the days when I was a freshman at the University of Wisconsin.

That's a pretty sweater," said Rose, our waitress, as she hovered about me with a pitcher of water.

"Mmmmm," I said, mentally calculating that I might as well sell it if she wanted it.

"You're about a size 34, aren't you?" she asked, pouring the water adroitly into my glass.

"That's right," I answered, as cannily as an old horsetrader.

"Five dollars?" she asked briskly.

"O.K.," I answered, just as briskly.

And the next week, when we all got our uniforms, Rose was richer by a sweater, and I had five dollars I hadn't expected.

The next day we really turned to at the business of being Apprentice Seamen.

We rose from our bunks at 0545. While you don't tell time in the WAVES by the ship's bell system, you do use the efficient twenty-four-hour method. Thus, one minute after midnight is 0001; one o'clock in the afternoon becomes 1300; and the witching hour of midnight turns up as an unromantic 2400. (Imagine Cinderella having to go home at 2400!)

"We rose" is a euphemism. What actually happened is that we were galvanized out of sleep by the insistent clanging of a bell, accompanied by a hearty, energetic voice shouting, "Hit the deck! Rise and shine! Fall out!"

I sat up in my berth, peered through the pre-dawn blackness at my shipmates, considered for a moment the advisability of handing in my resignation for the privilege of sleeping a little later, and finally decided it might be less trouble to get up. Miggs, in whose face I almost stepped as I began my descent, was telling nobody in particular to "call up the Admiral and tell him I'll be a little late for morning chow!"

Then came the general rush to the head. May I here assure all residents of crowded boarding-houses that they will find no surcease from their troubles if they join the WAVES.

In the half-hour before breakfast, we not only made up our faces—discreetly, of course—but also our rooms. Which brings me to the important subject of inspection.

In the WAVES, daily inspection takes place at noon, with a super-duper captain's inspection on Saturday. After noon, a room can let down its hair—girdles can dangle on the washline, a chair can be catty-cornered, a Coke bottle can ornament a desk. But for inspection, everything must be exactly shipshape, from the GI can down to the last microscopic pinch of dust. And even that shouldn't be there, because the inspecting officer usually runs his white-gloved finger across the most vulnerable surfaces.

Beds must be made in strict Navy style, with corners as sharp as those on a well-wrapped Christmas package. Locker doors have to be opened at exact right angles, with a line of well-shined shoes poking their toes out to be inspected. Even the chairs must be squared off at right angles to the wall, their legs exactly lined up with the boards on the floor.

About the only place in the room that's not inspectable is one's luggage—and therefore it's the "lucky bag" for any extra rations that happen to be adrift in the cabin.

Actually, policing quarters isn't too bad—even if, like me, you've always had someone else to pick up things after you. It's a bit difficult to get used to at first, but every time I started to feel sorry for myself, Miggs would read me excerpts from a letter one of her WAAC friends had sent her—enticing bits like:

"Was assigned to the WAACS museum today. That means lathering down the latrine, in case you delicate little WAVES have never heard the term."

or:

"Say, don't you finishing school sailor-girls ever get KP? Wondered about that as I scraped the khaki uniforms off some spuds today."

Then I'd sigh with relief that I had joined the Navy—and redouble my efforts on the washbasin bright work.

After morning chow that second morning we all posted our mail. I was slightly ashamed of the number of envelopes I slipped into the letter box, but evidently *everybody* had held onto their Christmas cards until the last minute to take advantage of the Navy's free mailing privilege.

At 0800 there was a muster again, and with a good attempt at *hup-two-three-four* (or *hup-two-hee-foh*, as it is more often pronounced), we hupped off to morning assignments. Mildred was our platoon leader, since she was the only one who had ever had parade experience. She used to lead the morticians' band at conventions.

For some of us, morning meant classes. For others, it meant drill.

I liked drill. We marched indoors, because there was snow on the ground, and we were asked to wear our galoshes to protect the schoolgirl complexion of the gym floor. This made our feet think we had transported them to the hot, damp tropics. But even that couldn't keep us from enjoying ourselves. Because there's something about drill that has the same effect on the heart and spirit as stirring martial music. Perhaps it's the sense of being a smoothly functioning unit in a smoothly functioning group. Or perhaps it's the physical uplift that comes from stepping out smartly in perfect rhythm, back straight, eyes front, arms swinging. At any rate, drilling is thrilling—especially when one is in uniform.

Of course, perfection in drill doesn't come all at once. At first, it takes a good deal of concentration to translate the incoherent, sea-lion barks of the drill officers into meaningful phrases like "Left flank!" "Dress right!" "To the rear march!" Once I found myself horribly alone in the middle of the gym because I didn't realize that Gene Tunney's trained chief petty officers pronounced the word "oblique" as "up-LIKE." I'm a literalist. I moved up-like while the rest of the platoon did a neat oblique maneuver.

Afternoons in boot training were flexible from the schedule point of view. There were classes and drill for those who didn't have them in the morning. Twice a

week there were calisthenics, including special posture exercises for girls who had
stenographer-droops and soda-fountain stoops. And then, of course, there was medical gunnery practice.

Here, a group of Navy doctors who had all been through a special course in
sadism (with post-graduate course in mass-mauling) lined up with a group of den-
tists and pharmacist's mates and calmly shot us. The targets were our arms, and the
ammunition consisted of typhoid, tetanus and smallpox vaccines. But while we
faced them, those hypos looked more formidable than 155-mm guns! We were very
touched by the Navy's solicitude about our future health, but somehow we weren't
very grateful when the reactions set in. At drill, for instance, the command "Dress
right!" would produce a unique scene. Hundreds of arms would make a feeble
attempt to stretch out at shoulder level. Some of them rebelled at the first movement.
Others would almost make it but at the last minute flutter down helplessly like dead
ducks. Finally even the tough drill officers were softened. We were allowed to measure distances with our eyes.

The time of day all good little Apprentice Seamen waited for, though, was
1630—4:30 to landlubbers. In New York harbor, it's a statue; on newsstands, it's a
magazine; but to us WAVES, LIBERTY was a precious slice of time in which we
could break away from our platoons for a while and relax. And "relax" to boots is
mostly a synonym for "eat."

Ah, liberty! The quick run down to the drugstore hangout which served as our
ship's service. The clamor for seats at the counter. The imperative, desperate, "Give
me a chocolate frosted!" ..."Make mine a hamburger and a lemon coke!" ..."Shoot
me some strawberry ice-cream with butterscotch sauce!" ... as if we were all drug
addicts pleading for our quota of stimulants. Then, the last-minute stop at the candy
counter as we took on provisions for the evening study hour, and finally, the quick
run back to ship before the doors were locked.

After liberty came evening chow, and then study hour from 1930 to 2130. At
this time, we were supposed to close our doors and bury ourselves in our books.
What we really did mostly, however, was shoot the breeze. We talked about our
shots, we talked about our beaux at home. We discussed the war and world affairs
as we hung our panty-girdles on the clothesline that stretched from the door to the
radiator.

Eventually, after about an hour of this sort of thing, someone would remind us
that we'd all better study for a while. Books in hand, we'd climb into our bunks and
plunge ourselves into the intricacies of naval organization or the fine points of sea-
manship. For fifteen minutes after that, there would be no sounds in the room except
the soft whisper of turning pages, the scratching monologue of a fountain pen on
paper, or the intermittent knocking of the radiator. Then breaking the silence, would
come Miggs' hesitant whisper.

"May I say something?"

We'd all look up from our books.

"You'll probably say it's just scuttlebutt, but I got it right from the radio shack
that—" which was Navy talk for an inside-story rumor, and meant our study was
over for the evening.

127

At the 2130 bell, there would be a mad dash down the ladders (we *did* call stairs "ladders" walls "bulkheads" and windows "portholes" most of the time) to the lounges, the only places we were allowed to smoke. If your eyes could pierce the thick blue clouds of cigarette smoke, it was a pleasant sight to see the girls in their non-regulation housecoats and slippers, looking for all the world like the senior class at a big boarding school.

Taps rang at 2200, and usually we were all so exhausted, we hit the sack gratefully. We had a roll-call, with the Mate of the Deck checking each room to make sure we weren't out gallivanting. Goodness knows where we could have gallivanted—Cedar Falls after sunset offered about as many diversions as a nice, quiet desert island.

You can imagine the general pandemonium when the first uniform notice was posted. Even an advertisement announcing a sale of nylon stockings could not have had a greater readership than those few bare mimeographed lines breaking the news to us about our Navy blues. Two shops had been designated to sell WAVE uniforms. The outstanding emporium in Cedar Falls was to provide us with accessories—things like shirts, hats, ties and hose. The Waterloo store was to sell us our suits and raincoats, using a whole floor of the County Relief Building as a fitting-room.

My platoon was assigned to get the accessories first. That afternoon we mustered and went downtown, with an Ensign along to make sure we didn't get off our course in the direction of any frills and furbelows.

Our first purchases were our hats. First we took off the various bits of headgear we had worn on the way down, putting them on the counter with hushed reverence.

"I'd like to see something rawthah tailored in navy blue, if you please," said Miggs, as though as she were addressing Lilly Dache.

"Here it is," said the saleswoman, handing her a bewitching little number. "And here's yours, miss."

I looked at it. Was *this* the hat that I was to face the world in—this glorified freshman cap, this shapeless receptacle with a brim—this limp, unflattering lid? Miggs didn't look so bad in hers. But her jaw dropped when she turned to look at me.

"Your face looks as if it's going down behind a mountain any minute. Try pulling the hat over one eye!" she advised.

"Sorry, Seaman Angel," warned the Ensign. "Regulations state hats must be worn straight."

We both shot her a withering look. The Ensign could afford to quote regulations; hers was the tremendously becoming stiff-crowned officer's hat.

"You can't fix it up with a veil or something, can you?" I asked the saleswoman.

"No," she said. "But you can try this on." She handed me a havelock.

A havelock is not, as one bright wit believed, a gadget invented by Havelock Ellis. It is best described as a weatherproofed piece of fabric which in stormy weather you drape like a miniature pup-tent over your hat and neck to keep out the elements. Actually, it is extremely cozy, and when I am demobilized I intend to have havelocks in all shades of the rainbow. But on this day the Arabian effect was startling.

"I look like a blurred scene from *Beau Geste*," I said. "I'll carry an umbrella, thanks."

"Sorry, Seaman Angel," gloated the Ensign. "No umbrellas."

I was beginning to feel the first pangs of regimentation.

"Cheer up," said the saleswoman consolingly. "My niece is a WAAC, and she looks even worse in *her* hat!"

The next step was the purchase of shirts, two in navy blue and two in the lighter reserve blue. After that came the ties, and Miggs astounded us all by her mastery of the regulation knot. After some pressure, she admitted she had been practicing with the washline.

Then we bought hose—beige lisle for duty, rayon for dress. Finally we splurged on the "uncontrolled" items—cosmetics, talcum powder, toilet water, cleansing tissue and all the other things that are as much a part of the female's daily life as food and sleep.

For the remainder of the week, we waited anxiously to receive the rest of our uniforms. Finally, the second notice appeared. Platoon 23, wearing girdles, was to proceed into Waterloo at 1930 for the issuance of suits and coats.

The County Relief Building had been organized as an outfitting mass-production line. First on the belt-system was a complete room filled with nothing but navy blue suits—racks and racks of them.

"I take a size 12 or 14," I said to the girl handing out the suits. She pretended not to hear and looked me up and down thoughtfully.

"I take a size 12 or 14," I repeated, as she turned around to the racks.

"Here you are," she said. "Sizes don't mean anything in these."

I soon found that out. For, when I finally slipped into my precious, long-awaited Mainbocher-designed suit, I could scarcely find myself in it. The skirt dragged down almost to my ankles; the jacket hung baggily from my shoulders as if it were carefully avoiding contact with any part of me.

"It's too big!" I complained to the fitter.

"Oh, no," she insisted. "That can be fixed beautifully. Regulations say your uniform must be loose-fitting, you know. And the skirt can be no shorter than mid-calf."

I understood that the Navy was trying to discourage any Lana Turners in the crowd, and I sympathized with its efforts to protect us from rude masculine glances. But I still took a strong dislike to looking like Dopey, the dwarf.

"I'm sorry," I said firmly; "this uniform does *not* fit."

"Now, dearie," said the fitter. "We mustn't get upset. Here, try on the raincoat."

I sighed and slipped the coat on. Its hem hit me somewhere in mid-thigh.

"Everything will be just fine!" bustled my lady tailor, popping pins into her mouth. "I'll just let down the hem and both of them will meet."

"These clothes do *not* fit me," I repeated firmly, a small crack in my voice.

"They will, dearie. They will."

Finally, I could hold it back no more. I had so looked forward to this moment—and now it was being ruined. Tears started to stream down my cheeks. Then, from the next booth, came my deliverer. She was a fitter, too, but a tiny white-haired one with a soft sweet voice.

"I'll take care of this little girl, Agnes," she said, and gave me a confidential wink.

"Now, miss, let's see if we can't fix you up." By some magic, she managed to get me a size 12 jacket and a size 14 skirt.

"There," she said, when I had put them on. "That's better. Just a bit of tailoring and that will be fine."

I looked at myself in the long mirror. By heavens, I *did* look impressive! The suit was beautifully cut, trim and efficient-looking without being stiff and masculine. It was the kind of tailored outfit I might have bought in civilian life—but in navy blue, with the fouled-anchor embroidery on the collar and black regulation buttons, it gave me the bearing of a woman in whom great responsibilities were vested. Unconsciously, I straightened and got a look of fire in my eyes.

"It's lovely," said my white-haired lady, "but I'm afraid I have to get on with my work. Now, just hold your breath while I pin this jacket and I'll see if I can't make it a wee bit tighter. And pull the skirt down an inch or so at the waist so I can cheat a trifle on the length!" Then as if in explanation, "You see, I had a daughter myself once."

Finally, approved by the executive officer, I was through with my uniform fitting. I clutched the merchandise coupon against which we were charging our purchases and found, with delight, that I hadn't quite totalled $200, even with my accessories and several other extra purchases counted in. What I didn't realize then was that at a later date I'd have to go through the whole business again for my summer outfit!

In the Navy they have a name for the awe-inspiring process by which a gal like me (previous maritime experience limited to such craft as the Hoboken Ferry) is turned into a true-navy-blue WAVE within the brief space of four or five weeks. It's called indoctrination.

Part of the WAVE's indoctrination consists, of course, of actually living under Navy discipline and rules at boot camp and of learning how to "Hup-two-hee-foh!" But just as important is the highly concentrated training program which gives every feminine boot a surprisingly complete background of naval traditions, customs and usages, and makes it possible for her to speak to anyone, from a seaman to an admiral, in his own language.

While we were learning, we were also being "screened." This does not mean that we aired our charms before a battery of movie cameras. It does mean that our skills, experience, personalities and personal preferences were weighed against the Navy's needs by the Selection Department to determine what the next step in our service careers would be.

In my own case, "screening" was not too difficult, since my medical technician's experience, plus the fact I passed the Navy aptitude test with what they tell me were flying colors, made it certain I would be assigned to the Hospital Corps. But with most of the girls, things were not so definite, as there was no way of telling what Washington would decide it needed most at that time. Thus when the assignments were finally posted on a bulletin-board in the lounge, there was a mad scramble to see what and where everyone had been tentatively assigned.

Only a few were disappointed at their assignments. "Darn it!" said one girl. "I used to take wonderful snapshots. I don't see *why* they didn't take me for Photography school."

Most, however, were excited and thrilled with their assignments. I was especially delighted to see that I had been billeted for further training at the Bethesda Hospital in Maryland, instead of at San Diego, the other possibility. I didn't feel like having all of the United States between my family and myself—not just yet.

Our graduation ceremony was a simple one. We all gathered in the auditorium, then Captain Davis arrived and gave a short address about our having successfully finished boot training, and the importance of the various billets to which we were assigned. It was his concluding words that I remember clearest.

"To the Navy, *each* of you represents a *fighting man*," he said.

Because I was up front, and his eyes momentarily rested on me, I felt as if I had been personally handed a great trust. My indoctrination was over; I was now a functioning part of the Navy. Mine was the job of filling a fighting man's job well, so that he in turn could get out to the front lines and help the Navy "seek out the enemy and destroy him."

# 3

# The War on Land

## RUSSIA, 1941

from
*PPG-2266:*
*A Surgeon's War*
by Nikolai Amosoff
Translated & Adapted by George St. George
Chicago: Henry Regnery Company, 1975

*Between the revolution of 1917 and the German invasion in 1941, Russia*
*had been on a crash schedule to bring all its 100 million citizens into the twentieth*
*century. It meant teaching people to read and write, building schools, roads, and*
*railroads. It meant building a commercial navy and teaching farmers to use*
*implements that would increase their production. It was the equivalent of bringing*
*a Stone-Age civilization hidden in the darkness of time suddenly into the bright*
*sunshine of the twentieth century. Perhaps this was one of the considerations that*
*persuaded Hitler that the time was ripe for invasion. Such a backward people*
*could never stand up to his war machine.*

*Creaking into the war, the Russian citizens found themselves relying on*
*wagons and horses against German trucks and planes. The Nazis had the latest-*
*model weapons from munitions makers in Germany and Czechoslovakia, while*
*the Russians had to rely on World War I weapons and the anticipated arsenal*
*from the United States under Lend-Lease.*

*The Soviet Union, however, proved a bitter pill for Hitler. The Nazi high*
*command had anticipated a quick victory that would give them additional slave*
*labor, plus oil, coal, and wheat. But they underestimated the will and the tenacity*
*of the Russian people. For hundreds of years Russia had been constantly invaded*
*by marauding bands and neighboring countries and had eventually driven each*
*invader out or absorbed it into the Russian way of life.*

*Hitler's blitzkrieg, after the initial surprise attack, crept along the vast areas*
*of Russia, meeting pockets of resistance that further slowed the advancing troops.*
*The Russians traded land for time. With the coming of winter, the Nazis literally*

*froze in their tracks. Long supply lines were paralyzed with cold, engines turned into blocks of ice, men died where they stood, frozen mummies, and the German blitz came to a halt. The fighting lines stabilized.*

*In a nation starved for knowledge, the medical community and medical care suffered along with the rest of the nation. The war caught them totally unprepared for the mountain of wounded that would need immediate attention. Field hospitals set out for the fighting fronts on horse- and mule-drawn wagons piled high with hospital equipment, while nurses and doctors marched the roads on foot. At night sleep was in tents or under the stars. Food was generally sparse, and cold— canned meat, bread and tea. Occasionally the cook would make some hot soup. The wagons rattled on. X-ray equipment rested on beds of straw. Medications were picked up along the way.*

*The story of the field unit PPG-2266 was "found" when Dr. Amosoff moved to a new home several years ago. He discovered his wartime diaries, about which he had completely forgotten. They show us the war as seen not by generals, but by a novice surgeon, twenty-seven years old and involved at the fighting front with all its filth, blood, and death. Here is an eyewitness story of a field hospital with all the sweat, chloroform, blood, pain, tears, and wonderment of what tomorrow may bring.*

## August 4, 1941

We are approaching the front. Before us looms a dark cloud—or a dense pall of smoke. A steady sound of artillery fire, for the second day. A continuous booming around the clock.

We are moving westward.

Our orders: "By 1800 hours on August 4 you are to set up a hospital near Roslavl to receive the wounded from front line medical battalions."

Our train: twenty-two sturdy carts, each pulled by two horses. We left the town of Zhizdra six days ago, and we are in a hurry. We have a little over an hour to meet the deadline.

The "staff cart" heads the procession. Khaminoff walks beside it. I know that he has varicose veins and is suffering. He hears the firing growing nearer and nearer, but he has to be in front. A commander. Our commissar is in the rear, running and shouting, seeing that no cart falls behind. A good man, but excitable.

Our horses are bearing up well even though the carts are heavy and we have covered over 110 miles in six days. At least our peasant drivers are experienced men. All the axles are greased, and the wheels are periodically doused with water to cool them down.

Now we are a true hospital. In Zhizdra we received all our surgical and hospital equipment. All of it was brand new, in wooden boxes—linen, bandages, medicines. We are ready.

As Head of the Surgical Department I also received a thick little book, *The Unified Surgical Doctrine*. Published by the Red Army Medical Department, it contained exact instructions for all surgical procedures. At first I was puzzled and even irked. What—no initiative? Everything covered by precise rules? But when I recalled that many doctors had been hastily mobilized, and that some of them were not surgeons, I had to admit the need for rules.

Russian military medical history is not brilliant. During the rule of the czars, the percentage of soldiers dying of wounds was appalling. "Evacuation" was the dominant principle: patch them up, load them into peasant carts, and send them back. There was a minimum of front-line surgery, only amputations when absolutely necessary (if gas gangrene developed later, well, too bad). There were always more *moujiks* to fill the ranks. The attitude of Peter the Great was typical: in one of his orders he decreed that medical personnel be kept out of soldiers' sight—"So that these scum would not remind men of death."

But this time, theoretically at least, we are ready. The Military Surgeon General, Professor Burdenko, had devised precise procedures for all emergencies, and these procedures had been tested during the clashes we had with the Japanese in Mongolia and Manchuria and during the Finnish war, when the percentage of the wounded successfully treated and saved was quite satisfactory.

In practice, who knows? This is a different war, invoicing millions of soldiers, thousands of doctors who have never done any surgery, and young nurses who have had no battlefield experience.

Then, too, the war news has been bad. We are retreating all along the front—if there is such a thing as a "front." The communiqués stress the enemy's losses—millions. Then why are Germans still advancing with such apparent ease? Where do they get the fresh troops?

During the last month we have seen many troop trains going to the front—young, eager men, well dressed (our supply services have done a tremendous job). But they say we have few tanks, few planes; so much was lost during the first weeks of the war. How could we have been caught so much by surprise? Had we no intelligence service? Someone must have blundered. Who? We can only guess.

Of course no one discusses such matters. Even those who dislike and dread Stalin have learned to trust him. Propaganda? Yes and no. He has succeeded in transforming the country, though often by savage methods. We have built mighty industries out of nothing. Our men are brave. They have always been brave. Suicidal Russian courage, some call it. But why are we retreating? Why don't we attack?

It is best not to think about these things. We just follow orders, blindly, uncompromisingly; history will judge later.

We are moving toward the war. And the war is moving toward us. Our armies are still retreating, and we are anxious to get into action. Those weeks of doing nothing, of being shoved around from station to station, were most unpleasant.

Once, three weeks ago, we were bombed by a single German plane. It dropped two small bombs. We had no losses, but there was panic. I remember lying down, in accordance with instruction, face to the ground. But some others ran into a nearby forest. We lost a day gathering them together again.

Was I frightened? I think so, even though I did not feel any conscious fear. And I was not hysterical afterward, as were some of our men. Oddly enough, our girls stood up better. None of them developed hysterics. Well, at least we have had a taste of war: our "baptism by fire."

The men walk beside the carts; even the drivers walk to save their horses' strength. Only those women whose shoes have given out and whose feet are bleeding ride. Some of the girls walk barefoot. We still have not received small-size boots, but they have been promised.

I walk beside the surgical carts. My team is all here: Lina, Liza, Tamara, Zoya. Good girls, all of them, though slightly afraid of the approaching action. Who can blame them?

We have been following small country dirt roads to avoid German bombers and to leave the highway clear for motor traffic. On those back roads we were quite unaware of the war until we heard firing. We did not even hear any communiqués. Our radio is out of order, and Commissar Shishkin could not get any news. Or perhaps he did not try to—he is responsible for our morale, and it has not been too high, anyway.

The introduction of commissars into the army has been widely criticized, but during the Civil War, when many Red Army commanders were old officers who did not sympathize with the Revolution, they were necessary, and I think that they serve a useful purpose even now. We have two political officers: Zvereff, the second in command, and Shishkin. Zvereff is responsible for overall political education, and Shishkin for the morale of every person in the unit. His duties resemble those of the old army's chaplains—with one difference. All political officers and commissars fight in the first ranks; they say that Germans shoot all of them out of hand.

We have become accustomed to walking. At the end of the day we fall down on the ground, exhausted, then wake up at night, shivering. The nights are quite cold here, in Smolensk province, and we wrap ourselves up in everything we can get. Every night Chapliuk cooks some soup, and we have water for tea. but often we are too tired to eat. The food is not too bad, but a bit monotonous.

Well, this is war. No time to think about feet or stomachs. The sound of firing is growing all the time, and the nervousness is spreading. There are grumbling voices: "Where the hell does he think he's leading us?... Can't you see? Straight to the Fascists. ... A home-grown Soussanin. [Soussanin was a Russian national hero. In the beginning of the 18th century, acting as a guide, he led a Polish detachment into a trackless forest where they all perished.] And where are those officers who are supposed to meet us? Probably running away like rabbits."

Here and there we see groups of soldiers and detachments, not only rear-echelon men, but guns and ammunition trucks. But no wounded. Khaminoff sent men off to gather news. Reports are contradictory. "There's fighting in Roslavl. ... The Germans broke through, going ahead like mad. ... Roslavl's burning."

It is almost eight o'clock, and it is growing dark. We are hopelessly late. We approach a village, and here we have to turn onto the Warsaw Highway. It is on this highway, somewhere near Roslavl, that representatives of the Army Medical Service are to meet us and give us further instructions.

Near a copse of trees, soldiers are fixing their field guns, the muzzles turned toward the sound of artillery firing. They do not speak to us—too busy. They just look at us in a puzzled way. Horses, carts, women. A gypsy caravan?

We turn north and approach the highway. The firing is very close. Someone says that he hears machine guns, but all I hear is a steady roar. From the highway we hear the sound of motor traffic—trucks, maybe tanks, a steady stream.

A road sign: "Roslavl—5 Kilometers."

Our heavy carts climb the steep highway slope with difficulty, but finally we are lined up along the road.

"Are you all here? Forwa-a-ard!"

We move for about a hundred yards, and there is a halt. I can just make out a light military passenger car. The headlights, mere slits on the painted glass, pick out a group: Khaminoff, Zvereff, and some officer, not from our hospital.

As I move up to get closer, I hear voices.

"Show me your orders and your map."

I see Khaminoff bring them out of his map case. A quick look. There! "Turn around and get out of here—at once."

A momentary pause.

"What are you waiting for? Issue the orders."

Zvereff: "And what about our orders?"

"I am ordering you. Colonel Tikhonoff of the army rear command. You can mention my name to your superiors. Clear?"

"Yes, Comrade Colonel."

Khaminoff gives the orders, and the carts begin to turn around. We get up on them. Overloading? Who cares? Fear does funny things. The drivers snap the reins, and we start off; it is easy going along the paved road, and we maintain full speed, covering seven and a half miles without a halt. Not a wheel broke, not a pack fell off.

The colonel was left standing on the highway. Probably laughing at our sudden mobility.

Finally, crossing the Oster River, we turn into a thin forest and stop there, exhausted.

No soup, no tea, not even bread and sugar. Everyone collapses on the ground. Sleep. Blessed sleep.

## Late August, 1941

We are retreating farther and farther east.

Today's communiqué: Smolensk has been "evacuated." There is fighting near Kiev. Uman and Bielaya Tserkov are mentioned.

Our hospital retreats with us.

After we turned away from Roslavl, we had a day's rest in a former agricultural college. Roslavl had been taken by the Germans just after we had turned back.

We stop at Sukhinichi, where we've been ordered to set up our hospital. We've even received a large motor truck with a driver. Moving past the railway station and oil tanks surrounded by poplar trees, we finally approach a line of large barracks. Khaminoff gets off the truck. We join him.

"Look, Nikolai Mikhailovich... a perfect place. Our orders say to take any empty buildings."

Suddenly: Bo-o-om! And immediately again: Bo-o-om! And then much closer: Bo-o-om!

Everyone jumps out of the truck. (Our carts are still behind us.) I crouch and instinctively draw in my head.

There are no more explosions, just a sound of a departing plane and several belated anti-aircraft gun bursts. Then, quiet and the sun. Peace.

We all get up, confused and a bit ashamed.

"Where the hell did they come from?" someone asks.

There is a small smoking crater near an oil tank. We were not the target, so the panic was unnecessary.

We inspect the place: two lines of twelve squat barracks, empty, not a stick of furniture inside.

"We can take a thousand wounded here."

"Yes, but look at our neighbors: the station and oil storage tanks."

"We must not expose the wounded to unnecessary risks."

Khaminoff brings out his map. We all study it. A couple of miles away we spot the village of Alneri. "A direct road from here," someone notices.

"All right, let's take a look at it. Get in," says Khaminoff.

We arrive in Alneri, take one look, and make a decision. This is our place—close enough from the railroad not to be isolated but far enough away from such tempting targets.

The village sits in a narrow ravine on both banks of a small river. Small neat houses, clean and pretty, clustered together. At the far end of the village stands a primary school in a large apple orchard. There are a few old barns and a squat brick building. Next to it is the village club, in a former church building. The caretaker explains: "This was a landlord's estate. During the Revolution they burned and looted it. Then they built the club. The orchard is so old that it produces no fruit."

The school, empty—vacations—is composed of four large classrooms and a small office. In one classroom—a group of small desks. On a blackboard—a round face: two eyes, nose, mouth, and two devil's horns. Probably some teacher.

We organize ourselves. The classrooms we'll reserve for bed cases. Lighter cases we'll handle in tents under the apple trees. The dressing station also will be in a tent. Dining tent and kitchen are also to be in the trees. We set up a bathhouse near the river, the staff quarters in a house nearby. All the rest of the personnel are billeted in the village.

It does not take long. Almost at once we begin to unload. At first the caretaker protests, but when we show him the requisition order, he helps us. He's a good old man and a former soldier from World War I. He was gassed near Riga.

We sit around waiting for the carts to come up.

## Early September, 1941

We have received our first wounded. We are working; we are finally in this war. My God, how difficult it all turns out to be. And we are only a GLR—a "hospital for the lightly wounded."

All my dreams about complicated surgery, for which I have been preparing in my mind, have evaporated. Khaminoff was relieved. "You're much too young to handle serious cases, Chief Surgeon," he said with a smile.

That is my official title now. I think Khaminoff was irked when they assigned it to me. A chief, indeed—so young and inexperienced. His attitude is understandable. Khaminoff is also a chief, so in effect we are addressed in the same way. But of course he is my superior.

Our hospital is part of a Field Evacuation Area. Each army has one. The main feature is the Reception Center, where all the wounded are processed, sorted, and sent to different hospitals. Our area has three of them; ours is located at Sukhinichi, and the hospitals are in neighboring villages. The wounded are brought in from the front in cars; some of them are sent to the rear in hospital trains, and others are sent to the hospitals to be treated, ready for evacuation.

That's what happens most of the time. We, however, have been assigned a special task. Our wounded are not going anywhere, except back to their units.

Before the war there were no special military hospitals for light cases; they were the product of the first war months. Our losses were large; replacements were slow to arrive; and in the general chaos men with light injuries were often sent beyond the Urals along with the seriously wounded. The chaos was too great, and the High Command put a stop to it. All lightly wounded were to be treated locally, patched up as quickly as possible, and returned to their units. There was to be no pampering; military discipline was to be maintained. Morale-building political education was to be administered, and there was to be no drinking or loitering.

So we are a GLR. Originally our unit was designed to accommodate 200 bed cases. But then we got our new orders: "reorganize PPG-2266 to GLR to accommodate up to 1,000 light wounded." Our base in Alneri has been approved. All recuperating cases are to be transferred to Sukhinichi, to the barracks near the oil tanks. There they are to be taken over by drill sergeants and political instructors, eventually to be returned to the front.

We sort all our wounded in the school corridor, where they are registered and given anti-tetanus injections. Then they are taken to the bathhouse and the delousing station that we have set up at the edge of the river. Only then do they get to our "dining room" in the garden under a canvas canopy. One corner of the dressing station— three tables in a tent—is screened off for our "operating theater." We do some minor surgery, after all.

Just as we finished getting everything ready, we had visitors—a very resplendent officer, the Chief of the Evacuation Area, accompanied by a very nonmilitary-looking army surgeon. We had already stuffed mattresses with straw and put clean sheets on the beds.

"Take it all off! No pampering of the men—this is not a health resort! Just straw! And watch for lice! We don't want a single louse here!" I knew I was in the army then—for real!

The doctor politely pointed out to us that we had no special place where the wounded could undress, and that our reception section in the corridor was too small. But he made no suggestion as to how we could expand the school building. They finally left in a small military car.

We sat in the former school office and waited for our first cases. We had been warned that they were coming "very soon." Suddenly a young nurse burst in, calling "They're here!"

Outside, filled to capacity, were three 1½-ton trucks with red crosses on the green canvas. The wounded were sitting on benches and on the floor. The medics helped them out, led them into the schoolhouse, and seated them,

There they were—the defenders of the Motherland. The first thing we noticed was that all of them were utterly exhausted—hollow cheeks, unshaven, dirty. The majority were wearing only shirts—no greatcoats. Some had canvas bags, others nothing. Many had gas mask cases but no masks. There were cutaway sleeves and trouser legs, fresh bandages, slings, makeshift walking canes. Most were middle-aged men, reservists.

Some fell asleep at once, leaning against walls or on the floor.

"Tired, comrades?"

"You'd get tired too," one said. "The whole day moving from place to place… some organization."

"We were already in a train. But then:—Get out!—Inspection! Why the hell can't they send us back into the rear where we could be treated properly?"

The man was angry, but it was understandable. Having gone through hell, he had had the good fortune to suffer a slight wound. Nearly a hero, he's suddenly thrown back into the mill.

"We'll treat you here, comrades," we said.

"You're kidding. Just behind the front? They'll bomb this place to hell in a couple of days!"

"What do they care? That would save them a lot of bother."

Our first patients. And now we are a real hospital, complete with paper work and routine. The nurse who accompanied each group hands over all the appropriate documents, military cards, tags. Everyone has to be registered and listed. No document may be returned to a man—the order is strictly enforced. They might run away and try to get on some hospital train going to the rear.

As soon as ten men are registered they are taken to the bathhouse near the river. The bathhouse is small, and men—emaciated, exhausted—wait outside on the benches, naked. All their things are taken away to be deloused; they are issued clean undergarments. There is plenty of hot and cold water, but soap and sponges are in short supply.

After the trip to the bathhouse, the general atmosphere is better. There are smiles and even jokes.

"Thanks, Comrade Doctor, for the bath. Haven't washed myself since the beginning of the war. Thought I'd get to Berlin stinking dirty."

"What about lice, men?"

"Sure, as many as you want. Government issue."

Our delousing station works slowly. Those who have had their bath sit outside in fresh undershirts and long underwear. There is some grumbling.

"We're hungry. Take us in as we are."

Fortunately it is warm. There is a large and growing heap of clothes near the delousing hut. How are we going to redistribute them? Well, that's not my problem.

In the dining room the soldiers are different again. For them it is the first hot soup they've had in many hours, even days. The food and the fresh undergarments make them cheerful.

"Just like Saturday night after a week in the fields. What about a little alcohol?"

No drinking is allowed.

Their wounds generally do not disturb them too much. To wash, to eat, to rest—those are their main preoccupations.

Of course all bandaging must be checked, and the dressing station works full blast. The tables are not used. Men sit on benches. Medical histories must be filled in: a slow procedure even though all the available doctors work on it.

According to the rules of military surgery, there is no needless wound dressing, just inspection and registration. But sometimes bandages slip or become soggy. When men specifically ask for redressing, we treat them.

They're all simple injuries; there's no surgery. All we have to do is keep the wound clean and it will heal by itself, but this is my first encounter with war injuries, and it is interesting.

Our specialty has rapidly become flesh wounds, small shell fragments under the skin. The rules say: small fragments up to 1/4 inch in size need not be removed. Larger fragments are different. They must be removed to prevent infection from setting in. All such wounds must be cut open and cleaned. We do not listen to the wounded men's descriptions. Some tend to exaggerate, others to minimize the extent of their injuries.

It's only minor surgery, but even that has its problems. I've had to learn the hard way.

One of my first patients was a man with a no-exit hip wound. Soft tissues. The entrance wound was about 1/2 inch in diameter. I examined it, dictated my diagnosis: no surgery required.

"Comrade Doctor, there's a piece right here—moving under the skin. Maybe it's better to cut it out?"

I felt the skin. "You're right, Comrade. Tatiana Georgievna, get the table ready. Local anesthesia."

The man was listening and became nervous: "What's that—local freezing? Oh, no. I won't allow it. I've seen what happens in medical battalions. They use local stuff and then cut them to pieces."

One must always consider the patient's mental condition. Generally, local anesthesia is not recommended under battlefield conditions. Men often are too emotionally disturbed and keyed up to respond to it.

"All right, sit here and wait," I said. "We'll finish with the light cases first."

In an hour all wounded debridement was finished. It grew darker. Finally it was time for my first bit of military surgery.

"Tamara, general anesthesia. Tatiana, cover the table with a sterile sheet."

Our man removed his underpants. His teeth were chattering. He was pale. "Please... be careful... I'm afraid," he said.

"Don't worry, Soldier. Lie down."

Tamara knows her business. Everything was ready—a mask, a chloroethyl spray, a wound spreader, a tongue depressor. She smeared vaseline around his mouth and asked a medic to hold down the man's arms.

We put the mask on the man and aimed the chloroethyl spray at it.

"Start counting!"

"One... two I'm choking!"

"Keep counting!"

The man jumped up, tore off his mask, face red, eyes wild. Gasping.

"I can't, Doctor,... can't! I'm choking!"

We calmed him down, put him back on the table, and secured him with belts.

"A stronger spray, Tamara."

Another attempt, another failure. The belts restrained him, but he jerked his head out of the mask. Such a humiliating struggle.

Other wounded soldiers crowded around the tent. "Operation... operation..." The word was out. Khaminoff came in, put on a white gown. He looked very unpleasant.

"Try ether. The man is too excited," he said.

We tightened the belts. Ether acts slowly, takes five or ten minutes. The man became excited again and mumbled something—the appropriate obscenities.

Finally he quieted down. I found the shell fragment, pressed the skin with a scalpel, but the damned thing was dull, wouldn't cut. The soldier started struggling again, screaming.

"Tamara, devil take you! Chloroform!"

Khaminoff ambled up to me, whispered, "Look, Nikolai Mikhailovich...it's been so long. ... you'd better do it yourself."

*I felt my cheeks flush with shame.*

"Lina Nikolaevna, put on sterile gloves. Give me chloroform."

While they prepared chloroform, I could hear voices outside.

"What do you think this is—a movie theater? Go back to your places." It was Kolia Kansky.

And there was a sarcastic voice: "Doctors! Cutting him up like a pig's carcass..."

Our patient kept muttering something. The ether had had no effect. Finally everything was ready. I began to drop chloroform, considered a dangerous anesthetic and not recommended. I had no experience with it at all, but I continued. We had to put him under. I remember thinking "And now his heart is going to stop. God forbid." There was no way out, of course. I had to go on.

"He has relaxed his muscles," Lina said, finally.

Thank God, I thought, and said, "Go ahead, Lina Nikolaevna." Lina made an incision, putting clamps on all the small blood vessels. But we were losing time. I couldn't find the fragment; my hands were shaking. Then I saw it, a very small piece of metal. We removed it. Then the final haemostasis, iodine under the skin, a bandage. The end.

"Stay with him, Tamara. He may start vomiting. He could choke himself."

The wounded outside went away: there was no real scandal. People love scandals, even if they are not malicious. Khaminoff walked away without saying a word. Only we, the surgical staff, stayed around, discussing our first operation. What went wrong? Chloroethyl did not work because of the man's overexcitement; it happens in civilian cases as well. Also, we decided, our mask was too small; we would get a larger one, perhaps even cover the patient's face with a towel. And use more ether. At last we knew that chloroform would be effective.

All in all a humiliating experience, especially with such a simple case. Some beginning.

## Late September, 1941

We've been working near Sukhinichi for over a month. The front has stabilized. More than that: we have retaken Elnya—a small town, but a big symbol. We too, can hit back! For two weeks we have been able to hear gunfire, and all our wounded come from the Elnya sector. On the day we captured the town, everyone became excited, happy, absolutely different. That is what victory means, even a minor one.

Down south things are not going well. Kiev seems to be lost; the news hits us hard. Odessa is holding, deep behind the German lines. Leningrad, too, is holding well. Generally the communiqués do not sound too alarming. England is with us, and Roosevelt seems to sympathize with us. It's good not to be alone.

I live with Khaminoff in a small house. We are fairly comfortable. He is a good man, Khaminoff, and a good physician. He likes to play the superior, he likes power, he likes flattery, but all within reason—he's an intelligent man. He can be argued against, and he treats me well.

We are now very busy. This morning we had 1,150 cases on our list, though only 420 were here, in Alneri. The rest are in our "recovery battalion" in the large barracks in Sukhinichi.

Besides the school, the club, and our tents, we have constructed several dugouts, accommodating fifty men each. Yesterday the dugouts got us in trouble. The commissar general of the army came in and raised hell with us because many of the men were lying on the straw in the dugouts. He was right, of course, but what about those orders "not to pamper the men"?

# TUNISIA—WAR IN THE DESERT

from

*The Battle Is the Pay-Off*

by Ralph Ingersoll

New York: Harcourt, Brace and Company, 1943

*North Africa became an active war theater in June 1940 when Italy joined Hitler in the campaign to destroy Britain. Italian forces quickly wrested British Somaliland from England in August. In September, Marshal Rodolfo Graziani's Italian forces launched Axis drives sixty miles into Egypt. A smaller but well-organized force of the British army counterattacked and drove the Italian army more than 500 miles down the coast, virtually destroying its fighting capacity. The Italian retreat ended once the German forces came to their aid and General Rommel took command of the African campaign in February 1941. The prize for the Axis, if they were victorious, would be the Suez Canal. The Mediterranean would become their private lake.*

*Battles seesawed on the flat terrain, which lent itself to tank warfare but left troops and machines vulnerable to air attack. It was a war of attrition, and the army that could keep its men supplied with machines and munitions would gain the advantage. Supply lines were strained as men and armaments were poured onto the battlefields. Rommel's forces rolled across the desert, destroying any troops and materiel that stood in their path until they reached Alamein.*

*Alaric Jacob, an English war correspondent in Cairo in July 1942, describes that battle: "The first battle of Alamein, which had been joined on the previous day, was raging with unabated fury, but so far without a decision. Next morning I drove up towards Alamein. I spent the night at Amriya with bombers taking off on the open desert all around us on nonstop bombing missions. The tired Axis troops were being pounded all the time from the air and blasted incessantly by our guns in the hope that they would be too harassed to carry their offensive right through to its end, but be obliged to halt at Alamein and re-form. By which time we hoped to be ready to deal with them.*

*"On the morning of July 4th I drove straight into the Alamein 'Box.' In an observation post just off the road I was able to watch an armored battle develop which led to a German withdrawal after a considerable loss of tanks and of men. Thirty German tanks were destroyed for sure and the enemy left five hundred vehicles in our hands by the end of the day. Out on a ridge to the south I could see tanks and vehicles burning. Our artillery was firing without let-up. With the naked eye I could see swarms of vehicles moving about on the ridge, and it was thrilling to see that the general tendency was westward—westward away from Egypt, and pushing the enemy back whence he came. Directly before me the flashes of our guns were like so many matches being struck in quick succession on the sandy plateau, which swirled with the dust kicked up by hundreds of trucks. The sharper, more staccato crack of anti-tank guns rose now and then above the general*

rumble of the battle. It was very much a gunners' show. Our precious tanks were not being hazarded; they were firing from hull-down positions or taking advantage of dead ground to maneuver close to the enemy, to fire and then withdraw again out of range.

"I thought of the prediction an important German prisoner had made the day before: 'Rommel has wonderful energy himself but he drives us too hard and some of us can't take much more of this. ... Rest we must have soon.'"

The dust of battle had barely cleared in Alamein, when in August, General Bernard L. Montgomery took command of a British 8th Army that had been resupplied, its ranks refilled. By October, the British opened its offensive with tanks, artillery, and air support. They cleared mine fields and chased the retreating German army out of Egypt, through Libya, into east Tunisia. In November the American troops landed in Africa and soon after, the Axis suffered total defeat on that continent.

General Rommel had little faith in the fighting ability of the Italian army. Whenever he felt the necessity to withdraw from a battle, any Italian units with the Nazi forces would be left behind to fight a rearguard action. To ensure that his allies would stay and fight, the general had the wheels removed or broken on all Italian vehicles. As a result, the Fascist forces had to either fight or surrender. In either case, it gave Rommel time to move his forces to another point, regroup, and continue with the war.

This ploy was evident when the American forces broke through the Italian lines at El Guettar. One of the soldiers with the American troops was First Lieutenant Ralph Ingersoll. A World War I veteran, and now at age 42 an enlistee again, he found himself on the hot sands of Tunisia. The unit he was with had prepared for a battle at Gafsa, but when they got to the city, it had been deserted by the enemy. Now they were moving on to El Guettar, the road to Sfax.

Enemy forces were reported along the road, which was referred to as "the funnel," for it passed through a steep valley without any possibility of escape. Reconnaissance indicated that all motorized equipment and military personnel on the narrow pass would be subject to ambush. The Rangers were going to try to circumvent the pass, and with the aid of a company of combat engineers, prepare the way for the infantry.

Lt. Ingersoll participated in this action; ex-World War I veteran, ex-managing editor of The New Yorker, ex-managing editor of Fortune, ex-publisher of Time, and ex-editor and publisher of the New York City tabloid PM, now an officer in the U.S. Army as part of a unit attacking the enemy. He reveals his age and generation when he refers to the G.I.s as "doughboys."

I t was like that, starting into battle. I did not feel a soldier, sitting in the plane from Algiers with orders which would take me into the line where the battle was. But when the actual march began, I felt neither soldier nor civilian. I do not remember feeling anything but some wonder at the scene around me and a simple and natural interest in finding my place in it.

The scene was complicated. Company D of the Engineers had moved from the rocks where I had left them resting and were forming by the side of the road, straggling in irregular columns. The captain appeared, said "Oh, here you are," and told me to wait with the troops for a runner who would tell me where the Rangers wanted us. He disappeared again. All about in the darkness, officers and men of other units were moving. The runner came purposefully through the crowd and I guessed it was he because he came from the hill where I knew the Rangers were. When he pushed to the edge of the road he stopped and looked uncertainly about him. I asked him if he was looking for the Engineers, and he answered me with authority.

"Colonel Chittenden wants you to bring your men up to the foot of the hill there. You are to follow me and I will show you where."

Both of the platoon lieutenants were with me now. We passed word down the column and set off after the guide, who had not waited for an answer but was disappearing into the crowd. He took us a short way up the side of the hill by the road, motioned to where he wanted us and went off at a trot. When D company got up there, its men fell into their places in columns of squads and I stood on a rock where they could see me and waved at them to sit down because I wanted them to rest until the last minute.

I could look back from where we were and see the slopes and the plain even more clearly. The foreground of the scene was beginning to make sense. From the milling troops near the road, files of men were breaking off and climbing up the slope parallel with the track that we took. Line after line formed and merged and was led up the slope. There was no clue to which unit was which, but these were infantrymen. The units were being sorted and runners were darting from one to the other, trying to find who was where and get word back to their C.O.'s. There were no orders called. The only sounds were still the scraping of feet, the small noises of metal and rock touching and far away the steady throb of many motors running.

The slope was now lined with columns as far as the shadows could be made out clearly, and the men were down off their feet and sitting or lying on the ground again.

I looked up at the hill under which we waited. Now that the moon was higher I could see that the hillside was marked with scores of small burrowings. This was the side of the hill that was away from the enemy and the burrowings were where the Rangers lived. As I watched, they were coming out from dugouts and striking the pup tents that they had set up here and there on scratched-out terraces. The hillside was alive with activity. The Rangers were dropping down out of their bivouac in twos and threes and ones, running rapidly down. When they came to where D Company waited, they pushed through and over us. Just beyond us they began their lining up. I thought of men coming out of their barracks for the chow line at home. It seemed the same except there was no horseplay.

Our men carried no packs but the Rangers had light packs attached to their shoulder harnesses. Otherwise, our uniform was like theirs—leggings, trousers, field jacket and helmet. When our men had first climbed from their trucks, the captain had noticed that some of them wore over their trousers the heavy, almost waterproof, ankle-tight overalls that was the bottom half of the armored force battle dress.

Most of the engineers had them and wore them in the biting chill of Tunisia's spring. The captain called in the sergeants and said rather sharply, "Tell them to take those things off. Nothing but leggings and trousers. They have a lot of climbing to do"—and the battle overalls had come off and had been sent back in one of the trucks.

I stood waiting there, watching the scene of ghostly preparation, of order emerging without orders. In five to ten minutes Captain Henry was back. There was a tall young soldier with him. Instead of a rifle, he had strapped over his shoulder the box with the long rod on it which is the 511 U.S. Signal Corps radio—the walkie-talkie. He held the microphone for it in his hand. The pair came up to me and the captain motioned to the two lieutenants.

"We are to be the third company in the line of march," he said. "Our line of march will be the two hell squads first, and then the mortars. I'll take the head of the column with Ingersoll and you two take your platoons. I want Sergeant Chervassy with me and this is our radio communication with the Rangers. The show starts any minute now."

And then, as a last thought, he motioned to the men for their attention and told them what Colonel Chittenden of the Rangers had said about keeping up.

Even while he was talking, I saw it begin, noticing that the columns nearest us were all on their feet and now first one and then another had begun to move up the hillside back away from the road. Now my only problem would be to avoid losing the captain. Seven hours' acquaintance had convinced me that he was an elusive fellow given to disappearing without warning. I looked at his silhouette. He was a small slight man, quick of movement. The best identification, I thought, was the gun on his shoulder. The lieutenant had been right. He carried a weapon the like of which I had not seen before. It had a long thin blue steel barrel, and I could make out only that it took some kind of clip. I said to him:

"If you like, I will keep the sergeant and the radio with me. We'll keep as close to you as we can but you will always know the three of us will be together."

He said, "O.K. Good," and his eye catching some movement in the column nearest us, he was off.

The tall young man with the radio, who had been listening intently, swung in behind me when I followed. The sergeant was already in motion. The columns around us had paid no apparent attention to us but there were whispered orders back and forth now, and as we drew farther up the slopes, the Rangers fell into their marching formation. They marched in two long, wavy lines about fifty feet apart.

Captain Henry was trying to find our place in the flotilla, and while I steered as straight a course as I could, he darted away to whisper to such Ranger officers he could identify. The Rangers were used to working together at night. They knew each other's sounds and shapes. But our company had never marched with them before and we could not tell who was who. Moreover, the Rangers had a way of starting a march at a pace that would be a jog trot for the average man. First one Ranger company then another drew away from us. You could tell when a company passed for between companies the line would be broken for a space of ten or fifteen feet. The Rangers' junior officers had not apparently heard that they were going to have company on the march. They met Henry's questions blankly with shakes of the head. Finally, the young man with the radio said very respectfully:

"That is E company going by now, sir. It seems likely that would be the last of the column."

Captain Henry said nothing about the lost marching order and we fell in behind E Company. The Ranger with the radio continued in charge. He said, again very hesitantly:

"It's the Rangers' custom, sir, to march with half of each squad in each column. That would be half of each of your squads in this column and half in the other."

Captain Henry took a few steps before deciding how to handle this and then, with a shake of his head, motioned me to do something about it. Splitting the squads in half was too complicated. I split the company instead by motioning two platoons out of line and waving them over into the wake of the second Ranger column.

During the time these simple things happened, we were all very busy. The men had been sprawled out, relaxed, and had only a moment's warning to be on their feet. They had their gear to adjust and all of them had then to get in rapid motion in an orderly column. It was immediately apparent—we could not know until that second—that we were to march over neither road nor trail but across country.

Marching across country there meant marching on a hard surface so littered with small and medium pebbles and rocks the size of two or three fists held together that there was nowhere space between them to set a foot firmly on the solid ground. Moreover, the ground beneath these rocks was not level but rising. As it rose, it seemed to weave and tilt from side to side, so that sometimes we walked up a slope and sometimes along one side of slope and sometimes along the other. The only thing that was constant at the beginning of the march was that at the end of any given ten steps we were several feet higher than we had been at the beginning.

Now, a little over half of the men in the Engineers column, like myself, carried only a rifle, rations, grenades and assorted ammunition, but this equipment was not packed in a carrier which could be ignored. It was stuffed into the bosoms of our field jackets, bulged from the pockets, was draped around the waist and over the shoulders. It would have taken some doing to settle all this gear for a march on a level highway, yet each man for himself had to arrange his gear for walking while moving at a rapid scramble over impossible footing.

The men in the other Engineer squads were, in addition, juggling thirty-five- to forty-five-pound pieces of mortars, trying to balance them on their shoulders or get them snug under their arms to find any way they could be held except by sheer power of finger muscles. And for the officers, who also each carried weapons, ammunition, and rations, there were these things to do and some way to find to give comfort or counsel to the men who were having the hardest time of it. Communication was by passing back messages whispered over shoulders. Captain Henry could do nothing but send back word that the men who were not carrying mortar parts should team up with men who were and that each should take turn and turnabout so that no one would have to juggle the mortars continuously.

Meanwhile, I had my own special distraction. Not having had a dress rehearsal, I had not foreseen the flaws in my costume that were presently to develop.

My pistol belt was too loose and, weighted down with pistol, ammunition and full canteen, it began to ride on my hips just where the motion of my legs began. This let the second belt, the one that had nothing but ammunition in it, inch down across my belly until it reached the bottom of the field jacket. As soon as it did so, all the truck that I had stuffed in the front of the field jacket began to jounce, jiggle, squeeze and wedge until first a can of ration and then a heavy grenade and then a stick of candy would come oozing out. This would then force me to hold the whole impending landslide in with one hand, which in turn threw my shoulders out of line, whereupon the M-1 promptly kited around on its sling and banged me in the back of the helmet.

I knew that I would never be able to regain my place if I stopped for even a few seconds to try to adjust affairs. One was barely able to manage the pace, fresh and untired, because of the treacherous carpet of loose rock. Walk over it one might, with God on his side. Run over it, never—and if one fell behind one would have to run to catch up.

All I could do, stumbling, too breathless even to curse, was to fish wildly in my breast with my one free hand and haul out items and try to stuff them in my already full pockets in such a way that they would stick there. And then laboriously work the top belt up to where it would hold together the walking sack that I had become. And next get some kind of a hitch in the pistol belt. And, finally, get my rifle slung off one shoulder and across to the other, in the hope that it would ride still for a few more steps. Within a hundred and fifty yards I was panting, and I do not remember really ceasing to pant, and breathing simply and normally again, until well after the battle was under way the next morning.

That was the way it was in the beginning of the march: everyone was so busy that time and space were lost completely and there was only the ludicrous motion of tripping and stumbling on, batting oneself in the head with a rifle or the barrel of a mortar and trying to stick things down in overfilled pockets and take hitches in belts.

When the world around me again became a reality, the scene had changed just as completely as the scene on the road between the time I had gone forward to the mine field and come back to the start of the attack. When I first got my head up and could look around, having so far seen only Captain Henry's heels and the rocks that rolled from under them to roll in turn under mine, the landscape around us was as bare and desolate as it had been alive and peopled with men when we had begun. There were only the bare sides of the mountains now on both sides of us. The moon that had been bright on the plains and in the foothills had gone. The moon had not really gone, it was we who had moved so deep into the mountains that the moon had not yet risen to where it could shine on us. It was dark and still. Looking ahead, beyond the shiny barrel of Captain Henry's Italian machine gun, I could see only the last two or three of the retreating figures of the company ahead. Behind, after a dozen or so men, there was nothing.

I had my first experience with a sensation that was to recur during the night, a sensation of awakening. I had been so wholly concentrated on keeping my place and my footing—like a man running across a river of logs—that I had become oblivious of everything else. Now, mastering my balance, it was as if I had awakened or come to.

I looked at my watch. It was a little after one. The pace was not as fast as it

149

had been, and the way here was almost level. I noticed that the moonless sky was still clear and perceived that when the moon cleared the mountain tops and shone down on the valley it would be bright again. I thought, "An hour out. We must be about in back of the first Italian wire on the other side of the mountain to the right— just beyond the place I walked out to our mine fields."

I could not judge how long our column was or how far ahead the first man in the Rangers Company would be now. It was very still and obviously no one was in trouble yet, for trouble is usually noisy and in those mountains even a small noise would reverberate. I observed that the temperature was ideal for climbing; it was neither too hot nor too cold, but simply fresh and clear. There was no wind where we were down in the bottom of the valley. I thought if I could only see men a few feet ahead, no enemy could see them any farther—but if there were listening posts about, the sighing shuffle of hundreds of feet and the little clickings of the rocks would not be hard to pick up.

I thought, "Good God, nobody can be surprised by this attack!" Only an hour ago I had stood on just a slight rise of ground and the whole plain back there was peopled with live and moving shadows. The movement on that plain must have been visible for miles in the moonlight. I could no longer hear the throbbing of motors on the road back near Gafsa. We were down inside the mountains now. I thought: "Well, I could not hear the motors when we were at the mine field, close to the enemy lines. No, from there I would not be able to see the motion at the Ranger post either."

So there was a chance that the advance had not yet been observed. I remembered the observation planes that had come over at dusk. I thought again that their photographs would show the roads empty and all the division's bivouac of the day before still in place.

I also thought, what the hell do I know about these things. I have never been in a battle before and this is all book talk. This is talk in the mess hall at Camp Edwards about maneuvers. God knows how it happens out here, either better or worse. We never really thought we were hot in camp. We always thought that out in the theater they would do it better—the sentry would never daydream, the communications would always work and our units would always be where and when they were supposed to be—we could see a hundred flaws in everything we did, a hundred ways in which an alert enemy could beat us by capitalizing on our errors. Sometimes we made big talk about what our outfit could do in action but we always knew it was just that.

Well, here I was, marching along behind a real live enemy's line. That wasn't big talk or little talk or any talk at all. That was just happening and it was happening the way it would happen and there was nothing I could do about it except tag along. We were all tagging along, after some battle plan that none of us then understood.

And now walking in the dark with a rifle on my shoulder, towards an enemy that was to be shot, I felt neither afraid nor unafraid. I could think back to that old feeling about a rifle but could not feel it again. It was only walking, walking, walking over loose rock on hard ground and it was purely speculation about how far away the enemy was, or where we were, or what would happen next.

These idle thoughts and lots of others passed the time as we marched. You can

150

think a lot of thoughts marching towards a battle because you are very wide awake, and because your feet are in the rhythm of walking and there's nothing else to do. Later on, when the moon came out and it was very beautiful marching through the mountain, I stopped thinking of anything at all and simply enjoyed the scenery.

Slowly the moon counted off the hours as it crossed the sky. It was after two, it was after three, it was after four. The column no longer moved steadily now but went forward fifteen or twenty minutes and then halted. Something ahead was holding the column up. It was the little halts that saved me. I could feel my feet wearing out and my legs began to ache steadily and what I carried was noticeably heavier. I wanted very much to smoke. The last of the orders passed back through the line was: no smoking and no talking. When we halted, each man dropped where he was. The captain and the tall young man with the radio and I were a group. One of us would take out a stick of candy drops and each of the others would pry one off the top and put it in his mouth. The radio was alive and when everyone was still you hear a high thin note from its speaker. About three o'clock, one of the lieutenants came stumbling up and whispered to Henry,

"How much farther?"

Henry shook his head and shrugged his shoulders. We had stopped and the lieutenant turned and looked at me. His face was full of concern. I looked at my watch. We had been marching over three hours but I did not think we covered more than two or two and a half miles in a straight line. He looked so concerned that I whispered, "Half-way, maybe."

The lieutenant looked back at the captain and said, "That's bad, that's very bad. The mortars are too tough for them."

The captain thought a moment and looked ahead into the moonlight. There was a climb and then there was a drop and as far as you could peer through the shadows only more hills, more valleys. The captain sighed and said, "Let them begin dropping back. Pull connecting files from the squad ahead."

Connecting files are soldiers spaced out between elements of a march to keep contact, to relay directions, and show the way.

Then he said to the boy with the radio, "Can you raise Colonel Chittenden?"

The radio man looked at his watch and when he nodded, I knew his little set was still out of the range of the enemy. I guessed, here in the mountains, that might be five miles. He spoke into the microphone. "Henry to Chittenden. Henry to Chittenden. Over."

Instantly the machine answered, "Chittenden to Henry. What is it?"

Henry said, "Let me have the microphone," and whispered into it. "The mortar squads are dropping back, the going is too tough. Connecting files out." And then, "Any instructions? Over."

There was a few seconds' silence on the machine. "Chittenden to Henry. O.K., do the best you can. Over."

The men in the column ahead got to their feet and moved silently away. The column was off again and we marched. Now I walked, watching the ground ahead, playing a game with the ground, trying to outwit it by finding spaces between the stones in which to place each footstep—or if there were no places, flat stones that would not tax my ankles. I could see now that it was going to be a question of how carefully I played that game for there was no reserve strength in my ankles, and if I put weight on a foot that was not firmly on the ground my ankle would go and that would be the end of it. And I knew, too, that small fractions of ounces of energy would count now. I thought, the top of me will be all right if my feet will get me there. The top of me is not tired.

The thought kept coming back to me that we were well behind the enemy's lines now, and were coming close to a place where the slightest slip in the discipline of the march would count. The shuffling whisper of the hundreds of footfalls blended into a monotone. But now and then, somewhere along the column, someone would hit a stone at the wrong angle and it would clatter down the hillside. Or there would be the little tinkle of a rifle barrel tapping a helmet. Then the heads in the column would raise in disapproval or listen more carefully. Each man in the column was feeling what I was beginning to feel, our nearness to the enemy. I began to be conscious of the blue steel of the barrel of Captain Henry's Italian rifle. It sparkled and glittered in the moonlight. I had been glad I could spot it before so that I could identify the captain in the dark. Now the barrel's brightness annoyed me. A man on one of those peaks who could not see the shadows of the men mingling with the shadows of the rocks would wonder about that flicker of light. The column became quiet; there were long intervals when not even a single stone rolled down. Each man was walking gently, gently.

The halts became more frequent and when it was almost five we sat, breathing heavily after an especially long climb, for many minutes. And then we moved up a few feet and sat again. There was a very heavy shadow just ahead and you could not see where the trail went. When at last we came to the edge of the shadow we saw why the column had been hesitating. There was a real cliff here. The men had to climb down it one by one. The men who were carrying more than their slung rifles had to pass the equipment from hand to hand. When each man went over the cliff he went rapidly, as the man ahead was melting into the darkness under his very eyes. A new fear, the fear of being lost or left behind, seemed to move each man and they went down the cliff as if it were not at the end but at the beginning of five hours of climbing up and down.

Captain Henry seemed as agile as a gazelle. He was gone before I could swing my legs over the edge of the cliff and look to see where I would jump, and brace myself for the jump to a rock three or four feet below, and then to another and another and another. Down at the bottom of the shadow the whole thing seemed to close up, to end against a huge boulder ten or fifteen feet high. Then, as the eyes became accustomed to the darkness there, I could see a crevice under the boulder, down to the right. It was the only opening. I twisted onto my stomach and stuck my legs through it and gradually, holding my weight with my arm, lowered through.

My feet touched something, then gave way, and I went down bouncing from rock to rock. And suddenly I was on the flat of a stream bed, quite alone, out of breath and panting.

There was no way to go but along the stream bed. A long way beyond I could see moonlight again and it seemed, from there under the cliff and the big boulder, as bright as sunlight. I ran towards it. The surface of the stream bed felt so flat and firm to feet that had been climbing so long over rocks that it was suddenly as if they had been bathed in cool water. I ran because I had not realized how much it had meant to be one of a column instead of being alone. I wanted to be with the end of the column ahead, and quickly. I did not want to be lost there.

Where the stream bed came into the moonlight I almost collided with a dough-boy standing. He whispered tonelessly, as he had whispered to hundreds ahead of me, "Climb to the little shelf there," pointing, "and then curve to the left around the base of the hill and then at the end of the plateau, go down in the valley to the right." And then, as if it could be done, "Keep closed up."

As I turned and left him, our boy with the radio came through and he was run-ning so he collided with the sentry. I motioned him to follow.

After we passed the big drop it went very quickly. The footing was better and they must have been urging the men ahead to move faster. We caught sight of Captain Henry at the far end of the plateau but only for a moment. The radio man stayed by me like a shadow. I didn't see the sergeant again. I was peering ahead always, to find the end of the column and somehow keep in touch and not lose the way. It was a race with the moon now for the moon was across the sky and close to the peaks on our right. There was just the first trace of growing light on the left.

I was almost up to Captain Henry again when, there on a little knoll of grass, we came abruptly to where Colonel Chittenden waited. I knew it was the colonel by the glob of silver on his helmet, and he had another walkie-talkie man with him and two officers. He spoke in a loud whisper and there was a note almost of exultation in it. He spoke as if to old friends, abruptly and without introduction. "Do you realize what we have done, men! Do you realize! We've got five whole columns through!"

There did not seem to be any answer to this. Captain Henry made none. The colonel stepped closer and peered at him, stooping a little to look under the shadow of his helmet. "You're Captain Henry, aren't you? You're the fellow with the engi-neers." And then, as if coming to from an ecstatic reverie, looking at the watch on his wrist, "We've got to keep going fast now. The attack begins at six. About eight we'll want your mortars, and will you leave out files, Henry, to show the infantry the way? They could get lost in here." Then the colonel's enthusiasm bubbled up again. "You know what this means to them out there, don't you? We've got to get this show under way on time. Their flanks will be wide open if we don't get this show under way on time. But I've got five whole companies past here and they are on up ahead."

Captain Henry continued to stand silently and I stood close by him, panting from the last hour. The colonel and his walkie-talkie and his two officers went off across the knoll of grass and disappeared rapidly. We followed, still not speaking.

After that there were no columns to follow. The Rangers were gone and we were simply coming up as fast as we could. It was well after five, it was five-thirty, it was a quarter to six. Now, the valleys we walked through were well defined and we could not lose our way.

You could not recall the moment it had happened, but the night had passed and it was light, even in the valley. It was fourteen minutes to six, it was twelve minutes to six, it was nine minutes to six. The head of our column had caught up with us and I could recognize the faces of the men of D company. They were expressionless. They looked neither tired nor tense now.

We saw the man who was waiting for us a long way ahead, standing at the top of a jagged pile of rocks. "Colonel Chittenden said to tell Captain Henry to keep his men down, behind those rocks there."

Captain Henry nodded. The runner turned and went off.

As his men came up, Sergeant Chervassy motioned them down behind the rocks. They went where he pointed and each man, as he found a place for himself, dropped down, taking his rifle from his shoulder and stretching out his legs, laying his rifle across him or putting it on the ground beside him, then lying back against the rock motionless. It was eight minutes to six, it was seven minutes to six, it was four minutes to six. In ones and twos, more men came up and these, seeing the others resting on the rocks, went there and rested too without being directed. Captain Henry and I stood and looked at the line of the hill against the sky. Chervassy was ahead of us. He had gone down on one knee and was resting on it, with the butt end of his rifle on the ground.

Almost as one man all three of us saw it and the sergeant flung out one arm pointing and turned his head back towards us, shaking it violently up and down. There was something moving on the top of the hill there. And all three of us held our rifles as if a clay pigeon were about to go up and we must be alert to shoot it quickly. I got my finger inside the guard of the rifle and pressed the safety off. It was a man, all right, on the hilltop, and now another and another. Each was doing something purposeful, running a little way, crouching, dropping out of our sight. The figures were too small and black for us to see more than that they were men. At that second I was not tired and I could not feel my body at all. I felt very wideawake and alert. Then, as we watched, we could see below the figures on the skyline other figures climbing towards them. We had not been able to make them out before but these unmistakably wore khaki, and we could see the shape of their helmets against the gray of the hillside. We put down our rifles.

I looked up at the sky and it was quite light. I remembered suddenly how much I had wanted to smoke and I found the cigarettes in my pocket and lit one. It was four minutes after six. It was very still in the dawnlight. Some of the men who had come up and were resting under the rocks were already asleep in these few moments. They would rest there or sleep till they were told what was wanted of them next.

Then in the stillness, like a perfect accent to it, there came, clearly and each note perfect, the sound of a bugle call. it came up from beyond where the men were silhouetted against the skyline, and it echoed once or twice in the valley where we were and then, before the sound was over, the shooting began, up there and over near where sounds of the bugle came from. Captain Henry looked at me and I looked at him, and said, "Come on, let's go up there and see what's cooking."

# RUSSIAN WINTER, 1942

from
*Diary of a German Soldier*
by Wilhelm Prüller
Translated by H. C. Robbins Landon
New York: Coward-McCann, Inc., 1963

*The boys and young men who grew up in post–World War I Germany knew the hardships of unemployment and hunger. They were also psychologically affected by being the war's losers. Hitler's simplistic explanation was that the war had been lost because the army had been sold out by non-Aryans. Germans of pure Aryan ancestry were superior in every way, and once they ruled the world, there would be paradise on earth.*

*Hitler instilled pride and purpose in the German people; soldiers responded to his "manly man" approach. Each fighting man had a mission, and with each victory, he was convinced that Hitler was correct. Germans were superior. They were Aryan heroes who would return to family and job when it was all over, and they would rule the world.*

*In June 1941, Hitler invaded Russia. The German soldiers saw themselves as liberators, and as the* blitzkrieg *continued, the feeling of invincibility swept through the ranks.*

*Russian strategy involved giving up ground in exchange for time to take advantage of the Lend-Lease supplies pouring in from the United States and build an army. As German troops neared Moscow, Russian resistance stiffened, and with the aid of the frigid winter, the battle lines stabilized with little movement in any direction.*

*This diary of a German soldier shows the influence of Nazi propaganda in his deep conviction of his superiority and in the belief that it is a privilege to die for the Fatherland. The fanaticism induced by self-hypnosis saw many a Nazi soldier through the grim Russian winter. He fooled himself into believing that there was nothing wrong in not receiving his winter uniform and other equipment to combat the cold. He did not question why armored divisions served as infantry troops. He couldn't see that there was a food shortage even when he was prevented from feeding those Russians who served the troops.*

*Prüller was so carried away with his Hitlerian mission that he had the audacity to describe to a grieving young woman the death and burial of her fiancé—of which he had no knowledge—so that he might spread Nazi propaganda: "A woman's place is in the kitchen and producing children—victory means a new and greater Germany and the small sacrifice she has made will come back a thousandfold in benefits for all."*

*The diary gives us a chilling insight into the thinking and character of a Nazi soldier, a man who would do his utmost to destroy a nation and its people,*

155

*and in so doing, would help create a new kind of world where it would mean slav-
ery or death to all who did not fit the Aryan mold of the "superior race."*

## Thursday, 1st January 1942

During the past days—quite often in the nights, too—the Russians attacked,
but were beaten back. They advanced in such a silly way that the whole
thing looked more like a demonstration than an attack. They would stop on
the incline, apparently to rest, and made a wonderful target for our artillery. And
after the first few shots they would disappear over the brow of the hill again, running like stuck pigs.

So it was today. At first we thought it was their revenge for our New Year's
barrage yesterday; we shot off every gun we had at them, using every kind of munition. They may have thought we had left, but we taught them differently.

The snow is very deep, and it's cold—often 35 or 40 degrees below zero
[centigrade]. But we must put up with it.

## Sunday, 4th January 1942

We are to change our position again. A few kilometres to the right where we
are to relieve the 2nd Company, who in turn are to go farther to the right. We find
the billets aren't bad, each troop has its own house. The civilians are still here, too.
which is a great help. In Ivanovka, I picked up a nice dog, who had been lying for
days—perhaps even for weeks—in a barn. I called him Ivan: he ran away from me
twice, but I always managed to get him again.

I hope that this will be our permanent winter quarters. We could stick it here.
This part of the front isn't bad either; the Russians can come and attack us here if
they want to—they'll see what happens!

## 23rd January 1942

I have just learned that all leaves have been cancelled for the whole
Wehrmacht. Probably the deployment for the offensive has started rolling; and with
it we hope that we'll be relieved. I expect this to happen about the end of March.

## 30th January 1942

For days now we've been having a huge snowstorm. The thermometer often
drops to 43 degrees below zero [centigrade]. It's quite beyond praise what our listening posts, often way out in front on heights lashed by the snow and wind, go
through, also the scouting patrols, who climb about the whole night in no-man's-
land.

Time is working for us now. Every day. New reserves are coming up, new
troop concentrations (they don't get to us!), so that it wouldn't be such a mess if the

Russians broke through now. All the rumours that we are to be relieved in March and be moved to the south of France get stronger all the time. It was even talked of recently at one of the C.O.'s teas. March! That would be only eight more weeks.

## 1st February 1942

This winter is terribly hard. And it can go on a good 6 or 8 weeks. It's simply a miracle the way the supply and munition people work. No vehicle can get from here to Shchigry—that's seven kilometres. No horse wagons either, because the animals sink up to their rumps in the drifts. No sleighs, either. And yet everything arrives. Not even the railway between Kursk and S. is open, but everything moves like a well oiled clock. The miracle of German organization again! I wonder though if we shall ever see anything of the winter uniforms, furs, wool things, &c., which people donated back home. Actually, we've managed to get through the winter all right up to now. If it doesn't get a lot worse, we can take it.

## 11th February 1942

If anyone had said to me in the summer that we would spend the winter in Russia, I would have said he was mad. We, an armoured division, who have been at the front the whole time, without vehicles and defending the whole winter? I would have bet anything that this wouldn't be possible.

And now February is almost finished, the winter is nearly at an end, and here we still are! Moreover, we've stood it marvellously up to now. The cold doesn't bother us any more, we've got used to it. Thirty-eight degrees or 40 degrees below? That's nothing. The worst was 43 degrees below.

The two retreats we went through were really shitty, but now we can understand better the morale of the Russians when they are chased hundreds of kilometres, often without food and without any hope whatever of getting in the ring again. We pulled back 40 km. and were quite desperate. And we've held fast for weeks now: the front is solid now.

## 12th February 1942

Wind, rain and warm weather has set in now. It's certainly not the end of the winter, but it's a sign that spring can't be far off. And then we'll roll on again, towards the east. Whether we'll be with them isn't clear as yet, but whether it's we or others the enemy will be chased, encircled, beaten, destroyed. Stalin and Co. will be awaiting the spring with horror. It'll be the beginning of the end for them.

*England will fall.* A long time ago the Führer made this prophetic announcement. Are there better days than now to confirm these three words? The Philippines, Hong Kong, Singapore, Burma, Borneo, Java, Celebes, Sumatra! The empire is cracking, breaking up. A whole kingdom will fall. And not National Socialism. That's the way the cards lie. What does it matter, our getting leave, being relieved, or no leave and further advance? The victory must be ours. All of us must serve this goal: every last man!

We've got our own tame house-partisan girl, who comes every day at 08.00 and works till 17.00. She never had food like that which our kitchen provides.

## 14th February 1942

Today orders come to have the civilians evacuated—for the umpteenth time. Probably somebody at the top level got the bright idea that we could be lapping up all the available food ourselves if the civilians weren't there.

Well, that order has been in effect a long while, but the inhabitants always returned, we quietly allowed this; for they heat for us, fetch water, wash for us, even bring milk from the two cows—well, and after all among the 230 men there are some who can't stand it without having female flesh about, even if it's Russian flesh. And so after a time we had them all over our necks.

Now the Herr General has put through the order himself. There isn't very much we can do to get out of it now. But the order was carried out as follows: the Herr Bataillonskommandeur allowed that each Company could keep three families who were to be used for work, and that each member of the family was to receive a permit signed by the Company C.O. Three families? That's not very much in relation to the needs of a Company. But: *we* put the families together ourselves! Nine inhabitants—men and wife—are included in one family, they all get their permit and each of them is called Ivanov. The next nine are called Baranova; and the others Vassiliev.

## 23rd February 1942

A long time ago a letter to an unknown soldier of the Company arrived in which a girl asked to have information about her dead fiancé. No one wanted to answer it, because there's no one here any more who was there when he fell. Thus the letter wandered about from one to the other till it finally landed in my lap. I wrote her the following letter:

Dear Mitzi Trunka,

After various detours I received your letter to an unknown soldier of the Feldpost No. 13694; no one dared to answer it. And I can't really blame anyone, for none of the Kameraden who were near your fiancé when he met his hero's death is with the Company anymore. He fell on 4th August in the great battle of Uman, as the Company was attacking Ternovka, and lies buried with other Kameraden who fell there in Tishkovka, 50 km. north-east of Uman. A shot in the lung robbed him of his life at the very height of his power. The death was immediate and without pain.

Believe me Fräulein Trunka, that I understand only too well how much you miss your beloved fallen man. But you are a German girl; and as such you are as enthusiastic about our fight for the life or death of our people as all of us who are here on the front. Later in your life, in a quiet hour, when you have your own family, you will remember with thanks beyond measure all the victims which this gigantic battle has demanded, and will demand. It is they, and only they, who will have saved us and our children from a life of degradation and shame, of distress and desperation.

I know that it is easy to speak of the sacrifice which the relatives of those who fell must take upon themselves, when one does not have to bear the brunt oneself; but as I think, so does each of us here. And every one of us is sure that the grain that is sown will one day be reaped.

Just as we here are proud to have taken part in this great fight, so you, Fräulein Trunka, must be proud to have made such a heavy sacrifice for this fight. It was not, it shall not be in vain! Your Martin shall be avenged! The survival of our great Fatherland, our imperishable people, and the victory over our accursed enemies shall have been accomplished partly through his death.

In our remembrance of the fallen Kameraden left behind I include you too, Fräulein Trunka; and greet you in sincere sympathy.

Long live the Führer!<br>Prüller

## 26th February 1942

After a cold day, snow and wind have set in again; immediately all the roads are full of drifts, the streets impassable. Let's hope that these are winter's last throes. We have finally received official confirmation—from Battalion—that we shall be pulled out of here in April. We are supposed to go back to Germany or Roumania and rest, and then to go to Turkey. It doesn't matter where so long as it's far away from this Russia. And back home again? That would be best of all.

Yesterday three deserters from the farm-house opposite us came over. The morale over there is very low; most of them would like to desert, but the commissar is standing behind them. They get little food, and that at rare intervals, but plenty of munition. Most of them are from penal colonies with ten or more years in front of them, and they are badly trained and equipped. A funny set-up. Well, it doesn't matter so long as they keep quiet.

Whatever the commissars tell them, they believe almost entirely; that we're about to collapse, that we're starving, that we would run like rabbits if they attacked, that we shoot all prisoners, that the Russians have 26 batteries (!) in Leshinki, that an armoured battalion of the Russians is advancing, etc., etc., etc. They're so silly! If they only dreamt what's going to happen to them in a few weeks!

Today we got a new gun, with a barrel out of cardboard. Don't laugh, it's *really* made out of cardboard. And it shoots, too—as far as two kilometres. The bullets are propaganda bombs which comprise more than 100 leaflets; at 2,000 metres, about 1.5 metres above the earth, they are spread all over the earth. Isn't that fabulous?

An important factor in this war thus appears on the horizon: propaganda. And in that respect, too, we beat the Russians, in fact we're miles ahead of them We've got a Goebbels, after all!

159

The mail is working, at least more or less, again; of course we're never satisfied with it and always think it could be improved.

## 16th March 1942

In the night of the 12th and 13th a snowstorm began and went on till this morning. We'd never seen anything like it. You couldn't see ten steps. If you had to go from one hut to the other, it was a real fight to get there. The huts were snowed in, right to the straw roofs.

In our hole it was so cold that we stood round the stove in furs—fur hats and ear muffs, gloves, two or three blankets and a fur; and it was still so cold you couldn't stand it. The wind whistled through the nooks and crannies and it was grim. It was a real Russian winter. If that had gone on for a few weeks, it would have been a pretty mess. And today everything was normal again. Our supplies, and even the long-awaited mail, is to arrive, and in Shchigry they will have mail tomorrow, also tidbits (Schnaps, cigarettes, &c.) How *do* they do it?

*On March 22, 1942, Wilhelm Prüller went on furlough. He spent his time with his family, in Germany, and returned to the Russian front April 29, 1942.*

## 20th May 1942

For some days now we have been having a near tropical heat wave. We're running round in bathing-trunks.

## 3rd June 1942

Today the C.O. of the new unit arrived. The infantry is to take over our positions in the night, and we are to leave tomorrow morning. We were five months in Semenovka—with many attacks, many small victories. We stood it, our first Russian winter. Will there be another? These huts and bunkers, these trenches, they were our home during this period. None of us can ever forget this hole. Despite all the difficulties, we felt well here—it was *our* place. And thus we take leave with curiously mixed feelings

## 19th June 1942

Big excitement for days now. We've been anxiously waiting, for since Monday we were supposed to move to our troop concentration-rendezvous. But it seems that the weather has put a spanner in the works, for it's rained without stopping for some time now. And anyone can picture the way the roads look—one single sea of mud. So it will certainly take some time before we go into action. We are reported to be the first unit which will advance.

## 22nd June 1942

It can only be a matter of days before we go into action. What's moving on our road alone is something fantastic—column upon column, artillery, infantry, new weapons (are they smoke mortars?), supply—without pause. On every road and cart-track.

## 23rd June 1942

We are filled with a proud, thankful emotion, for again we are to be the first to leap at the Soviets. At last we are again in our element, as attackers, as breathless pursuers. Thus it is we who are taking the initiative, Mr. Stalin. And neither you nor your beasts can stop us. The coming days will prove it.

If only the weather is good to us.

## 27th June 1942

If no orders to the contrary arrive before 18.00, the operation begins tonight. A burst of fire from the heavy guns—supposedly at 02.15—will give the sign for us to cross the Tim River. The dinghies are already lying in camouflaged positions and will be brought by Pioneers to the river's edge. Everyone has to rush across the Tim in double quick time, of course, and we have as our first target Nish. Dolgoe, as our second the edge of Gratschewka and as our third the heights to the south.

It is a warm moonlit night. The men up front move as silently as cats, and the 8.8 flak boys push their gun just as silently into position. Occasionally a noncom swears at one of his men when he lights a cigarette too carelessly, but otherwise the silence is almost corpselike.

To the right of us are two large red stone buildings. They stand on the Tim, lonely, and don't fit in at all, right in the middle of the countryside—they were once schools. Between the bushes you can see, here and there, the small glittering band which is the Tim. Tim! End of the year 1941, beginning of the year 1942! How much blood has flowed along your banks in the last half year! How often have you changed owners? Soon the change will be permanent, however, and no Russian soldier will ever shoot on your banks.

## Sunday, 28th June 1942

At 02.15 the artillery corps let off their first shot, and in that same instant, as the shell was winging its way towards the Russian installations, the heavy guns start a barrage the like of which none of us in the whole Battalion has ever heard before. Guns of every sort and calibre, batteries without number, spew their deadly shells at the enemy bank. The 8.8 flak barks, the 2 cm. flak .chatters, the heavy mortars roar, the artillery thunders—all in rapid-fire confusion. In between, the bombs of our new weapon howl—the rocket mortars (something like our "Stuka zu Fuss").

161

In the midst of this roar, the men are crossing the Tim with their little rafts in feverish haste. We are attacking on a broad front: many, many divisions are moving simultaneously across the Tim. Hundreds of thousands can now move again after the banishment of the winter, can move eastwards; we are so happy about it.

I'm still on this side of the Tim, clearing the Platoons so they can cross quickly at the appointed time. When the last Platoon hits the rafts, I rush into the water, and jump into one, already overfilled; but before I can even grasp what's happening, I'm on the other side.

The Companies are still lying in a protected position. We collect everyone and then move off towards Nish. Dolgoe, a village about 1½ km. from here; its capture is our first point of attack. The land is bathed in a thick fog, because of the many mortar, artillery and bomb hits, as well as the smoke-screen. You can't recognize anything at 20 feet.

All about us is still an ear-splitting, gigantic racket, shot after shot, the scream of rockets kicked off by rocket mortars, a never ending inferno. Meanwhile, we've fallen in, stormed across the enemy artillery and mortar fire, got through, as if by a miracle (or was it my nose?) the Soviet minefields, and landed in the middle of a Russian ditch shielded by a row of bushes. It's not easy to know where to make for now, because the fog doesn't allow you any sense of direction: people from another Company run past us—they belong over to the right—infantry tears right through our middle—they belong more towards the left—and at the beginning we are too far to the right ourselves, but during the actual attack we all got to our proper assigned places.

In another ditch which we are using to get out of the enemy fire, we find 70 or 80 Bolsheviks who have to be mowed down, driven off or taken prisoner. A man-to-man fight takes place, and only very few Soviets get away alive. We have some losses too, though: the best and most conscientious young chap I ever met in this war, our medical orderly, Gefreiter Handler, was badly wounded; several other popular men have been knocked out, too. In our neighbour Company the indestructible Lt. Näser fell—a wonderful chap. Now he lies at the Tim...

We reached our first target, Nish. Dolgoe, or rather the place where it used to stand, up till a few hours ago. The few wooden huts were blown to smithereens by our rocket mortars. Tiny remains—a few strong wooden beams and bits of household equipment—are all that's left. Frightened civilians, crawling out of the cellars, the fear of death in their eyes, weeping children, grown-ups shaking with fear, the apathy of the very old ones—that was Nish. Dolgoe. Dear God, we thank Thee that this war must not be fought on German soil.

The next target—Gratschewka—is now before us. First we must get to the south-east entrance. In a broad skirmishing line we attack again, comb the place, and have to use all our combined forces to root out some of the enemy who fight to the end in their fox-holes. But we're moving up fast. On past the Soviets, beaten and marching to the rear, past the dead, past trenches and bunkers, past enemy gun emplacements which they abandoned in an attempt to save their skins. We hardly waste a look: on, on, that's the motto.

Across hollows and valleys, over hills and rises, the forward troops wiping out pockets of resistance, and at a gallop we tear across a piece of land raked by enemy fire and reach our second target.

Then on to the third target, the hills south of Uspenskoye. It's only a few metres from there to the railway line Kursk-Voronezh and a few kilometres to Marmyzhi, the scene of such dreadful fighting in the second half of December 1941. How will it look now?

We push on, kilometre after kilometre. The Soviets seem to have withdrawn and as a result of our thrust to the southeast, we are now behind the Soviet echelons. It's oppressively hot, and we are sweaty, dirty, tired, and slowly getting hungry (it must be getting quite late). But on we go, on, on. I find myself remembering the first days of this war in Poland; they were similar. Again some tall wheatfields—I hate them so—have to be crossed. And it's curious (am I being silly?), I keep warning my men about mines, here 10 km. beyond the Tim.

Noon comes. And goes. On, on... Like everything in life, this march has an end, too. After 17 km., at 14:30, we finally reach the heights south of Uspenskoye. Hardly had I discussed all the steps to be taken—the C.O. is with the Battalion Orderly Officer over on the left wing—when it happened.

Suddenly an explosion very near to me. No whining of the shell, no whistling, just the muffled cough of a mortar shell. Is it air pressure or instinct?

In a split second I'm on my belly, just in time for a second explosion. My head roars inside, and I think my eardrums have burst. What's happened to me? I feel my skull—it's all right. Fine, in fact. Chest—nothing. Hands—nothing. I can move the upper part of my body. Legs—the trousers at the knee are ripped to pieces. Blood comes from the left. I'm wounded.

After three years at the front, after four campaigns, I've got mine.

I could weep with rage. Now, when we're moving again at last, when we could really ram our way eastward, something like this has to happen. Carefully, because I secretly hope that nothing serious has happened, I examine my left leg. Blood is pouring out of the knee. So it's a splinter.

I turn my leg over, but the splinter won't come out, it's sitting inside. Oh-oh! A medical orderly from infantry who got separated from his outfit, and whom I took along with us till he could be sent back via Battalion, bandaged me. I can't bend my knee. What will happen? Suddenly the worst thing occurs to me—you'll lose that leg! No, no! Then: it'll be as stiff as a board. Frightful.

After a while Lt. Schemm comes along. He's beside himself. Who shall take my place? I suggest my old Kamerad, Mayer II. Agreed. I have him come to me so that I can explain everything to him.

So: there's Mayer. Well, the daily reports are like this... here's my notebook with the leaves for everyone worked out.

"Hey, Prüller, Oberfeldwebel Heindl is wounded too, you can go with him."

"Yes, yes, just a minute. Now look, here is where the secret stuff is... munition... the supply..."

"Prüller, come on, will you?"

"The vehicles you'll have to... petrol. ... Now, another thing, you've got to take a scouting party into the woods and..."

"Dammit, Prüller, shift your arse over here..."

"Wait a second, for Christ's sake. ...now, don't forget to put in these promotion lists ... and ... and ..." There was so much I should have said.

Lt. Schemm wants to cheer me up, he says the splinter will be removed at the first-aid station and I can stay here with the Company. But I knew what a knee splinter meant. A Steyr is all ready for us, with two other wounded men aboard—Heindl and Pfc. Töpl from our 4th Platoon. With the medical orderly's help I manage to limp a few steps, then I'm through.

With a painful twist in my heart, I take leave of this wonderful Kameradschaft, in which I was bound to this Company for 3½ years, I take leave of the front. Shall I experience it again? God be with you, my dear 6th, may soldier's luck be with you always.

The main first-aid station is set up in several large tents. It takes some time till my turn comes. I get a real deal—my leg in a splint and one injection against tetanus and a shot of morphine against the pain. Then I'm taken to one of the large tents to await evacuation to the rear.

## 29th June 1942

It was an awful night. The splint allowed me to sleep only on my back, and in that position I can't sleep. Enemy bombers worked over us the whole night. Some bombs dropped dangerously near to us. That would be the ticket, to be wounded again here! Heindl, who had numerous splinters extracted, bears his pain with admirable calm.

Next to me is a *Feldwebel* from the 377th Infantry. He has a shot in the chest and lies in his own vomit. It has been raining since yesterday evening, and there's no hope of our getting away. The ambulance would get stuck in Shchigry, and that's 40 or 45 km. away. Thank God, I've still some cigarettes.

## 30th June 1942

Today we're supposed to leave in the early hours. If this proves to be true, I shall write it up later.

Later. That was a frightful trip from here to Shchigry. The huge holes in the roads keep making the vehicle rock, and we inside were more in the air than on our stretchers. We kept yelling "ow" at him, but the driver couldn't do anything but keep going at that tempo; otherwise we would have got stuck in the mud. We were relieved to get to the Army Hospital at S., but we weren't even taken out of the ambulance; they took down our particulars right on the street, and then sent us off to the station. A provisional hospital train—goods wagons with some straw on the floor—was standing on the tracks ready to leave. For Kursk. When we got there, on to Konotop. In Konotop, it was on to Gomel.

My knee hurts rather a lot, and in the night I took off the splint; but then I couldn't stand it. The trip seemed endless. Some of us were taken off in Kursk, others in Konotop. They were so badly wounded, the poor things, that they couldn't have stood the trip any further. Finally we arrived at Gomel at noon of 2nd July. There we were taken on stretchers to the Casualty Collecting Centre which is right at the station. Our bandages were changed, and the next day we were off again, in another provisional hospital train—but much better than before. We had straw sacks, at least, and a nurse in each car. The Red Cross took care of us at every station. We could not possibly eat and smoke everything they gave us.

On 5th July we arrived in Warsaw. They took me to the hospital in the Dobrastrasse. Right away we got deloused and bathed (that was marvellous). They gave me a new splint, much more comfortable than the old one. I felt as if I had been reborn: lying, washed, in a clean white bed, fresh linen, a wireless set in the room, attentive nurses—it was like a dream.

The X-ray pictures showed that the splinter was in two sections, and both the little things are stuck in my bones. I don't have any more pain, but I can't sleep—the damn splint.

Our stay in Warsaw, as planned, was not for long. As soon as you are capable of being moved, you go to Germany in a hospital train. The first time I had to give in—the train was going to Dresden. Meanwhile the splint was removed and I got a plaster cast. A day later I had to prepare to leave, and on the 9th in the evening I was on a train bound for the right destination—Vienna! In the night of the 11th we arrived in Vienna at the Aspangbahnhof. The next morning at 08.00 we were taken off, and when I got my hospital orders I almost fainted—Boltzmanngasse in the 9th district, ten minutes from my home! I managed to get the ambulance (it was one of the Vienna city vehicles) to go past my house and let my wife know I had arrived.

They decided not to operate, otherwise my knee would have remained stiff. Whether I shall ever regain its full use is doubtful; time will tell.

On the 30th (July) I received an airmail letter from Battalion in which I was informed that I had been decorated with the Iron Cross 1st Class. On 1st August I went out for the first time. I could barely move my knee.

*The American Red Cross provided no assistance to the German armed forces or civilian population during WWII. The German Red Cross was run by the Gestapo during WWII, and because of that was not recognized as part of the International Red Cross. The American Red Cross cannot say for certain that Red Cross societies in neutral countries (e.g., Sweden and Switzerland) provided no humanitarian assistance in Germany. The ICRC was involved in help for POW's, both Allied and German, but mainly in transmittal of parcels and letters, and exchanges.*

# 4
# The War at Sea

## BATTLE FOR THE PHILIPPINES

from
*South from Corregidor*
by Lieutenant Commander John Morrill, U.S.N.
and Pete Martin
New York: Simon and Schuster, 1943

*For the Japanese, the road to Corregidor, the last American bastion in the
Philippines, lay through Bataan. With the fall of Manila, enemy troops poured
into Luzon, while enemy planes pounded American and Filipino forces.
Thousands of Japanese troops marched towards Bataan aided by trucks, guns,
and tanks.*

*It was important to Japan to clean out all resistance in the Philippines as
quickly as possible. The islands formed the last barrier to Australia, the
Netherlands East Indies, and India, and Japan desperately needed those countries' natural resources to fuel its conquest of the rest of Asia.*

*As America concentrated upon the war in Europe, there were no supplies to
replace expended materials, no replacements to refill depleted ranks. The U.S.
had only ten P40 pursuit planes in the area: clumsy, slow-moving planes that
were no match for the Japanese Air Force. Hospitals and first-aid stations ran out
of medical supplies. Food and water were rapidly consumed. Guns fell silent as
ammunition gave out. The war of attrition bore fruit.*

*The Japanese marched on in the Philippines. Large fires could be seen at
night where they gathered their dead and burned them. But always there were
more Japanese soldiers, more arms, more trucks—always advancing.*

*As the Japanese smashed through the faltering defenses of Bataan, many
American soldiers tried to escape through the wooded hills. Others, using small
boats, tried to reach Corregidor, the rock fortress off the Bataan Peninsula guarding the entrance to Manila Bay. Those who made good their escape before the
American lines collapsed found Corregidor only a brief reprieve.*

*The Japanese placed their heaviest guns in the mountains of Mariveles on*

*Bataan, and on Cavite, and fired almost point-blank at the defenses of Corregidor, intending to silence all the gun emplacements in forts Hughes, Mills, Drum, and Frank and to destroy their barbed-wire enclosures. Slowly all the gun emplacements on the rock were silenced, and the barbed-wire entanglements destroyed. Fresh supplies were unavailable. Ammunition and food dwindled away.*

*After the fall of Manila, the U.S.S.* Quail *had been assigned to sweep mines seaward from Corregidor and to act as a watchdog to see that no Japanese forces sneaked up on the "Rock." The minesweepers attracted Japanese dive bombers, and the planes, insistent and accurate, met no opposition. The ships' crews were removed during daylight hours and slept in a cave in the "Rock" to avoid the constant heavy shelling. At night, skeleton crews took the ships out to perform their duties—as long as the fuel held out and the ships were in running order.*

*Lt. Commander Morrill's story of the last days of Corregidor's defenders paints a grim picture of the defeat that was to come.*

For three days and nights we worked dismounting the *Quail*'s guns and transporting them over to Corregidor. The Army Ordnance and the marines built mounts for them, and the sailors who had served them on shipboard went ashore to man them or teach somebody else how to do it.

Those of the crew who were left on board tried to cut the channel at night and sleep in the tunnel by day. We had spent so much of our time blacked out we had learned to live and work in darkness. Many of the sailors were so used to not seeing what their hands were doing they could handle a repair job by feel. They had literally trained themselves to see with their fingers.

Being under special orders, I had divided my crew into halves and used part of them on this work and the other part on the mine-sweeping chore. We lost the mine sweeper *Finch* on the eleventh of April, and the Commandant decided to disarm the others while we still had something to disarm.

On the eleventh we had anchored in such fashion that we served as a marker at the end of the channel we were sweeping. The *Tanager*, having no definite place to berth, chose the middle of South Harbor. The *Finch* picked out a spot close up against the sheer cliff of Caballo Island, where there was deep water within a stone's throw of land. She figured that dive bombers couldn't get at her there because they couldn't zoom down over Caballo. But on that same day heavy bombers gave Caballo a hell of a going over and in doing so some of the bombs spilled over the cliff and wrecked the *Finch*. When she sank she lay up against the island, all ripped apart.

We sent two-thirds of our machine guns ashore but were allowed to keep our three-inch guns. When the unloading was done, two-thirds of the men who had been doing it were ordered to stay on Corregidor at the disposal of the Army and help form a final defense man-power reserve.

Just before dawn every morning we went over to the Rock to make a full report of the progress we had made during the night.

Then I'd either try to sleep in the tunnel or climb up high on the rocks of Malinta Hill, where the marines had machine-gun dugouts. The thing I remember most vividly about them is the way they sighted along the barrels of their machine guns, figuring how many Japs they could mow down with the ammunition they had. They were very happy with the heavy machine guns we sent them from the ship, only they were a little rough in handling them. We had to lend them gunners' mates to teach them about the upkeep of the intricate parts.

A little farther down Malinta Hill there were emplacements with seventy-five-millimeter beach-defense guns, manned by marines and serviced by soldiers commanded by Lieutenant Crotty. It was a good fighting team and held a key position overlooking Monkey Point. Later on, when it was wiped out by artillery fire and the last submarine brought no replacement guns for it, we knew Corregidor was going to fall.

Whenever I could, I let my men sleep on the *Quail*. I had found out that after two or three days in the tunnel they got a disease which, for want of a better word, I called "tunnelitis." Feeling safe for the moment and huddling in tight sweaty groups with other men who felt temporarily safe, they let down their guards mentally. I sent brave men into the place, and after they had been exposed to whatever evil thing the tunnel did to them, they came back to the ship and sat and shivered on her decks, their nerves jangling at finding themselves out in the open again, with no rock roof over them.

I've read a lot about the Army tunnel but I haven't read much about the hole bored in the rock the Navy lived in. Because of the long dry spell and Jap high explosives, the dust was so thick in it, it was almost impossible to breathe. You sat in it and gasped for air. Flies were all over the place, little black ones that bit like mosquitoes. When you couldn't stand it any longer, you went outside, even during heavy shellfire, to fill your lungs with deep inhalations of something untainted and dust-free. A lot of men were killed just trying to breathe. Our latrine was a makeshift wooden affair with a shed roof over it, approximately fifty yards outside the tunnel. About the middle of April a bomb landed a few yards away from it. One of our men was in it occupying one of its lowly thrones, and when the dust settled we could see him sitting there still alive, but frozen into a horrified statue, with the debris draped around his neck. He was shell-shocked and dazed and suffered from concussion but was unhurt. Someone ran out and grabbed him and dragged him back into the tunnel, and it was hours before he realized what had happened or before anyone felt like laughing.

The piping for the tunnel sewage was impromptu, and the humidity made the place like a Turkish bath. The walls were always sweating and damp. The average temperature inside was around 98 degrees. When a bomb landed at the tunnel mouth, the concussion blew dust and trash right through the place from one end to the other. There was a makeshift ventilating system, but its main function was to pump dust-fouled air into an already dust-fouled place.

Corregidor had supplies for a protracted siege, but, not knowing how long a session we were in for, we were put on one-third rations after Bataan fell. Up to that time my crew on the *Quail* had made out better than the Bataan troops. But afterward, we turned our chow into the common pool and began to live on canned salmon and rice, twice a day. Even after that, we were still in better shape than most of the others, because our pharmacist's mate had been farsighted enough to lay in a store of vitamin pills before the war, and we had been throwing them into the crew like popcorn whenever we got a chance.

During the next few weeks, the Japs perfected their plan of controlled fire. They would put their guns on one spot on Corregidor until they had the range exactly. Then they wouldn't use those particular guns any more until the final assault. They did this again and again, so that when the last attack broke they must have had from three to four hundred guns trained on the Rock's vital spots. Also, by keeping their guns quiet after they had located their final targets, they could avoid counterfire.

During this process the Rock's twelve-inch guns were hit over and over again by direct hits from six-inch guns, but each time what was left of the gun crews picked themselves up to find that, aside from minor damage to the breech blocks, they could keep on firing a little longer. Gradually these guns were put out of action, until by the fifth of May there were only about two big guns still left on Corregidor and one on Caballo. The beach-defense guns, which were our main protection against barge-borne Jap landing parties, were used up one by one and abandoned. The Jap routine was one of creeping attrition. Our ships went the same way—one by one and little by little. Bombs got some of them, but most of the real knockout punches came in the form of shells from Cavite. There wasn't much we could do about it, since most of our ships were empty of oil.

To save fuel we didn't move the *Quail* during the day and used what oil we could spare to shift her out to the mine field at night. Our original idea had been to do our mine sweeping by day as well as by night, but we soon gave it up. On April 11, the *Quail* suffered three hits. It occurred to us then, as it should have before, that if the Japs could see us well enough to hit us, they could also see us well enough to figure out what we were doing over at the edge of the mine field. After that, we worked only at night, sweeping a channel four hundred feet wide. By May 3, we were ready to start widening it out to six hundred feet. That morning, however, the Commandant told me to have my men take a rest that night. We were in the groove now as far as that work was concerned and had almost grown to count on it as something regular and dependable in a confused and chaotic world. I was taken aback at his order and asked "why."

"Turn in and take a sleep," the Commandant said. "I'll tell you why later."

I grabbed my sleep and went back prick-eared for the "why." By that time he was ready to tell me. A sub was coming in to evacuate a group of nurses and officers from Corregidor, and the Commandant wanted me to pilot a boat through the channel we had swept through the mine field and ferry the group who were going out to the sub. He gave me the time and location and impressed upon me the need for secrecy about the undertaking. The thing was very hush-hush. The officers and nurses were given only one hour to pack and get ready to go.

After sunset, my passengers collected on the South Harbor Dock. The nurses wore khaki pants and shirts and dark-blue capes. They were calm and cool and talked very little. You don't feel like talking much when you're leaving behind you people you've known and worked with and grown close to, through common suffering, for a long time.

Thirteen nurses, sixteen officers, and one civilian and his wife herded into the little pilot steamer assigned to the job. Under my guidance, the steamer captain, a young ensign, picked his way gingerly through the hole we had bored through the mines.

Once we were through the opening, I told the passengers about it, because I knew they were on edge and that was one worry I could relieve them of at least. Then we lay to, to wait for our pig-boat date to show up. Presently she loomed up through the murk, looking bigger than a cruiser. She was blowing the top off her main ballast tanks, like a steel-plated whale coming up for air, and she lay low in the water, with her decks barely awash.

I climbed up on top of the pilot boat's deckhouse, where I was on a level with the conning tower, and while our passengers were being transferred, the sub's skipper and I had a chat. He turned out to be a Lieutenant Dempsey.

I called out "Hello-o-o" to him, and he asked, "Who's that?"

"Merrill," I said.

I didn't know Dempsey, but apparently he knew me or had heard something about my having been a sub skipper like himself, and wondered why I was there.

"I'm just working here," I told him. "What did you bring us?"

"We didn't bring much," he said apologetically. "The crew took up a collection and we've got some cigarettes and candy for your men. We've been busy. We haven't seen daylight for four weeks but we got a Jap flat-top—handed her one in the bellyband and touched off her magazine—and we got a couple of transports too."

It was exciting news, but there were things we needed even more urgently than good news.

"Did you bring us any guns?" I asked, and he shook his head regretfully.

It had been a forlorn hope. Still I had to ask him. We were getting down to peashooters. We had one Navy anti-aircraft gun on Malinta Hill which had been removed from the *Houston* before she left Cavite. Practically single-handed, this gun had shooed the Jap dive bombers away from Corregidor and the ships until about a week before, when the Japs had planted a shell squarely on the Navy gun mount and wiped it out.

Dempsey looked around in the night and asked curiously, "Don't they ever do any shooting around here? I thought you were having a war."

It was a natural enough question. By some freak of luck he had surfaced during the first two hours in weeks when there wasn't a lot of heavy stuff going off and the air crack-cracking with shells and the crump-p-p of bombs. I explained to him about his good fortune. Then I tried to sketch the Jap patrol lines out for him between Olongago and Fortune Island and the patrol between Fortune Island and Nasugbu and told him how we were hemmed in by a complete circle of ships. Meantime the sub's men were shuttling our passengers down the sub hatches and showing the officers and nurses where to put the ten pounds of clothing they had been allowed. The sub crew gave our crew the cigarettes and candy, and we said good-by and good luck to each other. Ten minutes later we were nearing the channel entrance in the mine field, homeward bound.

The lone civilian who had been given permission to get out to tell his wife good-by was standing looking over the rail, his eyes straining back through the night toward the spot where the sub had vanished into the darkness. I tried to cheer him up, but he was beyond cheering.

"The hardest thing I ever did in my life," he said, "was to climb up that conning-tower ladder and leave her down there."

At the last minute his wife hadn't wanted to go, and her arms had to be removed from his neck by force.

Just as we entered the channel, the Japs opened up on Corregidor for the first time with their full-dress-rehearsal barrage, to see how well all those guns they had been carefully spotting for three weeks would do. Corregidor was immediately transformed from a towering shape shouldering up into the night into a rock of leaping, flickering fire. It was like a mammoth Fourth-of-July set piece going off. Shells were puncturing the night close to us on all sides. The Japs scored a hit on one of the largest magazines on Fort Mills, and it erupted like a volcano. A roll of flame rolled right down Government Ravine, a steep gorge thickly inhabited by sailors sent ashore from the *Canopus.*

The young ensign of the pilot boat made a gulping noise in his throat. "There go a lot of our boys," he said thickly.

Horror and the crushing sense of the enemy's overwhelming fire power, to which we had no adequate return, pushed down on us like a heavy weight.

We were supposed to anchor at South Dock, but South Dock was almost hidden by shell bursts and leaping spouts of flame. I remember I said, "Dempsey knows *now* whether or not they do any shooting around here. He can hear it out there even if he's submerged."

We decided to take the boat over and tie her up to the stern of the *Quail* and wait and see what happened.

"If this keeps up," the ensign said, "there won't be any Corregidor to go back to."

We hailed the *Quail,* but even where she lay, shells were splashing around and bursting fragments were banging against steel plates in the dark, racketing a boiler-factory refrain.

I knew the little pilot boat didn't have splinter protection, so I took everybody off her and put them on the *Quail*'s gun deck. Three hours later, as suddenly as it began, the barrage stopped, and I sent the little boat to its regular anchorage.

Dempsey's sub was the last one to get through.

During the latter part of January and the first part of February it had been still possible for supply ships to run the Jap blockade by coming up from Cebu at high speed, making the trip entirely by night except for the last few hours. When they arrived off the Lubang Island group about daylight, our lookouts, three hundred feet up on top of Corregidor, would see them and we'd send out one or more PT boats to escort them in.

But after the fall of Singapore, the Japs gave the Philippines more attention with their dive bombers and warships. They bombed Mindanao and picked off our supply ships just off the Lubang Islands, where some of them sank before the agonized eyes of our lookouts peering helplessly through their binoculars.

After that, when we were mine sweeping at night and when we were holed up during the day, we could see and hear dive bombers dropping loads of eggs over Bataan for more than two weeks after its fall. It was mute evidence that large or small groups of our men had somehow escaped the holocaust and had taken to the hills, where they were being hunted down. This was particularly true of the western hills of the peninsula overlooking the west coast, where our Philippine scouts had been stationed.

The dive bombers came so close we could actually see them thumb their noses at us, which was a trick I hadn't realized the Japs knew. There was, however, another trick that belonged peculiarly to them. For months bodies had been floating past us in the water, some of them our marines, some of them soldiers, but most of them Filipinos, with their arms tied behind them and their legs tied together too. These bodies had all been literally cut to pieces by bayonet stabs.

When you've seen such things with your own eyes, your feeling is a deep conviction that you aren't fighting men but animals with men's bodies and dressed in men's clothes, but with strange, slimy jungle growths where their brains ought to be. My own feelings about them hardened into an intense desire to kill them and a stinging regret I couldn't kill more. From what my men said in my hearing, they felt the same way, except that many of them had dedicated themselves more intensively to the idea than I had, if that were possible.

The Filipinos felt even more strongly about it than we did. In the early days of the war we were talking one day in the *Quail*'s wardroom about the possibility of capturing Japs. My executive officer and I jokingly promised our Filipino mess boys they could have our first prisoners.

Much later a Jap aviator had his plane shot out from under him and parachuted into the water just off Corregidor. Only Jap officers had parachutes. The common or everyday Jap pilot was supposed to die if he lost his plane. We sent a boat out to pick that Jap up if possible, and while the boat was away, the mess boys sidled up to Lee, the executive officer, and myself and asked, "Mr. Lee, can we have him?"

Lee had forgotten the kidding in the wardroom by this time and asked, "What are you talking about?"

"You and the Captain promised us we could have the first prisoner," they said.

Lee noticed they were holding their hands behind their backs in a peculiar fashion and asked them what they were concealing. Eyes glistening, they brought out two long, sharp carving knives. Fortunately, we didn't pick that Jap up. He was gone when our boat reached the spot where he was last seen, thereby saving Lee and me from long explanations as to why we couldn't carry out our promise.

You couldn't be too careful about those Jap pilots.

Earlier in the winter they had come flying in an American plane at our boats tied up in the harbor and had bombed the hell out of us before we snapped out of our surprise at seeing one of our own crates with our own silhouette and our own marking on it doing unpleasant things to us. It was an old 1936 army training job which probably had been sold to the Japs in the trusting days when we sent them scrap iron and oil and other items to help them get ready for Pearl Harbor. But we got that particular one and arranged for him to take a long, deep sleep on the Cavite shore. From then on we make it a standing rule that if any plane, no matter what it seemed to be, came at us head on and persisted coming at us, we'd throw up a burst or two of A.A. in front of him to warn him away, and if he acted bullheaded about it we really got down to business.

Notwithstanding, we looked up one day to see a little Philippine training plane heading in our direction. We tried him out with a burst in front. He swerved and flipped his wings but kept right on coming. The Jap we had piled up on Cavite had flipped his wings too, so that didn't mean anything to us. Next we nudged this trainer craft with three-inch stuff and bolstered that up with fifty-caliber. He went back toward Cab Cabin in a hurry, and the next thing we knew, a telephone call came through to headquarters to tell us for God's sake lay off, that General MacArthur was in the plane and please let him come home.

When he came back the second time we kept our fingers off our triggers, but his pilot abided by the rules this time and gave us a wide berth.

The fact that we were never reprimanded by our Commanding General for almost rubbing him out was characteristic of him.

That incident seemed a long time ago on May 4. The General was gone now, and that last submarine which had brought us nothing and had only taken some of us away was a blow from which we never recovered. Many of the officers and men were low in their minds about it. They felt that they could have made out so wonderfully with such a little more. If, for instance, we had only had a pompom to replace that one lost on Malinta Hill or two or three more beach-defense guns, it would have made all the difference in the world.

On May 4 we worked feverishly all night long and well into the morning hours to finish widening that channel, as it seemed inevitable that the *Quail* had only a few more hours left, since she was the only ship still in commission.

But the eyes on the hills no longer followed our efforts. On shore the marines had stopped talking about how long they were going to stick it and talked only of how many Japs they could get before they were rubbed out. The soldiers and sailors on Corregidor talked only of hunger and food.

On the afternoon of May 5, I was walking around and talking to the outpost on Malinta Hill. The Japs were after the *Quail* hot and heavy. Every few minutes a messenger came panting up the hillside to say that headquarters had sent him to tell me that the *Quail* was reported sunk. And each time I told the messenger to tell headquarters that the news of her sinking was premature. I was watching her from the top of the hill. I moved around so much I guess the messengers had a hell of a time finding me. We were supposed to be asleep, but, as tired as they were, most of the officers and crew couldn't keep their eyes closed. It twisted our insides to see the *Quail* lying out there so helpless against repeated Jap dive-bombing attacks, even if she was cold dead, without oil, and useless to us.

Some of the other men begged to be allowed to go out to her and man her two remaining machine guns. Headquarters said no but that maybe if she survived throughout the day they would say yes tomorrow. That was all we could do about it.

*At midnight of May 5, the Japanese began landing troops on Corregidor. In a few hours the island was surrendered and the 7,000 Americans, soldiers, sailors and marines, plus 5,000 Filipino soldiers, were herded into the garage area of Kindley Field. It was an area 100 yards square. The 12,000 men were kept on this concrete floor without food for a week. There was one water spigot for the 12,000 and a twelve-hour wait to fill a canteen was not unusual. After seven days the men received their first food ration—one mess kit of rice and a can of sardines.*

# BATTLE IN THE NORTH ATLANTIC

from

*A Bloody War:*
*One Man's Memories of the Canadian Navy, 1939-1945*
by Hal Lawrence
Toronto: Macmillan of Canada, 1979

*Before World War II, a Neutrality Act obliged President Roosevelt to embargo any shipment of arms to a belligerent nation. This policy proved more painful for the French and British than to Germany, for the Nazis were regenerating their war machine with captured materiel and the manufacturing facilities of conquered countries.*

*In November 1940, before the presidential election, Roosevelt announced, "Our policy is to give all possible material aid to the nations which still resist aggression across the Atlantic and Pacific Oceans." The following day, Wendell Willkie, his Republican opponent, said, "All of us—Republicans, Democrats, and Independents—believe in giving aid to the heroic British people. We must make available to them the products of our industry."*

*England placed orders for munitions in the United States separately from, though in consultation with, the American army and navy. The ever-increasing volume of English needs led to friction at some points despite general goodwill. Three days after his re-election, Roosevelt announced a "rule of thumb" for the division of American arms output. As weapons came off the production line they were divided roughly fifty-fifty between the United States, and the British and Canadian forces together. But how was all this to be paid for? The Lend-Lease*

Act would not be passed by Congress until March 1941. Before that time, all British purchases had to be on a cash-and-carry basis.

Britain had entered the war with about $6,500,000,000, but by November 1940, had paid well over $4,500,000,000 for everything it had received. The British now faced three problems. They were running out of money to buy machinery, food, and munitions, the delivery of the material they had paid for was running into serious trouble on the high seas, and the enemy was advancing on all fronts. The Lend-Lease law relieved the financial pressure on the British, but getting the material delivered was becoming increasingly difficult.

The Nazis' program produced forty submarines a month. These submarines travelled in packs, attacking convoys and sinking ships loaded with vital supplies. Much material was shipped through Canada to England in convoys that ran the open seas, taking the shortest route to avoid exposure to enemy submarines. The path was to Greenland, Iceland, and then Britain. German submarines hovered in packs along the coast of Greenland picking off the loaded ships. What prevented a complete debacle was the Canadian corvette, a ship about 150 feet long, with one or (at times) two 4-inch guns (one fore and one aft) and capable of discharging depth charges.

The corvette was a primitive warship, and the job it had to do was next to impossible—seeking out submarines, discouraging or sinking them, and rounding up straggling freighters and keeping them in formation. The men on the corvettes, as well as those on the steamers that carried the supplies, served well beyond the call of duty. Young and inexperienced, they went into battle without firearms and gave their lives to support a cause they felt was just. These sailors are unsung heroes, who received neither medals nor recognition for the extreme sacrifices and hardships they endured. The dead were buried at sea. The living, after a convoy was safely docked, moved onto another ship, and their war continued.

One of the men who served with the Canadian naval forces was Hal Lawrence. In 1941, young Lawrence was stationed on a corvette assigned to ensure the save arrival of a convoy to England. The dramatic story of his voyage follows.

On a louring night in September 1941 two Canadian corvettes, HMCS *Moose Jaw* and *Chambly*, butted through a threatening sea off Greenland's bleak eastern coast. Our senior officer, Commander Prentice, RCN, in *Chambly*, was convinced from a study of U-boat dispositions that an attack was forming on Convoy SC-42. He was correct.

SC-42 had departed Sydney, Nova Scotia, eleven days earlier. Sixty-four deep-laden merchantmen covered twenty-five square miles of sea and carried nearly a million tons of vital cargo: fuel, grain, phosphate, lumber, ammunition, and iron ore. The voyage started quietly, except that the surly North Atlantic was whipping itself up to its months-long winter fury.

The first day found the convoy in the Gulf of St. Lawrence. Slowly, clumsily, the ships formed up on Commodore MacKenzie in the leading ship of the centre column. The sea was choppy, the wind had an edge, the sky was clear. Night fell. HMCS *Napanee*, *Matapedia*, and *Chicoutimi*, the local escort, were grateful for the good weather and for the brilliant moon that illuminated an ever-present danger at this season. Two large icebergs towered skyward taller than the largest ship. SC-42 sailed between them. Three hours later fog closed in. Were there still bergs around? We had no radar to detect them. The submarine-detection set, called "asdic," might give an echo, but more often one had to rely on the feel of a sudden chill, or hear waves breaking against the base of a nearby berg. The second day passed.

On the morning of the third day the fog lifted, luckily; a few hours later a berg passed through the centre of the convoy, and a lone polar bear gazed at us forlornly. There was the mid-ocean escort ahead: the destroyer *Skeena*, and the corvettes *Kenogami*, *Alberni*, and *Orillia*. They would shepherd the valuable flock from now on. Here, off St. John's, Newfoundland, the Commodore shaped a northeasterly course to Iceland. The latitude grew higher, the days grew shorter, the weather grew vile.

On the fourth day easterly gales set in, and so did the misery. Convoy speed slowed, seven knots to six, six to five. These wallowing, ponderous merchantmen have little steerage-way at low speed and they straggle. Escorts race to the rear, ordering them to "keep closed up," then adjuring them, then imploring them, all to no effect.

In the navy, we were taught to manoeuvre at high speed in close formation, about twenty-six knots and just three hundred yards apart. I remember Captain Woodward cutting obliquely through the convoy, ahead of one merchantman, astern of the next. The merchant-service captain finds this a nightmare. He is used to chugging quietly around the world with a whole ocean to himself: if another ship should climb the rim of his horizon, she will pass courteously about five miles off. But in wartime convoys, a merchant captain is surrounded by lunging ships just a half-mile off; the course must be constantly adjusted, now a little to port, now a little to starboard. The engine speed is always changing, now a little faster because his ship drops astern, now a little slower because she forges ahead. Some ships will take sudden unaccountable sheers and everyone scrambles out of the way. At night the ships are blacked out. Instinctively a merchant captain will try to give himself a little more searoom, a little further astern of his proper station in the orderly ranks of the convoy. Oh yes, merchant ships straggle. And then a corvette comes yapping around their arses. Ignore the bastard!

On the fifth day the gale increased slightly. The sixth day was about the same. The convoy slowed to two knots. The seventh day it hove to, the ships barely keeping steerage-way. By the eighth day the discomfort was acute.

Under such conditions it is impossible to keep food on the galley stove. The bread grows green mould. The cockroaches pit-pat around the decks and bulkheads energetically. The rats grow bolder as they grow hungrier. Dry clothes are forgotten. In the foetid, crowded messdecks exhausted men sleep where they can—in the hammocks if they are lucky enough to have a slinging billet, on the lockers, on the deck. Wretchedly sick men—landsmen just a few months before—lie in their vomit until the bosun's-mate hauls them up to push them on watch again.

It is fatiguing to be always grasping a stanchion, a table edge, a door-jamb, and to make progress only by short, lurching steps from object to object. On the other hand, most of our sailors were around twenty, and at this age physical discomfort is lightly borne. Many were not seasick. There was pride, exhilaration even, in seeing a small ship beating a powerful adversary. The sea is neither cruel nor kind—it is indifferent. When you are young, much of life can seem so dreadfully mundane. But a North Atlantic gale—that is something to pit your strength against. You could discern a sort of rueful happiness in the crew, and they drew closer together.

On the ninth day the weather let up a little and the slow crawl to Iceland resumed. The tenth day found SC-42 southeast of Cape Farewell, Greenland. We would traverse the Denmark Strait.

Here the Commodore altered course to the north, up the Greenland coast. Plots showed an ominous concentration of U-boats across our intended track, but the diversion was in vain. On the eleventh day we were sighted by a patient U-boat captain.

A sighting-signal flashed to Dönitz; back came terse orders to U-boats forming the Greenland-to-Iceland barrier. One by one they slipped in silently for the kill. Some had many miles to steam but eight had the convoy in sight that night.

Towards the rear of the convoy SS *Jedmor* was straggling. She spotted a periscope, saw two torpedo tracks pass close ahead of her, and bleated the alarm. *Orillia* (Lieutenant Ted Briggs, RCNR) swept back and, although she gained no contact, kept the U-boat submerged. It would be many tedious hours before this U-boat could overhaul the convoy and threaten again.

Midnight and the start of the twelfth day marked the beginning of our travail. The blessed moon that revealed icebergs was now a cursed moon that illuminated ships like sitting ducks in a shooting-gallery. This day was forty-six minutes old when a dull "whump" told of a torpedo striking home. SS *Muneric* had time to sound the tocsin on her wireless and then plunged to the bottom, dragged down by her cargo of iron ore. There were no survivors.

Battle was joined.

*Kenogami* (Lieutenant "Cowboy" Jackson, RCNVR) wheeled and sighted the U-boat making off to the west. She gave chase, firing as she went; the U-boat dived, no asdic contact was gained, and *Kenogami* shaped course to rejoin the convoy.

The object of the escorting ships was not to sink submarines; rather, it was "the safe and timely arrival of the convoy." Revenge was not sought, but protection for those ships that remained. A U-boat driven away and forced under was, temporarily at least, impotent, and would remain so for perhaps twelve hours. When you were outnumbered two to one, this respite was priceless. But if you stayed too long to hunt one U-boat, another could slip through the gap left in the screen.

*Kenogami* rejoined. Commodore MacKenzie sighted another U-boat ahead of the convoy. A few minutes later two merchant ships sighted a fourth. Slowly sinking flares threw a ghostly radiance over the packed ships; lurid tracer from machine-guns pointed a fiery finger to a fifth U-boat entering the columns of ships from ahead. This one *Skeena* (Lieutenant-Commander Jimmy Hibbard, RCN) pursued. As *Skeena* flashed by the merchant ships, their skippers bawled through megaphones the whereabouts of the submarine.

Commodore MacKenzie executed an emergency turn of all convoy ships of forty-five degrees to port. What had been an open lane for *Skeena* suddenly became an impenetrable wall of towering ships' sides. Impenetrable? Well, nearly so. By wrenching the helm over, by using full-stern power, then full-ahead, then full-astern, Hibbard squirmed through—sometimes by only a few yards. Though under fire from four convoy ships, the U-boats were doing their damage. SS *Winterswijk* blew up; a few minutes later SS *Tahchee*, then SS *Baron Pentland* burst into flames. *Skeena*'s depth charges arched out on the approximate position and exploded masthead high. No result.

*Alberni* chased a sixth U-boat on the starboard beam. *Kenogami* searched the port beam. *Orillia* took the damaged *Tahchee* in tow. There was a lull. *Kenogami* and *Alberni* dropped back to pick up survivors. Time: 0400.

At 0510 another torpedo struck. Star shell sought out the enemy. Thirty minutes later the familiar "whump" came again. A ship on the starboard side sighted a seventh submarine. Torpedo after torpedo tore into ships' vitals. Despairing rockets begged for help, but little could be given. Burning ships glowed red and star shell drifting down cast an eerie white light. Fiery tracer stabbed out, now here, now there; some seconds later the angry chatter of a gun was heard. Constantly came the rumble of depth charges exploding and, periodically, the thud of German torpedoes as the dogs of war harried the near-helpless flock. Wreckage littered the water: boats, floats, rafts, some with wildly waving men clinging to them, others empty. It's hard to say how many men were in the water, but the dull red flicker of the lights on their lifebelts seemed everywhere. Some men lolled limply, heads flopping. Some shouted weakly, hopefully, as an escort approached, and they yelled despairingly as she swept by. "The safe and timely arrival of the convoy" was the overriding consideration and an attack could not be broken off to rescue survivors.

On the convoy front, six miles across and on flanks of three miles each, the escorts fought on as best they could. By dawn, SS *Empire*, *Springbuck*, *Stargaard*, *Sally Maersk*, and *Empire Hudson* had plunged to the bottom.

The forenoon was filled with alarms, periscope-sightings, torpedo tracks, attack, and counter-attack. At 1445, SS *Thistleglen* was hit; *Skeena*, *Kenogami*, and *Alberni* searched the area. The rattle of machine-gun fire drew them astern.

A periscope! *Skeena* lunged for a pounce attack. The periscope coolly surveyed the situation for twenty seconds and then quietly slid down. Charge after charge rained down on the U-boat, held now by asdic. A large bubble of air rose to the surface, along with some oil. Asdic contact faded. A probable hit? A possible anyway. No time to wait, though; the convoy was unguarded. The three escorts bucked head seas back to their flock. There were no stragglers now. Dusk fell.

My captain in *Moose Jaw* was Lieutenant Frederick Grubb, RCN, the only pre-war officer on board. He regarded his officers with gloom, but also with the enthusiasm of a dedicated teacher who hoped to get his backward boys out of the primary grades.

The night before, I had had to call him because I lost contact with *Chambly*; she was guide and we were to keep station on her. I flogged around the ocean for thirty minutes before I told the Captain. That made it worse, and it was an hour

179

before he got me back on station. The night before that, it was the opposite. I was too close, close enough to make his experienced eye stare in horror while mine was tranquil with the ignorance of one who has never heard the grinding, tearing, and shrieking of metal in the agony of collision.

The twelfth day had not yet ended. About 2130 the Captain said, "I'm going to get my head down." (He never slept: he either got his head down or put his feet up.) "Aye aye, sir," I replied.

"About one-two-oh revolutions should hold her."

"Aye aye, sir."

"You shouldn't need to alter more than five degrees to keep station."

"No, sir."

"Zigzag Eleven we're doing. You're familiar with that one?"

"Aye, sir."

"You've read my night orders?"

"Yessir."

He paused. Was there anything else? There was so much else, but my training would take years. There was nothing he could do tonight. He sighed and went below. The rigging creaked rhythmically. The bow wave hissed. All serene.

We jogged along comfortably enough for ten minutes, then the radio telephone (RT) blurted a message from *Chambly*: "Have good contact; am attacking." She veered to port. I followed. I heard a dull thud, and felt a tremor run through the ship. Two white rockets streaked up ahead. *Chambly* said, "Submarine." I rang "Action stations." Four more white rockets to port. Star shell blossomed ahead in a sector search. Fireworks galore! A tanker was hit: the flame mounted. *Chambly* said "Firing now." and "thuck thuck" went her depth-charge throwers. Snowflake flares were everywhere, bright as day. The RT was a babble of messages; the ocean surface boiled white and soapy. A black metal snout reared out—U-501!

Just then the Captain arrived and in a tone of honest exasperation demanded, "Lawrence, what are you doing?"

Water streaming from her sides, U-501 set off in the general direction of Germany. We gave chase, the Captain manoeuvring to ram. With our primitive weapons this was the surest way for a kill; a corvette in exchange for a U-boat was a bargain. A white light blinked from the U-boat bridge; could it be the night identification signal? Could she be friendly? Impossible! What was the correct identification? Where was the signalman? The Captain was altering around now. Where was the bloody signalman? He arrived with a damp and grubby bit of paper and we peered at it in a dim light. Was the submarine one of ours? No!

The Captain roared, "Stand by to ram." U-501 altered away and we were staring up her stern tubes. The Captain eased over to her quarter, but she pointed her stern at us again. We eased back. Spinney's gun made a hit just for'ard of the conning tower. The Captain edged out again to U-501's port beam. U-501 swung violently to port and suddenly she and *Moose Jaw* were side by side about thirty feet apart, on a parallel course and at the same speed. Germans were on their deck, but our guns wouldn't depress enough to fire. For a few eerie seconds we regarded each other in silence. More Germans erupted out of various hatches; a long swell lifted us within fifteen feet.

"Stand by to repel boarders," sang out the Captain.

Now, there was a thought. U-501 was bigger than us, and probably had more men. A bit theatrical on the Captain's part, though.

The navigator was at my side. "Hal, have you the key to the rifle rack?"

"No, I gave it to Spinney."

"Oh, well, Father wants…"

"I know what Father wants but I haven't got it."

"Oh, all right, I'll ask Spinney, but he's pretty busy; his gun's stuck, I think."

I decided to do something myself about the Germans massing on the U-boat's bridge and deck.

"Lewis gunner," I shouted, "knock those Germans off."

No Lewis gunner.

I grabbed the strip Lewis gun from its rack, smacked on an ammunition pan, rotated it anti-clockwise (as taught by CPO Bingham, bless him), cocked it, hooked my arm around a stay to steady myself against the lurching of the ship, and fired.

Click.

No tension on the spring.

The Captain swung slowly to port to open the range. U-501's bridge was crowded with Germans. Both ships were rolling about twenty degrees in a beam sea. On opposite sides of a trough the superstructures were close now, although the hulls were thirty feet apart. One German climbed the edge of his bridge, balanced precariously for a few moments, then hurtled through the air in an astonishing standing broad-jump. He landed in the break of the fo'c's'le.

"See what he wants," said the Captain, putting on more port helm to open the range more quickly. At the break of the fo'c's'le I was met by a groggy figure struggling to his feet.

"We are not fighting. Let me speak to your captain," he said.

I led the way up the ladder, thinking half-way up that turning my back on an enemy at the height of an action was unwise. The Captain had manoeuvred into the position he sought, and was bearing in to ram. We hit, rocked over, metal screaming on metal. I arrived on the bridge with our guest.

"I am the Captain of the submarine. We surrender. Do not fire on my men, please. Do not fire any more."

There was no need. U-501's speed was reduced to about three knots, and beaten men crowded her decks. They jumped in the water and swam toward us. *Chambly* pulled up to U-501. Prentice shouted, "Stop your engines or I'll open fire."

*Chambly*'s boarding-party pulled over in a skiff. The boarding officer, Ted Simmons, grabbed a German who was speaking English.

"Take me below," he ordered.

"No, no. It is not safe. We will sink. We have opened seacocks."

Thrusting him aside, Simmons grabbed two more and, jabbing their back with his .45 and kicking their behinds, propelled them to the conning tower. On the conning tower the Germans refused to go below.

The swell was pounding the skiff badly; two seamen jumped in and lay off. A Lewis gunner covered the prisoners. U-501 was sinking by the stern; there was not much time. Simmons clambered down the hatch. If it were too late to salvage her, he might at least find code-books. The lights were out. By a dim torch he saw water gurgling up; then it flooded in with a rush. The stern sank further. Too late!

Pulling himself out, Simmons gestured the prisoners and his men over the side. Only the conning tower and the bow were awash now. With everyone off, Simmons jumped in the water. The bow reared and U-501 plunged down, sucking Simmons with her. He fought his way to the surface and struck out for the skiff. Hauling himself over the gunwale, he mustered his men. Stoker Brown was missing. Calling his name, they searched. No reply.

We in *Moose Jaw* had been circling the stopped *Chambly* and U-501. When we could we picked up prisoners. The U-boat captain, Hugo Förster, was uneasy about the lights we showed to do this. Twenty-nine Germans were plucked out of the water, frightened and exhausted. Two were dead and were dropped back in. Gunfire was continuous. And always there was the keening of the wind through the rigging and the rush of water down the scuppers.

The stunning fury of battle confuses inexperienced men. The cook blotted out the din and retreated in his mind to the safe, warm hash-house where he had been serving hamburgers only a few months before. In the white light of descending star shells and the orange glare of an exploding tanker, I spotted him. His action station was ammunition supply at the break of the fo'c's'le, but at the height of the action, 4-inch shells failed to arrive at the gun. Cookie was crouched in a corner under the gunwale, crying, head buried between his knees and arms over his head. A 4-inch shell splashed off the starboard beam.

I yelled, "Come on, Cookie, get on that goddam ammunition whip!"

I tried to pry his arms off his head but they were set like steel. He was a heavy man, about two hundred pounds, forearms as big around as my thigh. I kicked him in the ribs. No response. I kicked him on the knee. He gasped, raised his head, stood up slowly, and limped to the whip. Probably didn't get enough parade training, I thought; probably didn't get any. The supply of 4-inch to our forward gun resumed. Later the Cook went mad. It was only temporary—an hour or so—but it was a real enough example of shell shock.

On orders to take up station on the starboard bow of the convoy, we got under way. Men left in the water shouted for rescue. But there was no choice; the safety of the convoy was paramount. We closed our new position. Guns flashed and shells from the convoy whistled over our bridge; the merchantmen were thoroughly and understandably rattled by now. We flicked our navigation lights—high-up, far-apart navigation lights that could not possibly belong to a U-boat. Fire ceased. It was midnight.

At 0145 of the thirteenth day, we sighted the torpedoed *Brerury*, sinking by the head. There were several boats near her and many men in the water. Those in the lifeboats were embarked; one thrust up the ship's cat ahead of him. I was dropped in the skiff to aid those in the water.

Many were dead. You haul a limp man in. Is he dead or only unconscious? You can't tell. Anyway, that man over there isn't dead, he's shouting. So haul him in and push the first out; there's not room for everyone. Fend off that German with your oar. Buggered if we'll pick him up when we can't get all of our own. Those we pulled in were packed between the thwarts, one on top of another; a skiff is small but we jammed in twelve. Others clung to the gunwales. Rowing was difficult; our freeboard was reduced to a few inches and high waves threatened to swamp us. "Back port," "Give way starboard," "Harder!" Our bow rose reluctantly. Water splashed in. To bail was impossible. Star shell searched ahead. A ship blew up. Flares revealed the squat silhouettes of the merchantmen receding. *Moose Jaw* was called away.

"I hope she can find us again!" I thought.

The sea temperature was about fifty degrees, the air temperature about forty degrees, and some of the survivors we picked up must have been in the water an hour. They shook as with the ague. We covered them with our duffle coats but it did little good. One cried softly.

A corvette at speed was passing about a mile away. I flashed her. She altered, and, as her menacing bow bore down on us, I prayed that we didn't look like the conning tower of a submarine.

With a flurry of boiling water she put her engines astern and wallowed a few feet off. It was *Kenogami*. Unloading was tricky in that sea. One moment we would be level with her gunwale, frantically hanging on to a bow and a stern line thrown us; in the next instant we would drop dizzily and *Kenogami* would tower above us as we desperately bore off to prevent being tipped by her bilge-keel. The survivors had no strength to climb inboard. With lines secured around their knees and shoulders, they were hauled up. I found out, a year later, that only two of the twelve lived.

"Who's that?" asked an interested voice on deck.

"Lawrence, *Moose Jaw*."

"This is Peter Cock. How are things?"

"A bit bloody."

"Those chaps of yours are in bad shape."

"Yes," I said. "Where are you heading?"

"Reykjavik, to fuel."

"See you, maybe."

"Sure. I'll buy you dinner at the Börg Hotel."

The last body was swayed up.

"Can you tell *Moose Jaw* I'm here?" I asked.

"Sure, we'll ask her to come back. You'd better bear off before we swamp you."

In a few minutes *Kenogami*'s captain, "Cowboy" Jackson, shouted from the bridge.

"*Moose Jaw*'s coming. I'm off. Good luck."

*Kenogami* churned away.

In fifty minutes, willing hands in *Moose Jaw* hoisted the skiff inboard. We were wet, cold, tired. From the after end of the bridge, the Captain viewed the hoisting with distaste.

"No! No!" he rapped. "When you belay a boat's falls, the first turn is taken *inside* the cleat."

At the time, the niceties of RCN procedure were far from our minds.

The fight around the convoy was still going on but lessening in intensity now.

Survivors and prisoners crammed the upper deck and the Coxswain was trying to get them separated. The fore-upper mess was packed full also, as prisoners and merchant sailors shivered and stripped their sodden clothes. The Coxswain threw dry blankets at them.

The unconscious were stripped, bundled in blankets, and laid out on the lockers, and a teaspoon of rum was forced between their teeth. Some coughed and struggled up. Others didn't. We had no doctor, no sick-berth attendants, no medical personnel of any sort.

I climbed to the bridge. The convoy had closed the gaps in its ranks. The wind was freshening and the temperature had dropped. We went from action stations to defence stations. Eight hours had passed since we first sighted U-501.

After some twenty-five hours without sleep, I sought my bunk in the after cabin-flat. An armed sentry barred the hatch. "German prisoners down there, sir. Whole bloody flat's full of 'em."

These and thirty-eight merchant-service survivors put sleeping space at a premium. I lay on the wardroom deck; a bed at the Royal York Hotel couldn't have been more comfortable.

A few moments later, it seemed, the crash of our forward gun woke me. The wardroom was deserted. The gun spoke again and again. In a panic I rushed on deck. Another round; the acrid bite of burnt cordite stung my nostrils. About a hundred survivors and sailors were gazing intently off to port. They seemed strangely calm for a ship in action.

Of course, we weren't in action. The SS *Brerury*, loaded with lumber, had not sunk. The secret books had not been destroyed and it was too rough to put a boarding-party aboard. Round after round hit until she was ablaze. Her skipper, Captain Morgan, his officers and crew, watched impassively as their erstwhile home was destroyed. We rejoined the convoy.

The murky dawn gained strength. We counted the night's losses. Seven more ships sunk. This brought the total to fifteen. Fifteen merchantmen for one U-boat certain and one possible. Not a good score.

There were reasons why it was not better. The simple fact was that, even after two years of war, our ships were mainly manned by landsmen, some only a few months off prairie farms or city streets. In these two years the Royal Canadian Navy had grown from eighteen hundred to thirty-six thousand, the proportion of properly trained sailors to landsmen was one in two thousand. In *Moose Jaw* we were lucky to have two pre-war men on board, the Captain and Leading Seaman Nanteau. The Captain was twenty-six; the average age of the crew was twenty. That one can't make sailors overnight was proved presently. To me it was the most frightening aspect of the whole operation.

We ran out of feed-water for the boilers. In the excitement of the previous night the engine-room crew simply forgot to distill some. The heartbeat of the engine died away, the roar of the fans dropped, and we lay rolling heavily and silent. The survivors trickled up on deck and our sailors followed. From the upper deck they climbed to the fiddley one deck higher. Captain Morgan and some of his officers filtered to the bridge one deck above the fiddley.

That left only the Germans and the engine-room crew below deck. The engineers wouldn't come up until their honour was regained. The Germans couldn't because of the sentry. A merchant-service able seaman who's been torpedoed makes an excellent sentry; he's just trembling to jab that bayonet.

We fidget; conversation is jerky. The whine of the wind through the rigging and the rush of water as waves pass beneath us fills our ears. Never was there a better lookout kept; conscientiously our binoculars swept back and forth, back and forth.

"I presume that hands are standing by the boats and floats," said the Captain.

"Yessir," said the First Lieutenant, and slid below to make sure.

The Captain leaned on the bridge dodger and stared moodily at the receding convoy. There was a nasty set to his mouth. Thirty minutes passed. From the engine-room voice-pipe came a shout.

"Bridge?"

"Bridge."

"We're ready to go ahead."

The Captain nodded.

"Obey telegraphs," I said. They jangled. As the life-giving steam pumped through her veins, *Moose Jaw*'s heart throbbed again.

"Get back to station," said the Captain; "I'll be in my cabin. Give the Chief Engineer my compliments and tell him I'd like to speak to him."

Things were looking up. Four more escorts joined—*Gladiolus* and *Buttermere* (British), *Mimosa* (Free French), and *Wetaskiwin* (Canadian; her ship's badge, painted on the gun-shield, showed a shapely queen sitting in a puddle of water—the wet-ass queen). In the afternoon the 2nd Escort Group joined from Iceland—HMS *Douglas*, *Veteran*, *Saladin*, *Skate*, and *Leamington*. *Skeena*, *Chambly*, *Alberni*, and *Kenogami* detached to fuel in Iceland. We stayed. Peter owes me a dinner, I thought.

Regular watches resumed—four hours on, four hours off. The destroyers, *Douglas*, *Veteran*, and *Leamington* formed a forward screen. Inside were the corvettes. *Moose Jaw* was on the starboard bow of the convoy.

"Do you know your station?" *Douglas* flashed at me one afternoon.

"Affirmative," *Moose Jaw* flashed back.

"What is it?"

"Green six-oh degrees, two to three miles, leading ship, starboard column."

"Then go back there; stay there."

It appeared I'd wandered. It must be the radar in *Douglas* that tells when we are out of station. The clack of the signal projector had brought the Captain to the bridge. He looked ghastly, having had no sleep, or just fitful dozes.

"What was that about?" he asked pettishly.

"*Douglas* asked what our station was, sir."

"Doesn't *Douglas* know? He's Senior Officer."

"Apparently not, sir."

Watch on, watch off. And following us everywhere was the ping of the asdic set as our sound-wave searched below the water for submarines. Ping, and the reverberations came back over the loudspeaker; reverberations and tiny echoes from seaweed, small fish, debris, fainter and fainter as the pulse of sound energy went out from the ship. Then, ping, again. Hour after hour, watch after watch. The asdic set had been going since sailing and wouldn't stop until we reached a safe haven. Then it came.

Ping... beep. Ping... beep.

"Echo bearing Green three five" sang out the asdic operator, Gaudyk. I rang for the Captain but he appeared as I pushed the bell. I went to the asdic hut only a few paces away and put on my earphones.

"Extent of target?" I asked.

"Wait a minute. Right cut-on oh-three-oh." Gaudyk cut across the target, one step of two degrees for every transmission. Ping... beep. Ping... beep. Ping...

"Go back," I said; "you've lost her."

Ping... beep.

"Left cut-on oh-two-two. Extent of target eight degrees."

That could be a submarine with an extent of target of eight degrees. If it's too big it's not a submarine, nor is it if it's too small, unless it's a submarine bows or stern on. In that case one hears closing or opening Doppler, depending on changes in sound-wave frequency. This Doppler was slight high; that meant the target was approaching—a good solid, metallic echo, not fuzzy like a whale.

"Right cut on oh-two-five. Left cut-on oh-two-oh. Target moving left," said the operator. "Range eighteen hundred yards."

The Captain had hoisted the large black pennant signifying a hunting escort. He stuck his head through the window.

"Well, what is it?"

"Just a minute, sir."

The operator pointed. Although the beeps were coming back to our earphones, there was no trace on the range-recorder. The stylus moving across the chemically treated paper seemed to be loose, too slack. Metal fatigue? Ping... beep. Ping... beep. The echo was getting stronger, the range was closing.

"Sounds good to me," said the Captain. "How do you classify it?"

I looked at the operator. The picture was clear—extent of target, Doppler, range, movement, hardness of echo. He nodded.

"Submarine, sir."

About a minute had passed since the first beep.

"I am going in for a counter-attack," said the Captain. He rang full speed and *Moose Jaw* surged forward.

We started the sing-song chant of orders and information we had learned at the Asdic School back in Halifax.

"Centre bearing oh-one-six degrees. Moving left. Doppler slight high."

"Range?" said the Captain.

"Can't tell. The range-recorder's busted."

"Use your bloody stop-watch."

I did. "Range twelve hundred yards."

*Moose Jaw* was pounding at full speed, and bucketing about in the head sea. The resultant masking and quenching around the asdic oscillator, which protruded from the bottom of the ship, blotted out the echoes somewhat.

I'm going to throw off ahead of the submarine now," said the Captain. "Fire when we cross over."

"Can't fire without a range-recorder," I said.

"Then fire when you get instant-echoes."

Ping... beep. Ping...beep. Ping, beep. Ping, beep. Ping beep. Pingbeep. Ping-beep.

"Fire!" I pressed my buzzers to the depth-charge throwers port and starboard, and to the rails aft.

Thunk, thunk, went the throwers and, turning quickly, I saw the charges arch out, port and starboard.

"Get me a piece of string," I shouted to the signalman.

"Carrying out stern sweep," said Gaudyk.

The repeated crashes of the depth-charges assailed our ears. *Moose Jaw* bucked and surged. Relocating an echo through the noise of your own propellers and the turmoil of exploded depth-charges is difficult. The Captain swung around to give us a clearer arc of search.

"There she is," said Gaudyk as the beep reappeared through the noise.

"This what you want?" asked the signalman, holding up a four-inch length of unraveled hemp.

"It'll do."

I stopped the range-recorder, knowing we had no spare stylus. This present one, loose or not, would have to work. My hands were cold. The wind blew in the open window in front of me and out the open door behind. The Captain leaned in the window. He seemed to be enjoying himself. Nothing like a bit of adrenaline to perk up a man. With clumsy fingers I looped the string over the fragile copper stylus to the solid metal. Gaudyk kept his oscillator pinging back and forth across the fuzzy echo.

If there was a submarine down there, and one cannot be sure until it is blown to the surface, the U-boat crew would be hearing a crackling noise across their hull as the probing asdic finger of sound poked at them. The U-boat captain would know when I cut off and when on again, just as I knew. He would be measuring my range as I measured his. As I was listening for the whirring of his electric motors, he was listening for a speed-up in our thumping reciprocating engines. His hydrophone operator would be passing the same stream of information to him that Gaudyk and I were passing to Captain Grubb. His torpedo crews would be poised the way my depth-charge crews were. His heart would be pounding like mine.

"Range fifteen hundred yards," said Gaudyk.

I'm altering around and reducing speed," said the Captain. "This'll be a deliberate attack."

As I bent over the range-recorder, my head was near the wheel-house voice-pipe.

"What's going on?" I heard a voice ask.

"Lawrence is fixing the fuckin' range-recorder with string."

"He's what?"

"Christ! What a navy!"

Clearer came the beep. And strong and true the stylus marked the paper. As the paper rotated, the successive range-marks formed a slant to put the firing-bar on. This attack would be more scientific than firing on instant-echoes.

Our black pennant had brought a consort racing up to assist us. She angled out at ninety degrees from our line of attack. After we dropped the next ten-charge pattern, two asdics should be holding the submarine. The convoy had done an emergency turn of forty-five degrees away from us. The submarine was still heading in toward them. The U-boat captain should have a fairly clear picture. He knew we were two corvettes from the sound of our screws. He would therefore make his alteration of course and speed later rather than sooner, for we had a smaller turning circle than destroyers. He would know from the receding and slower thump of the merchant-ship screws, as well as from their slower rate-of-change-of-bearing, that the convoy had altered away from him. If our counter-attack had shaken him up, he could seek sanctuary in the boiling water of the wakes of some thirty large ships. All our asdic would get back from the wakes would be confused noise. Probably it was the best thing he could do now that he had lost the element of surprise.

The Captain studied the slope of the range-recorder trace through the window. In a conversational tone we fed him information on centre-bearings, Doppler, range, movement.

"I'll throw off twenty degrees," said the Captain. "Fire when you're ready. We're getting into the wakes of the convoy. Looks like this will be your last chance. If your submarine alters away it means he's going up under the convoy. What's the Doppler now?"

"Slight high. He's still closing."

Again the ping beep. Ping beep. The range-recorder trace crept under the firing-bar.

"Doppler same," said Gaudyk. "Slight low. He's altering away. Doppler marked low. Range four hundred yards."

Now we could hear the pulse of very rapid engines. The U-boat was making his move. Increasing speed and altering away, across the track of the boiling convoy wakes. I held fire until the range trace was lost in the transmission trace. "Hydrophone effect," said Gaudyk.

Again we heaved and shuddered as the ten depth-charges exploded. What must it be like below?

"Carrying out stern sweep," said Gaudyk.

But there was nothing. Or, rather, there was everything except a submarine echo. We nosed around for a half-hour and then took up our former station. Too many contacts ended that way. No escort saw this U-boat get out from under the convoy, if ever it did.

Our infinitely slow crawl across the Atlantic had finally brought us within range of aircraft from Iceland. One droned overhead now and disappeared in a search ahead of the convoy. It soon proved its worth. Back flashed a message—a submarine on the surface fifteen miles ahead. *Veteran* and *Leamington* creamed out. By dusk they were back and laconically reported the kill of U-207. Fifteen merchant ships for two U-boats certain and one possible. A better score.

The night was quiet and the fourteenth day dawned with no further losses, as did the fifteenth. On the sixteenth day three United States Navy destroyers patrolled about ten miles to the south'ard. Their role was ambiguous; the United States had not yet declared war.

This day the German captain and two of his officers were aired for an hour. HMS *Veteran* steamed across our bows on some little errand or other. Hugo Förster nudged his Executive Officer, Werner Olbring, and pointed. They talked excitedly.

"Speak English, please," I said.

"I was just saying," the Captain said apologetically, "that there is *Veteran*."

"Come on," I said; "anyone with a book of warship silhouettes knows it's a V-class. How do you know it's *Veteran*?"

"You see the galley funnel? How it crooks aft and then up again? None of the others is like that. Oh yes, that's *Veteran*. We've seen her often."

It made you think.

On the seventeenth day low fog set in. Above the fog it was glaringly bright; the sun was high in a cloudless sky and the mist lay just on the surface, perhaps to a depth of a hundred feet. Five U-boats still shadowed. That forenoon we spotted one. It dived. We creamed in with a counter-attack and dropped depth-charges on the swirl, but it took us over a minute to get there. In that time a U-boat could drop to a two-hundred-foot depth and make a speed of nine knots—in any direction. The search was fruitless. After dark a merchantman was sunk, but it was to be the last. As we laboriously climbed our great-circle course toward Scotland, the U-boats drew off, some to Germany to refuel and replenish torpedoes, some to re-form the Iceland-to-Greenland patrol.

At 0100 on the eighteenth day the dimmed lighthouse at the Butt of Lewis flashed out a welcome; one flash every twenty seconds. It was good to be "home." We thought of sleep—and food.

Owing to our hurried sailing, fresh provisions had not been embarked, and ten days previously we had broached the emergency rations. Merchant-service cooks had vied with our cooks to prepare tasty meals, but their talents were tested with only bully beef and ship's biscuits. Even those were scarce, since we were feeding a hundred and forty-nine instead of the usual eighty.

The Commodore ordered his ships into a narrower formation. We wheeled to starboard around the Butt of Lewis, and steamed south through the Minches. To have land on both sides was comforting. To see men walking across fields was amazing. A gentle east wind blew off-shore, moist and earthy.

The convoy dispersed under local escort, some for Londonderry, some for Liverpool, some for Southampton. In fives and tens they broke off. A few bore gaping holes in their sides, a few listed to starboard or down by the head, but they had made it. Skippers came to the wings of their bridges.

"Thank you for your escort," they bawled. We waved.

On the nineteenth day our anchor rattled down in Loch Ewe.

Captain Grubb was taken off to the hospital ship. He had been sick prior to joining *Moose Jaw*, but the doctors had pronounced him "fit for sea." Now, foul weather, bad food, and days of snatched sleep had taken their toll. Later that day we weighed anchor and proceeded on the last short lap.

On the afternoon of the twentieth day we secured at Princess Pier, Greenock. Armed soldiers waited for our prisoners; for them the war was over.

The U-boat captain stood by the gangway as his men went ashore. He offered his hand to the first, but the man brushed by him, as did the next. With heads averted, the U-boat's crew filed swiftly into the waiting vans. Their captain stood smiling fixedly until the last one was ashore and then, thanking us courteously, he followed. Can a captain ever be the first to leave his sinking ship? Even to prevent further deaths among his men? Years later we heard that in his prisoner-of-war camp he was arraigned for court martial by his brother officers. If found guilty of cowardice he would have been executed. Others were. But the prison authorities found out about it, and he was transferred.

Our survivors left with fervent thanks. One oiler hung behind the rest. He was a small man, with a scraggly beard. His pale eyes peered out of the hood of a borrowed duffle coat too large for him. He fumbled in his pocket and pressed something into my hand.

"Thanks for fishing me out. I'd like you to take this," he said; "I havena much. *Brerury* is the second ship I've lost."

I looked at the small pistol he had given me, a thirty-two. "Yes," I said, "I'd like that, thank you." We shook hands and looked at each other uncertainly.

"What will you do now?" I asked.

"Dinna fash yoursel'. I'll pick up another ship. They're short-handed and it's ma trade."

He jumped up the gangway and clumsily saluted the quarter-deck, a bit embarrassed, I think, at this momentary weakness to navy folderol. He trotted after the rest, turned, and waved.

"Goodbye," he called.

Goodbye.

# 5
# The War in the Air

## MEDAL OF HONOR

from
*Joe Foss—Flying Marine:*
*The Story of His Flying Circus*
as told to Walter Simmons
New York: E. P. Dutton & Co., 1943

*The Solomon Islands in the South Pacific could have served as a substitute for hell. The steaming islands were inhabited by screeching mynas and cockatoos. Lizards and crocodiles crawled through the swamps. Wild boars roamed the dank, impenetrable jungles. The native Melanesian tribesmen had once specialized in head-hunting and cannibalism.*

*Few who happened upon the Solomon Islands ever decided to stay. There were no coral beaches, only a few swaying palm trees and vast plains of tall razor-sharp grass that could slice a man's skin before he realized the danger of the cutting edges. There were dense rain forests and impassable jungles. The hot, stifling air was only occasionally broken by heavy rains, and the foul, stagnant landscape infested the visitor with tropical ailments and fatigue. The malaria mosquito would eventually deliver the coup de grace.*

*Surrounding waters hid reefs that tore the bottoms out of crafts that dared navigate the shoreline. Tropic winds turned calm water into churning maelstroms within minutes, and shallow waters often wrecked a ship in minutes.*

*These unappetizing volcanic rocks became important in 1942, when the Japanese recognized the proximity of these islands to Australia. Here could be a base of incalculable value in the capture of a continent.*

*A squadron of marine fliers was transferred to the Solomons to discourage the landing of Japanese troops and supplies. Their station was Henderson Field in Guadalcanal, the southeastern tip of the Solomons. It was the object of constant Japanese attacks.*

*Between October 9 and November 19, 1942, second lieutenant Joseph*

191

*Jacob Foss flew with Squadron 121 of the 1st Marine Aircraft wing in the south-
west Pacific. Foss rose to the rank of captain and, as executive officer of the
squadron, led escort, reconnaissance, and bombing missions over Guadalcanal.*

*Foss's official score of downed enemy planes was twenty-six. He was
awarded the Congressional Medal of Honor in 1943 and was at the time of his
discharge a major in the Marine Air Corps. Foss, one of America's leading aces,
tells of his everyday experiences on Guadalcanal at the time when the war's outcome in the Pacific balanced precariously on the bravery of the U.S. Army, Navy,
and Marines.*

October 6 arrived. We went aboard the carrier again, knowing this was no suitcase drill, and pulled out of the harbor. Next day, bound for action at last, we
were up at 4:20 A.M. and stood by all day in case of an alarm. There was
none. We checked our planes again and again.

The carrier nosed onward toward Guadalcanal, and we were up at 4:20 again.
There was a "bogey"—an American plane appeared. We were edging into the hot
zone, and everybody was on edge. All day we played cards without seeing the spots,
and listened to the phonograph without hearing the music.

The next morning we were up at five, had breakfast and packed. We took
plenty of pogey bait—candy—and cigarettes for the boys on Guadalcanal. Some of
us were on the list to fly over water to Henderson Field, while others, due to a shortage of planes, were to come in later by transport. A few of the men left behind actually had tears in their eyes.

The take-off at 12:55 P.M. was ideal. I'm not superstitious; I flew number 13.
Looking backward and down, we saw the deck of the receding carrier, ruled off like
a ping-pong table. Our heavy Grumman Wildcats, stoutly gunned and armored,
painted ocean blue on topside, sky blue beneath, purred along contentedly. A few
hours later we could see Guadalcanal. The boys had doubted my navigation, but fortunately it was right on the nose. We had hoped for a few enemy planes; there was
none in sight. All we could see was the luxuriant, peaceful green of the island, set
jaggedly in the sea.

It was so beautiful that war and bloodshed seemed impossibly far away.
Coconut Palms waved politely at us, cows drowsed in the green meadows, and
swimmers were splashing in a little creek.

When we neared Henderson Field, however, things looked different. We could
see hundreds of pockmarks left by bombs and shells. Besides the craters, there were
foxholes and slit trenches, and many wrecked planes ranged around the field, which
itself was a mere cow pasture hacked out of the jungle.

Rough-looking fellows with beards came running out of the woods to meet us.
They cheered almost hysterically, climbed onto the Wildcats, and seemed almost
ready to kiss us. Major John L. Smith, the famous Marine ace from Lexington,
Oklahoma, drove out in a jeep to say hello. They he took us down a peg or two by
pointing out that we had landed on the bomber strip. We had to take off again and
land on the fighter strip, three-quarters of a mile away. There, at one of the ready

tents, we met Captain Marion Carl, of Hubbard, Oregon, who was runner-up to "Smitty" in number of planes shot down.

Veteran pilots showed us to our camp—a few tents in the grove opposite the jungle. As green newcomers usually do, we secretly felt we were pretty good, but lost that cocky feeling completely after talking for fifteen minutes with the boys who had been through the mill. What dampened us most was the replies we got to questions about old friends. Several of them were dead or missing.

We were warned to expect shelling from the sea during the night. The warning was no joke, and neither was the shelling. Old-timers called it light, but the noise, intensified by the answer of our artillery, kept us awake nearly all night. Nothing fell close to us, however.

Next day was the saturnine Smitty's farewell to Guadalcanal. His boys of Fighting 23 wrote a good ending for themselves. Ordered to protect formations of torpedo planes and dive bombers in an assault on enemy shipping to the north, they were accompanied by another squadron of fighters led by Major Bob Galer of Seattle, Washington. Smitty and his men closely followed the torpedo planes as they skimmed the sea, looking for Jap ships. From above, a group of fifteen float-type Zeros saw them and dropped down in a savage attack, mistaking the wicked Grummans for torpedo bombers.

Out ahead, Major Smith gleefully noted this error and gave orders to capitalize on it. The Grummans split away from the formation and shot upward. Realizing his mistake then, the Jap leader turned his planes away, foolishly exposing their bellies.

"Give, 'em something to remember our last day," Smitty told his boys, and they did. They swept through the enemy formation like a hurricane through dry leaves. Nine of the fifteen Zeros were sent burning into the sea below. The torpedo planes and dive bombers succeeded in hitting a couple of Jap ships.

Smitty racked up a score of nineteen victims in his six weeks on the island and Captain Carl wasn't far behind with sixteen.

In the afternoon we went on our first flight mission—escorting bombers up the groove. We flew as high cover, then swept down, but did no strafing. I saw one of our bombers score a hit on a destroyer. There was a big explosion, blowing a lot of junk off the stern. Then I went into a cloud and didn't see whether the destroyer sank or not.

We scrambled next day when twenty-seven bombers and twenty-four Zeros approached the field, coming from their base on Bougainville Island, 260 miles to the northwest. Rain had poured down all morning, but now it was clear. After sparring around a little, the enemy fluked out on his attack, dropping the bombs two miles from the field and behind his own lines. It amused us to imagine what the Jap infantrymen thought when bombs from their own planes came raining down on their heads.

Our outfit got two bombers and a Zero. Galer's boys brought home seven bombers and four Zeros. We lost, for a little while, our first man—Lieutenant Art (Chongo) Nehf, of Phoenix, Arizona, son of the famous New York Giants' baseball pitcher. Coming in he ran out of gas and landed in the ocean back of the lines. Some Marine raiders went after him and later brought him back with a bad cut over his eye.

Ground troops pushed the Japs back across the Matanikau River that day.

That night was another wakeful one—there was a terrific naval engagement off Cape Esperance, the northwest hump of the island. In the morning the water was covered with heavy oil and filled with debris and swimming sailors—both American and Japanese. Boats were busy picking up survivors among the wreckage. It was much later before we connected the battle with the story of the light cruiser *Boise*, This ten-thousand-ton warship, armed with only six-inch guns, was instrumental in sinking six enemy ships in thirty minutes that night. The Japs lost two heavy cruisers, a light cruiser, and three destroyers. Our chief losses were a destroyer and 107 officers and men from the *Boise*—which thereupon became famous as the "One Ship Navy."

Despite their licking at sea, the Japs succeeded in landing thousands of troops on the island that night.

Again I saw a bomb hit on a destroyer. It is not a bad sight to look at. Eighteen of us got up at 4 A.M. and took off before dawn up the channel, escorting dive bombers assigned to chase away Jap ships remaining from the naval action. The bombers caught two Jap destroyers just off the coast of New Georgia—two little black splinters far below on the water. Decoying anti-aircraft fire away from the bombers, we saw a destroyer hit squarely, aft of amidships. There was a great belch of smoke and flame which died away slowly. Then the ship started burning fiercely. Torpedo planes at the same time attacked a cruiser and left it sinking.

We didn't lose anybody, though one burst of AA fire went right between our first and second sections, shaking up two of the boys. (Perhaps I should explain there are two fighter planes in a section, four in a division, and eight in a flight.)

The night was quiet. We really slept after that day's work.

American transports landed fresh troops in the morning. Bombs falling early on Henderson Field gave the ground crews some holes to fill up. We went up to meet the first enemy formation—twenty-two bombers—but failed to make contact. We could see them, too far away, gleaming silver against the cloudy blue sky, our anti-aircraft bursts puffing out beneath them. Bombs also fell on the beach, killing three of our men and wounding three others.

Two hours later came another attack—by eighteen bombers this time. As my flight climbed into position I felt excited and good, like a kid waiting for a big dish of ice cream. We climbed to the left of the big fellows before seeing five or six Zeros off to the right. I led my boys along the edge of some clouds, hoping the Zeros wouldn't see us.

In my excitement I guess I forgot to turn the radio on. Or maybe it wasn't working. Anyway, one of my boys flew alongside, waved urgently, looked up, and pointed. Thinking he was pointing at the Zeros we'd already seen, I smiled and waved back.

The first thing I knew my wingmen were gone. Attacked from above by a swarm of other Zeros, they had dived out of formation, and a Zero which had been hiding on top of the clouds was on my tail, sending a sizzling stream of tracers a few inches from my head.

The speed of his dive took him past, and he pulled up directly in front of me. I pulled up after him, got him squarely in the sights, and gave him a light burst.

With a great flash he blew into a thousand pieces. It was my first Zero.

I was conscious of a lot of things—my hair standing up, a dryness of the mouth, and a crazy desire to stand up in the cockpit and yell. That's the way you feel when a Zero blows up right in front of you.

But there was other business waiting. Pulling up to get this Zero had made me a setup for three others which now came in viciously, their guns blazing. As I pushed over into a dive I saw oil fly from my oil cooler, and a hunk of wing ripped out by a cannon shell. As I dove, the motor burned out in a flash and the pistons stuck. The propeller, however, kept windmilling.

Those Zeros chased me right to the edge of the field, and I didn't dare slow up for an approach. I came in like a rocket ship, sideslipping desperately at the last moment. The landing was so hot an ambulance was called out to pick up the pieces—if any. But by some miracle I managed to stop before running into the river or the stump patches at the edge of the field. I hooked a ride back on the side of the ambulance.

The old-timers laughed when I told them what had happened. "Bet that makes a Christian out of you. You won't pull that stunt again," they chuckled.

I didn't argue. I was a sad sack that night. True, I had my first Zero, but had made a boob out of myself getting him. The rest of the boys all came back, nicked and sore. They had been sprayed good, too. Our score was three bombers and four Zeros for the day. More important, we had all learned some good lessons.

I learned mine so well the boys were soon calling me "Swivel-neck Joe." The lesson was never get so intent on pressing home your attack that you fail to look around.

Lieutenant William (Big Bill) Freeman, twenty-five, from Bonham, Texas, learned something the same day. Slow, drawling, strong as a horse, and wise in the mysteries of engineering, Bill got separated from the flight led by Major Davis. Seeing a Jap bomber formation below, he went down alone to knock out the leader of the V formation.

In a way, Bill was successful. He got the leader all right, but in so doing he gave every side gunner in the formation a swell target. They laced him from all angles. he came down convinced the attack should be started at the rear of the formation and moved progressively up. We all took Bill's lesson to heart.

Bill later flew with my outfit. He was one of thirteen men who did at one time or another. I've worked with a lot of fellows and met a lot of people, but I've never encountered a gang with such spirit. They were a team out to win, and they just couldn't be beaten.

Mentioning the fact that thirteen men flew in our flight reminds me of another circumstance. I got my first Zero that day, October 13, flying the Number 13 Grumman I'd brought in from the carrier four days before. Only by that time it had been renumbered. We made it Number 53, because there was already a number 13 among our fighters.

Japanese land-based artillery, smuggled onto the island somehow within the last few days, completed our discomfiture at 5:30 P.M. by shelling us for the first time. In the distance we could hear a faint pop, then a whistle, getting louder as the shell approached, and finally an explosion. Our destroyers and land-based artillery answered, and finally the shooting died away.

After taking our lessons to heart and piling into bed, we were awakened at 11:30 P.M. by a tremendous bombardment from big Jap naval guns. It seemed as if all the props had been kicked from under the sky and we were crushed beneath.

The thing started so suddenly we almost broke our necks getting into fox-holes—and what foxholes! There had been no good tough shelling lately, and because of hot weather nobody had been inclined to do much digging. Duke Davis and I shared a hole six feet long and about eighteen inches deep. Lying side by side, squeezed together, we were pretty much exposed.

The ground was shaking and pitching from the violent concussions. We were shaking too—I'll admit that. We just about beat each other to death that night.

Jap planes overhead were dropping occasional white parachute flares and bombs. Fires set by the shelling lighted our area like day. A hundred yards away captured Jap gasoline in drums blazed with periodic explosions that shook our back teeth.

Shell fragments, slashing overhead after each burst, knocked down tents a few feet away, and the hot, jagged pieces cut off dozens of palm trees.

When there was a lull in the shelling, I crawled out of the hole. Suddenly I heard more big ones coming. I returned to the foxhole in a flying dive that just about killed Duke.

The worst of the shelling was in the two hours between one and three o'clock. Jap cruisers and destroyers were parading up and down the channel, throwing every-thing they had at us. Farther out to sea, an enemy battleship was working us over with fourteen-inch shells. Overhead, circling enemy planes dosed us with large bombs and small anti-personnel bombs.

At the height of the bombardment the express train roar of the bursting salvos was so loud that it overloaded the capacity of the human ear. Those two hours were simply indescribable. Nothing like them can be imagined.

Things quieted down after three o'clock, but the Japs made sleep impossible by nuisance bombing raids which continued till daylight. A series of air alerts began before breakfast. We walked around groggily picking up the pieces and viewing damage. A number of officers and men had been killed. One of them was Captain Ed Miller, my instructor when I was a cadet at Pensacola. He was a great guy and we all missed him.

Several of our planes were wrecked, and we found many deep craters in the field. These were repaired in short order. We picked up the heads from some four-teen-inchers and hung them up for gas alarm gongs.

At the edge of the field we saw several of the island's harsh-voiced, but beautiful parrots sitting on the ground, stunned by the explosions. Old-timers—the boys who had seen more than one war—said the night was the worst they had ever heard of.

Lieutenant Simpson, the Chicagoan, was the maddest man you ever saw. He had hung up his laundry the night before, and a jagged hunk of shell casing had gone right down the line, cutting hell out of everything.

Early that morning the dirt started to fly. Men were digging deeper foxholes everywhere. Nobody was going to be caught unprepared again.

Periodically Zeros broke loose from dogfights overhead and tried to strafe the field. Within a few hours the boys were up after a wave of bombers and had shot down a dozen.

At midmorning we went up to intercept a mass bombing attack. Dropping out of my flight due to a missing motor, I hid in clouds over the mountains because twenty-five high-flying bombers were loosing their cargoes on the field, and I could not come in. I looked up and saw a Grumman diving right in front of me with a Zero hot on his tail. The Grumman dove into a cloud and the Zero swung directly in front of me unknowingly. All I had to do was kick the plane around a little, and he was full in the sights. My touch on the trigger was as delicate as a drug-store clerk packing a pint of ice cream. The Jap's wing blew off, and he whirled into a cloud and disappeared. Afterward I saw the plane burning on the side of a mountain. It was Zero number two for me. I never got one any easier.

You might like to know how some of our combat victories were confirmed. Other flyers and observers on the ground with field glasses confirmed many. If a pilot happened to be alone and caused an enemy plane to explode or crash, he was entitled to claim it. But we were seldom alone. Lone Rangers made few successful rides in the sky over the Solomons. They had a habit of not coming back. The Japs were too alert for stragglers.

"Smokers"—enemy planes which disappeared in the distance, streaming smoke—were not counted, though they could not possibly have reached their base on Bougainville Island. Dark smoke meant a hit on the oil line and a burned out motor almost immediately. Light-colored smoke was usually not smoke at all, but escaping gasoline. That meant a sudden landing too.

Smokers often got away in hot combats when we were outnumbered. When we hit a Zero and saw him start smoking, we knew he was out of action and turned to somebody more dangerous. Sometimes we would have a Zero smoking nicely, then see a flight mate in trouble. Instead of polishing off the cripple, we rushed to the rescue. We never thought about personal scores in dogfights—there was too much else to do. It was weeks after my twenty-sixth credited victory, as a matter of fact, before I knew Captain Eddie Rickenbacker had shot down the same number of enemy aircraft in the first World War.

Later that day I led a raid on six troop transports which the Japs were trying to sneak in north of Santa Ysabel, accompanied by warships. We went through heavy anti-aircraft fire to strafe the decks, which were packed with standing soldiers. It was a slaughter—the slugs from my .50-caliber guns must have killed scores. I wish some of the boys we lost at Pearl Harbor could have been there to see it.

Lieutenant Edward P. (Andy) Andrews, a happy-go-lucky little daredevil from Liberty, Nebraska, went back alone and strafed all six transports again. He went right straight down the line, raked the deck of one ship, dropped over the stern, flying between that ship and the next so the two would not dare fire at him for fear of hitting each other, then raised up and dropped down on the next. He did this on all six. The convoy destroyers on each side did not dare shoot for fear of hitting their own ships. Our attacks badly damaged at least one transport. It was later found beached. For their part that day the Japs succeeded in setting fire to one of our cargo ships.

Japanese land batteries again shelled the airfield. A major land battle was obviously shaping in the jungle west of us. The Marines were reinforced now by Army troops under the command of Major General Millard F. Harmon of the air forces. It was plain that the Japs were assembling their forces for a heavy blow at the field. This was the very core of their strategy from the beginning—to recapture the field or, failing that, to reduce it to a condition useless for our purposes. Possession of that little cleared stretch was the only thing that enabled our out-numbered forces to hold out on Guadalcanal at that stage.

At 2 A.M. Jap warships gave us a light going over, but their enthusiasm of the night before was lacking. No fourteen-inch shells landed. We heard later that one of our bombers had laid a five-hundred-pound egg on a Jap battle wagon far off-shore—which no doubt explained the big boy's failure to take part in the nocturnal festivities. The Japs were successful that night, however, in landing heavy reinforcements. The estimates ran as high as 20,000 troops. Heavy artillery and tanks were also unloaded—a poor omen for the future.

Five Zeros flew high over Henderson Field early in the morning and scribbled a broken circle of smoke across our positions—apparently to guide following waves of bombers. Soon twenty-eight high altitude bombers appeared, and we were on our way after them. I remember slashing in to attack. There were Zeros and bombers on both sides, and I was twisting my head watchfully. The next thing I knew I was below a thousand feet and saw mountains on my left.

It was a narrow escape. Looking around, I had twisted my oxygen mask loose and lost consciousness without going through any stage of discomfort whatever. Occasionally we lost a man like that. The masks were pretty good ones but not entirely proof against carelessness.

Full of fear, my wingman, Captain Loesch, followed me down on that dive, and said I wheeled her out just before he gave up all hope. I landed after that.

When the boys returned, we went out to strafe transports and cargo ships which were unloading supplies between Henderson Field and Cape Esperance, about ten miles northwest of Lunga Point. That these ships were there at all was due to the fact that we were short of gasoline and couldn't keep up continuous aerial attacks. They were the five ships which had survived our attentions of the day before. Protected by eight destroyers, they were discovered at dawn, and our bombers began working on them without delay.

We strafed the decks as well as cutting up ground installations on the beach. Our dive bombers came over the hills, peeled off, and attacked from the northwest. They set one ship on fire, then a second, despite heavy anti-aircraft fire. Flame and black smoke came up in great bursts.

Meanwhile Major Cram, aide to General Geiger, loaded two torpedoes into the general's personal PBY. He had never dropped a torpedo before. Someone told him how to do it, and a couple of minutes later he was off, flying without a copilot.

He circled inside the bombers near the beach west of Kokumbona, taking advantage of every bit of cloud cover, then attacked from the opposite direction. He

198

was able to get in close before the destroyers saw him. They sent him everything they had, but he got down close to the water and came in, disregarding the fire. He lined up the transports and let go his first torpedo at about five hundred yards. Then he lined up the others and sent the second torpedo away. One of them got a solid hit. The transport blew up and sank within a few minutes.

# OVER THE NORTH SEA

from

*I Flew for the Führer:*
*The Story of a German Airman*
by Heinz Knoke
Translated from the German by John Ewing
London: Evans Brothers Ltd., 1953

*In accordance with the Versailles Treaty of 1919, Germany had to destroy all warplanes not already in Allied hands. Further, Germany was strictly forbidden to rebuild an air force. The treaty stopped just short of banning gliders and the construction of light sports planes. German aviation firms had to go abroad to work on new aircraft designs.*

*In May 1926, the Paris Air Agreement allowed Germany to build aircraft and create an air-raid early-warning system against a feared Russian attack. By 1932 the German air-warning organization was theoretically ready for deployment. Officially the purpose was to warn people and industry in the event of attack, but Germany was already preparing anti-aircraft artillery and fighter-plane defense.*

*The groundwork had been laid by the Aviation Department of the Reich Ministry of Transport, the German Scientific Society of Aviation, and the German Aviation Research Institute, all of whom were working on the problems of air combat. When Hitler seized power in 1933, the conditions were right for creating a strong air force. The Germans, however, underestimated the strategic importance of heavy bomber units. Göring stopped the building of experimental prototypes of the four-engine combat planes in 1937 and, under the influence of dominant army strategists, concentrated German efforts upon a small fighting plane that would give tactical support to ground troops. Blitzkrieg ("lightning war") depended upon an initial powerful and lightning-fast air strike, followed by tanks, artillery, and ground troops.*

*For some years, young Germans interested in flying had been encouraged to*

*meet in summer camps to build and fly gliders. If the interest in flying persisted,
application to become a pilot could be had through Lufthansa, Germany's commercial airline. Often the applicants were shunted off to military air schools, and
many were sent to Spain to get combat-flying experience. This was the evolution
of many of Germany's combat pilots.*

*The following excerpt is from the diary of a Nazi fighter pilot who followed
the trail from glider-plane student to combat pilot. Knoke downed fifty-two Allied
aircraft in combat—and lived to tell about it. He provides a revealing portrait of
one of Hitler's young men at a crucial moment in history.*

## 26th February, 1943

**W**hat a day!
I am feeling just in the mood for a good scrap with a swarm of
Americans. The weather is ideal, the sky a clear and cloudless blue.

Over Great Yarmouth everything is quiet as yet.

The pilots lie around outside on the tarmac, wrapped up in blankets, enjoying the warmth of the first spring sunshine. I relax beside them, squinting idly up
at the sky.

The two big loudspeakers blare out dance-music. We enjoy the B.B.C. musical
programmes for German soldiers. When the announcer starts his propaganda drivel
there is ironic laughter and applause.

"Shut your mouth, man, and get on with the music!"

Suddenly the music stops.

"Attention, all! Attention, all! Lieutenant Knoke is wanted on the telephone!"

Division is calling: fresh enemy concentrations are reported in map sector
Dora-Dora. So the Yank is getting ready off Great Yarmouth for another raid again.

At 1050 hours we are ordered to stand by. The Yank is off the coast and heading for Wilhelmshaven.

1055 hours: Intercept!

Canopies close. Mechanics swing the starters. My engine at once thunders into
life. I turn to watch the others starting.

All clear! The twelve aircraft take off together in formation.

I turn on the radio and call base:

"Elbe-one calling Bodo. Elbe-one calling Bodo. Report victor."

"Bodo calling Elbe-one. Bodo calling Elbe-one. Victor, victor."

Contact with the ground is good. We climb quickly up to 25,000 feet.

"Heavy babies in Anton-Quelle-eight. Remain over the airfield."

I turn north. Our engines leave heavy vapour-trails streaked across the clear
blue of the sky. Then I spot the enemy formation ahead.

It is an impressive sight. Some three hundred heavy bombers are grouped
together, like a great bunch of grapes shimmering in the sky.

I check my guns and adjust the reflector sight.

The enemy mass is still several miles away and heading south. I report my observations to base. It will be just like a beehive down there now: I cannot help smiling at the thought of the turmoil.

We draw closer to the bomber formation. I must have opened the throttle subconsciously. I can distinguish the individual enemy aircraft now. Most of them are Liberators. They look as if their fat bellies were pregnant with bombs. I pick out one of them as my target.

"This is where I settle your hash, my friend," I mutter.

I shall make a frontal attack. The Yank is focused in my sights. He grows rapidly larger. I reach for the firing-buttons on the stick. Tracers come whizzing past my head. They have opened up on me!

Fire! I press both buttons but my aim is poor. I can see only a few hits register in the right wing.

I almost scrape the fat belly as I dive past. Then I am caught in the slipstream, buffeted about so violently that for a moment I wonder if my tailplane has been shot away. I climb up steeply and break away to the left. Tracers pursue me, unpleasantly close.

Blast all this metal in the air!

Three hundred heavy bombers carry a total armament of 4,800 super-heavy machine-guns. Even if only one in ten have a chance to fire that still means we run into quite a barrage.

I come in for a second frontal attack, this time from a little below. I keep on firing until I have to swerve to avoid a collision. My salvoes register this time.

I drop away below. As I swing around I turn my head. Flames are spreading along the bottom of the fuselage of my Liberator. It sheers away from the formation in a wide sweep to the right.

Twice more I come in to attack, this time diving from above the tail. I am met by heavy defensive fire. My plane shudders under the recoil from the two cannon and 13-millimetre guns. I watch my cannon shell-bursts rake along the top of the fuselage and right wing, and I hang on to the stick with both hands.

The fire spread along the right wing. The inside engine stops. Suddenly the wing breaks off altogether. The body of the stricken monster plunges vertically, spinning into the depths. A long black trail of smoke marks its descent.

One of the crew attempts to bale out. But his parachute is in flames. Poor devil! The body somersaults and falls to the ground like a stone.

At an altitude of 3,000 feet there is a tremendous explosion, which causes the spinning fuselage to disintegrate. Fragments of blazing wreckage land on a farm 200 or 300 yards from the Zwischenahn airfield, and the exploding fuel tank sets the farm buildings on fire.

In a terrific power dive I follow my victim down, and land on the runway below. I run over to the scene of the crash. A crowd of people are there, trying to fight the fire in the farmhouse. I join in the rescue work and bring out furniture, animals and machinery from the burning buildings. Smoke blinds and chokes me, my flying-suit is scorched by the flames, as I drag a fat pig out by the hind-legs, squealing like mad, from the pigsty, which is completely gutted by the fire. The farmhouse and barns are saved.

Strewn all over a cow field lies the wreckage of the Liberator. The explosion threw clear the crew in mid-air. Their shattered bodies lie beside the smoking remains of the aircraft.

One hundred yards away I find the captain's seat and the nosewheel. A little doll, evidently the mascot, sits undamaged between the shattered windows of the cabin.

One hour later I land at Jever. My men carry me shoulder high to the dispersal point. That was my fourth combat victory, on my 164th operational mission and 1,004th flight since I started my instruction with Sergeant Van Diecken.

Dieter was credited with bringing down his seventh opponent: it was his second heavy bomber. In addition, Raddatz, Wenneckers and Dobrick shot down a Fortress each. That means a score of five combat victories for the Flight, as against nil casualties.

I cannot help thinking about the bodies of the American crew. When will our turn come? Those men share in common with ourselves the great adventure of flying. Separated for the moment by the barrier of war, we shall one day be reunited by death in the air.

## 28th February, 1943

All last night Lieutenant Gerhard and I sat together in my quarters. The Americans keep us bothered. The question is, what are we going to do about them?

Dieter comes up with a brilliant inspiration. Why not try using our own aircraft to drop bombs on the close-flying American formations?

All night long we sit up calculating velocities and trajectories. We both arrive at the same conclusion: that the desired result could be obtained by means of a simultaneous release of bombs from a Flight in close formation above the massed American bombers. This could then be followed up by an attack of a more orthodox character using our existing armaments.

The Messerschmitt 109G is capable of carrying a load of 500 lb. Thus it could be adapted to use either four 100-lb. bombs or a single 500-lb. bomb, or even a rack full of small anti-personnel bombs such as I used to drop on the heads of the Ivans in Russia.

We would require a fifteen-second time fuse. The altitude for releasing the bombs would be 3,000 feet above the enemy target formation.

I report to the Commanding Officer during the morning and tell him of our project. He thinks it is a joke, and begins to laugh. When our urgent entreaties convince him that we are serious, however, he agrees to support our project at Division.

In the afternoon, the Commanding Officer having previously telephoned, I fly to Division Headquarters at Stade. General Schwabedissen and Colonel Henschel (who is in command of the fighter pilots) hear what I have to say and agree to help.

I thereupon submit for approval an order for a hundred 100-lb. practice bombs, release mechanism for every type of bomb, and bomb-dollies for loading the aircraft. I also request the use for one hour every day of a target-towing aircraft, preferably a JU. 88, from the Air Servicing Command. This aircraft, with a speed approximately equal to that of the Fortress, is required to tow a ten-foot drogue for us to use as a practice bombing target.

No time is lost in putting my plan into operation. Colonel Henschel himself does not leave the telephone until all arrangements with the Regional Air Command have been completed for obtaining the necessary equipment.

We are going to make use of every opportunity during the next few days for perfecting the precision of our formation flying.

## 8th March, 1943

Forty-eight hours after my visit to Division Headquarters three heavy motor-trucks arrive with the practice bombs. The remainder of the equipment reaches us this morning.

Meanwhile, the Flight is kept busy with formation flying practice every day. All my pilots are capable and experienced, and we soon acquire high proficiency. We are able to fly wing-tip to wing-tip, steady as a board in the air. Every manoeuvre is executed with smartness and precision, including landing by Sections in formation.

For operational purposes I am on detached duty from the Squadron, which was assigned a few days ago for exclusive use as a tactical unit in operations against the massed enemy formations. I even have my own "Y" control.

In the evening Dieter and I drop our first practice bombs on the drogue target towed by the JU. 88. First results are far from satisfactory. We must remember that Rome was not built in a day.

## 10th March, 1943

Today we spend the entire day at bombing practice on the range at Zwischenahn. I am delighted with the results.

## 12th March, 1943

The first of the live bombs have arrived. The Flight is now ready for its new task.

## 16th March, 1943

The mechanics all work hard, practising bombing-up the aircraft at top speed. They are tremendously keen on the job, and I am delighted by their enthusiasm. They are really good lads.

## 18th March, 1943

During the morning Dieter and I each drop four of the 100-lb. practice bombs on the drogue. My third bomb scores a bulls-eye.

Without any warning, at 1412 hours operation orders arrive. We are to attack and intercept a formation of heavy bombers approaching the coast. The order to take off comes so quickly that there is no time for the aircraft to be bombed-up.

Before Dieter closes his canopy he calls over to me that he wants to bag the enemy formation leader today. I ask him, laughing, if the Yanks have recently taken to painting the wings of their planes with rank-badges.

At an altitude of 25,000 feet we establish contact with the enemy in the Heligoland area. I lead the Flight in close formation for a frontal attack.

I open fire on a Liberator from a little below. It immediately starts burning and sheers off to the right as it falls away from the formation. I come in again to attack from above the tail, and then turn for another frontal attack, firing from ahead and below the steeply diving Liberator. My aim has never been better. Suddenly there is an explosion, and the blazing crate disintegrates into a shower of wreckage above my head. For a few moments I am in danger of collision with falling engines or spinning flaming wings. That would mean certain disaster for me. Acting quickly, I slam the stick hard over into the left corner and go into a power dive. The falling fuselage of the Liberator misses me by inches as it hurtles into the depths. It falls into the sea some twelve miles south-east of Heligoland.

That was my number five.

I climb back to 25,000 for another attack at the massed enemy formation. Suddenly my heart almost stops beating.

Dieter is in the middle of the Yank formation holding his aircraft steady following the same course. His first Liberator went down a few minutes ago. Now he wants to put the formation leader into the North Sea. The lad seems to have gone out of his mind. He keeps hard on the tail of a Fortress, blazing away at it. Tracers from every side converge upon his plane.

He must have become completely insane.

I dive down through the formation towards Dieter, firing indiscriminately at any of the Fortresses flying in the vicinity.

Then Dieter suddenly breaks away in a steep dive. Three thousand feet below, his crate begins emitting a trail of smoke. He opens his canopy, then pushes himself up awkwardly in his seat, and the next moment is thrown clear. His parachute opens. I fly past close to him. His face is contorted with pain, he grips his body. Dieter is wounded.

Fifteen minutes later he is down in the sea in map reference sector U-R-9. He succeeds in getting himself clear of the parachute, his rubber dinghy inflates, and he drags himself into it. I fly down low over his head and wave to him. He does not respond. He appears to be either unconscious or in utter pain. He looks as if he has been shot through the stomach.

I immediately report by radio the position of our downed comrade and request help for him. Then I fly in and land. The mechanics look shaken at the news. I find no pleasure in my own success.

If only Dieter is rescued alive...

Alone I fly out to sea again. The others have not yet returned. I can no longer find Dieter. One of the crash-boats patrolling the vicinity will have noticed his parachute descent and hurried to his assistance.

Night falls. Still no news of Lieutenant Gerhard.

In his clothes-locker I find a bottle of brandy. There is another such bottle in my own locker. We have once agreed that these bottles are to be drunk by the boys in memory of whichever one of us should first fail to return from a mission. What can have happened to Dieter?

At midnight the telephone in my quarters rings.

Lieutenant Dieter Gerhard was found by the crash-boat *Falke*. He is dead.

Slowly I replace the receiver. Dieter is dead. He was my closest friend.

I remove the bottle from the locker and go across to Lieutenant Frey. He is in his quarters with his wife and Lilo. They also have been waiting anxiously for news of Dieter. There is no need to say anything.

I pass the bottle to Frey: "Come on, we may as well drink it up. We all feel the same—but that is the way we arranged it with Dieter, and that is the way it has to be."

## 19th March, 1943

They have brought Dieter in to Cuxhaven and laid out the body in the mortuary at the hospital there. I have had a large wreath made. My men place it in a Fieseler Storch, in which I am going to fly alone to Dieter.

My route crosses the Jadebusen and the broad estuary of the Weser. The water glistens like a mirror, smooth and calm, with the reflection of the rising sun stretching in broad bands of silver to the horizon. Over to the north lies the open sea, from which they brought in the body of my dead comrade.

I land in a small field near the hospital, and carry my wreath across to the tiny chapel. There, in the middle of a cold little whitewashed room, Dieter lies under a shroud.

Someone draws it back. The fine, tall lad lies cold and still. It is as if he were asleep, resting the strong body in exhaustion after the effort of that last battle and the final plunge. His eyes are closed, his features in an expression of something resembling defiance.

Good night, Dieter. You have earned your rest, after fighting and dying for our beloved German fatherland. You were my best friend: I shall never forget you. Alone now, I shall continue fighting this great battle for Germany, which we both started, you and I together, faithful to the same oath of service which we have sworn.

## 22nd March, 1943

1424 hours: alert sounds.

Blast! Once again there is no time for our aircraft to be bombed-up. The Americans are coming in from over their sea. They have assembled as usual in the same map reference sector Dora-Dora off Great Yarmouth.

Seven minutes later we receive orders to land. The enemy have turned about and are now heading back in a westerly direction. Will they return?

After landing, the aircraft are refueled immediately, with the pilots standing by. Another alert must be anticipated. The intentions of the enemy are never obvious, as they are in the habit of altering course all the time.

I have a 500-lb. high-explosive bomb slung at top speed under my plane. But in the meantime we are ordered to take off, and I am not yet ready to go.

"Flight Sergeant Wenneckers is to take over my command." I have the word passed down the line of aircraft.

Wenneckers waves his hand. He has understood, and rolls down the runway. The others follow. The Flight leaves the field in close formation.

Sweating mechanics work feverishly under the belly of my Gustav. I remain strapped in my seat, fuming with impatience.

"Come on, come on; hurry, hurry!"

The Flight disappears, climbing in the direction of the sea. The Yanks have crossed the coast of Holland.

"Ready!"

My weighted plane rumbles awkwardly down to the far end of the runway. With the bomb I cannot take off downwind.

Turning at the perimeter of the field, my aircraft suddenly lists heavily to port. A tyre has burst.

I fire off a red signal flare. My men over at the Flight dispersal point have understood. Twenty or thirty of them pile into a truck, which comes racing over to me. The left wing is lifted up on powerful backs, and the wheel is changed in a matter of seconds, with the engine still running.

"All clear!" They scatter. I open the throttle, start rolling with gathering speed, and then the crate again begins to list to port. I manage to pull it off the ground, however, after a run of some 600 feet, and clear the roof of No. 2 Hangar by a few inches.

I climb at full throttle up into the cloudless sky, heading out to sea. Overhead are the vapour-trails left by our own aircraft and the Yanks. They are already engaged in combat.

22,000 feet: my plane reacts sluggishly under the infernally heavy load. It climbs wearily up to 30,000 feet, taking twenty-five minutes to do so.

The Yanks have bombed Wilhelmshaven, as I can tell from the smoke and fires below. They are over Heligoland on the return flight now.

I edge forward slowly until I am over the tip of the enemy formation, which consists entirely of Fortresses. For several minutes I am under fire from below, while I take a very rough sort of aim on my target, weaving and dipping each wing-tip alternately in order to see the formation below. Two or three holes appear in my left wing.

I fuse the bomb, take final aim, and press the release button on my stick. My bomb goes hurtling down. I watch it fall, and bank steeply as I break away.

Then it explodes, exactly in the centre of a row of Fortresses. A wing breaks off one of them, and two others plunge away in alarm.

Twenty miles west of Heligoland my third heavy bomber crashes into the sea. There is no sign of fire. It is followed by the torn wing fluttering down like an autumn leaf.

The bomb had registered a hit. Not only on the Fortress, but also, it seems on our own higher brass.

Immediately after landing I am ordered to report to the Commanding Officer of the Wing. He himself was in the air at the time, and observed the crash of the Fortress.

"Good Lord, Knoke, you must do that again with your whole Flight!"

"That is my intention, sir."

"Do you believe that it will work?"

I am not too certain. "Today could have been just a fluke, sir; but perhaps we can bring down some more of the heavy babies this way."

Then Colonel Henschel telephones. "I am delighted, my dear Knoke. That was a magnificent show. Must congratulate you." He bleats away happily and sounds quite worked up. I hope his monocle will not fall into his cup of cocoa in the excitement.

The North Sea coastal area of Germany must have its little sensation!

Least fuss is made in the Flight. I find all this excitement over bringing down one single bomber rather absurd. Firstly, anybody could have dropped the bomb. Secondly, the original idea was not mine, but Dieter's. Thirdly, I have eight holes in my own plane where it was hit.

During the night I am awakened by the telephone ringing at my bedside. It is the station switchboard.

"Sir, there is a top-priority call for you from the Air Force High Command (OKL)."

"What! For me?"

I give my name.

A Major is at the other end, on the Staff of Reich-Marshal Göring. "You brought down an enemy aircraft today by bombing it, did you not?"

"Yes, sir."

I am asked for complete details: What type of bomb? What kind of fuse? How exactly had I carried out the attack? And just what had been the result?

"Who issued the order for this bombing operation?"

"No one, sir. I acted on my own initiative."

There is silence. For the first time it occurs to me that I was never authorized to lay so much as an egg on the head of the wretched Yank, and so they might consider that I had acted in an exceedingly high-handed manner.

Then the Major comes back on he line:

"I am putting you through to the Reich-Marshal."

This is the shock of my life!

I lie rigid, stiffening in bed to a horizontal position of attention, to report: "Lieutenant Knoke here, No. 5 Flight Commander, No. 1 Fighter Wing."

"I am delighted over the initiative you have displayed. I want personally to express to you my particular appreciation."

And that is that.

So there we have a full-fledged Prussian Lieutenant in the German Air Force talking to his Commander-in-Chief while lying in bed wearing nothing but a pyjama jacket.

Incredible!

If the Old Man only knew! I am not even wearing the trousers: the tight elastic irritates me. I cannot help laughing at the thought as I turn over again.

## 23rd March, 1943

When I arrive on duty out at the dispersal point there is a message from the station switchboard: "Sir, last night there was a call from the Experimental Station at Rechlin. They ask you to let them have a full report immediately."

Good God! If only I had never dropped that bomb!

At 1000 hours General Kammhuber calls. This poisonous little twerp, commonly known as "Wurzelsepp," is Commanding General of the Twelfth Air Corps.

I receive a terrific reprimand on account of my high-handed action of yesterday. He is incoherent with rage. I have to hold the telephone at arm's length from my ear until the din subsides.

"Where do you suppose we would get to if every Lieutenant just did as he damned well pleased?" shouts the irate voice at the other end. "What the blazes do you think you were doing?"

I knew that question was coming. It happens every time in our Services whenever the superior officer runs out of his store of expletives when administering a reprimand. Am I expected to answer that I cannot help playing with bombs because I so adore the funny noise they make when they go off?

"Well, do you have anything to say for yourself?"

I most certainly have!

"Yes, sir. Last night the Reich-Marshal telephoned me and personally expressed his appreciation of my initiative."

There! That takes care of Wurzelsepp. I hear him deflate with a gasp. One man's meat is another man's poison, according to the old German proverb.

## 17th April, 1943

The Americans made an attack on Bremen today. We take off with our bombs, which we have a chance to drop when the Flight is in close formation over the heart of Bremen. Not a single bomb registers.

We immediately go in to attack with our guns. I make three runs at a Fortress, and it finally catches fire. Southwest of Bremen, in a field near Bassum, it crashes. Four members of the crew parachute to safety.

The Flight is credited with three more victories.

## 14th May, 1943

The enemy raids Kiel. We go after him again with our bombs. Several times I attempt a formation attack 30,000 feet above Holstein. Every time the enemy formation weaves out of the way below. Apparently they have guessed our intentions.

Over Kiel we run into heavy flak from our own guns. The shooting by the Navy is unfortunately so good that we are considerably disorganized.

I observe the Yank bombing. They dump their load right on the German shipyards. I am impressed by the precision with which those bastards bomb: it is fantastic.

My chance of bringing off a formation drop has gone by now, so I send the Flight in one at a time.

My own bomb fails to explode. Hits are registered, however, by Flight Sergeants Führmann and Fest and Sergeant Biermann. Three of the Fortresses are destroyed in mid-air.

Once again relying on my guns, I dive for a frontal attack against a detached formation of some thirty Fortresses.

Almost at once I feel a hit in the fuselage, and as a result I have to abandon the attack. My engine continues running smoothly, however, and all the controls seem to be working.

I attempt another frontal attack. My first salvo registers right in the control cabin of a Fortress. It rears up, like a great animal that has been mortally wounded, and drops away in steep spirals to the right. At approximately 10,000 feet a wing breaks off. It crashes near Husum at 1217 hours.

I get home with several holes in my fuselage and tail.

Today my flight has shot down five heavy bombers. The total Flight bag credited has now reached fifty heavy bombers, and the fiftieth was brought down by Flight Sergeant Wenneckers. Thus my No. 5 Flight is now credited with shooting down as many heavy bombers as the Squadron Headquarters and Four and Six Flights all together.

During an inspection of the Squadron later in the afternoon General Galland, General Commanding the German Fighter Command, signs our Visitors Book with his good wishes and congratulations on our "Fiftieth Heavy Baby."

## 15th May, 1943

The Americans today repeated their attack of yesterday upon Kiel.

I could take only five aircraft into the air, since nearly all our planes had holes in them when they arrived home yesterday. We intercept the enemy formation off the St. Peter peninsula, before it is over the mainland.

The only one of our bombs to register is that dropped by Flight Sergeant Lennartz. One of the Fortresses goes down.

Twice I attempt without success to carry out an attack on one of the enemy formations. The Americans take evasive action by means of a sort of "weaving flight." That makes an accurate frontal attack extremely difficult to accomplish, when the time for firing is limited to three or four seconds only. Perfect timing is essential because of the terrific closing speed. Our own speed added to that of the enemy at an altitude of 25,000 feet amounts to more than 600 miles per hour.

Finally I succeed in getting at one of the Fortresses flying on the outer flank. I observe the inside right engine hit. The Fortress simply closes in and slides over into the well-protected centre of the formation. Another frontal attack on the formation produced no result. I narrowly escape a collision with the huge tail unit of one of the Americans. The rudder alone is as big as the entire wing-span of my Messerschmitt 109.

This seems to be one of those days when every blasted thing goes wrong. I lose sight of the Fortress which I have started to shoot up. By this time I simply could not care less. I dive steeply from behind at another Fortress flying at the tail end. At last my firing begins to have some effect. The two left engines begin smoking. The Yank loses height rapidly. Once he is out of the formation, it is all over. I fasten on behind his tail and blaze away with everything I have. Bright flames spread along the belly. All ten members of the crew bale out. The parachutes hang in the sky like washing on some invisible clothes-line, while the giant plane goes down trailing a long column of smoke, in a pilotless spin, falling out of control, and finally disintegrating in its descent.

It crashes at 1056 hours in map reference sector Toni-Siegfried-four.

## 19th May, 1943

At 1340 hours I bring down my seventh heavy bomber. During the afternoon an intruder on reconnaissance at a high altitude above Heligoland gets away from me. I am unable to make a positive identification: it is probably a Lightning.

## 1st June, 1943

The Americans once more come in over the sea. During the first attack in the Heligoland area my engine is hit badly, and the oil-pipe is damaged.

We were just getting into position for another bombing run. I am obliged to jettison my "egg," and it is only with the greatest difficulty that I succeed in limping back to our base.

Over Wangerooge Sergeant Kramer also is hit. With his tail shot away and out of control, he collides in mid-air with Sergeant Biermann. The two aircraft are locked together for several seconds and drop almost vertically. Then Biermann somehow gets his badly damaged plane clear, and brings it gliding down to the airfield. He attempts a dead-stick landing, but his speed is too great and he overturns. The aircraft is totally destroyed and Biermann is—uninjured.

Kramer bales out. He loses his nerve and tries to open his chute while travelling at a speed of more than 400 miles per hour. Two of the harness straps break. The chute is half open when he hits the sea. He is rescued spitting blood and taken to hospital.

## 11th June, 1943

The Yank does not come over again until this evening.

Twice we take off to intercept. Only on the second mission, when the formation is far out to sea heading for home, does my chance to fire come. One of the Fortresses goes down after my fourth run at it.

## 13th June, 1943

Today is the thirteenth of the month.

The Flight carries out a formation attack on a batch consisting of some 120 heavy bombers. There is a Fortress beautifully lined up in my sights. I press both firing buttons and—nothing happens. I check my magazine loader and safety-catch, press the buttons again, and—still nothing happens.

Seething with rage, I spiral down into the cloudbank below. Today is the thirteenth!

## 25th June, 1943

I am still feeling like death when I come crawling out to the dispersal point this morning. The other pilots and I all stayed in the canteen until daybreak. The bar is littered with a whole regiment of empty bottles.

The sky is overcast. We hope that this is going to be one day the Yank will leave us in peace. In the Squadron operations room no enemy activity is reported. I lie down to catch up on some sleep in the rest-room adjoining the crew-room.

The telephone wakes me at 0700 hours: enemy concentrations in map reference sector Dora-Dora.

As if they could not choose some other day!

The pilots are still asleep. I do not disturb them, but go outside to the aircraft. The chief engineer reports all aircraft checked and found serviceable.

Going into the dining-room, I order a fried egg and some white bread and butter, which I try to eat. The food seems to be quite tasteless. For the first time, I do not feel happy at the thought of the coming mission. There is a peculiar sinking feeling in the pit of my stomach. Is it fear?

No, I do not think it is fear exactly, so much as disinclination and indifference. Even a visit to the can fails to bring relief. I spend fifteen minutes running up and down the runway, trying to pull myself together. Turit, my dog, trots alongside. Now and again he dashes off, barking after a seagull.

From the operations room comes the order to stand by for an alert. The pilots are yawning as they come out one by one. After they have had something to eat, they crawl into fur boots, flying-suits and life-jackets. There is little talk. I stuff some emergency rations and a first-aid kit into my capacious knee-pocket.

Slowly we stroll across to our aircraft. The alert is due at any moment. The mechanics are there before us. My ground-crew chief dangles his legs as he lolls along a wing, chewing a blade of grass. What a picture of alertness!

Arndt fastens my harness, as I put on my helmet. He passes me the ground telephone extension. The Commanding Officer is on the line.

He asks if we are all set. The Flight Commanders answer in turn: Lieutenant Sommer, myself, and Captain Falkensamer. The enemy is approaching the coast: apparently today he is again heading for Wilhelmshaven.

0811 hours: take-off.

The Flights take off in succession, forty-four aircraft in all. The cloud ceiling is at 6,000 feet. We pass through it when we are over the coastline. Occasionally we catch a glimpse of earth through gaps in the clouds.

15,000 feet: another cloud layer is crossed in our ascent.

20,000 feet: there is no conversation on the radio. Only the enemy positions are announced.

22,000 feet: we may expect at any moment to sight the enemy.

I check my guns. My oxygen mask feels unpleasantly tight. I loosen and adjust it.

We fly between cumulus clouds. High above us spreads a third layer of ice-clouds. We fly through valleys and caverns, across gigantic mountains of cloud. Our planes seem absurdly small, dwarfed by this majestic background.

"There they are!"

The Fortresses are nearly 3,000 feet below us. They are not flying in massed formation today, but make their way, singly or in groups of threes and fours, through the magnificent cloudscape.

Peeling off, we go down diving.

"After them!" The chase is on.

It is a perfect surprise. Our attack throws the Americans into a state of utter confusion. They dodge and turn and dive for cover in the clouds as they try to get away from us. It is impossible to estimate how many of them there are. It is just as if a bee-hive was overturned. We call out to each other the best firing positions by radio.

In pairs our pilots attack the individual groups of Fortresses. As my wingman today I have a young Sergeant with me for the first time. This is his first experience of air combat. There is a good chance that it may also be his first victory, if he keeps his head.

I select two isolated heavy bombers flying wing-tip to wing-tip, and we go down to attack them from the rear.

"Dölling, you take the one on the left."

I call the Sergeant; but he keeps flying away off to the right and does not heed my call.

"Close in, man! Other side—over to the *left*! Get in and attack!"

I open fire at short range. My cannon-shells land beautifully in the centre of the fuselage. The rear gunner persistently returns my fire. I calmly close in, guns blazing. Holes appear in my right wing as I am hit. That sod of a rear gunner! He will not leave me alone—must have lots of guts.

Closer still I keep on blazing away at the Fortress, concentrating on the rear turret. It disintegrates under the salvoes from my cannon. More high explosives puts the dorsal turret out of action also.

We are between clouds, in a deep ravine, with milky walls towering high on both sides. It is a glorious picture. Dölling still keeps flying obstinately in his position to my right, calmly watching the shooting. Why does he not go after the second heavy bomber?

I lose my temper with him now.

"Attack, you bloody fool, *attack!*"

He still makes no move.

Woomf! Woomf! Woomf!

I am under heavy fire from the side. It comes from the right side turret of the second Fortress. I am in a position close alongside. The dorsal gunner also blazes away at me with his twin guns. Tracers pass close by my head.

Woomf! I feel another hit. We pass through wisps of cloud. My windows fog up, so I slide open the side window.

My Fortress is on fire along the back and in the left inside engine. Still the two gunners in the second Fortress keep on blazing away at me. They are only 100 feet away.

I continue firing at my victim. The bastard has got to go down, even if it means my own neck. I remain 150 to 200 feet behind his tail. The fire now spreads to his right wing.

I drop the stick for a moment and try to attract the attention of Dölling by waving and pointing to the second Fortress. There is a sudden flash in front of my eyes, and I feel my waving hand slammed violently against the right side of the aircraft. Alarmed, I reach for the stick, but drop it again immediately. My right glove is in shreds, with blood trickling out. I do not feel any pain.

Once again I grasp the stick with my injured hand, line up the sights on my opponent, and empty the magazine in one long burst. At long last the Fortress goes down, falling into the clouds like a flaming torch.

I go down after it, following as far as the sea. There all that is left of the heavy bomber is a large patch of oil burning on the surface.

By now my hand is starting to hurt. I take the stick in my left hand and find it smeared with blood. Shreds of flesh hang from the torn glove.

I lost my bearings some time ago during the shooting above the clouds. Heading south, however, I am bound to reach land somewhere. It is a miracle that my engine has not been hit. By a stroke of good luck the gunners on that Fortress were not good marksmen.

The pain in my hand is getting worse. I am losing a lot of blood. My flying-suit looks as if I had been wallowing in a slaughter-house.

How far out at sea can I be? Minutes drag by; and still there is no sign of that blasted coastline. I begin to have a peculiar hot, sickly sort of feeling: must be getting lightheaded.

This blasted pain in my hand!

An island looms up ahead: Norderney. Only seven or eight minutes more, and then I can land. The time seems interminable. Finally I am over Jever. In spite of the throbbing pain in my hand I dive low over the Flight dispersal point and announce my success with a victory roll.

The mechanics wave their hands and caps, as delighted as children. And now I need both hands for landing. I grit my teeth. My right hand is completely numb.

My ground-crew chief is horrified at the sight of my hand and the blood over my flying-suit. The mechanics swarm round my aircraft. The chief has been wounded!

At the station first-aid post the medical officer on duty removes the glove and places an emergency dressing on my hand. I also receive a precautionary anti-tetanus injection.

It is only 0900 hours. The last of the aircraft do not return until noon. Two more victories can be chalked up on the scoreboard at the dispersal point.

At noon I am finally taken to hospital. They have to operate. One finger-joint is amputated. The hand will be all right otherwise, unless gangrene sets in.

A nursing sister takes me into a ward. I am supposed to remain there until further notice. I look outside: my car is still there in the courtyard below. Jungmaier, my driver, has waited.

Cautiously I peep down the long corridor. The coast is clear: no one is in sight. I never could stand the smell of disinfectant in hospitals. Half an hour later I am back at my Flight dispersal point.

I cannot help laughing: they may be looking for me at that hospital to this day, for all I know.

## 2nd July, 1943

It had been my intention to remain with the Flight; but the Commanding Officer, Captain Specht (who assumed command of the Squadron two months ago), ordered me to take a few days leave, and together with Lilo and little Ingrid I went to Hamelin.

Three and a half years have passed since I left home. Then I had just taken my Senior Matriculation and was wanting to be a soldier. Now I am back as a Senior Lieutenant—I was promoted a month ago and confirmed in my appointment as Flight Commander—having been awarded the Iron Cross First and Second Class, the black wound-stripe, and the pilot's insignia. During the last few months, too, I have received operational wings in bronze, silver and gold, for having completed more than two hundred missions.

In those days I was in love with Annaliese, and today I am a married man and a father, too.

In our dear old rat-hole nothing has changed.

Every day the dressing on my hand is changed at the local hospital. I have my arm in a sling. Somehow I cannot help feeling rather proud of my first wound.

# 6
# Prisoners of War

## PRISONER AS SLAVE

from
*A Prisoner in Germany*
by Robert Guerlain
London: Macmillan & Co. Ltd, 1944

*In 1899, a general international convention met to discuss the treatment of prisoners of war. An agreement was signed at the Hague Peace Conference of that year. Another convention in 1907 at The Hague widened the provisions but did not allow for the neutral inspection of prison camps, the exchange of prisoners' names, nor correspondence with prisoners.*

*After World War I, it was evident that the Hague provisions were insufficient. The International Red Cross proposed a more complete code. The Swiss government invited 47 governments to Geneva in 1929, where they signed the Geneva Convention Relative to the Treatment of Prisoners of War. This document still remains the international law on the subject.*

*Chief among the nations not adhering to the Geneva Convention were Japan and the USSR. Japan did give a qualified promise in 1942 to abide by the Geneva rules, and in 1941 the USSR agreed to observe the Hague Convention rules of 1907.*

*The Geneva Convention laid down rules of conduct for captors to which they adhered. According to the signatories of the Geneva Convention, no prisoner of war could be forced to disclose to his captor any information other than his identity (his name, rank, and serial number). Every prisoner of war is entitled to adequate food and medical care, and has the right to exchange correspondence and receive parcels. He is required to observe ordinary military discipline and courtesy, but he may attempt to escape at his own risk. Once recaptured, he cannot be punished for his attempt. Officers receive pay either according to the pay scale of their own country or to that of their captor, whichever is less; they cannot be required to work. Enlisted men may be required to work for pay, but the nature and location of their work should not expose them to danger, and in no case can they be required to perform work directly related to military operations. Camps should be open to inspection by authorized representatives of a neutral power.*

*In World War II, Switzerland and Sweden acted as protecting powers. The United States and Great Britain fully honored the Geneva Convention throughout the war. Japan committed many atrocities, and it wasn't until a sufficient number of Japanese became prisoners of war that Japan, fearful of reprisals, softened its barbaric treatment of captured American personnel.*

*Germany did not treat all its prisoners alike. American and British soldiers received the best treatment, Polish prisoners the worst. The French had the Germans' contempt.*

*Robert Guerlain, a French prisoner of war captured during the Battle of the Somme in 1940 by the Nazi forces, tells of his experiences and treatment. In so doing, he reveals the bankrupt war strategy of the French in World War II and French ineptness in the field.*

*The "Maginot Line psychosis," the theory of defense lines backed by other defense lines with no plans for offensive action, doomed the French to defeat. The Germans pushed on as the French fell back to each designated defense system until there was nowhere else to go. The French distributed unusable ammunition, and food rations were scarce, but there was an abundance of chocolate and cheese. For a country that had experienced many wars in the past and had had twenty years to rearm and plan, the French proved to be abysmal failures on the fighting front. It was almost as if the entire army had been sabotaged from the inside, and from the top. The men who went off to fight for their country became a major portion of the slave force of Nazi Germany.*

W e had been told to hold. We had held. But all round us there was no longer any front nor any organized resistance. The German avalanche had long gone past us. The racket outside—merely mopping-up operations. For even our strong point, this village which we had fortified and held for days, no longer existed as such. In an hour or two we should be prisoners. Perhaps sooner. We could do nothing more about it.

Defeat? Thinking back on it, I can see that until, on that June day, in the cellar of a ruined house, we awaited our capture by the Germans, we had never dreamed of the possibility of a general defeat. We knew nothing of what was going on elsewhere. The Somme was lost. But behind that there was the Marne, the Seine, if need be, the Loire.

When we had left Alsace we had merely known that "things were going badly in Belgium." Belgium was a long way off. And then… Well, then, first came an interminable train journey, the marches, more marches, and still more marches, across the departments of Seine-et-Oise, Oise, Somme. Deserted fields. Evacuated villages. Silent radios. No letters. No papers. Somewhere, we came upon the Germans. Our advance battalion was trapped in an ambush and lost half its strength. We dug ourselves in, we fortified the villages in hedgehog style. To the usual fatigues was added one new to us—burying the dead. There were the anticipated skirmishes and patrols but there were also unanticipated German aeroplanes. There were five-cartridge clips for rifles designed for three-cartridge clips, but that was normal because confusion is a part of war; there were no supplies, but that was war; and there was no post, but that, too, was war. And then, one day the skirmishes and surprise attacks ceased and in their place came the big German push. It was June 4 and I know now that the newspapers at the time called it the Battle of the Somme. The Germans had tanks, Stukas, and much more besides. They also had a reconnaissance 'plane. We called it the petrol tin and at first it made us laugh because it seemed clumsy and ridiculous, but we did not laugh long, for the positions it flew over hadn't long to wait. We—well, the first day, we still had some artillery, but on June 5th, in the morning, our guns ceased fire, the 155's first because they were captured first, and at noon there were no longer even the 75's. And then, it was the Germans who began firing from the direction where our artillery had been. They fired from in front and they fired from behind, and there were the Stukas as well. At a given moment the German gunners fired in full sight and at close range. They were in their shirt-sleeves and appeared to be taking things easy. Their infantry travelled in lorries as far as what was called "the scene of operations." The German infantry had no junk slung around them and they utterly lacked that air of an overloaded mule which distinguishes the soldier in the field. They had come along like a football team, but they were never in any hurry to take a position before the arrival of their tanks.

We fell back from position to position, in ever-dwindling force, and finally found ourselves in this "hedgehog village."

There were barricades across the road and barbed wire behind the houses. That held as well as it might. And in the end, there was the cellar.

In the distance we could still hear the noise of battle. From time to time, too, there were bursts of machine-gun fire pretty close to us, from men who had barricaded themselves in a house.

It got darker and darker in the cellar. Little by little the sounds which came from outside grew less violent. Only a few hours before, it had been the dull explosions of mines, mortars, and cannon which had predominated, interspersed from time to time by those of bombs. These explosions first grew less frequent, then died down, their silence making audible the intermittent tac-tac of machine-guns and rifle-fire. With these mingled now, more and more frequently, the roar of grenades. We pictured them hurled into cellars like our own.

The day was dying but, after the hours spent in darkness, it was dazzling. I don't know whether I was able to discern the features of the two German soldiers who supervised our exit. I have no recollection of them. I know that one of them held a machine-gun, his finger on the trigger, and that the machine-gun shook. They were both drunk and shouting raucously. "Raus," they cried, and something else that none of us understood.

The village had been razed utterly in the "other" war. A few days of fighting had been enough to recreate what it must have been like at the end of 1918. But already there were great signposts everywhere with notices in gothic characters. An acrid smoke filled the air; the few houses which still stood were burning.

The road was pitted with craters and littered with debris, but it was not that which made it look so strange: it was covered with French soldiers. Not dead men only, as we thought at first. The dead could be distinguished from the living by their limpness, lying on their back or curled up in unmilitary attitudes. But the others were drawn up in fives, very carefully, lying flat on their stomachs with arms stretched out before them.

A gang of Germans were there to search us. They took away haversacks, caps, and belts.

"Down," said a non-commissioned officer, pointing with his revolver to the roadway, "by fives," he added, holding up his five fingers. Some German soldiers encouraged us with kicks—the order was quickly executed.

It was unwise to lift one's hand or move an arm. At intervals of about ten yards along the road stood sentinels to guard us. From time to time one of them would shoot over the heads of the prisoners—there's nothing like it for getting discipline.

Behind us we heard shouting. "Raus," cried the Germans. Other Frenchmen lay down behind us.

And while some monotonously shouted "Raus," others rummaged in the regimental lorries. It was, above all, the provision lorries that pleased them. The contents of one of these had been spilled on the roadway. There were tins of food, bread, bags of this and that, and a huge gruyère cheese, the size of a wheel, from which each German who passed cut a slice with his bayonet. But it was the chocolate which was the big success. The soldiers who found it distributed it generously among their comrades. The guard nearest us had his pockets filled to bursting. His sub-machine-gun under his right arm, the man held in his left hand a huge block of chocolate at which he gnawed from time to time. The expression on his face was divided between the martial sentiments of a conqueror intent on intimidating a contemptible beaten foe, and the delights enjoyed by his palate in contact with an unexpected prize.

There was a sudden upheaval, far ahead of us, at the entrance to the village. We made out a voice delivering a sort of speech in French. The voice drew gradually closer, obviously making the same speech at points nearer and nearer to us.

The voice was that of a gentleman dressed as a major of the French Army. The gentleman was spick and span and very elegant. He had a monocle screwed in his right eye, wore gloves, and seemed very much at ease at the head of a train of German officers who seemed to constitute his suite.

"Listen carefully to what I say," he began. "From now on, you only obey the German military authorities. You will be taken to the rear. The German military authority expects strict discipline from you. It is absolutely forbidden to leave the ranks on the march. The escorting troops have orders to fire without warning on anyone who lags behind. Get up, fall in by fives, wait for orders!"

An officer of the S.S. went by, accompanied by an interpreter.

"You wanted to go to Berlin," he told us. "Well, you're going, but it'll be a bit different from what you imagined."

"Fall in by fives; forward march."

It was the start of a long journey.

"Nach Berlin," said the S.S. men. They were very proud of their witticism and kept repeating it.

On leaving the village, there was a barrier. Yet another search. To make it simpler, we were relieved of greatcoats and tunics. Then came marching at the double. Nothing could have been simpler. The S.S. men were on bicycles and a bicycle is made for fast travelling. We had to go forward at the same rate as our escort. Along the road stood other members of this chosen band, sub-machine-guns at the ready, cheering us on with shouts and occasional bursts of lead.

Today I still cannot recall all the details of that progress. No episode of the preceding weeks nor of all those which were to come ever touched its nightmare quality. I can still see us running, worn out after days and days of fighting, weeks of watching and sleeplessness, and I know that we were haunted by one obsession: to keep in line, not to break the formation of "fives," not to fall down, not to give "them" a pretext to fire. To left and right, in front and behind, men tottered, fell. Shots cracked. The battle was over, but the death-roll was not complete.

I do not know how long this ghastly run lasted. I have no idea how far it took us. It ended not because we could go no further, but because, at a fixed point behind the lines, the rule of the S.S. troops ended.

They drove us, a wretched herd, into a cattle pasture. But before handing us over, they meant to take a worthy farewell of us.

They made us line up in five ranks. They counted us. With the remains of formations from other sectors which were already there when we arrived, we were about five thousand. A senior officer, with a whole cohort of fellow high-ups, reviewed us. Other conquerors photographed us. They have a mania for snapshots; already, on the way there, I don't know how many soldiers had turned their cameras on our column—they all have cameras; it must be the German tourist tradition flourishing on French soil.

The senior officer with his suite, having completed his inspection, stood a little way off from us. He gave orders to one of his juniors, who must have been an interpreter, for it was in French that he suddenly cried: "Jews, five steps forward, march!"

There was an interminable second's hesitation. The whole column seemed frozen with horror. Would anyone brave this fate? Yes. One man left the ranks, others followed, ten at first, then twenty, fifty. Finally, there were about a hundred, standing five paces off from their fellows.

The senior officer came up to them, strolled along the line. He took one by the hair, the smallest, the weakliest, the most "Jewy." He dragged him a certain distance away from the rest, so that everyone could see, pushed him forward and made a little speech. The interpreter translated. And the officer, treating his victim as though he were a stuffed animal, pointed out to us his "bestial face," his "vulture nose," all the traits of an inferior and abject race.

The officer was a big man, tall and very stout. He was the perfect gentle knight. He was Siegfried slaying the dragon. And he put heart and soul into his mission.

"You see before you," he cried, "what has brought you to your present pass.

219

This is what drove you into war. We are here to free you from him and his like. Victorious Germany will pardon you who went to war despite yourselves. But she will exterminate him" (as he spoke, Siegfried administered a kick to the dragon before him) "and them" (his gloved finger pointed to the others) "and all those of that foul race."

Victorious Siegfried finished his demonstration with a last kick at his victim. The beaten dragon, like a sleep-walker, fell back into line. The S.S. men went off with martial gait. Other Germans took over.

The march started again. It was night now. Kilometres and kilometres, but the pace was slower. Our present escort was composed of older men. We had no hopes, for we had seen enough to be prepared for the worst; so it was with grateful surprise that we observed that, though discipline was rigorous, it was administered without excessive zeal and without our captors, at least most of them, trying to improve on it by individual efforts. We were allowed to send parties in search of water. The walking wounded were attended to and put in lorries.

Péronne. In the town, the houses are still disintegrating within while their façades seem strangely intact. The streets are already cleared of rubble but absolutely deserted. Several kilometres out of the town another pasture where we are parked for the night. It is dark. Nothing to eat, no blankets. The men, whom the preliminary search has despoiled of everything, including their overcoats and tunics, wearily throw themselves on the cold, damp ground.

The next morning we start out early. There is still nothing to eat. On the road we form an endless column stretching for miles and miles and continually being swollen by fresh arrivals. Compared with the number of prisoners, the escort troops are negligible. But truckloads of soldiers are constantly speeding by the convoy, and every village is swarming with Germans. Nevertheless, escape would be possible were it not for the fact that we are so exhausted and weak that the thought does not even occur to us. Like a herd of cattle, we trudge on, ten, twenty, thirty, thirty-five kilometres. From time to time, in spite of the danger of being shot, men drop to the road unable to drag on another step. Here and there shots ring out; nearly always they are fired into the air. The escort does not show much enthusiasm. They are men well on in years, individually not harsh, severe only when they see an officer approaching. Once the officer has gone on, the storm quickly passes. Some of them even apologize afterward: "We have to obey orders."

And thus we go on for days and days. Sometimes in the evenings we are given a watered soup which has the tremendous advantage of being hot. Once we are even given a piece of bread. Many of us have lost all dignity and beg for something to eat from the Germans watching us go by.

At last one day we arrived at a station. Waiting for us was a train made up of fifty cars, most of them German and therefore slightly larger than the French "forty men and eight horses." Five thousand men were to be carried in these. I don't know how we managed to squeeze into our car, but I remember that the rifle-butts of our guards had a lot to do with it. For two days we rode in the car, 106 of us piled up on top of each other. The doors were shut and padlocked and it was impossible to get near one of the barred windows. There was absolutely no way of telling what zigzag course the train followed, bringing us finally to Givet in the Ardennes where we were to leave the train. On the way we were given a little bread and a piece of cheese. In spite of this however, we had reached the end of our tether, and the Germans had to resort to their guns again to make us march the fifteen kilometres to the transient camp at Beauraing, our next stopping place. Upon our arrival there were many who failed to answer the roll-call. Had they been shot? Or had they been picked up by ambulances? To this day no trace of them has been found.

We spent three weeks at Beauraing, the scene of one of the most humiliating incidents that happened during these demoralizing weeks. Standing in the station were several car-loads of shells. The Germans asked for a detail of volunteers to transfer the shells into trucks, holding out a promise of cheese and bread for those who would do the work. There was a wild rush. Several hundred prisoners fought for the job, men of every branch of the Army, of every rank. The Germans were obliged to send over two hundred back to the ranks.

The complete demoralization of a whole army is an amazing and frightful thing. It was to be temporary, but for weeks and even months it seemed to deprive some of us of our entire personality, or dignity as men, our whole background. I shall always remember an Alsatian quartermaster-sergeant whose father and two elder brothers had given their lives for France in 1914 and who, during the present campaign, had been one of the fiercest non-coms in my company. He had fought the Germans with a kind of personal hatred. I saw this man talking to some German soldiers and outdoing them in their own Nazi doctrines. He was denouncing democracy and making anti-Semitic speeches with such vehemence that the Germans themselves were showing a certain amount of reserve. It should be underlined that these were merely German privates watching us go by from the ground floor of the houses where they were quartered, and that the circumstances were such as to exclude any possibility of the sergeant's profiting by his attitude. There must have been a basis for this man's behaviour—resentment at having fought in vain, disgust for all the numerous obscure factors which were the cause of our disaster, and perhaps a feeling of despair—which led him and a great many others, seeing and, what is worse, feeling themselves beaten, to confide in a country, a regime, and a doctrine that has proved to be stronger.

Such incidents made our terrible journey far more painful. Although the majority of prisoners condemned the attitude of their "collaborationist" comrades, there were few who dared publicly express their disapproval. Yet it was not long before a number of incidents occurred which brought us hope and confidence. At Luxembourg it was the attitude of the population, who ignored strict orders not to go near the train in order to bring us bread and refreshments, and to encourage us, saying that we must not be disheartened because "the Germans, in spite of everything, will never win."

Later on it was the gallant attitude of some English prisoners of war at Trier, who, despite the opposition of their escort, marched through that first German town, column by threes, whistling "Tipperary" and keeping perfect step. It was almost a victory march, a march by men who were sure of themselves and of their cause, and the least bit affected by their status as prisoners. They marched down the street, heads held high, looking neither to right nor left, and bearing their dirt and rags magnificently, not like tramps but like soldiers returning from the battlefield.

And last, during a stop by the train that was taking us from Trier toward southwest Germany, it was our first encounter with Polish soldiers, a detail sent over to feed us, that also showed us it was possible to be prisoners without being conquered and that we could submit to the Germans without being dominated by them. They also showed us that, although beaten, France would always remain a source of hope for other nations of Europe. The confidence which they placed in our country, the friendliness which they showed, gave us back some of our self-confidence; and, when the train departed, we were in somewhat better spirits and feeling less humiliated.

That was the last night of our journey. We finally fell asleep after once more painfully struggling to create 106 "berths" in a box car.

"Wake up! Everybody out!" The men open their eyes slowly, as though coming out of an anesthetic; it takes quite a while for them to realize where they are. In the opaque blackness of the box car, 106 men seek painfully to disentangle themselves from the mass of arms, legs, and bodies.

Suddenly the doors, which have remained closed for so long, are thrown open with great clatter. A dazzling light bathes the interior of the car, throwing into sharp relief the silhouettes of the guards waiting outside. Helmeted and booted, they stand with fixed bayonets, a live wall stretching out of sight along the platform.

"Raus!" A raucous tone, and a word with which we have become all too familiar during the journey. "Column by fives!" German officers walk down the column. We are counted. Then recounted. "Forward march!" The line of German soldiers faces right and moves with us, squeezing in on us. As we march out of the rural station, they are joined by other soldiers looming out of the darkness with furiously barking dogs held on leashes.

Dogs. Bayonets. A road that never ends. A heavy rain pours steadily down. The ground is soaked and turns into bottomless mud under our feet. At last a huge gate before us. Barbed wire entanglements. More searchlights. A wooden observation post. "Halt!" A carved signboard, brilliantly lit up. It was placed there and illuminated for our benefit. It shows, in almost life-size figures, their outlines deeply marked in the wood, a file of French, English, and Polish soldiers, disarmed and in rags, stooping beneath an invisible burden. And a caption in gothic letters carved into the wood reads: Nach Berlin.

We looked at each other. And for the first time we became fully conscious of our situation. After two weeks of nightmarish marches and train trips, of nocturnal halts in cow pastures, of degradation and semi-consciousness, this signboard gives us an ironic and significant picture of our situation, its tragic outlines heightened by the harsh brilliance of the searchlights. We are prisoners, more than prisoners—symbols of defeat.

"Come and get it!"

Not much to get. But there was bread. A fortune in bread. Two hundred grams. This quantity was to last for the whole day. But it seemed enormous to us.

The bread came to us as a gluey substance that dried out in less than five minutes. Nevertheless, during the first two or three months of captivity, until the first packages from France arrived, the distribution of this bread was to become the most eagerly awaited moment of the entire day. At night we would go to sleep thinking of the next day's ration of bread, and in the morning it was our first thought upon waking.

"Assembly!" The 408 occupants of the barrack, lined up on the waste ground behind the building, encountered for the first time their new master, the Herr Gefreiter Hinterhuber. This Bavarian corporal, a choleric little man firmly persuaded of his own importance, after having carefully counted and recounted us, made a lengthy oration on the regime and discipline of the camp. It was *verboten* to leave the barrack between eight and twelve o'clock and between one-thirty and six o'clock. It was also *verboten* to go to bed except between nine in the evening and six in the morning. *Verboten—verboten—verboten.*

"You are in a prison camp and not in a hospital. If the regime does not appeal to you, it's too late to complain. You should have thought about it before you declared war on Germany. Dismiss!"

Here, then, is the barrack that will be our home for years and years. It is 180 feet long by 30 wide. It must serve as shelter and *lebensraum* for 408 men, crammed into two halls separated from each other by the washroom. From top to bottom and from end to end it is completely filled with a curious maze of scaffoldings: three platforms, one on top of each other. Each of these platforms is a bed for four men; each scaffolding holds twelve. Four tables and eight benches complete the furniture. Putting things in the best possible light, therefore, during the day there are seats for sixty-four men. Not another stick of furniture, no drawers, no shelves; the few personal things that remained to us, together with our clothes at night, had to be stowed away in the beds.

216 men are crowded into Barrack A, the larger of the two halls; Barrack B holds 192. Each of the halls is commanded by a French non-commissioned officer, usually a company or regimental sergeant-major. Under his orders are other officers, each in charge of twenty-four men; an interpreter, also prisoner, acts as intermediary in all contacts with the German officer in charge of the barrack or with other authorities. From where did these barrack commanders, these interpreters, all this personnel, spring? Often they were simply the greatest opportunists, the men who had obtained the soft jobs, the loudest mouthed, who had seen a chance to live on good terms with the new masters, to be exempt from work parties and from the majority of the inconveniences attached to our position. But also in a number of cases, particularly the lower ranks, such as the group commanders, they were men who had been put there in good faith by their comrades, and it must be admitted that often their job was neither easy nor enviable. For their principal task, especially during the first months, consisted in the distribution of soup at a time when hunger had wiped out whatever had been left of the men's solidarity and group spirit and when bloody battles were fought over potato peelings.

Life went on grimly and monotonously. Reveille at six o'clock. Two hundred grams of bread as daily ration, and an indefinable beverage masquerading under the name of coffee. In the lavatory, four hundred men battled around a single spigot for the privilege of washing without soap and cleaning their teeth without brush or paste. Assembly at seven o'clock. Until seven-thirty, waiting for the Herr Gefreiter to come to count and recount us. After this, back to the barrack until eleven o'clock—soup time. Indescribable hubbub around a pail of liquid made of fish powder or soya. Permission to walk about the camp until one-thirty. After that, the barrack again until evening soup. Another mêlée, and at nine o'clock lights out.

These were terrifying weeks. Hunger plagued us from dawn to dusk, and would often prevent us from sleeping at night. We spent our days in the cramped quarters of our barrack, where we were forbidden to lie down and where no more than sixty men out of six hundred could find seats, for there were far more prisoners in the barrack than had been expected. We lacked even the most elementary conveniences, but the worst thing about the whole ordeal was the demoralization of all these men. Two subjects dominated every discussion or conversation: food and freedom. And in spite of our gnawing hunger, it was the question of repatriation about which every thought revolved.

Liberation? Of course. Let France only capitulate, we were told, and everyone will be released. Look at the Belgians. Their country gave up, and none of their men were kept. (A few days later a hundred of them were to arrive in the camp.)

Defeated without yet realizing why, and believing everything lost, many prisoners asserted that absolute submission was necessary. It was the repetition in camp of the fatal *sauve qui peut*, that led to the collapse of so many sectors on the front. So there was nothing to be astonished about when the news of the signing of the armistice was in general hailed with joy.

But the armistice terms did not provide for the reparation of prisoners until "after the peace." After the peace with England, naturally. And, if the French prisoners were not yet back in their homes, they could blame the stubborn English, who continued to fight a futile war.

This argument soon threw a chill on even the most outspoken advocates of capitulation. But the Germans quickly brought up another point. Perhaps Hitler would now wink at the terms of the armistice. If France's conduct should be deserving, perhaps as a favour he would agree to liberate the prisoners according to their race.

Their race? Certainly. Didn't we know that the term "French nation" was a pure myth; that there was no such thing as a French people but merely a completely arbitrary agglomeration of varied and diverse peoples whose greatest desire was to be freed from the ancient yoke of a tyrannical central power? There were Bretons, Flemings, Normans, Catalans, Basques, and so forth, not to mention Alsatians and Lorrainers, who were Germans pure and simple, or Corsicans and the inhabitants of the Maritime Alps and Savoy, who were Italians. Therefore the Third Reich's generous gift of freedom would be measured, even before the total victory over England, by the creation of these new national states liberated from the French yoke and the return of the various races, together with the regions they inhabited, to the countries to which they belonged by right.

Apart from this, a whole series of departures had begun, but not for France. There was a heavy exodus of work battalions, sent either voluntarily or by force to the *Arbeitskommando*. These expeditions started at the beginning of July, and before long were going at such a rate that the camp would soon have been left empty had it not been for constantly arriving fresh batches of French prisoners.

All this movement did not appear to presage a forthcoming liberation. The prisoners still in camp were astonished witnesses of the continuous procession of tens of thousands of their comrades. They must have been the first among the tremendous masses of French prisoners to regain their balance and see things as they really were. For, although tightly enclosed behind triple barriers of barbed wire, guarded by an entire regiment surrounding the camp in a ceaseless watch, and closely watched on the inside by trained police dogs, they nevertheless had an observation post that enabled them to see certain things that escaped and that continue to escape the attention of many people living in the "freedom" of the new European order.

They had no newspapers to tell them what was happening in the outside world. But, even if they had, newspapers would have been poor substitutes for the numerous sources which every day brought them uncensored news.

First of all, each of them had his own administrative number plate. At the beginning of July, the Kommandantur had just handed out plate number 30,000. Toward August 15, the latest arrivals were given plates numbered from 65,000 up. In September, the 80,000 mark was passed. And the Germans continued to deliver more of them until February 1941, when the new prisoners were registered in the series ending with 125,000.

The men in camp remembered having read in the armistice terms that the troops not taken prisoner by June 23, 1940, would merely be disarmed and sent into the non-Occupied zone for demobilization. And so they wondered at seeing these tens upon tens of thousands of their comrades arriving in camp, the hundreds of thousands who kept arriving in the other German camps. Where did they come from?

It was not difficult to find the answer. It was found, in the barracks where men by the hundreds lay on the floor, the benches, and the tables, or in the infirmary, where were packed the hundreds of sick and wounded. There were thousands of new arrivals who had been made prisoners long after the armistice. Among them were men officially demobilized in the un-Occupied zone and then arrested, often by the French police or gendarmerie, upon returning to their homes in the Occupied zone. There were those who had been taken prisoner months after having returned to civilian life, and there were others who had never been soldiers. One day in November, a priest clad in his cassock arrived in the midst of a convoy of prisoners; the Germans in camp compelled him to put on a uniform so that he would bear more resemblance to a prisoner.

We called him "Le Négrier" (The Slaver). He was a prisoner like the rest of us, but he had a great deal of power. Quite stout and of middling height, he had a baby face with fat pink cheeks. It was easy to imagine him wheeling a perambulator through the streets of his little garrison town, with his fourth child, born just before the declaration of war. But I wouldn't know whether his friends in that town could have imagined him fulfilling the role in the prison camp which had earned him his nickname.

For this French regimental sergeant-major was the official purveyor of cheap labour to the Germans. I have no desire to pass judgment on him; that is a task for a French military court after the war. If I speak of him, it is because he and his colleagues in the other camps played such an important part in camp life that it would be impossible to speak of the prisoners without mentioning him.

He appeared for the first time at the beginning of July. He burst into the barrack one day, accompanied by two other French regimental sergeant-majors and a German sergeant, ordered an immediate general assembly, and, pulling a notebook out of his pocket, demanded fifty volunteer farm workers for a "job in the country."

The first time, he had no trouble at all in getting the number he wanted. Hoping to be well fed, happy to get out of camp and work at their trade, the men leaped at the chance.

The same thing happened on his second appearance. But when the slave-trader turned up for the third time to ask for a hundred volunteers, only six men stepped forward. The news had spread from men who had returned sick that the "job in the country" consisted of constructing a dam, that for ten hours a day the men had to toil up to their waist in a river, that they got no better food than at the camp, and that while they were not working they were locked up in a barrack without ever being allowed to go out.

"No volunteers? Very well, I shall pick the men myself." But that did not prove so easy. Some claimed they were sick and others based their refusal to go on their rank as non-commissioned officers. But the slave-trader ended up by getting his hundred men; the next day he came back with ten German soldiers to take them to work.

The sergeant-major very quickly earned himself a foul reputation. In a prison camp news spreads like wildfire. No sooner did he step into one of the barracks with his two aides than the neighbouring barracks were miraculously warned and the men concealed themselves as he made his rounds.

But one is not a sergeant-major for nothing. There are ways and means. The barrack commanders were threatened by the Kommandantur and made responsible for the volunteering of their men. They were obliged to draw up and keep open for inspection lists of their effectives, marked with the rank and peace-time occupation of each prisoner. In spite of all these controls, many men might have escaped from the Germans. But they could not escape from the slaver.

"So you don't want to go on Kommando? You say you're medical? What unit? Ha! Stretcher-bearer in an infantry regiment. You didn't belong to a medical section but you were a private. You have no right to belong to the medical personnel. Kommando."

"Sick? You say the major vouched for you? When? Barrack commander, let me have the list. Let's see now. ... Ah, here! Rheumatism. You reported sick on purpose. You're no more sick than I am. Fit for Kommando. You can leave tomorrow."

"You're a non-com? That's what you say. Your stripes? Anybody can wear them. Show me your Army papers. You don't have any? Well, that's just too bad for you. Come on, let's see your sleeve. You say you're a sergeant? Is that so! Now you listen to me. I tell you that you were nothing but a corporal. I can still see the marks of the woollen stripes you unpicked. Fit for Kommando. Out you go. And consider yourself lucky I don't report you."

The slaver could even find "volunteers" among those he was unable to take by force. I have seen him harangue a group of recently arrived non-coms, not yet up in the tricks of the prisoner's trade.

"You're non-commissioned officers. At present you cannot be compelled to work, for the Germans respect international conventions. But one of these days France will be signing an agreement to waive all privileges for non-coms. When that happens, you'll be sent to work in the Ruhr mines. Terrible. Constantly bombed. You'd do better to volunteer now to work in the country." Out of some hundred and fifty non-coms in that group, the slaver got eighty.

At the end of three months he had actually succeeded in eliminating every means of evading the work parties. The whole camp had been reorganized to facilitate his work. And that work was difficult. There were numerous categories of prisoners that should have been exempt from Kommando work. There were the unwilling non-coms; there were the employees in various camp services; there were those acknowledged to be sick; there were the "ethnic groups," in process of being "liberated," such as the Alsatians and Lorrainers, considered Germans, and the Bretons, who were being re-educated; there were the men of the medical corps; and, lastly, there were the numerous foreign volunteers held in camp for examination by the Gestapo. Naturally, the ordinary privates, liable to fatigue duty at the will of their captors, belonged to none of these categories and would often try to pass themselves off either as Lorrainers or as foreigners or as sick men, which never failed to lead to lengthy and tedious verifications.

With the object of putting a stop to these manoeuvres, the authorities reorganized the camp and placed each category of prisoners in a separate barrack. There were barracks for non-coms, for camp employees, for Alsatians, for Bretons, for foreigners, and there were barracks for "the others." The men in the latter hadn't a chance of escaping the labour draft. The slaver ruled supreme. Thanks to his zeal, the Germans had by November managed to draft 65,000 out of 80,000 men for Kommando work. Nevertheless, the Germans were still not satisfied.

Up till November 1940 the prisoners had been used solely in agriculture and public works. But from then on the needs of the Third Reich seemed to become so pressing that, contrary to all dictates of security, prisoners were put into war industries.

The first indication the camp received of this was in a considerable widening of the functions performed by the Labour Ministry, which had its offices at the headquarters of the Kommandantur. The hunt for labour, which till then had depended entirely on the cunning and zeal of the slaver, was put on a more rational and quasi-scientific basis. There was another general inventory of all prisoners, new cards were made out, and a great many new card indexes created. One of these classified the prisoners according to barrack and enabled the Germans to control at any given moment the number of men available in each one. These cards even had up-to-the-minute reports of doctors' visits, thus preventing any attempt to claim illness under false pretences. Another index classified the men by profession or trade. Hereafter the Kommandos were organized on the basis of these card indexes. Those who were not farm workers were taken out of the fields and sent to do work that corresponded to their civilian jobs. Tens of thousands of metal workers found themselves suddenly thrown into armament factories, while miners were sent into mines, and chemists were obliged to start working for the great I. G. Farben and Badische Anilin corporations. Rational exploitation of the prisoners thus reached a maximum degree of perfection.

But even that was not enough. Millions of French, Polish, and Belgian prisoners laboured night and day in factories and workshops, in railroads and in shipyards. Day by day the trains coming from every corner of occupied Europe drained toward the Third Reich thousands upon thousands of "voluntary civilian workers." Without halt the entire Continent, transformed into a gigantic war plant, kept pouring tanks and aeroplanes, and guns into Germany. But it was still not enough. More slaves were needed, and yet more slaves; there was no end to the number of slaves that were required.

Where was this additional man-power to be found? By December there were no more than 15,000 men left in the camp, in spite of new convoys of French war prisoners that brought the total of available workers up to 100,000. These 15,000 men were non-commissioned officers, camp employees from the various administrative departments, the workshops, kitchens, and so forth, and the sick or convalescent. How were they to wring another 5,000 men from this group? A very simple solution was found. This was to make the life of the non-coms as miserable as possible so that they would prefer Kommando work to staying in camp. Food rations were reduced. Fatigue duties were increased and made more arduous.

For, although international conventions do not permit the forcing of non-commissioned officers to do work outside the camp, they are liable to fatigue tasks in camp. And the term "fatigue" is not very closely defined. There was nothing to prevent their being made to do navvying inside the camp, nothing to stop their being compelled to dig holes one day merely for the pleasure of filling them up again the next.

At first this new regime applied only to non-coms up to and including the rank of quartermaster-sergeant, and for three days a week. But this got no results whatever. The same group of men that during the first weeks of captivity had been so docile and meek had acquired a fierce spirit of resistance. What! Do Kommando work? Give "them" voluntary assistance? Not a chance!

Food rations diminished still further. Still no result. "Fatigue duty" was extended from three days a week to four, and then to six. Still no result. Finally the exemption up till then accorded battalion and regimental sergeant-majors was lifted. But not one man left.

Every day now 8000 non-coms of all ages and ranks could be seen throughout the camp, digging in the ground, working with pick and shovel, hauling wheelbarrows—sergeants, master sergeants, regimental and battalion sergeant-majors, infantrymen, artillerymen, Chasseurs, Spahis, sharp-shooters, sailors, aviators, young and old, many of them wearing the Croix de Guerre, the Médaille Militaire, and numerous decorations from earlier campaigns, often from the last war. They are fighting today by refusing to do useful work for the Germans, by preferring to do far more strenuous work that is of use to no one, and by subsisting on food rations infinitely more meagre than what they would get if they were doing work useful to the Third Reich. Compelled to work, they do, but for their part they compel the Germans to assign them jobs that cannot benefit their enemies.

"There's the motorized corps," the prisoners would say upon seeing the long column of their comrades pass by, pushing hundreds of wheelbarrows before them, the sound of their wheels on the road resembling the dull rumble made by a truck convoy. But these wheelbarrows that serve no useful purpose, these shovels that dig up the ground, these picks and the hands that wield them, have become a symbol. And this work, meant to humiliate the prisoners, has instead become a humiliation for the Germans who have ordered it and supervise it, as they see it produce the reverse effect of what they had expected. No longer a coercive measure, it has become a joke. It is now a mute but eloquent demonstration before which the Germans are helpless. Work? Here you are. But it wont do you any good.

# BATAAN

from

*The Last Time I Saw Them*

by Lt. Col. Corey Ford and Major Alastair MacBain

New York: Charles Scribner's Sons, 1946

*Japan's military expansion began in the nineteenth century, with its invasions of Formosa, Manchuria, and Korea. The Japanese soldier used captives as "native slaves" for forced labor, and it was no surprise that Japan would not become a signatory at the Geneva Convention on the treatment of prisoners of war. All was going too well for Japan just the way things were. The Japanese made a habit of beating their "slaves" with bamboo sticks, rifle butts, and the flat ends of their swords. A twist of the wrist, and serious damage could be inflicted upon the "slave" who resisted.*

*The Japanese never concealed their brutality. Many American correspondents revealed the brutality of the Japanese in the lands they conquered. There were photographs of soldiers beating prostrate forms in rice paddies and of long lines of Japanese soldiers poking bayonets into crowds. There were pictures of executions: prisoner's hands were tied behind the back, then they were made to kneel before an open grave and coldly shot in the back of the head. But Americans paid little attention to these pictures. It was happening so far away to a people that did not excite their interest. Such cruel and inhuman treatment was a horrible shock to the Americans who found themselves prisoners in the early days of the war.*

*The Japanese demanded immediate respect from their American prisoners, and they demanded it with brutality, sadism, and barbarity. The experience of American captains Gene Dale, John Morrett, and Bert Schwarz as prisoners of war wasn't very different from that the Japanese meted out to other vanquished peoples, but Americans found the utter disregard for life and humane care shocking.*

*The captains were taken prisoner when Bataan fell. They saw fellow Americans die by the thousands of starvation and torture in disease-ridden compounds of O'Donnell, Cabanatuan, and Davao. This is their story as they lived it.*

We met at Davao. We happened to be assigned to the same work detail of American prisoners, planting rice; the three of us were side by side in line. We would bend over together and stick the rice seedlings into the black muck, take one step backward in unison, stoop and plant another row. The Jap guards walked the dikes above us, holding Enfield rifles with bayonets fixed. If we faltered, we would get a hobnailed boot in the ribs, or a rifle butt across a naked thigh.

We always worked naked: all we ever had on was a G-string. The Japs took all our clothes away when we worked outside the prison compound. They were afraid we would escape into the jungle, and they even took our shoes away. Going barefoot had a curious effect on the men's morale. Any good American likes to walk with his head up, but when he is barefooted and walking on rough stones, he has to look where he is going. He keeps his head lowered, as if he were cowed or ashamed. Maybe the Japs had that in mind.

They worked us from dawn to dark. The mud was hip-deep, and covered with blue slime; it stank like a carabao wallow. We could smell it a mile away as we approached the field in the morning. We would stand on the dike and touch our bare toes to the mud, like a kid testing the water, and the smell would almost make our stomachs turn over. But once we got covered with it, we didn't notice it any more. We rubbed it all over our face and under our arms and in our crotch, to keep off the red jungle ants and gnats that swarmed up our legs and bit us raw. It dried a gray-brown, like a mud pack, and after a while we looked more like natives than Americans.

We were getting to think and feel more like natives every day. It was over half a year now since Bataan had fallen, and what we had seen on the March of Death and later had left our minds sort of numb. All we thought about was eating and sleeping. We slept at night on the rough board floor, huddled together like animals to keep warm. Our food ration was only 600 grams of rice a day, and we were always hungry. We devoured any scraps the Japs tossed to us, a chicken head or a heap of *camote* peelings or sometimes a half-rotten squash that would float down the ditch into our compound from the Jap kitchen. Or, if we were lucky, would catch a lizard or a snake. There were always cobras lurking in the thickets around the rice paddies, and we would club them to death with a stick. We would wrap the dead snake around our bare stomach and smuggle it into camp so the Japs wouldn't see it, and that night we would roast it over the fire.

We must have been a funny-looking outfit, all skinny as skeletons except where our legs were swollen with wet beri-beri. The Japs got a laugh out of us, and we had to laugh at ourselves. There were colonels and majors of fifty or over, and kids barely eighteen. All of us had diarrhea or dysentery, and if we stopped to relieve ourselves, a guard would take his rifle by the barrel and swing the butt over his shoulder and bring it down hard across our naked backsides to keep us going.

We were not prisoners of the Japs; we were their slaves. They told us over and over that they hated us. "You are our eternal enemies," the little Jap CO told us when we arrived at Camp O'Donnell. "You will not like it here. If you try to escape, we will shoot you."

They promised they would make it tough for us, and they did. We had to empty their latrines, or do any other menial task they ordered. The highest-ranking American officer, even General Wainwright, had to salute the lowest Jap private, and, if he failed, he would be slapped or made to stand at attention in the hot sun. The only way was to shut our minds, and try to live from hour to hour. A man's mind is a funny thing, it operates in three worlds: the past, the present and the future. We lived in the past and in the future.

Mostly we lived in the past. We used to talk about the past together as we worked side by side in the rice paddies. Already it was getting harder and harder to remember all that had happened in the past six months, like trying to remember a nightmare after you are awake, or rather like a nightmare in which you try to recall snatches of an earlier dream. We would remember an incident here or a bit there, and begin to fit the various parts into place.

Johnny would mention some point where he had stopped along the March of Death, and Bert would say, "Hell, were you there? I was there, too," and they would compare dates. Gene would add some other detail, and gradually we pieced together a whole picture of the past. It helped to take our minds off the beatings and the hunger and the heat.

The Japs refused to recognize Wainright's men as prisoners of war. They crammed 10,000 American and Philippine troops into the 92d Garage Area, an enclosure less than 150 yards square, and held them as hostages without food or water. They stayed there two weeks with no covering from the sun, no sanitary facilities of any kind, no medicine to fight the epidemic of disease that was spreading fast in the filthy compound. The infections picked up in the 92d Garage Area accounted for hundreds of American deaths later in the prison camp of Cabanatuan.

The Japs looted the American prisoners constantly, taking their watches, rings and insignia, even their glasses. Gene saw a Jap soldier snatch the upper half of a set of false teeth from an old master sergeant, and smash them under his heel; he let the sergeant keep the lower half.

After two weeks, Gene said, the bedraggled and exhausted Americans were paraded through the main street of Manila. The Japs formed them in ranks and marched them past Manila's main hotel where the Jap officers sat in comfort and watched. The idea was to humble them in the eyes of the natives, but all along the line of march the loyal Filipinos would lift their fingers in a covert "V," and occasionally a native woman would risk her life by running out into the street and handing an American prisoner a cigarette or an ice-cream cone. The Japs would club the woman back to the curb with their rifles. At the other end of town, the Americans were loaded into cattle cars and taken to Bilibid and then Cabanatuan. Gene arrived at Cabanatuan four days before Bert and Johnny.

Johnny, meantime, had withdrawn with the northern and southern Luzon forces into Bataan, and for three months had engaged in a constant artillery duel with the Japs. The Philippine Scouts fought courageously, he said, but the Philippine army was a pitiful little outfit in their paper hats, cheap blue denim uniforms, and brown tennis shoes.

Most of them had never even heard a gun fired before. Johnny fought on the Orion Line until April 6th, and surrendered at Kilometer 167—some fifteen kilometers north of Bert.

"Destroying our own equipment was the hardest thing of all," Johnny recalled; "it made our surrender so complete. We destroyed everything we had. We put projectiles in the guns and blew them up, we beat up all the survey equipment—all our beautiful instruments—and we shot bullets through the truck tires, and poured sugar and water in the gas tanks with the motors running. There was a pay roll waiting to be distributed; we burned it beside the road. After we had destroyed all our weapons, the Jap tanks came up the road, strafing both sides of the highway. They killed our men as we lay flat or hugged the trees for protection."

After the surrender, we were all taken to a concentration camp and held that night without food or water. The following afternoon we started the March of Death.

The first stage of the Death March was the steep zigzag road leading from Mariveles to Little Baguio, almost a mile straight up. We marched in single file in the deep dust, against an endless line of Jap army traffic: cavalry, tanks, artillery mounts, caissons, military trucks. We must have passed 50,000 soldiers on that march, and every Nip who felt like it would shove us or cuff us as he passed.

Kicking was nothing; they all took sideswipes at us with their hobnailed shoes until our shins were black and blue. Some of our older men would fall by the wayside in the terrific heat, and the Japs would club the stragglers to their feet. We put our arms around one another and helped ourselves along, because we knew what happened to those who dropped out. The Japs would drag them into the bushes and we would hear screams, and we would not see them again.

The Jap soldiers would snatch things from us as they passed. Bert was wearing his silver pilot wings pinned to his shirt. A little Nip made a grab for them, and instinctively Bert half-turned and gave him the hip. It was a foolish thing to do, but for some reason the soldier just turned and walked away. From then on, Bert wore the wings inside his shirt where they wouldn't be seen.

As we progressed, we began to see more and more bodies in the road, crushed by the Jap transports, Bert and Johnny were at different places along the line of march, but they both remembered one particular Filipino body along about

Kilometer 160. It had been pressed as flat as a pancake by the truck tires, and, in flattening, it had spread about twice its natural size; it was as though someone had drawn a huge caricature of a Filipino in the road. It was so flat you didn't even see what it was until you were walking on it.

Now we were half crazy with thirst. We had to get water. We would stop and drink water out of a mudhole with a dead carabao lying in the middle of it; we would scoop the water up with our cupped hands and gulp it, regardless. At one halt, Johnny crowded with some others toward a stream to fill his canteen. The men upstream shouted that several Filipino bodies were lying in the water, but the others were too thirsty to let that bother them. Johnny had some chlorine tablets and offered them around, but most of the men didn't bother. They knew they were asking for dysentery, but they were beginning to feel it wasn't going to matter.

We made about forty kilometers that day without rest, and about ten o'clock that night we were jammed into the cellar of an old Spanish stone house. It had been used as a pigsty; it would hold about fifty pigs. They shoved five hundred of us in there and locked the door and left us standing in the dark, wedged so tight we couldn't move. Several men died that night of suffocation, but the dead stood all night with the living. There was no room to fall down.

We set out again the following dawn, and we marched all that day, and all the next day, and the next. Days were beginning to run together, and events were getting blurred in our minds. We staggered on mile after mile, too dazed to know what was happening any more. Americans would die and other Americans would demand a decent burial and they would be killed for demanding burial. Now and then we would run into friends in the line. Near Little Baguio, Bert passed Captain Ed Dyess resting with his men under some trees. Bert asked him why he didn't leave on one of the planes from Bataan, and Dyess said he was sticking with his squadron. Captain Dyess was with us until he escaped from Davao a year later.

The sun beat down, the dust choked us, the smell of the dead was everywhere. We didn't even think about the dead anymore. All we thought about was water, water. We would see a glass of water in our mind, and we could almost feel it run over our tongue and down our throat, but in our mouth there was nothing but dust. It was about this time that Johnny lost his precious canteen. A Jap soldier borrowed it to take a drink, and then hung it casually on his own belt and began walking away. Johnny doubled his fist and started after him, but the others grabbed his arm and dragged him back into line.

By noon of the fifth day we could make out the stacks of the San Fernando sugar mills in the distance, and we knew we were getting near the end of the march. A sprinkle of rain fell that afternoon; that was how we made the last few miles. We held up our mess kits to catch the rain, and we walked with our faces upturned and our parched mouths open to the sky. We were shuffling like drunken men, wandering from side to side of the road, but always keeping our eyes fixed ahead. Johnny almost passed out, and a little Air Corps pilot who was beside him put an arm around his waist and dragged him the rest of the way into town.

We arrived at Camp O'Donnell on April 15, 1942. We spent two months at O'Donnell and five months at Cabanatuan; and those seven months were the most unreal of all. We had no medicine, no bandages, no surgical equipment of any kind; we watched men die who might have been saved by a simple operation. Two thousand Americans died at O'Donnell the first six weeks. We had no clean clothing or sheets or mosquito nets: just the bare mud floor. The rain poured through the lean-to roof and soaked the ground, and pneumonia set in. All of us were covered with sores, and the floor was thoroughly infected, but we had no water to wash it. We had hardly enough water to drink; men would stand in the water line for hours in the hot sun.

The Jap medical officer made one inspection and ordered us to clean things up, but the Japs gave us nothing to do it with. They were thoroughly indifferent to everything that went on inside the compound. All they did was to nail up posters saying, "If you attempt to escape, you will be shot." We used them for toilet paper.

It was not that there was no medicine or food to be had. Once we saw three truckloads of supplies arrive at the camp—a gift to the Americans from a priest in Manila—and the Japs turned them away at the gate. It was tough to watch them leave. The Japs used our confiscated C rations to feed their dogs; they didn't care. Our only food was boiled rice, a soft, sloppy mess that went right through you. Some of the dysentery cases might have lived if we had had solid food. We had to cook the rice in iron *kawas*—big Philippine caldrons—and it was always watery and scorched on the bottom. You could hardly get it down your throat even when you were starving.

Some of the sick didn't want to wait any longer; they were tired of fighting to live. Eating the rice gruel only made their dysentery worse, and they were so weak they would have to lie in their own filth. The rest of us tried to feed them, maybe force a few grains of rice between their lips, and we held their heads on our laps and talked to them to give them hope. But we just didn't have enough hope to go around. When it gets that tough, you can't live for somebody else; it takes all you've got to keep alive yourself. We would nurse a man along a week or ten days, and then one night the place where he slept would be empty, and we would know where he had crawled.

There was a little shed at one corner of the compound, down near the latrine. It had a roof of thatched cogan grass, and three sides; the fourth side was open to the rain. We called it the Zero Ward. It was where the dead were taken so they wouldn't spread disease. They would lie there until the burial detail could dig fresh holes. When a man wanted to die, he would crawl on his hands and knees down to the Zero Ward, and take his place beside the dead.

We took turns heading up the burial detail each afternoon, but it was never easy. We had to remove all the clothing first, because we needed it, and we buried them naked in a common hole. We had to carry them past the barracks on the way to the burial grounds, and everyone, even the sick, would stand at attention and salute as they went by. Sometimes an enlisted man would step forward with a bunch of grass twisted together in the shape of a flower, and place it on the friend's body.

It was worst in the rainy season. We used to think about it as we worked in the rice fields at Davao; standing in the mud would remind us. The burial grounds were about a mile from camp in a low area without drainage, and a hole you dug in the morning would be flooded to the rim by afternoon. Johnny had a detail one rainy afternoon, and there was only one hole twelve feet square, half full of water. There were thirty-eight bodies to go in the hole. Johnny didn't have the heart to ask the exhausted men to get down into the water and place the bodies decently, so they had to roll them in. They would float back up to the top, and some of the men started getting sick, but Johnny said, "Everybody's in on this, everybody has to do his part," and he took a shovel and started throwing mud into the hole. Johnny wanted to say a prayer, but it was almost dark, and the Jap guards were yelling, so he said a prayer to himself as they headed back in the rain.

The rice fields were two square miles of solid mud, cut up by dikes into checkerboard paddies. One man would stand on the dike at each side of a paddy, holding a rope with knots every eight inches, to mark where the seedlings would be planted. The rest of us would take our places in the mud behind the rope. Each rope man would tie his end to a stake and jam the stake into the dike. When we finished planting a row, the rope men would yank up the stakes and move back, and the weight of the wet rope would almost drag them off the slick dike.

Before we started planting, we would go to the tin-roofed *bodega* and get the rice baskets, round two-handled laundry baskets made of woven *bajauka*. We would fill the baskets with rice seedlings, and put a bamboo pole through the handles of a basket and lug it a mile or so to the paddy we were assigned to plant that day. The basket was so heavy that the pole would cut into our bare shoulders, and we took some pretty good falls on the slippery dikes. There were always a few broken ankles and wrists around camp. Most of us had malaria, and wallowing in the cold mud was apt to cause a bad chill. That was what brought about Pete's terrible beating one afternoon, and gave us a new insight into the barbaric nature of the Jap.

We were learning more about the Japs each day. They were afraid of us. That was hard to understand at first, because the Japs were armed and had life-and-death control over us. But they were terrified of the Americans, and they would literally shake with fear if they had to take us very far into the jungle away from the rest of the guards. Maybe it was their inborn sense of inferiority. No matter how much they tried to shame us, they could never overcome their own feeling of being the low race. They could not break our spirit; that was what frightened them most.

The Jap is unstable, given to psychopathic fits of temper, ignorant, cruel. His barbarism shows in his treatment of animals. There was a sizable flock of chickens when we first arrived at Davao, enough to supply meat and eggs for all of us, but the Japs never fed them, and the hungry chicks began eating their own eggs. So the Japs decided to give the poultry a lesson and they cut out all food and water. The hens stopped laying altogether. The Japs, angered at this defiance, picked up the emaciated chickens, held them in their arms and solemnly slapped their faces one by one to punish them. It was funny, but it was also a little sickening.

Sergeant Hashimoto was the bane of our existence for two years, a vain, unpredictable, violent little man, a former judo expert. He was bucking for a commission and he sought to curry favor with the Jap officers at our expense. We called him Little Caesar. We had names for all our guards at Davao. There was Itchy Ape, the farming expert, a swart, ugly Jap with a face like Pluto the Pup. There was Five

O'Clock Shadow, who always carried the broken steel shaft of a golf club and who would hit the Americans across the face with its jagged end, opening a raw gash with each blow. Nishimura, the interpreter, was called Simon Legree: he could interpret the Jap orders any way he wanted, and he always made sure they were as tough as possible. There was another interpreter, Mr. Wada; we called him Running Wada because he had short legs and would trot after the Jap officers like a little puppy.

One Jap officer, Lieutenant Yuki, was a little more friendly than the others; he had been a Catholic before the war, but he had had to renounce his religion when he joined the Imperial Army. He told us one day that his brother officers had made him walk through a line of Chinese coolies, slashing their heads off, to prove that he was a loyal son of the emperor.

It was Little Caesar who did the brutal job on Pete that afternoon. Pete was a big, nice-looking kid from the Middle West, always willing; but he had had a stiff attack of malaria, and by noon he got to shaking so hard he couldn't control himself. He dragged himself up onto the railroad embankment, and started toward the *bodega*. Little Caesar was coming down the tracks at that moment. Maybe he thought Pete was trying to goldbrick, maybe he just figured the embankment was a good stage to put on a show; we never knew. He grabbed Pete by the shoulder without warning, threw a leg behind him, and flung him to the ground.

Little Caesar was proud of his ability at judo, and he loved to demonstrate it on Americans. He went to work on Pete, picking him up and throwing him down again and dislocating his shoulder; he twisted Pete every way but loose. Then when Pete was down for good, he began kicking him with his hobnailed boots in the ribs, in the face and in the groin, and beating him with the flat of his sword. He kicked Pete until he was unconscious.

Pete's mind was foggy after that, and his speech was impaired. All he thought about was killing Little Caesar.

A thunderstorm came up that afternoon while we were working. It had been raining for a couple of hours by the time we finished and got back to the *bodega* about 6:30, and the railroad tracks were as slick as grease. The Toonerville Trolley couldn't get traction enough to pull up the four-mile grade back to camp, and the Jap guards made us push the train all the way home.

It was pitch black, we had no shoes, we kept stubbing our toes on the protruding ties and slashing our bare feet on the rocks. The way back to camp seemed endless. We were nearly dead from hunger and exhaustion. The rain kept beating down harder and we were numb from cold in spite of all our exertion. The guards rode on the flatcars above us, yelling, "Push, push!" and leaning down to club us if we quit.

But we didn't quit, we got mad, We kept pushing, and we got madder and madder every step of the way, and the Japs began to get scared. We passed the house of the Jap commanding officer, and, as we went by, every last one of that bunch of tired, naked, emaciated Americans began to sing. We sang at the top of our lungs, and the Japs were too scared to stop us. We sang "God Bless America," and we made the night shake with it.

No matter what lay ahead, we were proud we were Americans that night.

Waiting was hardest. Or, rather, making ourselves believe that there was anything to wait for. We tried to keep our spirits up by inventing little rumors to give ourselves hope. We repeated the wildest latrineograms as though they were gospel. We would beg each other for news, any news, although we knew we were only making it up as we went along. We told ourselves solemnly that there had been a great naval battle, that the Imperial Fleet was retreating to the China coast, that the American destroyers were in hot pursuit. Ten Nip carriers had just been sunk. Russia had declared war on Japan. There was going to be an exchange of war prisoners, and we would all be home in a month.

Day after day we whispered to each other that the Americans were coming. But they never came. They did not come till three years later. Camp O'Donnell was deserted, the newspapers said, the Japs had burned all the barracks as they fled.

We talked about escape, of course. We made the most elaborate plans. We would overpower our guards and seize the narrow-gauge Toonerville Trolley that hauled us out each morning to the rice fields. But it was no good, we had no idea where to go. The compound was surrounded by a triple barbed-wire fence ten feet high, and Jap guards patrolled the area day and night. It was not only the barbed wire that kept us from escaping, for we often had chances to escape individually while working outside the camp. We knew what it would mean to those we left behind.

The Japs divided us into groups of ten, called blood brothers, and those ten were responsible for one another at all times. An enlisted man in one group at Cabanatuan made a getaway; he was on a firewood detail, and he just kept on walking into the jungle. We never knew what happened to him, but we knew what happened to the remaining nine. The Japs made sure we knew; they assembled all the rest of the men on the detail, and they kept their machine guns trained on them to make them watch. The nine men were lined up before a firing squad. One of the nine had a kid brother watching in the crowd. Just before the Jap squad was given the command to fire, he winked at his brother and said in a low voice, "Tell Mom I said good-bye." We used to think of that whenever we were tempted to escape.

Still some of the men tried to make a break. A lieutenant colonel and two other officers attempted it one night crawling on their hands and knees down the drainage ditch that ran beneath the barbed wire. An American private on guard—the Japs, in defiance of all international law, forced the Americans to stand guard over their fellow prisoners—halted the three officers, and pleaded with them in a whisper; he explained that if they were missing, it would be his neck. The officers shoved him aside, and started past him; but the commotion they made attracted the attention of the Jap guards. The three were seized and led back to the barracks, and a couple of Jap judo experts went to work on them, twisting their arms and throwing them down and kicking them in the head. After an hour they confessed.

We had an idea what would happen next. Luckily one of our medical officers had smuggled a small supply of morphine into camp; before the guards hauled the trio off, he managed to inject the entire supply into their arms. The shots made it a little easier for them to stand what followed. The Japs drove three stakes into the ground at the corner of the main highway leading past the camp. They tied the officers to these stakes, knotting their arms behind them and hoisting the rope higher, and higher until they could barely touch the ground with their toes: the full weight of their bodies hung from their shoulder sockets. A horizontal four-by-four plank was suspended in front of them, swinging freely; and every Filipino who came down the highway was forced to pull the plank back and bash it forward into the Americans' faces.

After a while their faces were unrecognizable; the colonel's left ear was torn off entirely, and dangled upside down beside his cheek. They hung there for three days, and all of us inside the compound could see them; we couldn't help it. The effects of the morphine wore off, and they went out of their minds with pain.

On the third night, the Japs cut them down and led them past the camp to the burial grounds. We heard two shots. We all listened, but we never heard a third shot. There were rumors that the colonel had been decapitated or else buried alive, but we never knew for sure.

The only successful break from prison camp was when Captain Ed Dyess and his group got away. Bert noticed Ed greasing his boots that morning and said to him, "Where do you think you're going?" Ed didn't answer; he just smiled. That same afternoon he gave away his extra soap to the other men in his barracks, and traded everything he had for some sacks of salt. Later the Japs told us Dyess and all his party had been executed. It wasn't until we got back to the States two years later that we found out he made it.

Things got really tough at Davao after Dyess escaped. Restrictions were doubled, and our rations were reduced from 600 to 300 grams of rice, a starvation diet. We were so hungry we ate rats, grubworms, even the little frogs that jumped out of the latrines. The Japs took away our shoes and even our shirts and made us go half naked day and night. They forced us to sign printed certificates stating that we would not escape, but we figured it was done under duress and our signatures weren't binding. If the Japs suspected anyone of plotting to get away, they would tie him to a post by the interior gate, with a sign around his neck, "I tried to escape," and force the Filipinos to beat him. If they didn't hit him hard enough, the Jap guards would beat the Filipinos.

Beatings were a daily occurrence now. Strafing—standing you at attention and slapping you back and forth across the face—was a favorite Jap punishment; though sometimes they would hit you across the bridge of the nose with the side of their hand, judo-fashion, or give you a knee in the groin. You very seldom saw a Jap use his bare fist.

We were transferred to Lasang on March 2, 1944. At first we were glad when we learned we were among the six hundred prisoners being moved. We thought nothing could be as bad as Davao. We were wrong again.

Lasang was a Jap fighter strip, from which their planes took off to attack our bombers and ships to the southward. Our job was to enlarge the runway—another violation of international law as we know it, since the Geneva rules state that prisoners of war shall not be required to work against their own country. Our barracks were located only four hundred yards from the strip. Either the Japs figured that our bombers would hesitate to hit the airfield for fear of killing their fellow countrymen, or they were determined we should be the first victims of an American attack. We were not even allowed to dig foxholes.

Five hundred and fifty prisoners at Lasang were assigned each day to work on the air strip. The Japs paid us by contract: a private received ten centavos a day, a non-com fifteen, a company-grade officer thirty pesos every two months Ten centavos is about a nickel a day, and a day at Lasang was twelve hours. We didn't get any time-and-a-half for overtime, and we didn't have swing bands to keep us working. But there were no strikes or job-shiftings or absenteeism under the Japs.

The other fifty Americans were taken each day to the coral pits at Tabunco. The job there was to dig the coral, break it up and load it into trucks to surface the new runway. The coral pits were eighty to a hundred feet high, dug into the hillside and closed in on three sides. All afternoon the tropical sun would beat against the dazzling white coral, and the inside of the pit was like a polished reflector oven.

You thought of a scene out of the *Inferno*, the Japs pointing their bayonets and prodding the naked men wielding sledges and shovels in the fierce heat. The flesh of our faces actually shriveled, and our throats were choked with the fine coral dust. We were half blinded by the white glare. We smeared charcoal over our faces to cut the reflection, but it was no help. We tried making sunglasses out of cardboard, with slits for our eyes, but we had to take them off because they cut our vision and we couldn't see to protect ourselves from falling chunks of coral.

The Jap planes were constantly practicing maneuvers over the airstrip, swooping low and buzzing us as we worked. The pilots tried to make us duck and scatter for cover, but we never budged. Sometimes a Jap fighter plane would run off the end of the strip and get stuck in the mud, and they would call a detail of American prisoners to push it out. We Air Corps men knew just what to do. We would crowd behind the plane where the pilot couldn't see us, and push down hard on the ailerons or bump the tail assembly to spring it out of line. We guarantee that some of those Nip fliers never got back from the next mission.

One night the first American bomber appeared over Lasang.

We knew it was an American plane the moment we heard it. We had waited two long years to hear that sound.

Every light in our compound was on. Maybe that would help the pilot find the field. We didn't care what happened to us. Nothing mattered now. We just stood and prayed for him to come.

We could tell by the sound how he was coming. He banked and came down in a dive, and we could hear the wind rushing past his wings. We could hear the roar of those American engines getting louder and louder. It was the most beautiful sound we'd ever heard in our lives. We couldn't shout, we couldn't say anything to each other, we just stood there with the tears running down our faces and waited for the bombs.

Those bombs were from home.

The American bomber that came over Lasang that night dropped four eggs on the far end of the Jap fighter strip, making several holes in the runway. They almost hit a gasoline tank, although they didn't know that till long afterward.

All work on the strip had been stopped the day after the bombing. The Japs held us in the compound, and cut our food down to a single cupful of rice and boiled *camote* peelings every twenty-four hours. We thought we'd been hungry before, but this was really a starvation diet. Groups of men would gather around the garbage pits each day, salvaging bits of vegetables which the Jap kitchen crew had thrown out. We began eating weeds growing inside the compound; we grazed that compound as bare as if we'd been a bunch of sheep.

After two weeks, the Japs told us we were going to be moved from Lasang. They tried to make us believe there was going to be an exchange of prisoners, but we knew the Nips too well to fall for that. They lined us up behind the barbed wire in columns of four, linking the outside men together by ropes tied to their wrists. As we marched barefoot through the rows of coconut trees, we wondered what lay ahead. Were we going to Manila, Formosa, Japan itself? Were we foolish not to make a break for it now, when the American forces were closing in? Would any of us live through this next one?

That noon we arrived at the Tabunco Pier, and were loaded aboard an old 5,600-ton Jap freighter. Four hundred men were crowded into one hold, three hundred and fifty into the other. The Japs loaded several tons of baggage in the hold with us, and there was hardly room for us to sit down, let alone stretch out and sleep. The heat was terrific, and there was no ventilation except the sides of the hatch covers; and the Japs piled sacks of vegetables on these, cutting off the air still more. Within an hour, we were running sweat, and we stripped off everything we had and stood packed like animals gasping for breath

We sailed from Tabunco about 6:00 that evening, and all that night we rocked and swayed with the creaking ship. Most of the men got seasick, but they were too empty to do anything but retch. The next morning we heard the roar of a plane, and through the ventilation hole beneath the hatch cover we caught a glimpse of a four-motored bomber about 10,000 feet overhead. We heard the swish and explosion of a bomb in the water. The machine guns on deck began to clatter, and the hatch covers were banged down and fastened.

All ventilation was cut off. Men began to pass out all around us due to lack of oxygen. Our bodies stung as all the excess water drained out of us in the terrific heat. After two hours of suffocation, our colonel began shouting for air, and at last the side covers of the hatch were taken off and we could breathe again. We just turned our faces up to the in-flowing air; we didn't say a word. Gradually the unconscious men began to gasp and stir again.

We stayed in Zamboanga Harbor ten days without being allowed off the ship. Twice they let us come on deck and run through a hose of salt water, and then returned us to the stifling hold again. On September 4th we were transferred to another boat. Two hundred and fifty of us were jammed into the small after-hold, the remaining five hundred were placed in the larger hold at the bottom of the ship. Most of the men never left that second ship.

Again that night we heard the hum of airplane motors and the clatter of machine guns. Bombs landed on the harbor installations right beside us, and the whole ship rocked and shuddered: the sides of the old tub seemed to buckle in. Some of the men were still bomb-happy from Corregidor. They started to scream, and the rest of us gripped their hands and held their heads in our laps and tried to calm them. There was a lot of praying going on, but by this time most of us were praying for a direct hit.

We had been under way a couple of days, and we were making pretty good speed that fateful afternoon of September 7th. Gene happened to glance through the ventilation crack, and he saw a curious sight: a Jap bugler was standing on deck sounding an alarm, his cheeks puffed out, his eyes straining sideways in terror. Then the Jap machine guns top-side broke into a loud staccato, evidently firing at something in the water.

The first torpedo struck with an explosion like the end of the world. Before we could gather our senses, there was a second and even bigger explosion, and the water rushed through a gaping hole in the side of the ship. Everywhere there was debris and thrashing arms and legs. Mangled forms floated in the water all around us, and the hold was full of screams and groans of dying men. Gene came to under water, and swam upward through the struggling mass of bodies. The hatch cover had been blown off in the explosion, and he could see light above him. The water was within three feet of the deck as he emerged.

Johnny was in the after hold when the torpedo struck. A flying section of beam struck him in the head; he regained consciousness lying on the floor, pinned under a dozen bodies. The hold was so full of cement dust that he could barely see. The face of the man lying on top of him was bloody, and Johnny put his hand to his own face and looked at it and decided that he was all right. He started clambering over the dead bodies. The Japs were firing into the hold, and they tossed a couple of grenades down among the mass of trapped Americans. A lieutenant was pinned under a beam and calling for help, and Johnny tried to work him loose, but the weight of the sagging deck held him. The boat was beginning to tilt and settle, and Johnny scrambled up the tumbled Jap luggage and made his way to the deck.

Seven Jap officers were lined up on the bridge of the ship with .30 caliber rifles, picking off the Americans one by one as they came up out of the hold. Little Caesar, our most hated guard at Davao and Lasang, was waving a pistol, and directing them in a high hysterical voice. Gene emerged on deck with two other men. Bullets were pinging past him and slamming against the deck. He heard a dull thud and the man on his right slid back into the hold. The deck was littered with mangled Jap bodies, laid open like butchered meat by the blast of the torpedoes. Gene stepped over the body of the interpreter, the obsequious Mr. Wada, who was lying dead across the cradle of a lifeboat, and vaulted the rail into the water.

Evidently the blast of the torpedo had locked the mechanism of the ship's whistle, and it screamed steadily like a child that has been hurt. The Jap officers stood on the bridge of the doomed vessel, still firing at the Americans in the water. The ship capsized so rapidly that they had no time to free the lifeboats from their davits; the boats went down with the ship. The Japs braced themselves on the slanting deck, singing a war chant as the water rose toward them. There was a crackling sound like crumpled tissue paper, and the ship broke in half and went down.

Small Jap patrol boats from other ships in the convoy were cruising in and out amid the debris, hunting down and shooting the swimming Americans.

Several seaplanes were flying overhead, dropping depth charges in an effort to hit the American submarine which had fired the torpedoes. One plane came right over Johnny and started strafing him in the water, but it quit because there were Japs nearby. The exploding depth charges had one advantage: they kept the sharks away. The water was filled with gasoline and oil from a Jap tanker in the convoy which had been torpedoed, and probably that also helped discourage the sharks. We could feel the gasoline sting and burn in our open wounds as we swam.

We were constantly encountering Japs in the water and fighting them with bits of stick and our bare fists. Bert and Gene saw Lt. Hosheda clinging to a spar, but he was too far off to get at him. The torpedoed tanker had run up on shore and beached by now, and her crew had broken out the twin .50 caliber machine guns and were training them on the American survivors. Bert and Gene realized they had to split up in order to present a smaller target.

The thing that saved the rest of us was the rapidly growing darkness. The Jap patrol boats couldn't spot the swimming men in the uncertain half-light. They cruised back and forth, announcing through megaphones that if the Americans would surrender, they would be shown mercy. Some of the men were so exhausted that they fell for it. We learned what happened to them from a staff sergeant later. He was one of the thirty survivors who were picked up by a Jap patrol boat. They were taken aboard a freighter, and their hands were tied behind them. Then the Japs lined them against the rail at the stern of the ship, shot them one by one in the back of the head, and pushed the bodies into the water. The sergeant managed to cut the ropes around his wrist with the frayed end of a steel cable, knocked down a couple of the guards, and raced the length of the deck to the other end of the ship. There he hid in the small compartment holding the anchor chain. After the guards stopped searching, he climbed down the anchor chain to the water, and swam to shore. He was the only one who lived to tell.

Johnny almost didn't make it. There was a strong tide running inshore, and he found himself being carried nearer and nearer the beached tanker. In the darkness he could see the red bursts of machine-gun fire, and he heard the bullets ripping into the water all around him. Somehow he managed to swim against the tide, and fight his way toward shore. He never knew where he found the extra strength. Perhaps it was the cold water that his parched body seemed to soak up; perhaps it was the sheer exultation of being free. The weight of those two and a half terrible years had been exploded in one shattering instant. It was like being blasted out the grave, he said. The torpedo had blown him back to life.

He reached the fringe of bushes at the edge of the beach, and something made him halt. He listened. From the thicket ahead of him came a low distinct hiss. The leaves parted, and a Filipino face poked through. He beckoned to Johnny, and his lips spread in a white-toothed grin.

Johnny threw his arms around him and kissed him.

The strong tide carried Bert and Gene past the tanker, and down to a narrow point of land that projected into the ocean. Several times the Jap patrol boats cruised near them in the darkness, but the boats changed course in the nick of time. They made the last hundred yards on sheer nerve, and clambered up onto the beach almost at the same moment.

They were making very poor time through the tangled underbrush that covered the low peninsula, and they forced their way to the water's edge, and splashed ankle-deep through the shallows. The jagged coral slashed their bare feet, and they left a wake of blood in the water with each step. By dawn they were safe in the jungle, and hid in a grove of wild bananas to rest up for the next night's march.

There the Filipinos found them. A young boy who spoke English assured them that the natives were their brothers. At first they were uncertain whether to trust them or not; but they decided to take a chance. The Filipino boy led them to his father's house where they were fed coconut, boiled bananas and water. They cautioned the Filipino family not to mention that Americans were hiding there, but the natives could not resist spreading the good word. That night the door opened, and Filipinos, young and old, poured in to welcome them. They held a big fiesta in the village, but the Americans were too exhausted and sick to take any part in it. They lay in the *nipa* leaf shack, praying that the Japs wouldn't hear the singing.

They learned from the Filipinos that another group of Americans was located in a village a few kilometers away, and next morning they started down the trail. The arrival of their party brought the total number of survivors in camp to forty-seven. All that night and during the next couple of days other stragglers arrived, a couple at a time, limping down the trail or riding on carabaos or being dragged on sleds when they were too sick to walk. As each new group arrived, the rest of us would look them over to see if some particular buddy of ours had made it from the torpedoed ship. A man would run from one person to another in the group, begging for news of a friend. "Did you see so-and-so in the water?" "Do you think he had a chance?" Altogether eighty-three Americans survived out of the seven hundred and fifty who had been aboard.

Most of the men were wounded by bullets or fragments of the hand grenades the Japs had thrown into the hold, and all of us were dazed and partly deafened by the explosion. Still we could laugh. A G.I. arrived wearing two Jap officers' coats; he explained casually that he had borrowed them from a couple of Japs he met in the water. A captain showed up with a Jap bayonet and a Jap pistol. He traded the bayonet to a Filipino woman for a souvenir knife, and swapped the pistol for a pair of shoes.

We stayed in the village until we were in shape to travel. We thought our troubles were over, but we had a grim reminder that we were not out of danger yet.

We had to cross a wide inlet, and that last lap of our journey was almost fatal. Jap airplanes were patrolling at tree-top height, still searching for any American survivors, and we kept under cover as much as possible. The Filipinos loaded all eighty-three Americans in a small sailboat, and started across the inlet. About halfway over, the wind died and the boat was becalmed.

We were like sitting ducks in the center of that flat stretch of water. The natives got out small home-made oars, and paddled us laboriously the rest of the way. We inched forward, holding our breath and scanning the sky for enemy patrols. We had just beached the boat and scampered up the shore to a fringe of bushes when three Jap seaplanes appeared, skimming the water. They circled the empty boat, while our entire party crouched motionless in the bushes, and then turned and roared away.

That night at the appointed hour we were rowed out to the sub in little Filipino *bancas.* We could see its dark shape looming up ahead of us, as big as a battleship in the tropic night. The natives held the little boats alongside, and the crew of the sub reached down and helped us aboard. Bert felt a huge warm hand grab him and pull him up. Bert didn't realize how thin he was; he was just skin and bones, and that big American sailor lifted him as though he were a little child. Another sailor steadied him and lowered him through the hatch.

We stood there and looked around us. We looked at the instrument panels, the dials, the wheels and compass and gadgets. Everything was American. The deck plates, the ladders, the steel hand rails were made in America. The sailors were American: husky, healthy, clean, not like the Japs. We looked at them, and they looked at us, but nobody said much. They said, "How was it?" or "How do you feel?" and we said "Okay," but it was hard to say anything. Then the mess cook stuck his head in the door and said, "Hey, youse guys, how's to make with some chow?" in a beautiful Brooklyn accent, and suddenly we wanted to cry. We stood there and blubbered like a lot of damned fools, and we couldn't help it. We had been away so long, and now we were home.

It's a funny thing, but you have to be away from America to find out what it means. Words like patriotism and love of country take on a different meaning after three years in a Jap prison. We had changed, but not the way you would expect. Our folks when we got back were afraid we might be tougher or harder, but it wasn't that. We were just bigger. The things we used to take for granted once, we didn't take for granted any more. We had learned a lot in three years. We learned about the Japs, but we learned more than that. We learned about Americans.

We sat down at the sub's long mess table, and they brought us vegetable soup full of vegetables, and pitchers of fresh milk, and plates of bread. We didn't wolf that bread, though. We just took a bite and sat back and rolled it around on our tongue and let it go down slowly.

That wasn't bread. That was cake.

# DACHAU, 1945

from

*The Day of the Americans*

by Nerin E. Gun

New York: Fleet Publishing Corporation, 1966

*In a few short years we will approach the fiftieth anniversary of the end of World War II. Generations of adults have little or no memory of the totality of that war. There have been many wars in the intervening years in which battling countries just withdrew their forces and declared a truce. But World War II was a conflict that could not end with just a withdrawal of forces. The aggressor was going to enslave all the vanquished. The population of the defeated countries would be slaves—or dead. No place to run, no place to hide. It is probably safe to predict that if Germany and Japan had been victorious, in a hundred years or less both countries, with new and improved weapons, would have been locked in battle for the title of "slave master of the world."*

*The Japanese had shown themselves as slave masters who gave no quarter. You either obeyed or were destroyed. Slaves led an animal-like existence. They were allowed to survive as long as they were able to perform their assigned daily functions. The Germans were a little more subtle, yet followed the same philosophy. As victors, they expected their commands obeyed unquestioningly. Punishment was swift and hard—and seldom just.*

*In this volume there has been very little about the Nazis determination to exterminate all Jews. This part of that dark period in the history of the world is amply documented by survivors of the Holocaust; their eyewitness stories of the torture and killing of millions of people are available in book stalls and libraries in most of the civilized countries of the world. While concentration camps were the sites for the torture and killings of Jews, they also held a percentage of prisoners of different faiths. Political prisoners, homosexuals, and others considered undesirable were incarcerated as well.*

*Nerin E. Gun spent time in eleven prisons and three concentration camps, the last being Dachau. He was one of the few international journalists imprisoned by the Germans. He had been a student in Berlin when World War II erupted, and as a neutral, he became a correspondent for Swiss newspapers and the Turkish press service. He attracted Nazi attention with his stories about the Warsaw ghetto and his prediction that the Russians would defeat the German armies. His story relates his liberation from the camp and the dramatic entry of American troops into one of the man-made hellholes of the world.*

O n March 21, 1933, just a few weeks after power was offered to Adolf Hitler, a short item appeared in the *Münchner Neuesten Nachrichten*:

"Yesterday, the first concentration camp was formally opened in the neighborhood of the city of Dachau. It can accommodate 5,000 persons. This measure has been taken, apart from any petty considerations, because we are convinced we are acting in the interests of national tranquility and according to the will of the population." *Signed*: Heinrich Himmler, Chief of Police.

The *Münchner Neuesten Nachrichten* was the most widely read newspaper in Bavaria, and it was obvious that Himmler, far from trying to keep this secret, was eager for all Germany to know of his initiative.

The city of Dachau was not long in publicly expressing its gratitude to Himmler. Its finances were in a pitiful state, and it was delighted thus to welcome the conversion of an old munitions factory, unused since the last war. The mayor had been promised that the political convicts to be housed there would be employed at draining the sinister Dachauer Moor, the notorious peat bogs of the region. The Hitlerites were anxious to emulate Mussolini, who had so brilliantly reclaimed the Pontine Marshes between Rome and Naples. But of course, the Germans brought greater perfection to the Fascist methods. Instead of calling for volunteers, they used slaves.

The one-time munitions plant was rebuilt, enlarged, re-equipped, and the KZ of Dachau became the model, the prototype of Nazi organization and subjection. It was to last a thousand years, like Hitler's Reich. Arrangements were made for important personages and foreign journalists to visit it. In 1938, the *Berliner Illustrierte*, which at the time was to Germans what *Life* magazine today is to Americans, was to publish a cover picture of the internees going to their work to the sound of bagpipes. Everything was alleged to be so impeccable in the camp that there had even been national elections, and the result of the plebiscite had gone 99 per cent for Hitler. And later, during the 1939 mobilization, the camp was temporarily emptied of its regular inmates, and it served as billet for an entire SS division, the *Eicke*.

Alas, all this admirable Prussian order had degenerated into disorder by the spring of 1945. Thirty-five thousand inmates in a camp originally intended for 5,000 are a heavy load, and first typhus, then hunger had completely upset the mechanism. To make room for a group of hostages of honor, it had even been necessary to move the girls out of Block 31 and thus deprive Dachau of its most original attraction.

For Block 31 was the Puff, the prisoners' brothel. In fact, only the VIP German jailbirds and criminals made use of it, the political prisoners having determined to boycott it as a matter of principle. This did not really represent a great sacrifice, for the majority of the incarcerated were so famished, so weakened and so terrorized, that the idea of going to the whorehouse could only rarely be a temptation to them. But in theory the area was accessible to all except the Jews.

Each inmate received two marks per week for his work. During the earlier years he was able to use this money. It was not legal tender, but scrip that was honored in the camp, for which newspapers or toothpaste could be bought at the canteen. But soon these became unavailable, and the only place to spend the money was at the brothel, where the rate was two marks a trick. This worked out very well for the SS administration, for the whorehouse was self-supporting and the salaries paid to prisoners came right back to their source. The inmate had to put his name down in advance and then go for a medical examination. He presented his certificate to the Puff Führer, who, after the usual sarcastic comments, had him draw a number out of a hat. The number designated the girl he was to have. Then he had only to wait his turn.

But even in a concentration camp, prostitution followed its own rules. Soon, the customer developed preferences, even a favorite. To achieve his ends, he had to subvert the SS man and then buy the favors and the silence of the girl so she would accept the infringement, agree to spend more time with him and be more complaisant. So he brought tobacco, food, stolen clothing, and it even happened that somehow he produced a Parisian gown, a well-known perfume, or a piece of jewelry. It seems that one of the Kapos succeeded in keeping one of the fifteen girls in the Puff all to himself for a whole year. She was off limits to all others.

However, the girls did not keep their earnings: just as in Montmartre, they had their "sweet daddies." For there were pimps operating in the camp: professionals who were inadvertently caught in a raid or picked up because they were also pushing drugs, or perhaps had "taken" some Nazi big shots for whom they had been procuring; and amateurs also. They could be seen at nightfall loitering near the windows of the whores' barracks, bargaining, checking on the "work" of their fillies, receiving their tribute. They were strong and good-looking, for with what they got from their women they could afford to eat well at the black market of the camp. They did a bit of white-slaving, and sometimes were able to transfer a girl from some other camp, sometimes succeeding in convincing a woman prisoner to volunteer for the Puff, perhaps by promising to save the life of her husband or child.

Normally the staff of the brothel was made up only of professional prostitutes, girls from houses in Warsaw, Lodz or Prague, who simply had been moved in to Dachau. Rarely were the women political prisoners forced into such pursuits. In the eyes of the Gestapo, that was no punishment, and moreover they would not have been satisfactory. As in any other craft, they wanted only experts at Dachau.

That there were pimps at Dachau should surprise no one. I would like to be able to say there had been nothing but heroes in the Lager, but that, unfortunately, would be untrue. We were a heterogeneous group. Among us, there were some of everything: Communists, members of the underground, criminals, anarchists, homosexuals—these wearing a little pink triangle, while the political prisoners wore a red one, the criminals a green one, and the admirable Jehovah's Witnesses a black one. The members of Jehovah's Witnesses, it must be said, showed such courage, daring, virtue, and stoicism in adversity that they deserve a special salute. They were rocks in a sea of mud.

Even among the "politicals," it was to be noted that sharp distinctions existed: for instance, among the Frenchmen, there was an abyss between the early Gaullists and those who had seen the light only after the landings in Normandy; between the Vichy vassals who had fallen into disfavor with the Germans for some reason and the volunteers of the Charlemagne Legion; the French SS men who had fought in Russia and who could no longer take it, as against the illegal wheeler-dealers from Paris, the stool-pigeons, the volunteer workers who had turned saboteurs or girl-chasers, the black-market boys, and those who had been arrested for pillaging after bombing raids.

Beyond these, there were German deserters, courtmartialed SS men, people who had simply been picked up on the street during indiscriminate roundups, or, as happened every day, drunkards or curfew-violators, who somehow found themselves in Dachau simply because their local jails were overcrowded to the bursting point. We were the Court of Miracles of Munich.

And then there were all those who actually felt completely innocent—in a word, those who had no idea what had landed them here. I had occasion to read a large number of their dossiers before they were destroyed, and I would guess that at least a thousand of these internees of the final period had been stupidly denounced by a wife, a girl friend, a secretary or a relative. Jealousy, spite, hurt feelings, meanness, whim—whatever the motive, there is nothing more dangerous than a woman who knows a way to get rid of a man without running any risk herself. Some of the captives did not even know who had accused them. A neighbor woman, living across the corridor, might have seen the man going into the apartment of his girl friend, whom she secretly hated. Why was he there with the other woman when she herself was lonely that night?

All she had to do was pick up her pen and a sheet of paper, or just call the Gestapo. An old woman in the Briennerstrasse opened the telephone directory at random, let her finger fall somewhere on the page, and copied off the names. In this way, she turned in some 150 suspicious characters. All were arrested and then forgotten in confinement by the Gestapo, which by this time had more than it could handle.

These simple-minded creatures of course imagined they would immediately be freed, as soon as the mistake had been cleared up. The favorite game in camp was to impress the fact on them that they were here to stay and to paint a vivid picture of all the horrors of the place. The rookies hardly believed us, so we trotted figures out for them and showed them proof. It was cruel, it is true, but in a way practical, for they were then not too paralyzed when faced with the harsh reality.

Practically all nationalities were represented there and, according to the time and season, some were looked up to and some looked down on. In Dachau at first it was the Poles who were insulted, then came the turn of the Frenchmen, then the Russians, and finally the Italians and Hungarians occupied the bottom rung.

The only missing great nationality was the American. In one way that was unfortunate, as Edmond Michelet noted:

"Whereas all of Europe was represented in Dachau, not a single American citizen, not one fighting man from the U.S.A. experienced the hell of the German concentration camps. I have often regretted that not one of our friends from across the sea had the possibility day after day to meditate upon an experience similar to our own. That he could not see the black science to which we were exposed. ...I am afraid that Nazi barbarism will seem no nearer to them than that of the Assyrians. ...On that score, there will be more than an ocean between us, there will be a whole world. ..."

Alas, we could scarcely imagine then that in barely twenty years the President of our liberators would declaim in the middle of a public square largely filled with the accomplices of our former jailer, *"Ich bin ein Berliner!"* How much more secure the peace of the world would be if, instead, John Fitzgerald Kennedy had been able to say, *"Ich war in Dachau. ..."*

There was a black market, with headquarters in the shower rooms, the same place the prisoners chose for having it out with knives when they were bent on killing each other. Brisk trade went on in canned goods received in packages, foodstuffs stolen from the SS men or the prisoners, hard-to-get daily necessities, and all sorts of trinkets. The medium of exchange was tobacco. There were real cigarettes, reclaimed butts, and ersatz smokes made from old newspaper and stable straw.

At Dachau, these smokes were perhaps responsible for more deaths than typhus and hunger. The smoker found camp conditions ten times harder than the nonsmoker. He was ready to betray, to kill, to sell himself for a cigarette.

I was sharing my bunk, a few weeks before the liberation, with a very nice Italian fellow, a Milanese, father of seven kids. Every day, he swapped his midday soup for one cigarette—that was the going rate—and there was no making him listen to reason. One morning I woke to the strange sensation of blood clotting on my chest. This was not my bedmate's usual hemorrhage. He had died during the night. In my arms. Of hunger.

News from the outside had a tremendous influence on the morale of the camp: when Paris was liberated there was dancing on "Liberty Street," but when the Rundstedt offensive scored its breakthrough toward Bastogne, everyone was downcast, there were suicides, and some of the sick refused treatment. At that time, a large number of German prisoners, dishonoring themselves and us at the same time, volunteered for the SS Dirlewanger Legion and went to fight on the Eastern front.

I still remember the excitement on the occasion of the attempt on Hitler's life on July 20, 1944. At that time, I was at Maria-Lanzendorf, a camp near Vienna, and the panicky commandant suggested that we take over the "management" of the camp while he, temporarily at least, took shelter. We were all convinced that Hitler was finally *kaputt*, so we were in no hurry to get out of camp and we decided to throw a huge banquet, with roast chicken and the varied wines of France that were to be found in the SS cellars. Unfortunately, the same night, everything was called off: Hitler was alive, the commandant came back to camp, and we went back to our cells.

At dawn on April 13, 1945—we were six hours ahead of American time—Dachau had the saddest moment of its whole history. The news came in by short wave. Roosevelt was dead. This was a terrible shock. To us, Roosevelt was more than a father; he was the man who had promised us freedom, not as a gift but as our right. There were twenty-five suicides in camp that day. I think that nowhere in the world was Franklin Delano Roosevelt mourned as he was at Dachau.

Mass was said in the chapel of Block 26, the priests' block. Entry to this chapel was only given to a privileged few, selected as carefully as applicants to the exclusive Jockey Club, and even these were allowed in only during the final months.

This Block 26 had at first been open to all Catholic priests, as a kind of concession to the Vatican. Conditions there were better than elsewhere, and many packages were received from outside, thanks to the Archbishop of Munich. Then the German priests decided that all foreign priests should be excluded from it. It was equally off limits to all the rest of the camp's internees. A Bavarian priest stood guard outside the door, blackjack in hand, and woe to anyone who tried to get by him to take part in the religious service inside. Even old Schmitz, the ancient and highly likable Burgmeister of Vienna, had to kneel and cross himself from outside. These antics gave the SS men a good laugh.

Once more, I quote Edmond Michelet on the subject, since he, as a member of the hierarchy of the French Catholic Party, cannot be accused of religious irreverence: "Perhaps I am wrong to appear to hold a grudge against these poor German priests, subjected as they were to discipline. ... We were thrown out of the chapel, sometimes with punches to boot. ... The captive Church of Block 26 was a pitiful thing to see. ... Of course, the Block was full of packages, the parishioners did not forget their *Pfarrer*. Where might it not have led if all the camp's starvelings had suddenly felt overcome by piety and thereby come into contact with the stores of foodstuffs kept in the priests' lockers?"

It is difficult to give credit to any one person for the idea of setting up a prisoners' committee which, should the occasion arise, might take over the running of the camp. There was Patrick O'Leary, who claimed to be English, Canadian, Australian, and sometimes even Swedish, but whose real name was Albert Guerisse and his real nationality Belgian. Then, there was Haulot, who later became a minister in the Brussels government; the Pole Nazewsky; the amazing Albanian, Ali Kuci, who maintained to me that he was a direct descendant of Alexander the Great; and later, General Delestraint. The committee wanted to create a "Resistance brigade," avoid too much confusion in camp if it came to a pitched battle between the Americans and the SS men, set up an intelligence service, and especially, keep up the camp morale.

The International Committee needed weapons. We had made a few Molotov cocktails, found a bayonet, a few knives, and also—treasure of treasures—a Luger automatic. O'Leary had a Canadian pal, an aviator, Pat, a very handsome fellow. He had succeeded in attracting the interest of a big, strong, red-headed SS woman warder, who sometimes came to the infirmary supposedly to get medicines for the brothel girls.

The German woman in her death's-head uniform and the wretched prisoner took a fancy to each other. They would discreetly hold hands in an isolated corner of the Revier, and I think they even had a few rendezvous, very secretly, in a hothouse where exotic plants were cultivated. The Dachau nursery was one of the most flourishing enterprises of the SS empire.

The German woman not only gave her affections, but also her promise to find us some arms. That was how we came to have the revolver, which was hidden under the bolster of a hospital bed. The Canadian prisoner had convinced his SS belle that the Führer was done for and it would be all to her advantage to be on the good side of the International Committee. Whether out of love or self-interest, the Fräulein Unterscharrführer became a precious ally to us. In exchange, we saw to it that she was not molested when liberation came, and I have been told that her one-time Canadian admirer still writes to her from time to time.

The fever was mounting, the camp was rife with unfounded rumors, and everyone was astir. Already a first convoy of Russians and Germans had been ordered out of camp, in the direction of Mittenwald. Going on foot, it was to be decimated on the way. The final Thursday, general evacuation of the camp was ordered. We dressed in all the clothes we could get on our backs and put our blankets around us. At my waist I had my messkit, my fork, my knife (they might be useful, my committee superior had pointed out to me; they were weapons, and we had decided to attack the SS men at the first opportunity). But O'Leary, tipped off by the Canadian flyer's German girl, decided it was better not to try anything yet. Instead, we sabotaged the roll call. After four hours of trying to get us started on our way, the SS men got discouraged with the whole idea, and sent us all back into our barracks, possibly because they were too anxious to go to join their fellows in the storehouses and offices who were stealing civilian clothing and even prisoners' passports and identity cards.

Ten times a day, we thought we saw the Americans coming. It was exactly the same hallucination as the Crusaders had had before Jerusalem, when they thought they saw St. George on horseback opening the gates of the Holy City to them.

The least sign was interpreted as the harbinger of imminent liberation. "Hope shone like a blade of straw," as Verlaine put it.

I can still hear, on that last evening at Dachau, the singing of the SS recruits who, after training exercises, marched back into their barracks as if nothing untoward were happening, their black figures silhouetted against the wild redness of the twilight.

No one that evening, not even O'Leary, was aware that at the very moment when Himmler was trying to negotiate an impossible armistice with Count Bernadotte, the camp commandant had before him an order signed by the selfsame Himmler:

> "Flossenburg, April 14, 1945.
> To: Commandant, *KZ Lager*, Dachau.
> Surrender of the camp to the enemy is unthinkable. The whole camp is to be immediately evacuated. Not one prisoner is to fall alive into the hands of the Americans."

And this order was confirmed by another telegram, telling the commandant that, in case of necessity, he was authorized to use several military planes, which still remained intact at the air base of Schleissheim, near Munich, to massacre the entire population of the camp with napalm bombs and gas.

During the night of April 28, a ragged Jew, his face peppered with smallpox scars, knocked at the door of the camp. An old reserve soldier, attired in an SS uniform, opened the door to him, and was amazed to hear him say:

"I don't know anybody in Germany. On the outside, there's pandemonium. I'd rather go back in."

He had been in a convoy that had left Dachau three days earlier by rail. When the locomotive was hit by a bomb, the SS guards had taken to their heels. One of the prisoners, a priest, had taken refuge at a peasant's, and another stopped a passing truck to have the wounded loaded on it. The rest went ahead on foot foraging off the countryside as best they could. They grabbed whatever foodstuffs could be "liberated," put the fear of God into girls who saw them passing by, and had the unheard-of luxury of bathing in the large stream called the Amper. That was foolish: three of the escapees died of exposure and cold. The Jew who came knocking at the gate had wandered astray, terrified. Stones were thrown at him by civilians, and so he had decided to come back to the camp because, as far as he could remember, the prison was his only home.

The poor wretch was not entirely wrong in feeling bewildered when exposed to liberty. On this last day the murderous chaos which always precedes a victoriously advancing army had engulfed the region. That very morning the last detail had gone out of the camp to work in the town's shops. It was made up mostly of

Germans and Austrians, tough nuts, some of whom were veterans of the International Brigade of the Spanish Civil War. The road from the Lager to the city of Dachau was lined with corpses—evacuees from other convoys who had died along the way of exhaustion or typhus or had simply been expedited by an SS bullet in the nape of the neck. It looked as though this was what was in store for this last work detail and its members decided to gamble everything in a desperate effort: they entered into negotiations with their SS guards, promising them immunity when the Americans arrived. The latter agreed, and turned their arms over to them. Otto Jendran, a veteran of the Spanish Civil War, took command of the troop and impressed some passing Volkssturm (uniformed German civilian home guards) into lending a hand. His men took control of the Rathaus, and he sent an envoy out to carry the word to the Americans, who he hoped were very near. But the SS at Allach, when the rebellion was reported to them, arrived posthaste by truck, and a furious battle ensued. It was to last for five hours. More than half the prisoners of this work detail died during its course. The rest tried to get away into the countryside. But the skirmish served one very useful purpose. The camp commander, intimidated by this revolt, decided to give up any idea of mass evacuation of prisoners.

The Americans, meanwhile, knew perfectly well what was going on. Their reconnaissance planes had been flying over the camp continuously and had seen all these comings and goings. Alerted to the fact that a detachment of SS men had left its quarters in Munich to proceed up the fateful Dachauerstrasse and perhaps make a deadly assault on the camp, they interdicted its progress with artillery fire. This was the source of the cannon thunder we were hearing at Dachau.

The whole world was talking then of Buchenwald, which had been liberated by the British. It would have been humiliating if the American army, for its first great camp liberation, found nothing but smoking ruins.

Fortunately, the situation in the German ranks was tumultuous. The former commandant of Dachau, Weiss, now inspector general of all camps, countermanded the orders received from Berlin. He informed the Americans by phone—yes, the general confusion was such that it was perfectly possible to establish telephone contact across the lines—that Dachau would be handed over to them intact. The Red Cross would act as the delivery agent. But the SS officers preferred not to wait for the surrender to take place. They deserted during the night. Command was turned over to a young survivor of the slaughters of the Russian front, a man who, as a result of administrative delays, had arrived at Dachau only two days earlier to spend his "convalescence" there. It was the Lieutenant Heinrich Skodzensky.

He was given a brand-new SS uniform, of which the warehouses were full, and he looked as though he had just stepped out of a bandbox. His decorations stood out richly against the gray-black color of the uniform. He was a hero from the front. He therefore was in no danger, for it was well known that the Americans handled real fighting men with kid gloves. He knew little about Dachau. He never even had a chance to set foot into the confines of the KZ proper.

He was the one who gave the orders to raise the white flag over the Jourhaus. He was to spend the entire day there in the guard headquarters, awaiting the arrival of the conquerors.

252

The Jourhaus was the main gate of the camp. Its binational name was a throwback to the Napoleonic era, when the Prussians borrowed the French word *jour* from their opposite numbers. Through its portals, since 1933, each of the camp's damned had entered into this land of horrors. The entrance gate was made of wrought iron, the work of an Austrian deportee, and it bore the high-sounding legend: "Work will make you free."

In the city of Dachau, where there is a great, long-distance view from the malls of the chateau, the first American tanks had already been spotted, and bells had begun to ring. In the camp itself, an excited prisoner had pulled the switch of the alarm siren. Patrick O'Leary decided to call a full meeting of the International Committee in the library of the Schreibstube, which was the building closest to the Jourhaus. A large part of the garrison, like its officers, had bolted from the camp, but there were still several hundred SS men left; the machine guns in the watchtowers were still trained on the camp, and in the general confusion one could never tell what might happen. So, the committee had been in continuous session since 9:00 A.M., sending out repeated calls to remain calm, with sentries on the rooftops relaying its messages around the camp.

The Americans were not simply advancing; they were running, flying, breaking all the rules of military conduct, mounting their pieces on captured trucks, using tractors, bicycles, carts, trailers, anything on wheels that they could get their hands on. The Second Battalion, 222nd Regiment, 42nd Division, was coming brazenly, impudently down the highway, its general in the lead.

At the same time, the 45th Division, with its dauntless First Battalion, was coming across from the east. They were the ones who were to meet the greatest resistance, for the SS men, who had decided to impede the enemy's progress as much as possible, had massed in that sector. They preferred to make their stand here, with the Lager filled with prisoners at their backs, rather than in the western part of the compound, where their houses were and their families lived.

Inside the camp, the International Committee was wondering whether or not it should order an assault on the watchtowers and try for a breakthrough to establish contact with the Americans.

Since dawn, two men, stark naked, had been standing near the Jourhaus gate. They were Mandzourian, the prisoner who had been the "administrative head" of the camp, and Wernicke, a Gypsy, who had run the internees' "self-police" force. Both of them for years had acted most barbarously toward their fellow prisoners. They had wanted to flee along with the SS men, but these, having other things on their minds, had left them behind without another thought. The International Committee, wanting to foil their escape, had confiscated their clothes, and they were thus readily identifiable. They stayed near the gate, shivering with cold and turning blue with fear. But if they had remained inside, they would have been pitilessly lynched. They, too, were hoping for some kind of miracle.

Then came the first American jeeps: a GI got out and opened the gate. Machine-gun fire burst from the center watchtower, the very one which, since morning, had been flying the white flag! The jeeps turned about and an armored tank came on. With a few bursts, it silenced the fire from the watchtower. The body of an SS man fell off the platform and came crashing loudly to the asphalt of the little square.

Patrick O'Leary had knelt behind the windowsill to protect himself from the bullets. He was never to forget the scene that ensued:

"At this point, the young Teutonic lieutenant, Heinrich Skodzensky, emerges from the guard post and comes to attention before the American officer. The German is blond, handsome, perfumed, his boots glistening, his uniform well-tailored. He reports, as if he were on the military parade grounds near the Under den Linden during an exercise, then very properly raising his arm he salutes with a very respectful 'Heil Hitler!' and clicks his heels.

"'I hereby turn over to you the concentration camp of Dachau, 30,000 residents, 2,340 sick, 27,000 on the outside, 560 garrison troops.'

"Am I dreaming? It seems that I can see before me the striking contrast of a beast and a god. Only that the Boche is the one who looks divine.

"The American major does not return the salute. He hesitates for a moment, as if he were trying to make sure that he is remembering the adequate words. Then, he spits into the face of the German,

"'*Du Schweinehund!*'

"And then, 'Sit down there!'—pointing to the rear seat of one of the jeeps which in the meantime have driven in.

"The major turns to me and hands me an automatic rifle.

"'Come with me—'

But I no longer had the strength to move.

"'No, I stay here—'

"The major gave an order, the jeep with the young German officer in it went outside the camp again. A few minutes went by, my comrades had not yet dared to come out of their barracks, for at that distance they could not tell the outcome of the negotiations between the American officer and the SS men.

"Then I hear several shots.

"'The bastard is dead!' the American major says to me.

"He gives some orders, transmitted to the radiomen in the jeeps, and more officers start arriving, newspapermen, little trucks. Now the prisoners have understood, they jump on the Americans, embrace them, kiss their feet, their hands; the celebration is on."

Lieutenant Colonel Will Cowling, who was among the first of the liberators, came very close to being mobbed by the mangy mass of humanity that swept him along like a tidal wave. The GIs had to fire into the air to make room around him. All the prisoners wanted was to get his autograph.

The detachment under the command of the American major had not come directly to the Jourhaus. It had made a detour by way of the marshaling yard, where the convoys of deportees normally arrived and departed. There they found some fifty-odd cattle cars parked on the tracks. The cars were not empty.

"At first sight," said Cowling, "they seemed to be filled with rags, discarded clothing. Then we caught sight of hands, stiff fingers, faces. ..."

The train was full of corpses, piled one on the other, 2,310 of them, to be exact. The train had come from Birkenau, and the dead were Hungarian and Polish Jews, children among them. Their journey had lasted perhaps thirty or forty days. They had died of hunger, thirst, of suffocation, of being crushed, or of being beaten by the guards. There were even evidences of cannibalism. They were all practically dead when they arrived at Dachau Station. The SS men did not take the trouble to unload them. They simply decided to stand guard and shoot down any with enough strength left to emerge from the cattle cars. The corpses were strewn everywhere—on the rails, the steps, the platforms.

The men of the 45th Division had just made contact with the 42nd, here in the station. They too found themselves unable to breathe at what they saw. One soldier yelled: "Look, Bud, it's moving!" He pointed to something in motion among the cadavers. A louse-infested prisoner was crawling like a worm, trying to attract attention. He was the only survivor.

"I never saw anything like it in my life," said Lieutenant Harold Mayer. "Every one of my men became raving mad. We turned off toward the east, going around the compound, without even taking the trouble to reconnoiter first. We were out to avenge them."

"Now I know what we're fighting for," exclaimed Corporal Eagle—our friend Chief Glorious Eagle. "We can't live in the same world with them. They are nothing but animals. They must be destroyed."

In this very same station, at the very same time, German men and women, peasants or burghers from the town of Dachau, were in the process of looting the depot and the neighboring buildings. Their children were with them. The children played within touch of the corpses, while their parents piled their loot up on little carts, or on their bicycles, totally indifferent to the dead on the train and the nauseating stench of rotting flesh.

The ire of the men of the First Battalion, 157th Regiment, was to mount even higher as they got closer to the Lager of the deportees. The dead were everywhere—in the ditches, along the side streets, in the garden before a small building with chimneys—and there was a huge mountain of corpses inside the yard of this building, which they now understood to be the crematorium. And finally there was the ultimate horror—the infernal sight of those thousands and thousands of living skeletons, screaming like banshees, on the other side of the placid poplars.

When some of the SS men on the watchtowers started to shoot into the mobs of prisoners, the Americans threw all caution to the winds. They opened fire on the towers with healthy salvos. The SS men promptly came down the ladders, their hands reaching high. But now the American GI saw red. He shot the Germans down with a telling blast, and to make doubly sure sent a final shot into their fallen bodies. Then the hunt started for any other Germans in SS uniforms. Within a quarter of an hour there was not a single one of the Hitler henchmen alive within the camp.

In the SS refectory, one soldier had been killed while eating a plate of beans. He still held a spoonful in his hand. At the signal center, the SS man in charge of the switchboard was slumped over his panel, blood running down to the receiver, the busy signal from Munich still ringing in his unheeding ear. At the power plant, the SS foreman had been beaten to death with shovels by a Polish prisoner and his

Czech assistant. After that, they had been able to cut the high-voltage current from the barbed-wire fences around the camp.

When there were no more SS men to go after, the GIs machine-gunned the dogs which were kept in the camp's huge kennel.

Then came the time for fraternization with those who had just been saved, the mass of scarred, pate-shaven ones with their haggard, livid faces, their smiles grotesque because of their broken teeth, these human wrecks who embraced you, threw themselves on you, tried to tell you their stories in sign language, led you by the hand to show you the hovels they lived in, the dead outside the barracks, the dying in the hospital. The Americans gave them cigarettes, their rations, their chewing gum, their addresses, even the jackets or overcoats off their backs, or simply emptied their pockets to them.

During all this, at the Jourhaus, Patrick O'Leary was talking things over with the American colonel.

"We must press on to Munich," the colonel told him. "I will leave you a squad, to be under your command. But the camp gates must be kept closed. Nobody is to move away. You have carte blanche to enforce that."

"We need rations," O'Leary insisted.

"I have nothing with me," the colonel answered, "but I am advising headquarters. In the meantime, you are authorized to requisition whatever is necessary in the neighborhood."

The colonel went to his jeep to get two bottles of bourbon, which he gave to O'Leary. "To celebrate the liberation," he said.

Now Patrick O'Leary, who only that morning had been a prisoner like any other, was master of the camp. He sent out two deportees, escorted by American soldiers, to bring back some cows that were still on the special SS farm. During the night, they would be slaughtered and a first meat ration would be ready for the sick. He also authorized the confiscating of all supplies at the small canning factory at the edge of the compound. The contents were at once distributed to the freed prisoners, with what bread was left over in the SS refectory.

He was informed that Mandzourian, the Armenian Kapo, had been found hiding under a roof, and been rather severely beaten by his former fellow prisoners. With the help of the soldiers under his orders, O'Leary was able to save the Armenian, and he lectured his comrades: "We are civilized, don't forget. We do not kill out of hatred."

The Kapo was turned over to the American authorities. Two nights later he was shot down by a firing squad. The other murderer, the Gypsy, met the same fate.

O'Leary then went about disarming those prisoners who had got hold of revolvers or automatic rifles. There was to be no summary settling of scores at Dachau.

This was an admirable and courageous decision. Elsewhere, at Mauthausen for instance, there were veritable massacres among inmates, each wanting to get even for a beating, a piece of stolen bread, or an insult received. It was disgusting, for that was just what the Germans had wanted to make of us: stool pigeons and killers.

We had no right to take into our own hands the punishment of those who had made us suffer. First of all, because they were prisoners like ourselves, victims of the same circumstances; and secondly, because we were all guilty—all of us, at one time or another, out of selfishness or blindness or sheer madness, had wished for or brought about the death of a comrade. If we were alive this glorious evening, it was only because others had died in our place. In truth, the only ones responsible were those who had reduced us to this state.

In Reims, in the "little red schoolhouse," headquarters of SHAEF, a short paragraph was being dictated, for the communiqué of April 30, 1945, over the signature of General of the Armies Dwight D. Eisenhower:

"Our forces liberated and mopped up the infamous concentration camp at Dachau. Approximately 32,000 prisoners were liberated. Three hundred SS camp guards were quickly neutralized."

# 7
# The Home Fronts

## TOKYO, 1940

from

*Blind Date with Mars*
by Alice-Leone Moats
Garden City, NY: Doubleday, Doran and Company, Inc., 1943

*An American weekly magazine,* Collier's, *was looking for a correspondent who would send it exclusive reports from war-torn Russia in the waning months of 1940. Getting into that country presented many difficulties, and the paperwork seemed insurmountable. At a time when the magazine had almost lost hope of getting someone into the Soviet Union, a young society woman convinced the editors at* Collier's *that since she had published several articles she could handle the assignment and, more important, she was going to Russia as the guest of the American ambassador and his wife. This twenty-nine-year-old woman seemed to be the answer to* Collier's *prayers, and she was hired.*

*Alice-Leone Moats was five-foot-six and weighed a hundred and thirty pounds. She came from a very wealthy family and had been educated in Europe as well as in the United States. She had a keen ear for languages, but was more addicted to fur coats, jewelry, and bath salts than to writing about war fronts. Suddenly she had the assignment of her life. She later said, "Looking back, I wonder who was crazier,* Collier's *for giving me the assignment, or I for taking it. A combination of the gambling spirit and ignorance made me a foreign correspondent. The gambling spirit belonged to the editors of* Collier's Weekly; *the ignorance was mine. I had never worked on a newspaper; my writing had consisted of one light satirical book, many articles in the same vein, and five 'profiles' of well-known personalities."*

*Unfortunately, even as a guest of the American ambassador, Moats met with delays getting the necessary documents to cross from Japan into Russia. While she and the editors of* Collier's *waited for the paperwork, Moats traveled to Japan and managed to capture a picture of a people at war.*

259

*Japan had been at war since 1937, when it had invaded the northern
provinces of China. Chinese resistance flared into a full-scale, though undeclared
war. In 1938 and 1939, while still fighting the Chinese, Japanese troops clashed
with Russian troops on the Manchurian border and, much further to the south,
invaded Indochina. The Japanese lines were stretched thin, and there was heavy
demand for men and materiel.*

*The demands that Japan made on the United States in December 1941 were
undoubtedly predicated on their desperate situation. The United States was well
aware of conditions on the Japanese mainland and turned down all Japanese
requests, deliberately hoping to provoke that Asian nation into war.*

*The following excerpt details Alice-Leone Moats's observations of life in
Tokyo in November 1940. Almost a year before the attack on Pearl Harbor, she
notes food shortages and inconveniences of all kinds in Japan. This saucy, sharp-
tongued correspondent gives us a stark look at the heavy dictatorial hand that
managed the everyday lives of all its citizens.*

T he ship reached Yokohama on September 4. After a forty-minute ride by rail
I arrived in Tokyo and went directly to the Imperial Hotel. There are certain
hotels in the world which, for one reason or another, become famous as centers of cosmopolitan life and gaiety. The Imperial in Tokyo is (or should I hopefully say was?) one of these. After reading and hearing so much about it I don't
quite know what I expected to find, but certainly nothing ever prepared me for the
grisly reality.

When I drove up to the Imperial for the first time it struck me as one of the
ugliest buildings I had ever seen. After two months I was still of the same opinion.
Mushrooming over an entire block, with innumerable wings and ells, it was low,
squat, and built of narrow brownish bricks unevenly set so as to form a design reminiscent of Assyrian architecture. The walls and pillars of the lobby and corridors
were of the same brick, and one had the definite impression of being inside a tomb.

The first evening, in spite of the heat, I put on a black day dress and a small
hat. Although I had seen the hotel, I still imagined that I was in a social center. In
comparison with the other women I was decidedly overdressed; they had the air of
having loosened their corset strings for the duration. There was quite a crowd sitting
around the wicker tables in the lobby, but it was the saddest-looking aggregation
that ever met a traveler's eye. In accordance with the regulations for the trial black-
out which began that night, the lights were even dimmer than usual. That made the
people look as dejected as they felt. Voices were muted, there was no laughter, and
later, when the orchestra began to play waltzes at a funereal tempo, the atmosphere
became really dismal.

At that time the housing question, always acute in Tokyo, had become worse
because the Japanese didn't want to rent their houses to foreigners, and most of
the Imperial guests had been living in the hotel for several months. It had become
just one big, unhappy boardinghouse where everybody knew everybody else, at
least by sight. A new arrival attracted immediate notice, and the appearance of a

female, young, unaccompanied, and togged out in Bendel's best, created a wave of excitement.

The next morning I started out to look over the city. It reminded me of a German provincial town. Once in a while, by glancing down narrow side streets, I had a glimpse of low wooden houses with paper windows, which indicated that I was really in Japan. Very few passers-by wore kimonos, although most of them stuck to the *geta* even with their European garments, and the clack-clack of wooden clogs on pavements could be heard above all the other street noises at any hour of the day or night. There was little of the cherry-blossom atmosphere that I had expected and none of the much-touted "glamour of the Orient." Foreigners who had lived in Japan for some years assured me that both of these had once existed; their disappearance was due to the New Structure. I was to hear that expression again and again. The New Structure cropped up one way or another ten times a day; the newspapers were full of it, and all the changes and discomforts in the country were ascribed to it. For that reason, before recounting my personal adventures in the land of the Mikado, it seems better to sketch in the background by describing some of the new laws and regulations which thoroughly did away with the country's former charm and glamour.

The first word of Japanese that I learned was *arimasen*. It means "there isn't any." The second and third were *nai desu*. They combine to mean "there isn't any." Usually the waiter or room boy or shop clerk just let it go at that, but sometimes, in an expansive mood, he would amplify it by adding, "New Structure." That was supposed to make everything clear, in spite of the fact that no one had a definite idea of what the New Structure actually was. That it formed an integral part of the New Order in East Asia just made everything so much more confusing.

Premier Konoye, in a speech, had announced that the New Structure was neither Nazi nor communist. In his own words, "The goal of the movement in its ideological aspects is to give a clear-cut idea of the Japanese national character to official, financial, and all other circles and strata in this country. It is designed to embody all the finest points of Nazism and communism, but the fundamental objective is a strictly Japanese ideology according to the principle of fulfilling the duties of subjects of the Emperor."

The definition may have been intelligible to Japanese used to struggling with imperial rescripts which sound like so much double talk. To Occidentals it was a bit vague, but after a short time it became quite clear to me that the "proposed" New Structure, as the papers cautiously qualified the term, was responsible for the lack of everything: food, luxuries, most necessities, comfort, transportation, pleasure, and even common civility. Always great admirers of the Germans, the Japs were not only imitating the Nazi spirit; they were going it one better by adopting a program of Strength *without* Joy.

Under the rules of the New Structure no dish in a restaurant might cost more than one yen (about twenty-four cents); the price of breakfast was limited to one yen, luncheon to two-fifty, and dinner to five. At those rates the food couldn't possibly be of first or even second quality, and it wasn't. Real butter was a commodity never encountered in a public eating place and seldom even in the house of a foreigner; olive oil was never seen, and the coffee was made of soybeans or barley. The bread was soggy and gray; when ordering "*à la carte* the customer paid fifteen sen for each slice, which had to come out of the two-fifty or five yen he might spend on lunch or dinner.

In October the price was reduced to eleven sen and a slice of bread increased to a thickness measuring about three inches. Every guest in the hotel objected to this and tried to have it cut in half. The waiters refused; it was against the law. So, in an effort to save bread, three times as much was served for four sen less. Of course the authorities may have been farseeing enough to realize that no one would want to eat those thick slabs.

The egg shortage in Tokyo was admittedly the worst ever; matches and sugar were rationed under a ticket system; whale meat was sold instead of pork. Every now and then a few stale, dusty, not-too-sweet squares parading under the name of candy would appear on store counters, but the Chocolate Shop had no chocolates to sell.

Fresh milk was a rare luxury. Condensed and powdered milk might be sold under a system of cards issued by the mayors of municipalities exclusively for the use of infants under one year of age; that is, if the request was accompanied by a doctor's certificate stating that the child couldn't get sufficient milk from its mother. On the other hand, mothers were urged to feed their babies as long as possible, and it wasn't at all unusual to see women in trains and other public conveyances giving the breast to children two or three years old.

The lack of commodities such as milk, butter, and eggs was a hardship to foreigners; the Japanese wouldn't have minded if they could have obtained enough of their staple food, rice. The trouble was that they couldn't. Due to poor crops, the great amount of rice that had to be exported to feed the troops fighting in China, and the farm-labor shortage resulting from the "Incident," there wasn't enough native rice to go round. It had to be mixed with grain imported from Indo-China and Siam, which didn't suit Japanese palates, or with barley and wheat, which suited their palates even less. Anyone sufficiently foolhardy to complain over the poor quality of the rice found himself locked up in jail for three days without food. At the end of that time he would be let out with the question, "Don't you find that the quality of the rice has improved?"

The more expensive brands of cigars and cigarettes had been done away with to "relieve the shortage of cheaper brands," but even with that measure a week or two often went by when it was impossible to buy either Hikaris or Cherries, the two most popular cigarettes. The tobacco monopoly's bland answer to that was a claim that there had been no reduction in output; the shortage was due merely to an increased demand. The government authorities attacked the problem from another angle by enlisting the support of the National Spiritual Mobilization Headquarters in a campaign to induce moderation in consumption of tobacco by inveterate smokers and abstention on the part of minors and women. Smoking during working hours or on the street was frowned upon, and those who indulged in this appetite were ticked off for flouting the spirit of the New Structure.

October 7, 1940, was the date originally set for the ban on the sale of luxury goods. In the end, at the pleas of the merchants, an extra year's grace was allowed; but the prices were fixed by the government, and luxuries might be sold only under special license, which meant to foreigners. An *obi*, for instance, couldn't be sold for more than a hundred yen. The ones of best quality were, therefore, put away to be sold if and when the laws were changed. The same had happened with other expensive goods. In some cases they were still left on display, but when it actually came to purchasing them it turned out to be impossible for obscure reasons. A friend of mine looking at a cabinet for gramophone records was told by the shop clerk that he had better make a decision immediately because next month it would be half price. To an occidental mentality that didn't make good sense, but he eventually caught the point—next month the cabinet wouldn't be for sale.

Several large department stores were closed, and the buildings had been taken over by the government for offices. In keeping with the spirit of the times, the display windows of those still operating showed only the cheapest, least gaudy wares. Nothing must be done to tempt the purchaser. Women's hats, for instance, had to be either black, brown, or navy blue, and of only one model—a round, schoolgirl type with rolled brim, not exactly becoming to Japanese faces. According to the newspapers, a salubrious effect was evident as a result of the luxury ban—people were proud to wear old clothes and happy to flaunt patches instead of expensive finery.

The ones who weren't either proud or happy to disport themselves in worn or mended garments were usually cautious enough to do so. Women who appeared in the streets too expensively dressed ran the risk of being slapped by some ardent patriot or being handed a ticket by a member of one of the feminine organizations.

It was impossible to buy a yard of pure silk in Tokyo. The foreigners who needed to replenish their wardrobes or who were furnishing houses had to send to Shanghai for dresses, upholstery, or curtain materials. The same was true when it came to purchasing sheets or towels. The natives made do with a staple fiber material known as *sufu*, which had only one quality—unexpectedness. Sometimes it shrank to half size, sometimes it stretched, and sometimes it just disappeared. The Japan Women's Federation actually dared to stage a revolt against *sufu* and called a meeting inviting many government officials and representatives of textile manufacturers to be present. There was an exhibit of eighty-six *sufu* garments sent in from all over the country, eighty-two of which had been rendered completely useless by one washing. *Sufu*, the women said, was not any good for baby clothes, not only because of its poor durability, but also because it wasn't absorbent. Therefore, they added, the government's campaign to popularize the material was inconsistent with its earnest desire to increase the birth rate. Faced with such arguments, the authorities yielded ground before the determined ladies by giving assurance that more liberal amounts of cotton would be allowed for particularly vulnerable articles such as socks, shirts, students' uniforms, and babies' pants. The newspapers termed this surrender "A disorderly retreat from the *sufu* battle line."

September 16 was set aside as a date for honoring the rabbits who had given up their skins to keep the army warm. Prayers were to be sent up yearly for the eternal repose of the souls of those heroes among rodents who were doing their bit for the fatherland. It looked as though "Dog Day" would come next for, by order of the

Ministry of Forestry and Agriculture, the canine population was to be cut down with a triple objective: (1) using the hides for soldier's shoes and gloves, and thus relieving the leather shortage, (2) saving rice, (3) protecting the public from mad dogs.

For a while even women were regarded as heroines. The widow of an officer killed in China committed suicide after reading his last letter in which he asked her to follow him into the next world if he were to die in action. The newspapers played up the story of her great sacrifice with such praise and enthusiasm that all the widows wanted to become heroines, and an epidemic of suicides broke out. Within a few weeks hundreds of children were orphaned and left on the government's hands. Something had to be done about the situation, and the newspapers received orders to publish articles pointing out that it was more courageous for a woman to live on after her husband's death than to kill herself.

Only diplomatic, government, army, and navy cars were allowed an unlimited supply of gasoline. No private automobiles were permitted on the streets unless they had been converted for charcoal consumption or other gasoline substitutes. Seventy per cent of the busses ran on charcoal; that is, they did when they could get it. When the authorities passed this law it seemed a brilliant idea; they didn't figure on the charcoal shortage which occurred that year. Sight-seeing busses were prohibited, no matter what they burned, and taxis were rationed to seven gallons of gasoline a month. As a result, taxi drivers refused to carry a fare further than a few blocks, a run which took much longer than it would have to cover on foot because the driver turned off the motor every few yards with the naive idea of saving fuel. With truly touching faith he would usually even try to coast uphill. Pressure had been brought to bear on all hacks not to convey their fares to waiting houses, theaters, race tracks, or other places of amusement, and none might go within a block of a licensed quarter. Since there is at least one of the latter in every district of Tokyo, it didn't allow the taxis a very wide range of operation.

Even telephones had come under the rationing system. There was such a shortage of instruments that it took at least six months to get one installed. According to the new law governing Mr. Bell's invention, telephones were installed only in offices where a definite need for such communication with the outside world existed and it was announced that none would be put in the homes of private citizens or "in the houses of their concubines."

The New Structure allowed no place for amusement or relaxation. Restaurants, bars, and ice-cream parlors had to be closed by ten at night. Japanese restaurants had a rule that rice and geishas couldn't be provided at the same meal; a patron paid his money and took his choice. When I asked a Japanese woman what the men would do in that crisis she replied: "Oh, it's quite simple. They will eat rice at home before going out and order geishas at the restaurant."

No liquor might be served before five in the afternoon. Then one almost regretted that it was, as the liquor to be had was native. This was due to the fact that the law forbade charging more than fifty sen a glass for any drink. It was a simple manner of doing away with imported liquor.

There were only three rat- and cockroach-infested restaurants serving foreign food in the capital and not one place with music for dancing. Bridge and other games of chance might not be played in public places, and although there were three theaters and a few movie houses still operating in Tokyo, the public was offered every discouragement against attending them. It was one of the best examples of the government's policy of discouragement rather than prohibition. When I went to see *Camille* one afternoon I found an S.R.O. sign at the box office. I decided to go in anyway and take a chance of getting a seat when someone left. When I got into the theater I found it three-quarters empty.

Most of the moving pictures shown were five or six years old, and, aside from the dimness and flickering due to their age, it was difficult to see what was happening on the screen because the lights had to be left on in the auditorium. This was to prevent any surreptitious love-making, which would run counter to the spirit of the times. Lights had also to be kept on in taxis and cars, partly for reasons of morality and partly to allow the police to see at a glance who was riding in the car.

The police also clamped down on "insincere" mind readers, astrologists, and fortune-tellers who bilked the public. Those who were sincere and considered harmless to public order were allowed to continue their trade under a license system which also forced them to charge uniform fees. Soon after, the Tokyo Association of Fortune-tellers decided to see only happy omens in cards, stars, and tea leaves, so the patrons might not be unduly discouraged in these times of emergency and stress.

Skiing simply for fun was frowned upon. The sport was all right if undertaken only with the idea of hardening the body. Those who went to mountain resorts and appeared to be skiing merely for pleasure were ticked off by members of the Young Men's Association. If their attitude remained unchanged after an official rebuke, they were dealt with in the "proper" manner by the authorities. That, in Japan, has an ominous sound, and one could be sure that the snowy slopes were covered only with solemn little figures sliding down, grimly determined to harden their bodies with the least possible enjoyment.

The Spiritual Mobilization authorities in Tokyo found that elaborate weddings ran counter to the new spirit and recommended that they cost no more than twenty yen. This ruled out any entertainment or exchange of gifts. *Sake* and food for attendants at funerals had to be done away with, as well as the custom of exchanging condolence presents.

There were 1,500,000 girls working in factories in Japan when I was there, with pay ranging from sixty-five sen a day for twelve-year-olds to eighty-five sen for those over eighteen. It was expected that this number would probably be doubled, for in its moral drive the government was making an effort to cut down the number of bar girls, geishas, and prostitutes who would then have to seek new lines of endeavor. The choice was limited to taking a job in a factory or finding a husband. The second alternative was quite possible, since virginity hasn't a high market value in Japan.

The police were taking vigorous measures to do away with or, at any rate, cut down prostitution, which they referred to as "this shameful relic of feudalism." In Tokyo alone the official figures numbered the geishas at 12,000, licensed prostitutes at 7,000, with about the same number of unlicensed. Just to prove that this time they meant business the police announced that they would refuse to recognize a contract for the sale of a girl into prostitution made by anyone except her real father, and that for proper reasons. "Improper" reasons were such things as the settlement of gambling or other frivolous debts; if Papa wanted to sell little Kiku San to buy a government bond, that was all right.

Brothel business hours had been curtailed—they could be open only between 5 P.M. and midnight. No licenses for new houses were being granted. This system, it was hoped, would cut down the number of ladies practicing the world's oldest profession, and, besides, a gradual decrease was expected through marriage, bought freedom, retirement, or death.

Since going out with a girl brought on so many complications, university students solved their sex problems with true oriental philosophy—they switched to boys. Homosexuality had reached extraordinary proportions, but that didn't seem to trouble the authorities.

The anti-foreign campaign begun at the start of the China Incident had been renewed and was proceeding briskly in the autumn of 1940. Its most violent manifestation was to be found in the spy phobias which possessed all inhabitants of Nippon. Things had come to the point where no one believed that a foreigner could possibly be living in or visiting Japan for any simple reason such as business or pleasure. He must be in the pay of a foreign government—any government. This entailed a counterespionage system in which every Japanese joined with enthusiasm.

One of the reasons why the service was so bad in the Imperial Hotel was that the room boys and waiters were too busy keeping an eye on "spies" to have time for the performance of their regular duties. I gave them plenty to do by leaving all my things in great disorder but took the precaution of always carrying my papers with me. The cooperation of even school children had been enlisted; they were offered a monetary reward for turning in suspicious characters. One tattletale tot at a summer resort rushed to the police with the report that he had seen two Europeans photographing a fortified zone. The guilty pair—a German couple—were promptly taken into custody and held until the film were developed. It turned out that the "fortified zone" they had photographed was themselves romping over the beach with all the zeal and exuberance of Teutons on holiday. They were released, but the officious child was given ten yen, a pat on the head, and the admonition to keep on with the good work.

The Military Secrets Law made it a crime to take pictures from any height above twenty yards. The penalty was a year's imprisonment or a thousand-yen fine. If the pictures were shown to the public or published in newspapers, it meant two years' imprisonment or a two-thousand-yen fine. Exportation of the films incurred seven years' imprisonment or a three-thousand-yen fine. In the end what it boiled down to was that it was wiser never to produce a camera at all in Japan.

Villagers were warned against fishermen who arrived complete with rod and reel and asked the depth of the ocean at that particular point. They were not interested in fishing, what they really wanted to know was whether the water was sufficiently deep for an attacking submarine or battleship.

To keep the public continually awake to the spy menace, posters had been put up in all cities and towns warning the inhabitants against foreign agents. Most of them showed a man in full evening dress (no doubt the "uniform" of the Westerner) peeping furtively through the illuminated window of a Japanese dwelling. Matchboxes bore such slogans as "Beware of Spies," "Let No Spy Escape," and some were decorated with reproductions of the posters. The national broadcasting company put on a nightly program devoted to teaching to listeners the words and music of an anti-spy march with innumerable verses repeating that there were spies everywhere and that friendly smiles and gestures were dangerous.

A great point was made of the fact that the foreign agent got his information from a woman. The Japanese lady is such an amiable creature that she is far too willing to be helpful, and therefore every effort must be made to prevent her meeting strangers. The authorities infinitely preferred foreigners to talk with men rather than with women, but even that wasn't encouraged. The result was that Japanese were afraid to be seen with any foreigners, particularly diplomats. The few I happened to become acquainted with all asked me to be good enough never to communicate with them by letter or telephone.

A foreigner residing in Japan did well not to have too much to do with his own embassy or legation, as that was considered very suspicious. A young American told me that he had been studying pottery making in Kyoto but had had to leave the town because his presence was making life too difficult for his teacher, who was accused of harboring a spy. By chance the American was able to see his police dossier and found that the charges against him were based on three counts: he had been seen walking on the main street in his undershirt (actually it was a sports shirt with short sleeves); he had lunched at the hotel with some American tourists; he was on too good terms with one of the secretaries at the American Embassy in Tokyo.

This was the sort of thing that made life unpleasant for foreigners living in Japan. They never knew what action of theirs was going to tag them as dangerous spies and get them into the clutches of the police. Once there, it was not easy to get out. Strangely enough, in such a regimentalized country, each policeman had his own interpretation of the law, and he reigned supreme in his particular bailiwick.

Through these various methods a strong feeling of hatred for all Westerners was produced in the people. Most of the foreigners I met had grown almost afraid to go out on the streets for fear of demonstrations against them. When they had to ride in busses or streetcars they were careful not to push or shove and never to take a seat away from a Japanese. A Dutch woman riding on a trolley in Kobe was severely beaten up by the other passengers even though she was sitting quietly and minding her own business. A Canadian girl in Tokyo was stoned one evening on her way home. One woman told me she was continually being spat at in the street, but she may have been hypersensitive and imagined the passers-by were aiming at her. It would be difficult to be sure in that country where the people hawk and spit all the time.

The servants in every household reported luncheon and dinner parties to the police, with a list of guests who were present. Mrs. Grummon, the wife of the First Secretary of the American Embassy, was approached after a luncheon party by her number-one boy, who said, "There is a policeman in the kitchen who wants to know the names of the people who were here today." He was unusually naive; apparently too much for his own good, since about a week later he gave notice, sobbing with grief as he did so and leaving a garbled letter of explanation which made no sense whatever.

All the "boy sans" and the "chauffeur sans" working for foreigners belonged to a sort of club which met twice a month to report on what their masters had been doing. None of the victims enjoyed this close watch in their own houses very much, but most of them endured it with fairly good grace. Only the Soviets objected vigorously, and they put up such a fight that they were fully allowed to have Russian chauffeurs and a Russian telephone operator. However, this meant that they were under even closer surveillance outside the embassy. When they made up a golf foursome, for instance, four men were sent along to keep an eye on them. One wasn't considered enough to keep watch on the party, for supposing the player were to go into the rough, what would the other spy do then? If he followed into the rough, that left the other three unwatched. With the caddies, this made twelve people on the course in the same group and slowed up the other players. Finally the club passed a ruling excluding all diplomats from its membership list.

Persecution of the Christian churches was a part of the anti-foreign campaign. The idea back of it was to stamp out the outside influence which, through missionaries operating with money sent from abroad, had been exerted over Christian Japanese. Members of Christian institutions in Japan were advised to leave them; Christianity, it seemed, ran radically against the guiding spirit of the national structure. All Christian educational institutions were ordered reorganized speedily so as to conform to the fundamental policies based on the Imperial Way.

The first direct shot was fired at the Salvation Army. It was ordered to reorganize completely, changing its name (the word "army" grated on the ears of a militaristic nation), severing its ties with the world headquarters in London, and abolishing its military structure. When all that didn't take place overnight the organization's immediate dissolution was demanded as well as "complete repentance." Its social and welfare activities were transferred to the Japanese government, and all forms of spiritual and material assistance extended to the Salvation Army by any individual or groups were ordered to cease. Then, just to make sure that it couldn't continue to operate, the leaders were accused of British espionage activities. The Salvation Army, it was announced, was nothing but a blind to cover British spying, and if it was not put out of existence, a victory would result for the pro-British groups which would be detrimental to the establishment of the proposed New Structure.

Sixty thousand Korean Christians had been brought into a group of a completely Nipponized nature. Christian schools in Korea were reorganized, and the reformed doctrines condemned communism, individualism, and democracy as inconsistent with the Japanese national policy. The Christian principles of self-sacrifice, being in conformity with the traditional Japanese spirit of patriotism, were allowed to remain, and all Korean Christians were encouraged to enlist in volunteer services in times of emergency.

Soon after the anti-Christian campaign started forty-eight Protestant families in a village in Japan gave an example of the "right" spirit which the rest of their fellow believers would eventually have to follow. They built god shelves in their houses on which to place newly acquired Shinto sacred objects. Until then they had made a point of maintaining no accommodation for Shinto gods and had forbidden their children to attend shrine festivals. Then suddenly the light broke and they allowed the spirit of the times to prevail.

Having disposed of Christianity, the government moved on to a campaign to do away with all English words that had crept into the language. At one moment the authorities announced that station signs in English would disappear. Not only would such directions as "Way Out," "Entrance," "Station Master," and so on be removed, but also the ones with the names of the town written in Roman letters. Just before the impetuous railway officials began to tear down signs some practical soul pointed out that it might be rather an expensive proposition. The Japanese characters were on the same signboards as the English ones, and it would mean putting up all new signs in some four thousand stations. Regretfully the plan was abandoned, but every time a sign wore out and had to be replaced the new one bore no English words.

Baseball was also remodeled to conform to the New Structure. The fundamentals of the game were left fairly intact, but American phrases, scoreboards, and regulation caps and uniforms were discarded. However, the officials struck a snag when it came to ousting all baseball jargon. They found a phrase to take the place of "Prei boru" but were completely stumped when it came to finding substitutes for "out" and "safe" and concluded that perhaps they had been too hasty in deciding to do away with all Americanisms.

# THE WAR EFFORT AT HOME

from
"Be Thankful for a Ration Book"
by Alice Fraser
*The Parents' Magazine*, February 1943

*Whenever disaster strikes, be it natural or man-made, there will always be those who take advantage of the victims. Someone else's calamity becomes their profit. During war, when there are shortages of everyday essentials, there are many opportunities for the unscrupulous to make a profit. In war-torn countries, black-market operators flourish and, at times, may even control the necessities of life.*

*In the United States, black marketeers, when caught, were faced with fines, and sometimes jail sentences, depending upon the scale of the operation. But the Americans who paid high prices for scarce material often bragged that they knew where they could get as many tires as they wished, as much gasoline as they needed, or pounds and pounds of extra sugar. They felt that "beating the system" gave them status. War industries had around-the-clock work schedules. Men and women worked overtime, boosting their salaries to heights never dreamed of. Money was available, but there was little to spend it on.*

Sugar, meats, fats and oils, fresh and processed fruits and vegetables, dairy products, and coffee were in short supply. Gasoline, automobiles, tires, fuel oil, rubber boots and shoes were also on the restricted list. To be fair in the distribution of scarce materials, a system of rationing was introduced that not only made available that which was scarce, but also put a cap on prices so that manufacturers, wholesalers, and retailers could not profiteer.

The Office of Price Administration (OPA) was established in April 1941. The U.S. Congress gave the OPA broad authority to fix maximum prices and the power of enforcement. Because consumer purchasing power was rapidly rising at the same time that supplies were dwindling due to Lend-Lease, the OPA, in April 1942, issued a maximum price regulation that set the prices charged in March 1942 as the ceiling prices for most commodities. Ceilings were also imposed on residential rents. By 1946 almost 90 percent of all retail food prices were "frozen."

Stamps were issued for scarce foods, and little red cardboard coins were issued for the purchase of meat and fish. Stamps were issued for gasoline, and they had to match the sticker on your windshield. If you had an "A" sticker you could only purchase your gasoline with "A" stamps. If you needed tires, you had to go to the local rationing board and get special dispensation to buy them.

The government had to sell this program to the American people. One approach was to describe the program as being good for children. If the government could persuade families to observe OPA rulings, then a good chunk of the American public was accounted for.

Rationing was a shock, and although it met with opposition in the beginning and never did quite lick the black market, it proved very effective in the end. Many publications stressed the importance of rationing to persuade the public that it was important to the war effort. The following article was read and approved by the Office of Price Administration and the Office of War Information prior to its appearing in a popular magazine.

T he long arm of war reaches into every home and in its hand is a ration book. Rich and poor, famous and obscure, none escape it. And children are no exceptions. For this is a children's war as well as an adult's war.

It is a little more than a year since Pearl Harbor. Yet already, our children know something about rationing. Cissie and her gang have to go easy on the sugar cookies that they used to gobble up by the dozens. Bud must apply to his ration board if he needs a bicycle for that after-school delivery job. Neither of them is allowed to poke at father's typewriter anymore because father can't get another. The old inner tube is now too precious for fooling around in the lake and has probably been turned back to the Government along with the tire that was last year's backyard swing. As for Bud's dates, they ride the streetcar to the movies instead of going in the family car, and there's no more fun in the third-floor playroom this winter because the fuel oil ration won't heat the whole house, and the playroom is closed.

And even as you read this article a new form of rationing—point rationing—is being put into operation. Which means that in addition to the now familiar straight coupon technique of rationing used for single commodities such as gasoline, sugar and coffee, American families will soon learn at first hand about a new system. Children will soon see their mothers figuring household food budgets in terms of "points" as well as pennies, and when a favorite item is missing from the dinner table, the reason may well be that mother couldn't afford to spend the required number of points out of her set point allowance to obtain it. Thus, to children, as to the rest of us, rationing is a nuisance, rationing is a depriver.

But to them, as to the rest of us, rationing is also much, much more than that. It is a sinew of war, a bulwark against economic chaos, an equalizer of sacrifice.

It is a sinew of war because without it the war machine couldn't keep going. It is a bulwark against economic chaos because without it the price ceilings that keep prices within range of father's purse wouldn't stick. It is an equalizer of sacrifice because without it others greedier or richer than father might monopolize all of the things that are scarce.

When the Japanese took Malaya and the East Indies, this country lost well over 90 per cent of its rubber supply—and war is a glutton for rubber! A four-motor bomber gobbles as much rubber as three dozen passenger cars. One battleship needs more rubber than 4,000 automobiles. It takes three unbuilt passenger cars to put wheels on a 37-mm. anti-aircraft gun.

The same situation holds true for sugar. Much of our sugar was imported and is now lost to us either through military defeat or through shortage of ships to carry it—and war is a glutton for sugar! One shot from a 16-inch gun eats up a whole acre of sugar cane. Fighting men need quantities of sugar because sugar is energy food.

Thus rationing at home "keeps 'em flying" on the battle front.

And while it is doing so, it is also helping out on the home front, and one of the ways that it helps is with price control. For experience shows that price control without rationing is Gilbert without Sullivan, Barnum without Bailey, Crusoe without Friday.

Take England for instance. England tried price control without rationing—and prices kept right on rising. It was only after key supplies were rationed to the consumer that the upward push slowed. For price control without rationing encourages buying.

The controlled prices made it possible for almost everyone to "lay a little by," and almost everyone does. Goods grow scarcer and scarcer. Buyers, more and more frantic, offer more than legal prices. Soon the black market flourishes. And daily, more and more is bought there at higher-than-legal charges. Price control, unaccompanied by rationing, has defeated itself.

With rationing, however, price control can succeed. Consumer demand does not outstrip supply because demand is balanced with supply. Consequently, since goods in excess of the ration allowance are not to be had, there is no reason to pay illegal prices. It is a case of check and double check. Violators of price control must not only flout the price-control law, they must also flout the ration law in order to get the additional, illegally priced goods.

Thus, children have a great stake in rationing over and above that of "keeping 'em flying." If price control fails, children of low-income parents will be underfed, underclothed, underprivileged and all children will know the hardships of economic chaos. For economic order in the world that will be theirs as adults after the war depends to a great degree on the success of price control now. If it fails, the dollar will be worth only a fraction of today's dollar; the war debt they shoulder will be far more crushing than it might have been; their country, when the price bubbles burst, will be plunged into an even more terrible depression than the last one.

Against such disasters, rationing is a bulwark.

The first settlers of this country used rationing when their food and clothing ran low and they pooled what they had and apportioned to each his share from the common pool. In England, "fair share," as rationing is called, was demanded some months ago by the people, not foisted upon them by government, when low-priced clothing became scarce while high-priced clothing remained plentiful, when cheap staple foods disappeared while the larders of expensive restaurants were loaded.

Now Mr. Churchill's ministers no longer wait to ration until after an article becomes scarce. They ration it before there is any real economic need because they have learned that nothing is more destructive of national unity than leaving the degree to which individuals sacrifice in the common cause to the accident of pocketbook.

In this aspect of rationing, rationing as a democratic divider, children have a peculiar stake. For children are less able than adults to look after themselves; moreover, they have special needs.

The importance of their stake has everywhere been recognized in countries pinched by war shortages. Russian children receive supplementary rations of sugar, meat, cereals, and fats. Dutch children are the only Dutch population group accorded shoes with rubber or leather soles. English children's clothes coupons have a higher purchasing power than adults', and, to cope with the "outgrowing problem," special allowances have been made.

In particular instances, however, special allocations for children may be necessary, and in one instance have already been so, the homes where there are children under four being authorized to receive special allocations of fuel oil.

Even in the case of dire emergency, of which general differential-rationing will be a sign, however, children have less to fear than anyone else. In England, in fact, much that is good for children has come out of the grim compulsion of differential-rationing. The most striking development is the National Milk Scheme, under which one pint of milk a day is subsidized by the government for expectant and nursing mothers and children under five. The milk is free to those with incomes below a certain level; to others, it is four cents a pint. Thus, out of war has come acceptance by England of the principle of public responsibility for the nutrition of her children.

This principle England puts into practice in a number of ways. Free to all children under six is cod-liver oil; to all children under two and over six months, black currant purée; to all children under six months, black currant juice. No one is allowed to pay—thus removing the stigma of charity.

In addition, the English government has assumed the burden of child feeding

272

at school, paying up to 95 percent of the cost of the milk and hot meals that are pro-vided at noon. Furthermore, children have priority in the purchase of oranges, when available, and eggs.

The almost unbelievable result is that, despite blitzes, shelter crowding, and war tension, English children are in better condition than ever before. The reason is that children in low-income homes, among whom formerly came the high incidence of disease, are now eating almost like children in high-income homes.

Rationing is something more than a negative grinding form of self-discipline. It is a requisite of military victory, a requisite of decent and healthful living while victory is in the making. From rationing, children have less to fear than grownups, more to gain. It is one of their most powerful safeguards, and it will be used to pro-tect them to the utmost.

# 8
# The War's End

## THE BUNKER

from
"The Final Hours of Adolf Hitler"
by Sigrid Schultz
from *I Can Tell It Now*
by members of the Overseas Press Club of America
edited by David Brown and W. Richard Bruner
New York: E. P. Dutton & Co., Inc., 1964

*The beginning of 1945 saw many vital changes in America's strategic position. In three years the army had grown from 1,600,000 to 8,000,000 and the navy from 430,000 to 3,800,000. War production had increased 680 percent!*

*New airfields had been built on Saipan, and now Japan was within air range of American bombers. One hundred eleven planes took part in the first bombardment of Tokyo, pounding strategic targets in November 1944. Four days after the initial run, bombers flew over Japan once more to bomb the industrial waterfront. On December 3 Japan was hit again.*

*Superfortresses were conducting almost nightly reconnaissance missions over Japan, constantly dropping incendiary bombs. Japanese homes were tinderboxes built close to one another along cramped, narrow crooked streets through which flames could eat their devastating way quickly.*

*Carrier-based planes bombarded Tokyo in February, followed by more than 200 superfortresses from Saipan. This raid was followed shortly by a 300-superfortress raid, dropping a 1,000-ton load of the new type of jelly-fire bombs for the first time and wiping out the heart of the city. Not a building was left intact in an area of fifteen square miles. A million people were homeless, industrial plants were in ashes, and the A-bomb was yet to come.*

*The war stepped up on the islands in the Pacific as the Americans took Iwo*

Jima, Okinawa, the Philippines, the Marshall Islands, and the Marianas. The Australians invaded New Guinea, driving out the Japanese. Akyab, the last big Japanese naval and air base in western Burma, was captured by British and Indian troops.

In Europe, by January 1, 1945, Berlin was doomed. The Russians had advanced speedily on an unparalleled scale, completely liberating Poland and much of Czechoslovakia. They had driven deep salients into the German homeland in Silesia, East Prussia, Pomerania, and Brandenburg. Berlin, with candor intended to stiffen national resistance, outdid Moscow in describing the fury of the Russian attack and the appalling accumulation of German disasters. The German radio first pictured the Red Army's surge as a steamroller, then as a landslide, next as an avalanche, and finally as an Apocalyptic "Bolshevist flood."

Terrified refugees by the tens of thousands rushed towards Berlin from the far reaches of the collapsing empire. As the city was rapidly being reduced to rubble under ceaseless air attacks carried out by the Royal Air Force at night, and the American planes by day, women manned anti-aircraft guns while children and the elderly helped to dig trenches and antitank ditches.

Much of the Netherlands had been liberated by Anglo-Canadian forces. In Germany, American armies scored many triumphs. Forces under General Hodges captured Leuna and besieged Leipzig; General Patton reached Chemnitz and swept through the Bavarian town of Bayreuth, while the Seventh Army under General Patchwas marched on Nuremberg.

All this bad news was transmitted to Adolf Hitler, who was bordering on a nervous breakdown. Some of his generals advised him to surrender or begin negotiating for peace, but he would have none of it.

Chicago-born Sigrid Schultz, a journalist and author, was bureau chief in Berlin for the Chicago Tribune before and during World War II. She was one of the first American journalists in Germany to predict the coming of the war, and she interviewed Hitler several times. She freely discussed her opposition to Nazism with him, and he patiently explained to her, "You cannot understand the Nazi movement because you think with your head and not with your heart."

Hitler compelled Sigrid Schultz to leave Germany in 1941 because of her unfavorable opinions. Back in the States, she wrote Germany Will Try It Again. She returned to Germany in 1945 to cover the aftermath of the last days of Adolf Hitler.

About two hours after the first big American convoy of victors had pulled into the Berlin suburb of Zehlendorf on July 3, 1945, correspondents who had covered Germany in the days of the Weimar Republic and during the reign of Adolf Hitler jeeped at top speed through the Brandenburg gate. We were headed for the Chancellery of the Führer on Wilhelmstrasse and the underground shelter where he was supposed to have committed suicide.

"Kolossal" had been the word for the new Chancellery that Hitler had erected on this historical street, convinced that it was as impressive as the glorious buildings of the Eternal City of Rome. Now, despite its massiveness, it was in ruins.

A little old man who had been an attendant at the Chancellery for eight years, and who said that he was glad to see it smashed, led us across the rain-soaked yard to the famous underground "bunker" that had been Hitler's last headquarters in the tense, stormy days of 1945 when armies of the countries the Germans had invaded or challenged were advancing deeper and deeper into Germany, closing in on him and his cohorts.

Before the entrance we saw empty jerricans, reminders of the reports that the Führer had ordered a Viking funeral, with a flaming funeral pyre for himself and his bride. The inside of the bunker was dank and cold. The floor was soggy. The last guards on duty after the Führer killed himself had started to set it on fire before fleeing, but hungry Berliners who had been lying in wait in nearby cellars for the moment when the mighty would decamp noticed the flames and rushed in to douse them. They were not going to let a little fire prevent them from trying to get in ahead of the Russians and to grab some of the food that had been trucked into the shelter in vast amounts to provide generous rations for Hitler's crews.

The simplicity of the cramped cubicles of the bunker were in stark contrast to the new-rich leftover furnishings in the undestroyed parts of the Chancellery. Even the suite of Hitler and Eva Braun looked drab. Only one elegant piece of furniture seemed to stand out in their living room. It was the sofa on which Hitler had shot himself after he and Eva had swallowed their capsules of poison. It was spattered with reddish brown streaks—Hitler's blood, said the attendant.

We knew a good deal about what had happened in the bunker by the time we could inspect it. Between VE day and our arrival in Berlin most of us had interviewed every German we could find who had been in that underground shelter in the days when Hitler's Thousand Year Reich was foundering. One point that puzzled most of us was: why had the Germans fought on after there could not be any doubt in the minds of the German generals that the war was lost?

One of the escapees from the bunker whom I interviewed was General von Hofmeister, chief of the Berlin garrison between July, 1944, and April 15, 1945, whom I found in a hospital in Bad Toelz in Bavaria. He moaned: "For six months I begged the Führer to have Berlin declared an open city. Hitler had become a shaking wreck of a man by March, racked by fear and distrust. I actually saw him make Martin Bormann sample his food, then lock the dishes in his bedroom and come back to watch Bormann like a hawk. After a few hours he decided the food must have been all right. He went back to his room and wolfed down the whole cold mess.

"My fellow officers who were with Hitler were even harder to take than he was. They knew as well as I did that there was nothing to stem the Russian tide—that the war was lost. They also knew what misery lay in store for three million Berliners if it ever came to a real siege. I made my last try to talk sense with them on April 15th. I was turned down cold and became so upset that I suffered a stroke.

"Maybe that was lucky for me because my friends packed me on a plane and flew me to Bad Toelz, otherwise Hitler's toadies might have tried the same stunt on me as they did on General Rommel, forcing him to swallow poison after he had warned Hitler that it was time to sue for peace.* Instead of upholding military integrity, these pet generals of the Führer joined in with Goebbels, Martin Bormann, and similar odious characters to convince him that the East-West Alliance was bound to crack any minute. Their theory was that once this happened it would be easy for Germany to make a deal with the side that seemed strongest and thus end the war at the side of the winner.

"That was irresponsible gambling. It meant more battles and hadn't our people suffered enough? My answer to the question of why Hitler and his pet generals forced us to carry on after the war was lost is that to the last minute they believed that the Soviets and the nations of the West would turn on each other before they had scored their final victories."

Hofmeister rambled on: "I'm the one who talked Himmler, the Gestapo chief, who, I admit was a friend of mine, into trying to sue for peace through the Swedes. I myself talked about these efforts with Hitler. He did not protest against them, but when the world press reported on these moves, Hitler kicked Himmler out of the Nazi Party. Why? I think, partly, because the gang in the bunker knew that peace would end its days of power, but mostly, because the death of President Roosevelt revived Hitler's hopes for a split between the Soviets and the bourgeois nations before a total, final defeat of all German forces."

I found ample confirmation of Hofmeister's views about why the Germans had fought on, despite their spectacular retreats, after we left the Chancellery and I discovered the whereabouts of Germans I had known as trustworthy for many years. There was, for instance, Dr. Wilhelm Ziegelmeier, star nutritionist in the Quartermaster Office of the German Army, who because of his many years of service had participated in a good number of secret discussions among leading German officers. He also believed that Hitler had known about Himmler's conferences with Swedes.

"It so happens," he told me, "that in early April I phoned to Himmler who was in northern Germany to ask him to let General Schneider have part of a certain building as an emergency hospital for 250 wounded. He told me we could not have it because it was the only office he had left in Berlin—after all the bombings— which had the telephone lines and radio equipment needed to reach the Führer in the bunker—that he was negotiating with Swedes to pave the way for peace—that he had to keep the Führer informed of every step so that Hitler could issue the final orders at the right time.

"Whether Himmler was lying or not is unimportant now," said Ziegelmeier, "but the building we wanted was interesting in other ways. General Schneider and I found most of it served as storage center for all the files which German Intelligence had accumulated on the United States. They had been moved from the regular building in a much-bombed area of the town and cached in this plain apartment building across the street from my home. And because of this location I know what happened to them."

---

* Most writers state that Hitler decided Rommel had to die because of the general's complicity in the July assassination plot.

What had happened to the German Intelligence files on the United States? Four days after Berlin surrendered to the Reds, a group of Russian officers entered the building, led by German officers. The next day Russian soldiers came and packed all the files into trucks. Within three days there was not a scrap of these intelligence reports left. The Russians had carted everything eastward.

"This was a carefully planned move," explained Ziegelmeier, adding: "We know that by invading Russia, by declaring war on the United States, Hitler drove both countries into a synthetic alliance that might work as long as their attacker was a menace, but not after he was licked. We used the mutual distrust of the Reds and the Capitalists to good advantage after World War I. We can do it again. especially since there is not the slightest doubt that a victorious Stalin won't be able to resist the temptation of making the kind of moves of aggression, of infiltration that will infuriate the West. The files that were handed over to the Russians are meant to bolster the position of those German officers who are with the Russians and who, like General von Seeckt did, believe in Russo-German cooperation.

"But we also have presents in store to woo the Western nations. Starting in January, 1945—if not earlier—the offices of the Army's Eastern Intelligence Department had many copies made of its most important information on Eastern Europe and Russia. They were cached in southern Germany, in areas which Army leaders figured would be taken over by the Western armies. In time they will be used to bolster the position of German military experts in the eyes of the Western Allies—and let us have no doubt, intelligence, spying is the most sensitive area in a world shaken by distrust."

Ziegelmeier's forecast proved correct. It did not take long until the wartime chief of Eastern Intelligence of the German Army, General Reinhard Gehlen, and his friends managed to put over a deal with the Americans by using his ample files as bait. Germans boast that he never actually turned them over to the United States, but that we allowed him to set up his own "Gehlen outfit" that retained its files, sent out its own agents, and handed over to the Americans only what Gehlen himself considered suitable while we were footing the bill for all these operations. By 1955 the Gehlen outfit had become the Intelligence Service of the West German partner in the NATO alliance.

In 1945 it was not possible to publish the frank statements of General von Hofmeister and Dr. Wilhelm Ziegelmeier and others like them without endangering their lives at the hands of fanatic Nazis or fanatic Reds.

While German military experts made good use of parts of their Intelligence files in their postwar political game, the thousands of agents and spies who were trained in Nazi organizations secured jobs with Eastern and Western Intelligence outfits regardless and often because of their shady pasts. Members of the sinister Security Service of Himmler fared specially well. On occasion they managed to get on American and Russian payrolls at the same time, to create enough havoc to delight Neo-Nazis. This was shown most clearly at a spectacular trial in West Germany's Supreme Court in July, 1963, when three agents who had been on the American payroll for five years under Gehlen, then were switched to the German payroll, were sentenced for their well-paid cooperation with the Reds.

Nazis assembled in the bunker in the second half of April would have found some consolation in the thought that the East-West break they hoped for had merely been delayed. Instead, they were wrapped in deepest gloom, interrupted only by the wildest scenes of fury Hitler had ever staged in a career marked by many stormy outbursts. Yet some of the men remembered lighter moments that amused them. The ladies in the shelter engaged in feuds. These reached dramatic heights after Eva Braun arrived on April 15, determined to show one and all that she was the only important woman in the life of the Führer.

Until Eva turned up, beautiful Magda Goebbels, wife of Nazi Germany's star philanderer, Propaganda Minister Joseph Goebbels, had held the limelight. Hitler had named her "High Priestess of Nazism," and every time she begged him for permission to divorce her husband and marry another man, he managed to convince her that it was her duty to give the German people an image of a happy family, all fired by the high principles of Aryanism. Apparently Hitler never realized that this "image" had vanished as long ago as the middle 1930s, when most Germans had juicy tales to tell about "clubfoot Jupp Goebbels" and a succession of stars, starlets, and would-be starlets.

Eva and Magda had fought a tug-of-war for years. It was a minor affair as long as Eva centered her life almost entirely around pretty clothes and enjoying major shopping sprees thanks to the ample funds with which Hitler provided her. But in 1940 Eva suddenly felt the urge to join in the diplomatic game to win friends for the Fatherland.

She had overheard a member of the protocol office complain of the deterioration of official relations with American correspondents. She saw herself as the glamorous woman who could remedy the situation. It was at this time that I first met her.

Eva approached a friend of mine and asked him to fish for an invitation to dinner at my house. He told me all about it, but before I had decided whether it was smart to entertain Hitler's official mistress, my friend turned up in my office looking sheepish. Eva could come only if I gave the Chancellery an advance list of my guests. This was against *my* protocol and any question of a dinner was dropped. I decided to meet Eva behind the backs of her supervisors, however, because it might be useful to know the "lovelight" in the life of the strange man on whom we were all reporting.

I had many reasons for assuming that this was her real role. For instance, there had been the time when Eva, in a fit of jealousy over the attention Hitler was paying to a number of actresses, had tried to commit suicide. No devoted husband could have been more frantic than Adolf. With tears streaming down his face, he came to her bedside, grabbed her hand, kissing it over and over, and making Eva promise never to do such a thing "to him" again. The scene finished with his placing a huge square emerald on her ring finger.

How do I know? From the nurse who had been sent to Eva by her only close friend who did not belong to the official gang. The nurse was a fervent Catholic and hated the Nazis. She disapproved violently of "that" man who made poor little Eva live in sin. On the other hand, the emerald looked like an engagement ring to her and that improved matters as far as she was concerned.

She helped arrange my "accidental" meeting with Eva after I assured everyone involved that I would not write about her because if I did her non-Nazi friend would be in danger. There was nothing striking about Eva's face, but she had a nice figure and moved with exceptional ease and grace. Since Hitler admired dancers of the Tiller-girl type, she had obviously spared no effort to conform to it. To the very end she was to retain that Tiller-type figure. She apologized profusely for the party mix-up. "You see," she said, jingling her bracelets and trying to look soulful, "that is the tragedy of being a historical personality. Whenever I try to emerge from my womanly sphere, that peroxide blonde, who can't even hold her own husband, Magda Goebbels, sees to it that somebody interferes. She is jealous of me. I can understand that all right, because after all there are few women in this world who become historical personalities."

She had obviously planned a number of roles for our meeting. The woman of the world did not go well; she did better with the somewhat helpless, but oh so eager, admiring young thing. Then there was the woman of destiny on whom greatness had been foisted, which seemed either funny or pathetic, depending on your own mood. In between she acted like a happy adolescent, or even a trusting young puppy. In all her transparent histrionics there was a certain playfulness which I have no doubt provided one of her holds on a man like Hitler who drove himself incessantly. One could not escape the picture of the pliable, smart chorus girl amusing a tired tycoon.

At the time Eva was full of her newest discovery. The Führer was susceptible to perfumes. He would become gay and relaxed when he found her rooms filled with a scent that delighted him. She was busy mixing fragrances. Since this meeting took place after the conquest of Paris Eva experimented with the best perfumes France had to offer, not by the ounce but with quart-sized bottles.

When I asked about her "historical personality line," the tough, determined woman emerged, as she replied with the haughty air that used to infuriate the women at Hitler's court: "As the only woman who is important to the Führer, I shall take my place in history."

This conviction did not prevent Eva from having a good hot time when the all-important Führer was not around. She attended parties at Dr. Brandt's—Hitler's physician who had a villa on the grounds of the Chancellery. They were so wild that one of my German legmen who was a very gay blade in his own right would be petrified for days after attending one of them, with fear that Hitler might find out about what actually went on.

When I saw Eva, she was not worried about her unmarried status. In 1939, before he started his war, Hitler had promised her mother that he would marry Eva in the most spectacular wedding ever staged and that it would be part of Germany's victory celebration. During most of the war, Eva acted as the Führer's official hostess, supported by a retinue of her relatives and friends of her own choosing, generally in the "Obersalzberg," Hitler's favorite home in the Bavarian Alps.

By April, 1945, it was clear that there would be no victory celebration nor any spectacular wedding rites. Eva was ready to settle for a plain wedding ceremony. Without it, she feared she might not rank as a "historical personality." She refused to obey Hitler's order to return to the comparative safety of her native Bavaria. Though

281

by now she had become a tragic figure, the devoted woman volunteering to die at the side of her man if need be, Eva chose to stage a show of her own—a fashion show in the grim setting of the underground bunker.

"You never saw anything more incongruous," Hans Doering, one of the last German reporters with access to the bunker, told me. "We could hear those horrible Russian pipe organs that split your eardrums. Artillery fire seemed to creep ever closer. Hanna Reitsch, the aviatrix, had flown the plane of General Greim of the Air Force to the Berlin Tiergarten after it had been hit by the Russians and the general had to drop the controls because he was injured. She was storming around weeping and screaming for permission to die with the Führer. Magda Goebbels was planning how she would kill her six children before seeking death with her husband. The secretaries were working overtime, fully aware that they might not escape death. The Führer was staging fulminating scenes, deciding on the last moves of his remaining armies, with generals, politicians, couriers, officials running back and forth. And against this background Eva would emerge every few hours in some elegant new outfit, like a bride showing off her trousseau and wafting big clouds of perfume ahead of her. The irritated women could avoid looking at her, but they had to smell her too. I don't think Eva realized that some of us were amused, but she had no doubt that she was annoying the female contingent."

Eva's great day came when Hitler, after blaming everybody else for the tragedy Germany was experiencing, declared that Eva and his dog were the only ones who were really loyal to him. As a reward Eva would be allowed to share his death as his wedded wife.

The wedding had the distinction of being perhaps the most macabre on record. Instead of staging the traditional rehearsal party, most of the men and women who formed Hitler's last court held a suicide rehearsal party during the night of April 27–28. They explained in detail how they would end their lives as soon as Russian infantry could be seen, and discussed what could be done to prevent their remains from falling into the hands of the victors.

The actual wedding ceremony in the early hours of April 29 was a perfunctory affair, with a minor Nazi official supervising the signing of the document that gave Eva the coveted title of Frau Hitler. The only traditional symbol of gaiety at the feast that followed the ceremony was free-flowing champagne. The bridegroom himself reminisced about the past and concluded with an oration about his readiness to die.

In the early afternoon of April 30, Hitler walked down the corridor of the bunker with the hand of a calm-seeming Eva on his arm. They both shook the hands of the men and women who had assembled for this last farewell. Then the couple with-drew to their suite.

Everybody stayed in the corridor waiting for the shots that were to end the lives of Hitler and his wife. They heard only one. Eva had relied on the poison her husband had given her. I like to think that in those last hours the young woman who had babbled so happily in 1940 about becoming "a historical personality" had the consoling illusion that she had fulfilled this lifelong dream.

Hitler had issued detailed orders for his and her cremation. As the battle for the conquest of the German capital raged over most of Berlin, and centered all around the bunker, the attendants rolled Hitler's remains in a rug. Then they carried the two corpses into the yard, poured the gasoline secured hastily for this last rite over the bodies, and threw a burning rag onto the pile. Goebbels and others extended a last Nazi salute and quickly withdrew to the comparative safety of the bunker to plan their next moves.

Marshal Vasily Chuikov of the U.S.S.R., to whom the forces in Berlin surrendered on May 2, 1945, believes that Hitler's staff announced his death two days before it actually took place. He writes that the Russian units that seized the Chancellery area on May 2 "found a still smoking rug and in it the scorched body of Hitler."

He suspects some sinister plot behind this discrepancy in dates—but it is very possible that the Viking fire Hitler had ordered did not fully consume his remains. Some of the German attendants say that when the first fire they had started near the bunker burned out, they placed the remains in a nearby bomb crater and that they poured some more gasoline over them in the course of the night. Thick rugs burn very slowly and Hitler was rolled in one. He was a heavy-boned man. Rain always accumulates in bomb craters and even under normal conditions the ground in Berlin remains moist through the most of May. All this was bound to slow up the cremation of the two bodies.

That the Russians actually seized the remains is certain. I found evidence to prove it. The day after we had seen the bunker in July, 1945, a trusted Berlin friend of mine, the vet who used to take care of my dogs, advised me to try to find the assistant of Hitler's dentist, Frau Kaethe Haeusermann, née Reiss. She had been on duty in the Chancellery to the very last day and had been one of those honored by Hitler with the present of a capsule of poison to use in case she wanted to end her life.

Frau Haeusermann felt no such inclination and returned to her home and friends. On May 9 Russian Intelligence officers picked her up and took her to a hospital in Buch, a suburb of Berlin.

They led her up to a big table that was covered with broken-out teeth, with smashed and half-burned jaws, with dentures of all descriptions. She was asked whether she recognized anything in that pile.

When she returned to her home two days later she told her closest friend—whom I interviewed—that she had actually identified two of Hitler's bridges and a "window crown" of his, on which she had done work as assistant of Hitler's American-trained dentist. She also believed that a bridge of Eva Braun's was in the pile—but this had been made by a technician, Fritz Echtmann. The Russians took him to Buch, too. He confirmed Frau Haeusermann's findings, then both of them were sent home with a big sack of potatoes—a most welcome reward for their help. Some days later she and Echtmann were again summoned by the Russians. They had not returned to their homes by the time the American convoys reached Berlin.

By then Joseph Stalin had decided to shroud the whereabouts of the remains of the Führer in mystery and to use the ghost in his political game at home and in foreign lands. The days of the victorious East-West alliance were ended. The era of mutual distrust had started.

# DEFEAT FOR JAPAN

from

*I-Boat Captain*

by Zenji Orita with Joseph D. Harrington

Canoga Park, CA: Major Books, 1976

*In June 1945, American forces captured Okinawa, giving them a base for the invasion of Japan. By July, devastating American bombing missions were being launched daily against more than sixty Japanese cities. A full-scale invasion was scheduled for November. However, the use of atomic bombs on August 6 on Hiroshima and on August 9 on Nagasaki hastened the Japanese surrender. On August 15, Emperor Hirohito called upon the Japanese people to accept surrender, and on September 2, the formal document was signed aboard the U.S. battleship* Missouri, *anchored in Tokyo Bay.*

*Zenji Orita, the author of the following excerpt, was second-in-command aboard a Japanese submarine at Pearl Harbor in 1941. He served in the Japanese navy throughout the war, and in August 1945 he was stationed near Hiroshima, where he served as a submarine-school instructor. Near the end of the war, the Japanese government destroyed its naval records. Orita's account may be the only existing history of the role of the Japanese navy during the war.*

*Several terms untranslated from the Japanese should be explained for the reader.* I-Boat *is a first-line, class "A" submarine;* tokko *means "suicide";* kaiten *is a rocket-propelled, human-piloted bomb.*

On July 2, the American submarine *Barb* used a new weapon for submarines—rockets—against targets in the Japanese homeland. Three days later, Gen. MacArthur announced that the Philippines had been formally liberated from Japan. On the next day, *I-351* arrived at Singapore. This was Lt. Cdr. Noboru Okayama's second fuel run there. He took aboard 500 kiloliters of aviation gasoline, as before, and started for home on July 11. Three days later, *I-351* and all her crew were scorched into eternity. Torpedoes from the American submarine *Bluefish* tore into her, and the transport-converted-to-tanker blew up. Next day a force of enemy surface ships shelled our northern island, Hokkaido. The net was closing.

On July 15 the 6th Fleet added six submarines to its roster, but only on paper. They were the German submarines *U-181, U-862, UIT-24, UIT-25, U-219* and *U-195.* The first two were confiscated at Singapore, the next pair at Kobe, and the others at Jakarta and Soerabaya, respectively. We renamed them *I-501* through *I-506.* All were out of service when we confiscated them from our surrendered ally and still undergoing refit when the war ended.

On July 16 the world's first atomic bomb was exploded successfully at Alamorgordo, New Mexico, in the U.S. On the same day USS *Indianapolis,* which had been waiting for word of this, left San Francisco for Tinian, carrying a special cargo of uranium. Battleships and cruisers were shelling our main island of Honshu not long after that. On July 16 and 18 enemy carrier planes swept, one wave after another, over the Kanto Plain. Described to Mr. Harrington by a Yokosuka resident as "filling the sky in every direction you looked," they hit Tokyo, Yokohama, Yokosuka, and the nearby airfields defending our capital city. *I-372*, which Lt. Shingo Takahashi commanded, was getting ready for a sortie at Yokosuka and was sunk in the July 18 raid, all hands miraculously surviving the bomb hit that sent her down. Just before and after *I-372*'s loss, however, we scored two minor victories. *I-53* sent a *kaiten* into the attack transport USS *Marathon* on July 12, damaging her, then sent another into the destroyer escort *Underhill* on July 24. Lt. Dr. Oba hit *Underhill* right in the middle of an attack on him. *Underhill* was so badly damaged that she had to be sunk by friendly forces.

Carrier aircraft hit Kure on July 23–24. When they flew back over the horizon, Japan had practically no navy left. Battleships *Hyuga*, *Ise* and "lucky *Haruna*" (the ship Americans claimed to have sunk about as often as we claimed to have sunk USS *Saratoga*) settled right at their moorings, only portions of their superstructures thrusting above the surface. That left Japan with only 1 of her 12 battleships remaining, IJN *Nagato*, and she was damaged. Also, while those carrier planes were hitting Kure, Japan was being invaded—by submariners! A party of Americans had paddled ashore from USS *Barb* at Karafuto and blew up a railroad train.

*I-402* was completed at Sasebo on July 24. Neither she nor her sister, *I-404*, saw action. The war was over before *I-402* completed her shakedown training, and *I-404* was sunk by bombing at Kure on July 28. She was moored offshore awaiting completion when carrier planes swooped in to give our navy its final blow. Carrier *Amagi*, ancient cruiser *Izumo*, light cruiser *Oyodo*, and destroyer *Nashi* went to a watery grave with *I-404*.

Meanwhile, in *I-58*, Lt. Cdr. Hashimoto had cruised for a week without sighting anything. On July 28 he spotted a tanker and, a few minutes later, a distant explosion was heard. *I-58* surfaced for a look, but a rain squall obscured vision in all directions. Hashimoto dived his sub again, estimating there was a "very dim possibility" that he had sunk a tanker. At that moment in time, in spite of duty in a total of five submarines since the war's beginning, Hashimoto had yet to fire a conventional torpedo at the enemy. The following night, he scored Japan's last success of the war.

"A messenger waked me as I had ordered, at 10:30 P.M.," he said. "The moon had then been risen for 30 minutes." Hashimoto threw some water on his face, then stopped for a few moments of meditation at his ship's shrine. This, a 10" by 16" box of white paulownia wood installed by workers at Kure, contained a few mementoes and charms from Ise Grand Shrine, where the Emperor's goddess-ancestor, *Amaterasu*, is venerated. Then Hashimoto went to the conning tower, accepted a routine report from his watch officer, and assumed the conn.

"Night action stations!" he ordered, and took *I-58* up from the depths to where he could scan with his periscope. He also ordered the air and surface search radar antennas elevated and, when nothing could be detected either visually or electronically, called out,"Surface!"

*I-58* had hardly come to rest when one of her lookouts reported seeing a ship, 90 degrees left of the bow. Hashimoto was then steering almost directly south. The sighting was to the east.

Hashimoto said he heaved his "thick body up the ladder to the bridge," to confirm the sighting personally and issued a rapid series of orders. "Dive! Level off at 60 feet! Man all *kaiten*! Make ready all torpedo tubes!"

The enemy ship, which had been a black blob on the eastern horizon, slowly took on a triangular shape. Hashimoto began to make out a large ship with a high superstructure. It was either a battleship or a cruiser. As it kept plowing through the sea toward him, neither changing speed nor appearing to zigzag, he kept saying to himself "That ship is dead!! That ship is dead!"

All six of *I-58*'s tubes were loaded and readied, at which point Hashimoto grew fearful that the enemy vessel might pass too close to him for his torpedoes to arm. Like Tanabe approaching USS *Yorktown* at Midway, Hashimoto needed to make sure the run from his tubes to the target would be long enough for his torpedoes to arm themselves, which they did after a specific number of propeller revolutions. He quickly ordered a 180º- turn made to the left. Then he ordered another, to the right. This long S-turn put him back on his original course, but along a path more to the east and somewhat more distant from the enemy's track than he had been earlier. The cruiser-or-battlehip was now about 2-1/2 miles away, angling across *I-58*'s bow from the left. Hashimoto could now make out her two towering "islands" clearly, as well as her turrets. He decided, because of her high freeboard, that she was an *Idaho*-class battleship.

The four *kaiten* men were in their weapons, all clamoring to be fired away, now that the size of the target had been announced. Hashimoto curtly told his torpedo officer, Lt. Toshio Tanaka, that the *kaiten* men could wait. He had a perfect firing setup now, and was waiting only for the range to shorten a little more before emptying his tubes at the target. If he took time to launch *kaiten*, the target might pass and be gone into the night. Also, launching human torpedoes was a noisy operation that might be picked up on enemy sound equipment. And the visibility had begun to vary. *Kaiten* pilots might not be able to see a thing through their short periscopes.

When the enemy ship was about 1500 yards away and *I-58* on a line 60 degrees off his starboard bow, Hashimoto shouted "Fire one!" In quick succession, a half-dozen Model 95's leaped from their tubes, spaced 3 degrees apart, set to run at 19 feet. Three missed, running across the enemy ship's bow. Then, one after another, the other three hit. The first slammed into the bow, and the second hit under the first turret. The final torpedo struck under the bridge, according to Hashimoto's report. He could see a third column of water in the light of explosions caused by his first two hits.

*I-58*'s torpedo officer, gunnery officer and two communcations petty officers kept scrambling for turns at the periscope while Hashimoto was using the night one. Their cries of joy were repeated throughout the submarine. Hashimoto kept sweeping the horizon with his periscope. He could not believe that so big a ship was traveling without escorts and recalled the time off the Marshalls when a line of destroyers appeared out of nowhere while he was working into position to torpedo two aircraft carriers and a battleship. After a short while he dived his boat and turned to the westward, to keep clear of any escorts while his torpedo tubes were reloaded. An hour later he was back on the surface, sweeping the area with both radar and binoculars. The radar showed nothing and the visibility had closed down to 100 yards. Hashimoto wirelessed Kure, saying "Have just torpedoed and sunk *Idaho*-class battleship." Then he turned north and made full speed for several hours on the surface, getting as far away as possible before diving again.

On Aug. 10 the captain of *I-58* launched two more *kaiten* at enemy ships, with results doubtful. On Aug. 12, the last *kaiten* of the war was fired. Hashimoto had two remaining, but Petty Officer Ichiro Shiraki's was found defective. The other, manned by Petty Officer Yoshiaki Hayashi, was sent away at what Hashimoto thought was a large seaplane tender. Actually, it was the dock landing ship USS *Oak Hill*. Hayashi may have actually scraped this target's side with his *kaiten*, but he did not sink it. Destroyer escort *Nickel*, trying to locate the human torpedo, saw it explode about a mile astern of *Oak Hill*.

Hashimoto had set out on July 16, but had had to put about and return when several *kaiten* periscopes were found to be defective. A week after he left this second time, Japan received word of the Potsdam Declaration, which demanded unconditional surrender from Japan. To some of our high-ranking officers, this was unthinkable. A group of them, later called *kichigai* ("the insane ones"), plotted to seize rule of Japan. They claimed that this would foil the "Badoglio-type" statesmen surrounding the Emperor who, they said, were acting like the officer who had surrendered Italy to the Allies. Gen. Korechika Anami (Minister of War) was the leader of this no-surrender faction. His followers went so far as to forge an order giving them command of the Imperial Palace guard, then searched the Emperor's residence on the night of Aug. 14, trying to find the phonograph record of the surrender announcement the Emperor had made for broadcast the next day. Posters suddenly appeared everywhere, denouncing the Emperor's closest advisors as traitors and urging people to provide themselves with bamboo spears for repelling expected Allied paratroopers. *Mainichi*, one of our larger national newspapers, carried announcements of government orders that indolent workers would be punished and showed pictures of large underground factories being constructed. Workers, fearing bombs, had not been reporting for work at industrial defense plants, so threats of fines and imprisonment were used against them. Absenteeism had become a civil crime.

Then came Aug. 6, the day when "two suns," one natural and the other man-made, cast their fiery glow over Hiroshima, not very far from my place of duty. An air raid warning sounded at 8 A.M. at Otake, but I did not pay much attention to it. There often were false alarms and the radio at the time was reporting that only one lone B-29 had been sighted in the sky. I had gathered up my books and was about to head for my classroom when, at about 8:15 A.M. a terrific explosion was heard. A short time later, all the windows on the north side of my building were blown in by an air blast, the great pressure wave emanating from where an atomic bomb was first dropped on human beings. I looked toward Hiroshima. A large cloud was spreading over the city. It then seemed to zoom upward with ever-increasing speed, after which it topped off at a great height, giving it the appearance of a giant mushroom.

"Atomic bomb!"

I don't think I spoke the words aloud, but I know that I spoke them in my mind. I had heard from time to time that Japan's scientists were studying how to make atomic bombs. And the matter had been brought up for discussion in the National Diet during 1942. At once I realized that America had perfected her bomb first. Two other things came into my mind at the same moment. My family was safe, but the war was lost. Should America continue to drop bombs like that one, Japan was truly doomed.

I went on to my classroom, but had difficulty concentrating on the curriculum. *What is the purpose of what I am doing?* I asked myself. There I was, teaching students how to make a submarine attack, when B-29's were spreading mines so thickly that even Japan's fishing fleet was decimated, and could not bring food to our people. Submarines had difficulty clearing Kure, letting alone reaching and hitting the enemy. They had to pass through Bungo Strait submerged, out of fear of lurking enemy boats. And America had the atomic weapon! What chance was there for victory?

Whenever my glance moved in the direction of Hiroshima that day, I was thankful that none of my family, relatives or friends lived there.

On Aug. 7, with several other submarine school instructors, I drove into Hiroshima. We were curious to see the effects of an atomic weapon. So small was our knowledge of it, that we didn't even know about danger from radiation and rode blithely into what would be later called the danger area. Horrific sights met our eyes. Everywhere there was desolation. All that remained standing of Hiroshima's structures were the shells of concrete buildings. Everything else was flattened over a wide radius from the explosion's center. Fires were still smoking, and charred bodies of men, women, children and horses lay everywhere. A few live people, haggard-eyed, wandered about poking through the wreckage, trying to find the remains of lost ones. A sickening stench rose from everything. We soon realized that this was no time for satisfying scientific curiosity and, after offering a few of the more wretched ones our condolences, we got back into our car and returned to Otake. No one spoke during the ride back, but I am sure that my comrades had the same thoughts as I—radar, blockade, bombs, fire raids, and now this. No doubt of it, the end could not be far off!

On Aug. 8 [sic.] a second atomic bomb was dropped, on Nagasaki, and Russia declared war upon Japan. The first was expected sooner or later, and the second surprised no military man. For forty years the Russians had been waiting for an opportunity to take revenge, ever since our military and naval forces had smashed them at Port Arthur and Tsushima Strait. Few of the world's white men (other than diplomats, historians and political scientists) are aware of how much that defeat rankled, especially since it had been achieved less than 40 years after Japan had emerged from a supposedly "barbarian state."

The world's colored peoples are aware of it, however. One need only discuss history for a few minutes with leaders of any backward nation before learning that scholars from such nations mark the Russo-Japanese war of 1905 as a "tide-turn-ing," the first time in history that a colored race defeated a white one. Every Japanese military man was constantly aware of the "great bear" at our backs, ready to pounce should we ever grow weak.

In class that day, I told my students that we should fight on for Japan so long as breath was left in us. In Tokyo, the Emperor was telling an Imperial Conference that "the time has come to bear the unbearable." Lt. Cdr. Yukio Inaba took *I-373* out of Sasebo on Aug. 9, heading for Formosa. Four days later the U.S submarine *Spikefish* torpedoed and sank her, the last Japanese submarine destroyed or sunk in the war. Early in the morning of Aug. 10 our Emperor demanded the unanimous consent of his closest advisors for accepting the terms of the Potsdam Declaration. Japan, he said, must surrender unconditionally. There would be no more quibbling. And, on the next day, the American Secretary of State announced that, from the moment of surrender, our Emperor would be subject to the orders of the Supreme Allied Commander in the Pacific. This was Gen. Douglas MacArthur, who later thwarted Russian attempts to seize Japan by simply ignoring whatever the Russians requested or said.

Not knowing what else to do, I continued my submarine classes. At Otake we had no knowledge of what was occurring in Tokyo; the plots, the promises, the planned revolts. Then, at 7:15 A.M. on Aug. 15, we heard over the radio that the Emperor would speak to all of his subjects at noon. It was something that had never happened before; His Majesty's voice coming to all Japanese at the same time. We didn't know what to make of it, except that something of great and special impor-tance was bound to be said.

By that time, bomb damage had hurt Japan so badly that electrical power was rationed. It required a special allotment of electricity to bring off the broadcast. When the appointed time arrived I gathered with other Otake officers and men in front of our main building, where loudspeakers had been set up. Vice Adm. Noboru Ichikawa stood facing us. None of us had any idea what was coming. I expected the Emperor either to issue an imperial order, or make a personal appeal for all Japanese to unite in one final stand against the enemy. There was a lot of static in the broad-cast, making it difficult to hear, and every account I have read since states that this was "interference" caused by unkown persons who were trying to jam the broadcast. Nevertheless, all of us could make out enough of it to understand that the Emperor was telling us that he meant to end the war.

Earlier, while some of us were still in the school instructors' office, Lt. Cdr. Genbei Kawaguchi, former skipper of *I-44*, had burst through the door. In an agitat-ed voice he said that advisors to the Emperor had told our ruler lies about the true state of Japan and overseas. He claimed that the Emperor, misled, was about to make an announcement of surrender. This was appalling news to all of us. How Kawaguchi received the word in advance, I do not know. Perhaps he had been told by representatives of the Army officers in Tokyo who were planning the *coup d'état*. They hoped to seize control of the empire, fight on, then turn control back to the Emperor after winning the great victory they were sure they could bring off.

We became confused upon listening to Kawaguchi. The confusion increased

289

when we later heard the Emperor's broadcast. Some wanted to fight on, including myself. But a few (again including myself) also began to think of our duty to the Emperor. He said that he was going to end the war and that made us bound to assist him, to carry out whatever orders were given toward that end. Nonetheless, Aug. 15, 1945, was a day of insanity. No voice of reason could be heard. Anyone who dared mention the word "surrender" would have been fighting his own comrades for his life. After a lot of speculation, I and others took refuge in indecision. We decided to wait until some kind of official word was sent down through 6th Fleet from the Naval General Staff. Meanwhile, business as usual. We returned to our classrooms.

The next day, *Gekko* night fighter aircraft from the nearby air base at Iwakuni flew over Otake, dropping handbills. Each bore a message from Capt. Yasuna Ozono. He was at the air base in Atsugi, southwest of Tokyo, and commander of the aircraft charged with defense of our capital city. Ozono refused to surrender. He had sent men to other bases, too, to take over planes from those men who were surrendering. His leaflets urged all of us to fight on with him "to a certain victory."

Only a small minority at Otake were influenced by Ozono's message. The time between the Emperor's broadcast and the dropping of the leaflets had given us a chance to think. At Hirao, Lt. Takesuka Tateyama, determined to fight on, took the old *I-159* out, with a pair of *kaiten*, and headed for the Inland Sea. But he came back in two days. On Aug. 17 I was ordered by Rear Adm. Mitsuru Nagai to take over as disciplinary commander at Otake. "You will be responsible," he said, "for calming the wild spirits of young submarine men and students. It will not be easy. You know that their spirit is the highest in the Imperial Navy. They will not want to give up."

My duties also included the burning of all official records and documents, and I also had to see to it that submarine men were released from active duty. I also had to see to the discharge of all civilian workers without incident. These were not easy tasks. Many men and women had worked long and hard in hope of a Japanese victory. Telling them that all was lost and they would no longer be needed was a hard thing to do. I had to calm many people, soothe many disturbed feelings.

Hashimoto got back to Kure with his *I-58* on Aug. 18. On the way up Bungo Strait he'd met six HA-Class submarines that had left Kure, their captains determined to fight to the death. Hashimoto, having already received the Emperor's broadcast on his radio, was reserving decision and action until he arrived in port. When his boat glided on past them, the six HA-Class boats put about and also returned.

Hashimoto reported that *I-58* had sunk a battleship. He found a very tense situation at the Kure anchorage. Submariners had earlier provisioned and fueled every boat there. A delegation of young officers, led by Lt. Akira Kikuchi, met with Capt. Shojiro Iura, of the 6th Fleet staff and asked him to convince senior officers to keep on fighting. Iura disagreed (risking his life) and reminded those men of their duty to the Emperor. The delegation left, but a few submarine captains tried to change Iura's mind. "Let them go!" they urged, "Those men do not want to live. They can fight the enemy for as long as two more months before committing *seppuku*. They wish to die in battle, like true *samurai*. Why not let them do it?" Again Iura demurred, and it was about that time that the six HA-boat commanders took matters into their own hands and headed down Bungo Strait.

When a third group came to him in the afternoon of Aug. 18, Iura went to Vice Adm. Daigo that evening, and Daigo summoned all concerned to his headquarters the next day.

"For nearly three years," he told them, "I had official duty that put me in close attendance on our Emperor. I know what he is like. I understand his feelings. You men obviously do not understand them. He is very humane, very concerned for all of his people, not just us few in the military forces. If we continue to fight, the enemy will continue to fight. And what will happen? Many thousands of innocent ones, women and children, will die because you are so headstrong. If you sink even one enemy ship, death will shower down on the innocents who have no weapons at all. Think! Try to understand the deep sense of humanity that made the Emperor come to this precedent-shattering decision!"

Daigo's words were enough. All present apologized, and begged his forgiveness for causing him and the Emperor concern. They promised to make no more trouble. That ended the problem at Kure. Except for an occasional raised voice, disbanding of the forces there went ahead with no difficulty. Disturbances occurred among submariners at Yokosuka, Maizuru, Sasebo, and the places where *Tokko Squadron* 11 had positioned *kaiten*, *koryu* and *shinyo*, but everyone eventually calmed down after a few days. Men began to think about their families, left alone to face an occupation by the enemy. They began drifting away from Otake and other bases, toward their homes.

# 9
# The Occupiers

## SOVIET OCCUPATION

from
*Russian Zone of Germany*
by Gordon Schaffer
New York: SRT Publications, Inc., 1948

*If we consider the time of Hitler's influence as dating back to January 1933 when he became Chancellor of Germany, then in twelve short years Hitler and the Nazi philosophy managed to corrupt many German citizens.*

*Word leaked out over the years of the German looting of homes, museums, and art galleries in all the conquered countries. Books and magazines carried stories of people being falsely imprisoned, tortured, and murdered. Slave labor was imported, people were jailed and killed because of their political and religious beliefs. This was happening not only in Germany but in the countries it had conquered and occupied. Gradually, the average Nazi accepted this brutal behavior as normal. Just how callous the average German had become was brought savagely home when the Allied armies occupied Germany. Bribery and black marketeering were rampant. Teenagers, without any vocational training, ex-members of the Hitler Youth Movement who were to have been cared for by the state, were now adrift in a country that held no promise for them. The adolescents joined political gangs, stealing from and, on occasion, attacking occupation forces. They longed for the old days of Hitler.*

*Many German adults had accepted the Nazi decree that they were all soldiers in the war—even those who worked in the factories. Doctors and health officials had implemented directives that workers in the factories had to continue working even if they were ill, that the factories must be regarded in the same way as the front, and that if workers died while working when unfit, they would be regarded as soldiers in the battlefield, casualties in the fighting line.*

*Although this order was in the main directed at slave labor used in the factories, Nazis in the production centers saw themselves as unsung war heroes.*

*They, too, longed for the good old days of Nazi rule where even the lowliest among them had a goal. Some German citizens had difficulty accepting the Nazi defeat. Let the Americans, British, French, and Russians feel they had won the war. Adolf Hitler would be back.*

*Once-proud Germans, while marking time, now sought special privileges through stealth and craftiness, or as informers.*

*Correspondent Gordon Schaffer was the assistant editor of* Reynolds News *and its special writer on political and industrial questions. He covered the Spanish Civil War for his paper and reported Britain's war effort for the Ministry of Information. Here he records the conditions he found in the Soviet-occupied zone of Germany during a stay of ten weeks. In that time, he studied the life of the people and assessed the changes that had taken place since the Russian occupation.*

*He was trying to set down a previously untold story which the world, he felt, ought to know if it were to judge the pressing problems of Germany aright.*

On the train from Osnabrueck to Berlin, I met a Danish singer who had lived in Germany before the war and was on his way to a job in Berlin. He had called that morning on a pre-war friend in Hamburg and had breakfasted with him on eggs, bacon, white bread, real coffee, and other luxuries unknown to the German compelled to live on his rations. This particular German was a dealer in carpets and tapestry, and was trading entirely on the black market. He reckoned his weekly family expenditure on food at 10,000 marks, more than most honest persons in Germany can earn in a year after payment of tax. In Berlin I met an Englishman who showed me a beautifully turned-out cigarette case priced at 42 marks. He had paid for it in cigarettes at the current price of 7 marks each and was very proud of his bargain. It did not occur to him that his action was plain looting.

I met an English official on the way home on leave who explained to me that he had left his dog to be looked after by some German friends. "Can they feed it?" I inquired. "They're not short," he said. "They've got everything. They even keep me in cigarettes." I asked how they achieved this miracle in starving Germany. "Selling fake antiques to Americans," he replied. "They are making very good stuff and only experts can tell they are not genuine. As a matter of fact, they needn't bother, for the Yanks will buy anything. My friends are making 140,000 marks a month and they're salting the cash down in genuine antiques against the time when the American demand dries up."

"How do they get raw materials?" I asked. He chuckled. "You can get anything in Germany if you know the right way. Why, look at my hat. It was specially made by hand. My friends paid twenty cigarettes for it. Of course, I wouldn't go in the black market myself, but after all, this was a gift."

These are just cases met at random which could be repeated endlessly in Germany today. The pegging of wages and prices imposed by the Allies has prevented inflation in the legitimate market, but in the black market there is a completely inflationary situation. Cigarettes have become a universal currency and the newly arrived visitor is soon reprimanded by his friends if he spoils the market by tipping to the extent of more than a couple of cigarettes at a time. The cigarette currency arouses far more confidence in the West than the mark, and cigarettes will pass through many hands. In fact, most fantastic of all, sometimes they will pass around to the point when they fall to pieces and are never smoked at all! This situation means that goods are simply being looted by anyone, German or foreign, who can secure cigarettes, soap, liquor, or other commodities from the occupation troops to exchange for goods.

That is one form of black market. The other arises from exchanges of manufactured goods from the factories and sales of foodstuffs by the peasants. With black market prices ranging at 500 to 600 times the controlled price, the diversion of goods from legitimate channels, unless sternly checked, goes on increasing and with it comes a disruption of the whole economy. It becomes increasingly difficult to induce the peasant to deliver his proper allocation to the State, while absenteeism leaps in the factories and mines because it is far more profitable to concentrate on securing a packet of cigarettes or a few pounds of potatoes than to put in a week's work. As confidence in the currency declines, black market prices rise even higher and the incentive to work grows steadily less.

These problems faced the Soviet Zone equally with the rest of Germany, but the method of tackling them in the East was entirely different. The Russians began with the stopping of bank accounts and the registration at the Labour Exchange of all holders of ration cards with the exception of old people and women with children. This meant that from the outset there was some check on the money available for black market operations and supervision over the people who would otherwise take the opportunity of deserting work for black market activity. Even those people who retained a certain amount of cash could not make it last long at the prevailing black market prices.

In one village the peasants told me with great gusto the story of one of the richer farmers who, in common with everybody else, had his banking account stopped. He discovered a method of getting some of his money paid out by a branch of his bank in the American Zone. Accordingly he got across the zonal frontier, drew his money and proceeded to have a good time. Within a few weeks he was back grumbling more than ever. He described the fantastic prices he had been obliged to pay on the black market for foodstuffs available on his own farm, and indicated that he now proposed to settle down. It was then that he received the news that since he had been away a better tenant had been found for his land.

Others got away with it for longer, like the former manager of an insurance company in Saxony Anhalt who succeeded in making frequent journeys along the Elbe to Hamburg in the British Zone. When these trips at last became the subject of investigation, it was found that he was drawing cash from a branch of his company still operating in the British Zone and returning only after he had had a good fling on the black market.

There are examples of the small racketeers. Bigger leakages occurred through the activities of criminal gangs, many of them led by Nazis and former S.S. men. An exhibition at Leipzig Police Headquarters gives an interesting cross-section of the underworld of the Soviet Zone. It takes the form of posters published by the police all over the town with the object of bringing the public behind the authorities in the fight against the black market. Here are some of the case sheets:

Fritz Keittel—former compositor, forged 15,000 three-pound bread coupons and a large number of meat and sugar coupons. The poster explained that he took to crime because of a "morbid desire to show off, instilled by Nazi methods of education, particularly the Hitler Youth." Fritz had three associates, all named in the poster, who traded the forged coupons in public houses for money, liquor, and cigarettes. Later, he grew bolder and, with an American uniform, secured with the help of his girl friend, Annelies Wasserfall, he went into the black market in an even bigger way. "Our whole supply plan is seriously endangered by such conscienceless forgeries," the police statement declared.

Alfred Pazsch—aged twenty, had set up as a burglar and enlisted four other youths from sixteen to eighteen in his gang. "All these youths," said the police poster, "had gone through the Hitler Youth and were left without any desire to lead a decent life."

Eldebrant Schroeder—the girl who appears in the next poster, secured a haul of 3,000 pairs of stockings, nearly 1,000 yards of curtain material, and half a ton of wool. She had a confederate in a factory in the Saxon town of Zwickau and disposed of the swag through another girl.

Another gang got away with a big haul of foodstuffs under the leadership of a former police officer presumably dismissed as a Nazi, who used his uniform and forged documents to enable his confederates to pose as members of the criminal police.

The file also includes the case of a butcher named Kalat who killed off dogs, selling the flesh on the black market as veal for about a hundred times the rationed price, and a gang who wore Soviet army uniforms and got away with a vast range of goods varying from jewellery to noodles.

Inevitably, in conditions of acute shortage, the black market offers rich rewards to the many criminal elements in the Zone and gives an opportunity for revenge to the large numbers of dispossessed Nazis, who are determined not to redeem their past by hard manual work. The problem of juvenile crime is also acute. Large numbers of boys and girls had no schooling at all during the last years of the war. Boys were enlisted in the Wehrmacht at fifteen and sixteen, and since the collapse have been living on their wits. Cases are constantly coming to the notice of the authorities of prostitutes at the ages of thirteen and fourteen.

To these demoralised youngsters the black market is a constant attraction and the authorities in the Soviet Zone have set up a number of youth reclamation centres where attempts are being made to bring them back to a normal life. Under a law dating from the Weimar Republic children in need of care and attention may be compulsorily sent to these homes.

"The greatest difficulty in reforming these juveniles is the lure of the 'golden West,' " a worker in one of these homes said to me. "The boys' one idea is to get over the zonal frontier and to live on cigarettes and other goods cadged from the American and British soldiers. The girls are obsessed with the idea that they may succeed in marrying a British or American soldier if only they can reach the West."

Social workers are emphatic that this youth problem must be solved, and a campaign is going to secure more of the big houses of the confiscated estates as centres where the reform of youthful delinquents can be tackled thoroughly and scientifically. The fact that the authorities in the Soviet Zone are making a genuine attempt to deal with a problem which is acute all over Germany has not stopped certain British newspapers from indulging in the most grotesque campaign of lies about the treatment of children in the Soviet Zone.

Shortly before the Berlin elections in 1946 the British, American, and French licensed papers came out with stories of children in the Soviet Zone being collected in the streets and taken away to concentration camps. The story began with "hundreds" but it soon increased to thousands. Mothers were supposed to be throwing themselves in front of the cars which were carrying away their children. Newspaper readers who are constantly being fed with stories of this kind must have been prepared to believe that some Bolshevik pied piper would soon come on the scene to lure away every child in the Soviet Zone. All that really happened was that about fifty-four youths of between thirteen and sixteen were arrested in Brandenburg following the discovery of three secret organisations headed by former members of the Hitler Youth. They had several machine-guns, rifles, and other weapons, and openly confessed that they intended to carry out a campaign against the Russians.

There have also been arrests of students at the universities for pro-Fascist activity, and although these cases have been very few, they are invariably the signal for another spate of terror stories in the anti-Soviet newspapers. While I was in Dresden, stories appeared in the Western newspapers about arrests of students in the town which were denied by every responsible official to whom I spoke.

On this matter, as on others, the question may be asked how an investigator can be certain of his facts in turning down such reports. The answer again is that it is inconceivable that Germans of all parties, as well as ministers of religion, government officials, and police—who are perfectly willing to criticise the Russians on other matters—should conceal the truth, particularly on a matter affecting children. It must also be remembered that, while a big proportion of German youth is being swung into the movement for national reconstruction, the Nazi tradition is probably stronger in a section of the former Hitler Youth than anywhere else in Germany. These young criminals have been detected in the other zones of Germany, and the Russians, equally with the other occupying powers, have a duty to stamp out their activities.

Hans Kahle, who commanded the German division in the International Brigade and who is now police chief of the province of Mecklenburg, told me that the problem of juvenile crime is the most difficult task he has had to tackle since he returned from London to Germany. "The moral deterioration during the Fascist period, and particularly during the war years, presents us with a constant problem," he told me. "It shows itself in widespread thefts among people who, in former times, would never have thought of indulging in petty crime, and in an acceptance of the idea of corruption in the most unexpected circles. Youngsters who have lived in this atmosphere for most of their lives and who ran wild during the war are already confirmed criminals. We have had a number of cases of murder by youths of seventeen and all sorts of other offences can be traced to these youngsters. They resent any attempt at discipline and are easy prey for the Nazi propaganda. We had one case of two boys in a country town who sent through the post crude leaflets, decorated with pictures of the Nazi leaders cut from old newspapers, and ending with 'Heil Hitler!' Maybe this was purely bravado, but it is dangerous in a country which is only just emerging from Nazi dictatorship."

The criminal underworld is one of the constant problems in post-war Germany and in the Soviet Zone it is sustained by all sorts of people who are only too anxious to sabotage the administration by undermining the economic and agricultural plans. For them, too, the black market has proved a powerful weapon. The activities of these elements consisted mainly in diverting goods from the factories to the black market. It began with apparently innocent "compensation agreements." These worked in this way:

A factory making stockings would barter some of its output with a neighbouring factory making pots and pans or an enterprise turning out electric lamps would make an exchange for soap. Almost any undertaking would try to get coal in return for some of its products, while the miners, who in the cold winter were the masters of the whole situation, would collect foodstuffs and consumer goods from all over the Zone.

In a number of factories the shop stewards were drawn into these agreements. In many cases they acted quite innocently, thinking only of securing essential supplies or of giving some incentive to their fellow-workers. But the system soon grew into a gigantic racket and round about the end of 1946 and the beginning of 1947 the figure of production diverted in this way rose in some areas to as high as 30 per cent. There was plenty of ground for suspicion that numbers of employees saw in the procedure a method of sabotage. Some factories, for example, handed out rolls of cloth or articles of clothing to their workers, thereby drawing them into the racket. But a big part of the diverted material found its way on to the black market.

The authorities acted swiftly. They banned all "compensation agreements" within the Zone. During the cold spell the agreement under which the mines were allowed to dispose of half their production over the plan was cancelled and the trade unions were mobilised for a campaign to explain to the shop stewards that "compensation agreements" were destroying the whole economic structure of the Zone. The regional conference of the trade unions in Thuringia and Saxony took the lead by passing resolutions condemning the practice, and the zonal conference of the trade unions in Berlin followed by adopting a statement declaring that the method was "unjust and undermined economic planning."

"Compensation agreements," said the statement, "cannot safeguard the supply of industrial goods to all workers. They are unjust because only workers employed in factories producing household articles, clothing and similar goods, can profit. They endanger supplies because a fairly large quantity of goods is being withheld from general distribution." The conference suggested that, as an alternative, goods produced over the plan should be fairly distributed among the workers in all factories over-fulfilling their quota.

The campaign was not a hundred per cent successful. In an economy in which everything is short, the temptation to secure additional supplies overshadows everything else for a good section of the population, but it reduced the evil to a very large extent. Certainly, it could not have been tackled without the trade unions and the collaboration of other mass organizations. And here again one must note that, in the Soviet Zone, the creation of mass democratic movements has provided the only machinery capable of dealing with problems of this kind.

I found general agreement in the Zone that the Russian occupation troops and officials are not pumping goods into the black market to any considerable extent. One reason is that the Russians do not receive more than their minimum needs of goods susceptible to black market sales. Another is that control of the movement of all goods is extraordinarily strict. A Russian car driver might get hold of a few litres of extra petrol to swop for a bottle of schnapps, but he has no opportunity to secure any quantity. In the early months there were cases of Russian officers taking supplies illegally from the factories, but subsequently the most stringent checks were introduced.

Moreover, the control of raw material begins from the moment it leaves a factory in the Zone or is imported either from a foreign country or from the Western Zones. The central planning office has a list of factories requiring the raw material, but deliveries are only made on receipt of detailed specifications of the purpose for which it is required. Once the raw material is handed over, the factory is compelled to deliver manufactured goods in accordance with specifications. Thus, allowing for normal margins of error, it is theoretically impossible for anything to be diverted from the agreed purpose. All imports to the Zone are handled either by the Zonal Imports Board or by private firms working on direct instructions from the Board. No financial transactions with the Western Zones can take place except through the Berlin State Bank. Thus, really big black market operations which can only now be based on illegal trading involving a constant supply of raw material have been made virtually impossible either for Germans or Russians.

Whatever checks may be introduced, the problem of corruption remains, and to counter this the Allied Control Council issued an order in April 1947, providing drastic penalties for the illegal use of controlled foodstuffs, consumer goods, or documents concerned with these commodities. Sentences of from six months to life imprisonment may be imposed on persons concerned with the production, administration, transport, or protection of these goods if they steal or misuse them, or the documents connected with their disposal. In addition to imprisonment, offenders can be fined from 5,000 to 5,000,000 marks—a salutary way of getting back black market fortunes. Smaller penalties are imposed for neglect of duty. There is no doubt that in the Soviet Zone this law will be resolutely applied.

They all talk food! Everyone in Germany—except the occupation forces—talks about food. Go to any home, and however important the subject under discussion, the conversation will sooner or later turn to rations. The Soviet Zone has been hungry—no hungrier than a number of countries which suffered from aggression, but nevertheless sufficiently hungry for food to overshadow everything else in the minds of a big section of the population.

In the early months of occupation the Russians brought in considerable quantities of food to tide over the complete breakdown brought about by looting, transport chaos, and other accompaniments of the collapse. Then the Soviet administration and the newly found German authorities settled down to organizing a proper system of distribution. The supplies available in the Zone had to provide for the existing population, for an ever-increasing stream of new settlers, and for the main demands of the occupation force.

From the beginning, ration cards were allocated on the basis of work, the various categories ranging from the heavy worker with the highest rations to the person without work (including housewives) on the lowest category. The first peace-time winter was exceptionally difficult and there were gaps in the allocations, but early in 1946 supply became more regular. During my visit I received the same reply to my inquiries wherever I went—that though rations might be late, the cards were always honoured. Whatever is on the ration card is always ultimately available in the shop.

Rations are paid out for ten-day periods and the delays can mean hardship. Two weeks' supply of meat may come all at once, or the fat ration may be carried over to the next ten-day period so that again the housewife draws double quantities. Most families get through these double allocations in the single period and may then be left for days with little more than dry bread. Unlike Britain, there is literally nothing off the ration, except for those fortunate enough to be able to buy on the free market and those with friends in the country.

Everybody has a potato card entitling the holder to about eight pounds a week. This was paid out in hundred-pound allocations until the spring of 1947, when supplies failed in many areas because the clamps were ruined by frost. Vegetables are distributed to all groups on a special card according to available supplies. Eggs, fish, or cheese will sometimes replace meat, but quantities are increased to make up protein value. Four times the amount of cream cheese, for example, is issued against meat coupons.

Milk is issued for three months at a time to tuberculosis cases and is also secured on a doctor's certificate by expectant and nursing mothers.

Certified victims of Fascism receive one grade of rations higher—that is, workers receive heavy workers' and dependants receive workers' cards.

Vouchers for clothing, household articles, and other consumer goods are given out by the local authority on proof of need, settlers from the former territories, bombed-out families, and victims of Fascism being given preference. These vouchers are strictly limited to available supplies, but in shop windows all over the Zone one can see articles of clothing for sale against coupons.

Gas and electricity are technically rationed but supplies have generally been so limited that households seldom get an opportunity to use their full amount. Gas is available at rare intervals and I met numbers of families who made a habit of getting up in the middle of the night in order to cook their weekly joint when gas was on tap. Electricity cuts are frequent, industry being given preference over the domestic consumer.

Some towns adopt the practice of dividing the areas into two parts. One half is allowed to use electricity in the morning and the other half in the afternoon, the whole town being switched on in the evening. Inspectors detecting anyone using current outside permitted hours have the right to switch the offender off for any period up to a fortnight without further argument. In one or two areas an experiment was made with a special fuse, which can only be fitted by the local authority and which blows out if more than a given number of electric appliances (except lights and radio sets) are in use at the same time in a block of flats. The residents are expected to sort out the period between themselves, and if the fuse blows they can wait up to fourteen days before the inspector comes along to put in a new one.

The frequent breakdown during the times when current was supposed to be available provided the main hardship. Meetings would have to be abandoned because the light failed; scores of families simply went to bed as soon as the lights went out. In a hundred ways life was disorganised because there were simply no supplies of candles or oil to provide alternatives.

Berlin gets a slightly higher ration in all sectors, although the four powers bring in different types of supply. In the villages of the Soviet Zone and in the semi-rural areas, workers not employed on the land get a rather lower ration because it is assumed they can supplement their supplies from allotments and peasant friends. Peasants receive normal rations of foodstuffs which they do not grow themselves and sometimes are given extra supplies in return for extra deliveries to the State. They take their own flour to the baker for bread, and receive butter from the dairies in return for additional deliveries of milk.

Everybody receives a quarter of a pound of ersatz coffee a month, one piece of poor-quality soap and some soap powder. Various "teas" made from herbs are sold freely. Neither real coffee nor tea is available except on the black market at fabulous prices. Cigarettes and tobacco are on ration but are seldom available. An enormous number of people grow their own tobacco. There is a tax on such plants over a certain number. Peasants who bring in their crop of tobacco to one of a list of tobacconists are given cigarettes in exchange.

Coal is on separate ration cards which were honoured until the cold spell of 1947 shut down many mines. The ration is not sufficient even for one warm room during a normal winter.

The universal shortages show themselves in various ways. For example, for a shampoo at a hairdresser's the customer has to bring his own soap and his own towel. Laundries demand soap powder before accepting any work. Restaurants serve meals in return for coupons. Quite substantial meals are on the menus but they take a couple of days' meat coupons as well as those for fat and potatoes. In consequence no one can dine out except on rare occasions, and social life has transferred itself from the restaurants and tea-shops to the factory or office canteens, where meals, consisting mostly of vegetables (except when supplies are coming from the peasants), are served for a much smaller number of coupons. People's restaurants were opened during the winter of 1947 because families could not cook owing to the fuel shortage. These provide meals at a low coupon rate.

A surprising number of small manufactured articles—picture frames, candle holders (but no candles), cigarette lighters (but no flints), ornaments, and so on—are to be seen in the shops. Clothing, handbags, shoes, slippers, knitted goods can be made in shops all over the Zone from customers' own material.

The standard of living represented in these rations is low, but by no means catastrophic. Families in the Soviet Zone with some members on heavy workers' and workers' cards are probably the best off of any in Germany—always excepting those living on the black market and the peasants. The real hardship is suffered by the old people unable to work and people on the lowest ration who are living alone.

Until February 1947, non-employed people, including housewives, were on a lower category—"cemetery ration" as it was called by the population—and those not living in families were very near to starvation. The abolition of this card, which brought several million into the present lowest category, was a tremendous concession and was made at a time when other zones were suffering cuts.

Prices of rationed goods are rigidly controlled, with the result that rations take a very small proportion of the average income. Heavy workers' rations for a month cost only 21 marks (about 30s. on 1936 values) and those of children and the lower ration groups a few marks less. Spirits are much more plentiful in the Soviet Zone than in England (or in Scotland!) but they are heavily taxed, costing 42 marks (60s.) a bottle. Beer (very weak) is served freely. These figures mean that even the poorest, including those on the lowest scale of public assistance at 90 marks a month, can afford their rations. One woman said to me, "There is less food now than after the first war, but then the unemployed could not afford to buy even the present ration."

I visited a number of hospitals and talked to many doctors in the Zone. Their reports all agreed that, though there are extensive signs of malnutrition, there is no great evidence of starvation. Hunger edema has occurred, mostly in the older people without work who lived for many months on the lowest ration card. When cases do occur among children and young people they are treated with a special protein food manufactured in the Zone, supplies of which are too short for all to benefit.

The children's physician at one of the big Dresden hospitals told me that young children are receiving sufficient and are able to maintain full health on their rations. Complaints due to over-feeding have disappeared. After six years of age, however, the children are showing the effects of a diet which is deficient in a number of body-building foods. Infectious diseases take a heavy toll and there is a prevalence of skin ailments. Tuberculosis is on the increase among children as in every other section of the population and is aggravated not only by shortage of food but also by appalling housing conditions and lack of cod-liver oil and vitamin preparations.

Drugs generally are desperately short. People have died through lack of insulin. Penicillin is being produced in the Zone but supplies are limited. Sulphonamides are also limited. Dr. Runja Scheuer, Pathologist at Dresden hospital, brought a small quantity of M. and B. with her from England. "I just keep it for the worst cases," she told me. "It's a terrible decision to have to make, but until we get normal supplies of drugs we have to accept the fact that patients who could otherwise be saved must die."

# AMERICAN OCCUPATION

from
"What Are the German Civilians Like?"
by Corporal Leslie Lieber
*Tricolor* magazine, June 1945

*The Allies were pouring troops and tons of war materiel into Europe as they pursued the German army in early 1945. The Nazis were on the run, and although some surrendered immediately, there was fierce fighting in isolated pockets.*

*In the spring of 1945, advance infantry of the United States First Army crossed the Ludendorff Bridge at Remagen. That was the first crossing of the Rhine in force. In one week, the Remagen bridgehead was extended to the autobahn connecting Frankfurt-am-Main with the industrial Ruhr. The entire Western Front was now moved east of the Rhine. Montgomery's Twenty-first Army Group, comprising the British Second, Canadian First, and U.S. Ninth Armies, pushed on through Wesel in the north. In the center, the U.S. First Army extended the Remagen bridgehead 33 miles. In the south, the U.S. Third Army crossed the Rhine and moved on Frankfurt. Even farther south, the U.S. Seventh Army cleared up the final German pocket east of the Rhine.*

*As the Allies advanced, so did the personnel of the AMG (American Military Government). Their job was to establish law and order in conquered villages and cities and create some semblance of normality for the German population.*

*Corporal Leslie Lieber, a member of the AMG, acted as an interpreter in a village whose name was deliberately omitted in his dispatch to* Tricolor *magazine. One interesting aspect of this report is the robotic responses to authority of the defeated Germans after twelve years of Adolf Hitler.*

303

## March 15

When I crossed the German border, I tried to summon all the different emotions assailing me at the moment—just to see which one was dominant. There was nothing to indicate a crossing into enemy territory except the rousing signs in big white print splashed on every wall: *Es Lebe Hitler* (Long Live Hitler), *With Hitler to Victory, The SA is giving everything, what are YOU giving? Germany will never again be a slave.* Many people had hurriedly blurred out these signs which, on the walls of their houses, betrayed their own feelings.

White flags flapped from nearly every street corner, and nearly every house—and every floor of apartment houses—had something white, usually a pillowcase, dangling from the window sill. The first thing that struck me, after crossing the border, was the soft green-felt hats (Bavarian style) worn by most of the men. Green seems to be the prevailing color in clothes. A lot of men are wearing green pants or sweaters.

The men don't look at the American trucks rushing past. In other words, they are behaving toward the occupant with the same indifference that is supposed to have characterized the French toward the Germans. Many of the women, however, have a hint of a smile on their faces that seems to be waiting for a little encouragement from the American soldier to bloom into quite a friendly expression. They aren't getting any smiles back, however, the Army's admonition against fraternization being buttressed by a $65 fine.

These people are still firmly believing in victory for the Germans!

## March 17

German soil and the sky above are about all I've seen of Verbotenland thus far. We don't venture out of camp, and very few things venture in. Even the water supply from the outside has been cut off to prevent possible intentional pollution. We have to dip our helmets into a well for washing water, and the potable liquids come from our own Lister bags. This will be supplemented by beer in a few days.

There are German laborers on the grounds, scooped up off the street in the best Hitler-taught style. They are contented conscripts, however, because they get American K-rations for lunch, complete with stray cigarettes. They also get the opportunity of picking up cigarette butts dropped from the mouths of their democratic conquerors. Most of these laborers are old men and they respond willingly, smile easily, and show no emotion of either resentment or hurt pride at their new situation.

## March 21

For the last two mornings I have been interpreting and gradually handling more and more problems of civilians at the Military Government office. They are swamped with work, and there are hundreds of people lined up at the door every morning. I am very happy to be able to get acquainted with what's on the Germans' minds, how they act and feel. In two days I have spoken to about a hundred. They are almost invariably old people, or past military age.

Many Germans have been hired to work as stenographers and interpreters, and they seem to enjoy their work. Everyone knows there are Nazis among them, but no one seems to care, because they are not in a position, because of the nature of their jobs, to do any harm to the Allied cause—and in cases where their talents are needed, they are put to work. This causes consternation in people who claim to have hated Nazism (of whom there will soon be 65,000,000) in this country!

Two women who have helped the Allies by denouncing outstanding Nazis around here came in this morning, and casting a side glance next to them, whispered to me, "What's that Nazi, Herr——, doing here?" I asked a couple of our officers, and they said not to worry—the place is full of them.

So far, I have not seen a scowl cross a German's face. Sometimes our treatment of them is mild and considerate, sometimes rough and tough. The reaction of the Germans under the two extremes of treatment is exactly the same. You can yell at them, bark at them, treat them like dogs, and they don't bat an eyelash. That intuitive knowledge one has sometimes of what must be flitting through the mind of a person, even though he succeeds pretty well in masking his face, doesn't apply here. The German doesn't seem to resent being lambasted at all. He displays no emotion and returns a civil answer. He seems to be completely cowed by the sheepish policy of follow-the-leader practiced for so long in this country. For one thing, they were all primed to being cut up and quartered like so many ribs of beef—by German propaganda warning them of our coming. They all seem pleasantly surprised at being alive and seem to feel that a little bellowing on our part is the least they can expect. All they want is the right to stoop for American cigarette butts as they follow in our footsteps.

As I say, these people are from forty years of age, on up. But even on the streets, the younger people seem to be containing their desires to give a friendly greeting. But they get no encouragement from the Americans. There is a certain amount of stone-throwing by civilians at soldiers riding in jeeps. A fellow driving me was hit by a stone a few days previously, The culprit ducked out of sight before the American could stop the jeep. But the latter unslung his Tommy gun and let fly in all directions—as a warning that the rewards for stones are bullets.

Many of the local citizenry prelude their requests at the Military Government office with avowals of how anti-Nazi they were under Hitler. They invariably whisper this about two inches away from your ear, from force of habit. For many years no anti-Hitler utterance has been made in Germany more than two inches removed from a friend's ear. The typical line goes like this: "The Gestapo wanted to hang me for listening to foreign radio stations. ... How's the chances of my getting a special pass to do this, or special permission to do that, etc."

The following happened to me yesterday—my first morning at the AMG. A well-dressed middle-aged, soft-spoken man stepped up to say that for several months he had worked for the Nazis in a near-by city, had hired a group of men to work with him in some construction project. Then we came along and drove the Nazis out before he could be paid for the job. His men were clamoring to be paid. So, would we please tell him whether we intended taking care of this obligation incurred by the government with which we are still engaged in a life-and-death struggle! No use dwelling on the reception this proposition got in the office. The man didn't do it with any sly intention of tricking us into paying. He just wasn't able to see how ridiculous his proposition was.

Today a man, who looked as if he could never smile again, walked in with a dazed-looking boy who seemed to be seeing the world for the first time. He said his wife was Jewish and his four children half Jewish. He had hidden them, more or less, for the last four years in something resembling a stable. For the last year, the most terrible conditions prevailed, because of the Gestapo, so that they had to disappear off the face of the earth, to all intents and purposes. All six had to live on his Aryan food and clothing card and whatever else a desperate husband in those circumstances could scrounge. They have all been sleeping and sitting on the floor for four years—that is, when they weren't standing up. What he wanted was a couple of beds and chairs. Like all cases having nothing to do with military or general food and health questions, he was told to make these requests of the burgomaster, who has been instructed to see that all civilians have sufficient food and lodgings.

The principle on which the AMG is run here is this: refusal of all requests for special permission to be on the streets during other than prescribed hours, refusal of all requests to leave one town for another (even if the other should be home), denial of permission to ride a bicycle, drive a car, push a cart, or be seen on the streets except for extremely rare cases. A woman had to sweat for hours and see clusters of officials before being given a pass allowing her to travel four miles to visit her child who was going blind in a near-by hospital. The penalty for being on the streets five minutes after curfew is usually a couple months in prison, preceded by at least two weeks in jail, waiting for the trial to come up. It causes a lot of tear-shedding, but there's no monkey business going on, as a result of this strictness.

## March 22

Spent another interesting morning interviewing German civilians. I am coming to the conclusion that what's missing in the German people is the ability to have a sense of guilt. I made an interesting discovery this morning. I had been wondering whether the people here realized what hardships they had imposed on the rest of the world. Twice today, some of the local residents remarked that the Allies were being very strict, after a couple of their requests were turned down. I generally treat them very politely, but if there's one thing that infuriates me it is to hear the slightest tone of indignation in their voices or to hear some remark about how tough it is to be a German civilian now.

So I reminded a few of these complainants that we are doing nothing that hadn't been learned from the actions of the German army when they occupied a downtrodden country, and I asked them whether they didn't think the Poles, the French, the Dutch, and so on hadn't suffered. In each case, the German said, "Yes, I know, that's true," and then walked away—satisfied that he was doomed to retaliation. But there was no feeling of guilt or surprise or attempt to deny that Germany had caused woeful misery in Europe. They must be fully aware of that and feel no remorse. But they realize what the medicine has to be.

One farm woman came in with a long face and a sad story about how hard it was now to plow the fields—because all the French slave labor is gone. Now isn't that a rotten shame! But imagine a person coming in to the American authorities and making a wry face about the disappearance of the foreign serfs. Why? Because the idea of slave labor and all these Nazi innovations are now considered so natural by the Germans that they've lost the moral significance.

Another thing, which seems to be true of all Europe, is the increasing emphasis on and clamoring for *things*, and the diminishing emphasis on human beings. Today, for instance, a man came in to get permission to have his wife transported here from another war-struck place. Why? "Because she has my food card and I have to get it from her." Several wives came in, saying their husbands had reported to the American authorities on our arrival some time ago and had never returned home. After three weeks the wives came down to find out what had happened. They didn't seem to care, but it was the thing to do. They weren't affected by the news that nobody could tell them where their husbands were, that they were probably prisoners. They smiled gaily as they left, with a look of a person who has done his duty. On the other hand, there's a general tendency to break down and start crying every time they start talking of how cold they are at home, how they were made to leave their houses before they could gather up enough extra clothing and must, consequently, go around with nothing but the clothes on their back. (This to the German is the greatest humiliation of all. It makes them all burst out crying in a tidal wave of self-pity.)

## March 28

I continue to be impressed by the poker face with which the Germans accept our denial of all their requests. Even though they've lost the war and can expect treatment fitting a defeated people, it's natural that they should attach a lot of importance to their individual problems and entertain hope that perhaps some of their requests will be granted. But I've yet to see one person lose patience, give anybody a dirty look, or make an "aside" to another German when a request, which he thought was reasonable, was turned down by order of the American authorities. He might be a little persistent and ask to see the Commandant. But if that fails, he never fails to say, "Thank you." "Good day." observing all the amenities, and going away satisfied with their failure. The difference between that sheepish submission to authority (which I am not lamenting, only observing) is the exact opposite to the reaction of the French.

307

Whereas the French would have the wrath of the righteously indignant if somebody plundered their premises, the Germans seem to regard it as a natural instinct and place no moral stigma on it, but simply ask for an *Eintritt verboten* sign to keep prowlers away. One woman has a garden where soldiers were wont to come in and play football. She applied to Military Government for an Off-Limits sign in English, which was granted. The next night, the soldiers returned to their *Kartoffel* Bowl, jerked the Off-Limits sign down, and continued their playing. The woman came back, saw the head of the Military Government office, got another sign, and posted it on the garden gate. Next night, the varsity returned, took the sign away, and made end runs on the spinach. Today, I was there when the vegetable lady returned for her third Off-Limits sign. She wasn't angry, she wasn't vindictive about the "gangster soldiers" Hitler had warned her were coming. She just wanted another Off-Limits sign—that's all.

One out of every three German petitions to the Military Government has something to do with potatoes. Many of the inhabitants had to move out of their dwellings so that our soldiers could move in. Invariably they had to leave so quickly that they left all their belongings in their house. And in the cellar of every German house, it appears, there are bushels of potatoes. When a German leaves home without his potatoes, he is glum, he broods, he becomes a man of action. Like a magnet, the spuds pull him back to his old neighborhood. He begs the soldiers to let him fetch his treasure trove of potatoes. And since no one can enter a house occupied by our troops, the potato chase inevitably leads back to the Military Government. The saddest expression on a German's face comes when he finds out that he can't go back for his potatoes. "But my potatoes are in the cellar," he says—half to himself and half to fellow Germans, as he walks partly dazed (but not angry) out of the AMG office.

An interesting sidelight on the sort of treatment we could have expected, had Germany won the war, is the way the chief German receptionist acts toward his countrymen who come in with their woes. This German is a big-shot now because he's in with the Americans and acts as a sort of shock troop to answer the simpler questions. He's one of those "trusted" civilians who wear a *Polizei* (police) armband. It would be natural to suppose that, being one of them, he would be the kindest in his treatment of those who had lived and lost with him. Far from it. Here we see the German victorious, the German still in a position to give orders, the German who still represents authority. What is his vocabulary? Hardly listening to the individual pleas, he splutters a series of words which range from *Ausgeschlossen* (Out of the question) to *Verboten*—peppered with such variations as *Keine Moglichkeit* (No possibility), *Keine Erlaubnis* (No permission), *Wir geben keine Genehmigung, wir geben keinen Schein* (We give no authorization, we give no permit). Sometimes, in the case of a cripple or a matter of life or death, the American authorities try to make an exception in granting a request. But not so the German. He's having a great time turning down his *Landsmann* at the door.

## March 29

Today at Military Government I had, as usual, several noteworthy experiences. One was translating for a major who had summoned an old red-faced tycoon to the office to form a local Chamber of Commerce. The man had been president of the Chamber of Commerce before Hitler. He wasn't very happy about his being chosen. "Why do you choose me?" he asked. "I am an old man." He was chosen, said the major, because he had held his position before Hitler came in. There was an expression on his face that seemed to say, "Well, that's just because I got old enough and rich enough to retire after Hitler came in. I have nothing against Adolf." Anyway, his job will be to make a census of all the raw-material supplies and manufactured goods lying around the city which can be used to feed and clothe the populace. He is to form a committee of younger employees who will do the actual running around and canvassing of factories and warehouses.

When the major asked him when he could come back again with something to report on the first steps, the German, showing the usual local brand of submission to authority, asked when the major wanted him to come in. The major confused the issue by saying he wanted the president of the Chamber of Commerce to use his own judgment. Using his own judgment, the not-too-bright retired industrialist said he'd be back in ten days (probably wanted to stall awhile, to make sure Hitler wasn't coming back). This didn't satisfy the American officer, so he told the man to come back tomorrow—with some results. On the way out of the office, the rather befuddled patriarch seemed so glum that I thought I'd appeal to his *Volksgemeinschaft*, that love of one German for all Germans, by reminding him that on the success of his quest depended the well-being of the city's populace. That didn't seem to thrill him at all, but he said thank you and stumbled out of the door.

## March 31

A few days ago I went with some correspondents, as interpreter, to interview a Catholic priest on what message he was going to give his flock on Easter Sunday. He replied that he wasn't going to give his flock any message of cheer but would stick strictly to the religious story of Easter.

He told us that the Catholic Church in Germany had never prayed for German victory, only universal peace. They had never mentioned the Führer in a prayer, but had prayed that the leaders of all nations might be guided by God's wisdom. We asked several Catholic luminaries present what the solution to Germany's present problems was. One of them surprised us by saying, "Roosevelt had the right answer when he said in a speech years ago that the only solution was for all nations to seek their salvation in Christ. Roosevelt said it—I heard him."

The Protestant minister said he was going to give his people a definite practical moral in his Easter sermon—saying that in this war the only victor was Christ, and if this was true, then Germans should take heart. Because if Christ was the victor, then there could be hope for the future. He, too, said that his church, which belonged to the Niemöller group, had never prayed for a German victory, but only for peace. He said their prayers were under constant perusal by the Nazi party; that Germany was divided into the Christs and Antichrists, and that the schism was unbridgeable. There are more people for Christ than against Him still in Germany, he said. But the religious leaders need a helping hand from the Allies if they are to triumph. He said this with a meaningful glance, and it turned out he was hinting around for special permission to ride a bicycle to visit his parishioners.

## April 3

The cases are becoming more and more stereotyped. Potatoes in basements still continue to play an important role. Several people come in daily, beseeching permission to go into the basement of a Nazi who fled the city—and take away the man's potatoes.

One good thing resulting from the German defeat is that *das Volk* is waking up to the realization that the Aryan race isn't quite so angelic and spotless as Hitler bluffed them into believing. For the main complaint now is not against the plundering of the Allied soldiers, but against the wholesale thefts perpetrated by the Wehrmacht against German civilians in the last hours before they pulled away under the Allied onslaught. All this will help the Allies when it comes time to break down the people's belief that all that is German is beyond criticism.

# Afterword

*A* *Taste of War* is meant to give the reader glimpses of World War II in a collection of segments. After World War I, the thoughts of politicians and the scheming of world leaders give us a picture of a world ready to explode. When the explosion occurred, the world leaders were unprepared. They should have known what to expect—or did they? Was their unpreparedness a deliberate ploy to sway emotions, to line up the proper allies, to pursue the old war to a successful conclusion?

It is doubtful that the world will ever see a war again fought on such a vast scale, where the stakes are so great and the instruments of death so lethal. The universal brutality shown to noncombatants as well as combatants reached a new high. Military prisoners of war endured incredible pain and torture. Civilians captured by the enemy were reduced to slave status. The entire structure of civilization crumbled beneath the weight of warfare.

The importance of books about the war years is to hold up before us the horror of battle. For those unborn at the time, it is necessary to learn that war unleashes indiscriminate terror that once set loose, is impossible to contain.

Unfortunately, memory is short among world leaders. President Ronald Reagan, during his term in office, visited the cemetery at Bitburg and paid homage to German SS troopers. These were the vilest of men, noted for their torture and killing, and there stood the President of the United States, at the foot of their graves, with his hat reverently placed over his heart.

Emperor Hirohito of Japan, a declared war criminal along with Adolf Hitler and Benito Mussolini, was allowed to die in bed 44 years after the cessation of hostilities. George Bush headed a delegation to Tokyo to pay last respects to the head of the Japanese empire.

Already forgotten were the atrocities endured by American and Allied armed forces on both sides of the world. These were affronts to the men and women buried in mass graves, victims of Japanese brutality and the savage barbarism of the German SS troops. The free people of the world must never forget what happened and must always be on the alert, for to let our guard down in the protection of freedom for anyone chips away at freedom for all.

# Index